Machine Translation Summit 2023

Volume 2: Users Track

Macau, China
4-8 September 2023

ISBN: 978-1-7138-9037-9

Printed from e-media with permission by:

Curran Associates, Inc.
57 Morehouse Lane
Red Hook, NY 12571

Some format issues inherent in the e-media version may also appear in this print version.

Printed with permission by Curran Associates, Inc. (2024)

For permission requests, please contact the Association for Computational Linguistics at the address below.

Association for Computational Linguistics
209 N. Eighth Street
Stroudsburg, Pennsylvania 18360

Phone: 1-570-476-8006
Fax: 1-570-476-0860

acl@aclweb.org

Additional copies of this publication are available from:

Curran Associates, Inc.
57 Morehouse Lane
Red Hook, NY 12571 USA
Phone: 845-758-0400
Fax: 845-758-2633
Email: curran@proceedings.com
Web: www.proceedings.com

MT Summit 2023

MTS Machine Translation Summit 2023

September 4-8, 2023 Macau SAR, China

Proceedings of Machine Translation Summit XIX
Vol. 2: Users Track

September 4 - 8, 2023

Preface to the Users Track

Every new edition of the MT Summit brings innovation to the history of MT conferences. The 19th edition, which is held in September 2023 in Macau, has at least two distinguishing factors: after the COVID-19 pandemic, researchers will again have the opportunity to meet face-to-face to discuss the MT landscape, and this is the first MT Summit in which large language models (LLMs) will occupy the central stage on an MT event.

The question everyone asks at the moment is whether LLMs have come to replace MT as a set of methods for language-pair-based training and translation inference. In other words: will MT simply become one of many downstream applications of powerful LLMs? This year's edition of MT Summit will contribute to this discussion, but it will very clearly not close it. Another observation is getting clear: MT is not a solved problem, not even with LLMs, as there are many gaps that ask for in-depth investigation, and new questions arise all the time. The uses and applications of the wealth of technologies that is currently within reach of researchers is one of the most relevant directions for the required new waves of research.

The organisers of this year's Users Track see this moment in the evolution of MT and of language technologies as an opportunity to bring the people who use the technologies back to the centre of all research and discussions. Our perspective is that MT must always be seen as an instrument of communication between humans. The more advanced this technology is, the more prevalent the role of humans becomes. We see the presence of Users Track in MT conferences as an opportunity for computational research to listen to and incorporate the concerns and research avenues opened up by Humanities and Social Sciences, from Linguistics, Psychology, Sociology and most important, because it integrates all these disciplines, from Translation Studies.

In organizing this Users Track, we have called for contributions that debated how MT is used in translation workflows, by translators and post-editors, but also how raw MT is used by end users, in companies, public institutions and in education. We believe that the collaboration of researchers and scholars from around the world has created the conditions for this to be a remarkable moment of knowledge sharing in such an important moment in the evolution of our disciplines.

The Users Track of the XIX MT Summit will count on a group of distinguished invited speakers, led by Dorothy Kenny, who will present a keynote which will help us find the ground in these turbulent times, supported by theoretical clarity and keen observation of practice. The track will also feature a panel debate with specialists from industry, academia and research, who will raise fundamental questions for the proper future use of MT and language technologies. Akiko Sakamoto, Chan Sin-wai and Kirti Vashee will bring their views on the sustainability of the current professional and business models of translation, the different ages and types of translation technology, and the perspectives of professionals and of the industry over this technology. Besides these, 21 innovative papers will be presented across 7 sessions, focusing on themes such as MT applications in education and subtitling, advancements with LLMs, MT quality challenges, professional workflows, and Asian language translations.

We thank all organisers and sponsors of the MT Summit for the opportunity to bring this wealth of knowledge together at this event and for the many hours they dedicated to the organisation of the event. We also thank all authors and co-authors, some of which we will meet in Macau, others who will present their papers online, and others who will keep on working in the background for the progress of MT and translation. We want to express our special appreciation to the keynote speaker and panellists. We finally thank all reviewers and members of the committee for their contribution to the selection of a rich set of perspectives on such an exciting subject. To them and to everyone who will read these proceedings, we wish this is a fruitful experience.

Masaru Yamada and Félix do Carmo

Organizing Committee

General Chair
Eiichiro Sumita, National Institute of Information and Communications Technology

Steering Committee
Eiichiro Sumita, National Institute of Information and Communications Technology
Kozo Moriguchi, Kawamura International Co. Ltd.
Derek Wong, University of Macau
Sadao Kurohashi, National Institute of Informatics & Kyoto University
Hideki Tanaka, National Institute of Information and Communications Technology

Research Track Chair
Masao Utiyama, National Institute of Information and Communications Technology
Rui Wang, Shanghai Jiao Tong University

User Track Chair
Masaru Yamada, Rikkyo University
Félix do Carmo, University of Surrey

Workshop Chair
Jiajun Zhang, Chinese Academy of Sciences
Thepchai Supnithi, The National Electronics and Computer Technology Center

Local Arrangement Chair
Derek Wong, University of Macau
Hou Pong Chan, University of Macau

Publication Chair
Katsuhito Sudoh, Nara Institute of Science and Technology
Xuebo Liu, Harbin Institute of Technology, Shenzhen

Sponsorship Chair
Kozo Moriguchi, Kawamura International Co. Ltd.
Jaap van der Meer, TAUS
Tong Xiao, Northeastern University

Conference Manager
Andrew Jiang, Macau Expo Group

Program Committee

Akiko Sakamoto
Ana Guerberof-Arenas
Callum Walker
Carlos S. C. Teixeira
Celia Rico
Constantin Orăsan
Dorothy Kenny
Fabio Alves
Jianwei Zheng
Joke Daems
Joss Moorkens
Jun Pan
Kirti Vashee
Lieve Macken
Lucas Nunes Vieira
Lynne Bowker
Maarit Koponen
Masaaki Nagata
Michael Carl
Mike Dillinger
Nora Aranberri
Rei Miyata
Sanjun Sun
Sergi Alvarez-Vidal
Tomoki Nagase
Yuxiang Wei

Table of Contents

Conference Program

Wednesday, 6th September

16:00–17:00 User Track Session 1: MT in the classroom

Exploring undergraduate translation students' perceptions towards machine translation: A qualitative questionnaire survey
Jia Zhang

MT and legal translation: applications in training
Suzana Cunha

Technology Preparedness and Translator Training: Implications for Pedagogy
Hari Venkatesan

16:00–17:30 User Track Session 2: MT and Subtitling

Reception of machine-translated and human-translated subtitles – A case study
Frederike Schierl

Machine Translation Implementation in Automatic Subtitling from a Subtitlers' Perspective
Bina Xie

Improving Standard German Captioning of Spoken Swiss German: Evaluating Multilingual Pre-trained Models
Jonathan David Mutal, Pierrette Bouillon, Johanna Gerlach and Marianne Starlander

Thursday, 7th September

10:30–12:00 User Track Session 3: New workflows with MT/LLMs

Leveraging Multilingual Knowledge Graph to Boost Domain-specific Entity Translation of ChatGPT
Min Zhang, Limin Liu, Zhao Yanqing, Xiaosong Qiao, Su Chang, Xiaofeng Zhao, Junhao Zhu, Ming Zhu, Song Peng, Yinglu Li, Yilun Liu, Wenbing Ma, Mengyao Piao, Shimin Tao, Hao Yang and Yanfei Jiang

Human-in-the-loop Machine Translation with Large Language Model
Xinyi Yang, Runzhe Zhan, Derek F. Wong, Junchao Wu and Lidia S. Chao

The impact of machine translation on the translation quality of undergraduate translation students
Jia Zhang and Hong Qian

16:00–17:30 User Track Session 4: Exploring applications of MT

Leveraging Latent Topic Information to Improve Product Machine Translation
Bryan Zhang, Stephan Walter, Amita Misra and Liling Tan

Translating Dislocations or Parentheticals : Investigating the Role of Prosodic Boundaries for Spoken Language Translation of French into English
Nicolas Ballier, Behnoosh Namdarzadeh, Maria Zimina and Jean-Baptiste Yunès

Exploring Multilingual Pretrained Machine Translation Models for Interactive Translation
Angel Navarro and Francisco Casacuberta

Thursday, 7th September (continued)

16:00–17:30 User Track Session 5: Challenges in MT quality

Machine translation of Korean statutes examined from the perspective of quality and productivity
Jieun Lee and Hyoeun Choi

Fine-tuning MBART-50 with French and Farsi data to improve the translation of Farsi dislocations into English and French
Behnoosh Namdarzadeh, Sadaf Mohseni, Lichao Zhu, Guillaume Wisniewski and Nicolas Ballier

KG-IQES: An Interpretable Quality Estimation System for Machine Translation Based on Knowledge Graph
Junhao Zhu, Min Zhang, Hao Yang, Song Peng, Zhanglin Wu, Yanfei Jiang, Xijun Qiu, Weiqiang Pan, Ming Zhu, Ma Miaomiao and Weidong Zhang

Friday, 8th September

10:30–12:00 User Track Session 6: MT quality in professional workflows

Enhancing Gender Representation in Neural Machine Translation: A Comparative Analysis of Annotating Strategies for English-Spanish and English-Polish Language Pairs
Celia Soler Uguet, Fred Bane, Mahmoud Aymo, João Pedro Fernandes Torres, Anna Zaretskaya and Tània Blanch Miró

Brand Consistency for Multilingual E-commerce Machine Translation
Bryan Zhang, Stephan Walter, Saurabh Chetan Birari and Ozlem Eren

Developing automatic verbatim transcripts for international multilingual meetings: an end-to-end solution
Akshat Dewan, Michal Ziemski, Henri Meylan, Lorenzo Concina and Bruno Pouliquen

Friday, 8th September (continued)

14:00–16:00 User Track Session 7: MT and LLMs in Asian Languages

Exploring undergraduate translation students' perceptions towards machine translation: A qualitative questionnaire survey

Jia Zhang jia.zhang2@unsw.edu.au
School of Humanities and Languages
University of New South Wales, Sydney, 2052, Australia

Abstract

Machine translation (MT) has been relatively recently introduced in higher education institutions. However, MT courses are often offered to students at the postgraduate level or in the last year of an undergraduate programme (e.g., Arenas & Moorkens, 2019; Doherty et al., 2012), and most of the previous studies have surveyed the perceptions or attitudes of these students towards MT via quantitative questionnaires (e.g., Liu et al., 2022; Yang et al., 2021). The present study investigated undergraduate students' perceptions of MT in the early stages of translator training via qualitative questionnaires. Second-year translation students (n = 20) were asked to complete a questionnaire with open-ended questions, the responses to which were analysed manually using NVivo to identify themes and arguments. It was found that MT was used more often as an instrument to learn language and translation rather than as a straightforward translation tool. While the students were willing to experiment with MT as a translation tool, they were doubtful that MT could be introduced in the classroom. They had a neutral attitude towards the quality of MT but agreed that MT increased the speed of their translations and their confidence. It is hoped that the findings will make an evidence-based contribution to the design of MT curricula and teaching pedagogies.

1. Research background

The term 'machine translation' (MT) includes various activities related to translation that are performed by computers. A widely used definition provided by Hutchins and Sommers (1992, p. 3) is that MT systems are 'computerised systems responsible for the production of translations from one natural language into another, with or without human assistance'.

The increasing accuracy and fluency of MT have recently led to MT being included in translation programmes in higher education institutions, with specialised courses for students being provided. However, such courses are often offered at the postgraduate level or towards the last year of an undergraduate programme (e.g., Arenas & Moorkens, 2019; Doherty et al., 2012). One of the concerns is that technologies such as MT might be too difficult for undergraduate translation students to learn. The other concern is that the students' translation performances and their translation competence could be negatively impacted by MT because they might not have the ability to evaluate the output of the technology (Bowker, 2015). Therefore, MT training is not usually available to undergraduate students. In addition, teachers or management may formulate policies that forbid students from using MT in their assignments.

There is a lack of sufficient evidence in academia to conclude that MT has a negative impact on novice translation students. Most of the previous studies have focused on postgraduate students or undergraduate students in the last year of their programmes (e.g., Jia et al.,

Proceedings of Machine Translation Summit XIX, Vol. 2: Users Track, pages 1–10
September 4–8, 2023, Macau SAR, China.

2019; Wang et al., 2021; Zaretskaya et al., 2016). Little research has targeted undergraduate translation learners in the early stages of their training.

However, it has been observed that students have been interacting with MT in contravention of official instructions. With MT systems and abundant information about them being freely available on the internet, it is unlikely that students would be unaware of MT or would not be interested in experimenting with it. As the quality of MT increases, students might have strong intentions to use MT when learning to translate. The author thus argued that novice translation students' knowledge about and experience of MT could be of value in the curriculum design and pedagogical development of MT courses.

In previous studies, the participants' perceptions were often solicited via closed-ended questions (e.g., Liu et al., 2022; Yang et al., 2021; Yang & Wang, 2019), the answers to which were later analysed as quantitative data. However, as the participants answered questions on a scale or according to the available choices, their views were limited. For example, Yang and Wang (2019)'s study focused exclusively on students' intentions to use MT; their study was based on a technology acceptance model in which an individual's intention to engage with technology was linked directly to their attitude. A questionnaire using a 5-point scale was developed in accordance with the model and was answered by 109 Chinese student translators. The results supported and verified the technology acceptance model in that the students' perceived ease of use and perceived usefulness of MT were correlated positively with their intentions to use MT.

Based on the above discussion, little is known about how undergraduate students in the early stages of translator training perceive and use MT or what their training needs may be. Therefore, this research intended to survey translation students in the early stages of their translator training to solicit their attitudes towards and perceptions of MT via a qualitative questionnaire survey. This research included open-ended questions, thus allowing the participants to express their opinions freely. Furthermore, unlike interviews, questionnaires with open-ended questions could be self-administered without the researcher's presence, thus avoiding researcher bias.

2. Research questions

This study investigated undergraduate students' perceptions of MT in the early stages of their translator training via a qualitative questionnaire survey. It is hoped that the findings will make an evidence-based contribution to the development of MT curriculum design and teaching pedagogies.

The research questions (RQs) are as follows:

1) How do translation students in the early stages of translator training interact and engage with MT?
2) What are their attitudes towards MT in translator training and professional work?
3) What are the pedagogical implications of students' perceptions of MT?

A questionnaire survey with ten open-ended questions was sent to second-year undergraduate translation students (*n* = 20) who were attending a Chinese university. Their responses were collected and analysed manually with the assistance of NVivo. Major themes and arguments were then identified for further discussion.

3. Methods and data

After ethical clearance was obtained from the university, 20 students from an Applied Translation Studies programme at a university based in China were recruited.

The participants were all in the second year of an undergraduate translation programme; they had similar educational backgrounds and hence comparable language proficiency and translation competencies. They had taken three translation courses covering fundamental translation theories and practices. No specialised training in MT, post-editing (PE) or translation technology was provided in the classroom.

The survey included ten open-ended questions to solicit the participants' knowledge, experience, perceptions of and attitudes to MT. As few previous studies have used open-ended questions, the design of this questionnaire mainly drew on González Pastor (2021)'s paper, which had a similar design and goal as the current project, and referenced three other relevant papers (Çetiner & İşisağ, 2019; de Faria Pires, 2020; Schmidhofer & Mair, 2018). González Pastor (2021) investigated students' attitudes to and perceptions of translation technology before and after being taught about translation technology. The questions were adapted and narrowed down to MT- and PE-specific questions. Questions regarding the students' understanding of translation concepts, processes and products were added as answers to these questions provide an alternative perspective to understand the impact of MT and PE on students' translation processes and products.

This paper mainly analysed answers to questions regarding the students' knowledge, attitudes to and perceptions of MT. Therefore, only the answers to the following six (out of 10) questions were analysed and presented.

1. Can you tell us briefly about your technical knowledge of MT and PE?
2. Do you have any experience with MT? What do you use it for? Can you explain this in detail?
3. Based on your knowledge and experience, in what way do you think MT is helpful in translation tasks (either for your translation assignments at school or real-life translation tasks in the industry)? In what way do you think it is unhelpful? Why do you think so?
4. Do you think that MT might have an impact on the quality of your translations? Why? If yes, in what way do you think the translation quality is affected?
5. At what stage of translator training should teachers introduce MT and PE to translation students? Do you think there are some prerequisites for learning MT and PE?
6. Do you think there are ethical concerns related to MT, such as legal or moral issues, biases, justice or privacy? Can you explain your thoughts in detail?

The students were told that they could answer the survey in Chinese or English, whichever they felt most comfortable using. The answers in Chinese were translated by the author, a certified translator in China and Australia with over 15 years of professional experience.

All the data were de-identified with students' names being indicated as "s + participant number" and were imported into NVivo 14 for thematic analysis. The author conducted the analysis twice at two different times to ensure the reliability of the results.

4. Analysis and discussion

4.1. Students' knowledge of MT

The students were asked how much they knew about MT (and possibly PE) and what they considered the advantages and disadvantages of MT to be. Even without proper training, the students did know about MT and PE, as all of them provided relevant definitions correctly. The students also mentioned the ways in which MT was helpful or unhelpful, as summarised below.

Students' perceptions of the advantages of MT:

1) **MT can be used to evaluate the difficulty of a translation task.** Poorer MT translation quality means that the translation tasks are more complicated.
2) **MT can help to improve translation efficiency.**
   It can save the translators' effort to understand the source text, for example, some professional or complex texts that are written in a second language (L2), and help translators to express themselves quickly in the target language.
   It also increases translators' translation speed, particularly when translating informative texts, such as government documents, or when translating demanding or urgent translation tasks.
3) **MT can help to improve translation quality.**
   It assists translators to quickly locate idiomatic expressions, fixed combinations, slang and grammatical sentence structures when translating into the L2.
   It improves translators' understanding of difficult content, such as long and complicated sentences in the L2, thus ensuring correct translations.

Students' perceptions of the disadvantages of MT:

1) Although the MT quality appears to be good at present, translation errors still occur, particularly word-for-word translation errors. More effort is sometimes needed in PE when the MT quality is poor.
2) MT may fail to convey contextual or emotional meanings in literary and cultural translations.
3) Over-reliance on MT may impede translators' critical thinking and creativity.
4) MT cannot be generated to meet special requirements, such as desktop publishing issues.

It can be seen that, even without formal MT training or professional translation experience, all of the students had some basic and correct understanding and perceptions of MT. For example, the students noted MT's usefulness in translating texts in different genres. They were aware that MT could translate informative texts better than it could literary texts and that MT could not convey implied meanings. They also saw the value of MT in improving efficiency and quality.

Such knowledge is reasonable in this digital age. The present generation of university students has grown up with many disruptive technologies, such as personal computers, tablets and mobile phones, and students have extensive experience interacting with numerous software programmes and electronic tools, including MT. Furthermore, they have been exposed to a large amount of information on the internet. As MT often makes headlines and there are many free lectures on MT, it would be difficult for the younger generation to ignore such a development.

This knowledge shows that students' opinions regarding the integration of MT in translator training could be valuable. Trainers and teachers are not encountering groups of students who barely know anything about MT. Due to the students' knowledge of MT, they also have training needs for MT, and they may have intentions to experiment with MT at some point during their training as translators. Simply preventing them from accessing MT online is useless. Instead, their voices should be heard when making decisions regarding the design of MT curricula and pedagogical developments.

4.2. Student's interactions with MT

The students were asked how often they used MT in their translation assignments or actual translation tasks (if any). They mentioned mainly using MT in reading, writing and translation. Some of their responses are presented below.

S14: 我使用MT的次数很多，几乎每天都会用，查一些不认识的单词短语之类的。(I use MT many times, almost every day, to look up some unknown vocabulary or phrases.)

S15: I used it for the words I am familiar with and the translation of proper nouns in translation exercises.

S08: When encountering idioms, slang, or so, I also sometimes resort to machine translation. I use machine translation to help understand some complicated sentences.

S03: 可以更加快速地掌握学习内容…不用逐字斟酌词语的具体意思是什么，帮助我梳理知识结构 (to master the content I am learning more quickly…I don't have to read every English word to understand the exact meaning of the text. Machine translation helps me easily sort out the structure of the knowledge.)

S11: 今天我的论文中间出现了一些不太懂的生词，会用到机器翻译来翻译出它的意思，并且运用到我的论文句子中间去。(Like today, I need to use some vocabulary that I don't really know well in my English essays. I will use machine translation to translate the Chinese words and use the English words in my essay sentences.)

S10: 参考翻译软件是否可以给出不同的句子结构或词组 (I use machine translation as a reference to see if it could provide a different sentence structure or expression.)

S17: 在做翻译作业时，有时不知道该如何表达更通顺时，会使用一些翻译软件翻译句子作为参考，有些翻译的不错的会进行PE。(When doing translation assignments, sometimes I don't know how to express a sentence fluently. I will use machine translation systems to translate the sentences and use the translation as a reference. I will only post-edit when the quality looks good.)

The most frequently mentioned uses of MT were summarised based on the responses.

1) The students used MT as a dictionary to look up vocabulary, phrases, cultural words, terminology, and proper nouns in the L2.

2) The students used MT as a reference to understand the meaning of a complicated sentence or a difficult text in the L2.

3) The students used MT as a reference to look up idiomatic expressions in the L2 at the word, phrase and sentence levels.

4) A few students used an MT of the entire text as a benchmark reference to check the quality of their own translations.

It was found that MT was used more often as an instrument to learn language and translation rather than as a straightforward translation tool. None of the students reported using PEMT at the text level in their translation assignments. Instead, they referenced MT output to understand terms, fixed combinations, complicated sentences and texts and to produce accurate, authentic and varied phrases and sentences.

The reasons that they chose to use MT as a reference tool rather than as a translation tool can be seen in the following quotes.

S09: revise的过程很痛苦！ (The process of revision is painful!)

S04: 难度较高的内容的翻译准确度还是欠佳…这种情况下更浪费时间降低输出质量。(The translation accuracy of some more challenging content is not good enough ... In this situation, it is a waste of time, and our output quality might also be reduced.)

S03: 有时候我们的翻译会被机翻所局限 (Sometimes our translation might be limited by machine translation.)

S04: 在看了机翻之后，脑子里对于原文的翻译会形成一个基础的输出表达方式扰乱和禁锢自己的思路，可能自己潜在的更好的表达会被抹去或者遗忘 (After reading the translation generated by the machine, a basic expression will be formed in our minds for the translation of the source text. It's likely that a potentially better expression of mine will be erased or forgotten.)

When the MT quality is low, more effort is required in PE than is needed in from-scratch translations. However, the students did not attribute such increased effort to their insufficient language proficiency or their translation competence but to their lack of MT and PE training. In addition, they were afraid that their creativity might be limited.

S01: 它有一个基点，给了一个参考，愿意相信它的大意会是正确的 (It serves as a starting point, and provides a translation. I would believe that most of the meaning of the machine translation is correct.)

It could also be said that the students trusted MT output to a certain extent. When they encountered difficulties in a translation assignment, they trusted the translation provided by MT to either help them to understand the source text or to locate idiomatic expressions in the target language. There was very little mention of making more mistakes due to their insufficient language proficiency and their competence in identifying errors in MT translations.

4.3. Students' perceptions of the translation quality

Students were asked if their translation quality would be impacted by MT. Five out of 20 students believed that the quality of their PEMT-assisted translations would be the same as that of their from-scratch translations. Fourteen out of 20 students suggested that the quality of their translations would be improved with the assistance of a machine. The following quotes represent their perceptions of the translation quality.

S12: 我认为不会。因为在机器翻译后，我会人工进行检查和修改，把里面没翻译出来的意思或是翻译不好的地方改掉。(I don't think my translation quality will be negatively impacted. Because after the machine translation is generated, I will manually check the translation and revise it. I can add the meaning that's not translated or revise the poorly translated parts.)

S18: Yes. Because using MT and PE can help my vocabulary, grammar, sentence structure and so on, which can improve my translation quality.

S16: 因为我现阶段已经具备了语言敏感度，我知道怎么翻是好的，怎么翻译是奇怪的，能够形成自己的判断，所以我觉得我会择优，而不是一味copy. (Because at this current stage, I have trained to be sensitive enough to language issues. I know how to translate in a better way and what kind of translation is strange. I can make my own judgement. So I think I can identify a good machine-generated translation instead of only copying the MT.)

It is worth noting that the students' thoughts about MT were positive, as they thought that referencing MT or engaging in PE would improve the quality of their translations. They were confident about their language proficiency and translation competence and believed that they could identify MT errors and would not be affected by them. They believed that they could judge the quality of MT and decide whether it was sufficiently good to be used.

> *S20: 翻译结果变得像流水线生产出来的，虽然质量都差不多，但缺少了翻译本身的意义。(The translation output becomes something coming out of the assembly line. Although the quality is almost the same, translation has lost significance.)*

Only one participant said that the quality might be negatively influenced by MT. However, what this participant meant was that translations generated by machines and then edited by humans would be homogenised and that the meaning of the translation activity would be lost in this case.

4.4. Students' attitudes towards MT and PE training

The students were asked if they wanted to receive specialised MT and PE training at their current stage of translator training. Curiously, 13 of the 20 respondents said no, even though they believed that MT was beneficial to learning how to translate and had already made extensive use of MT as a reference. The students also expressed a certain degree of trust in the quality of MT. While they were willing to experiment with MT as a translation tool and to perform PE in future tasks, they were doubtful that MT could be introduced into the classroom at their current stage of translator training.

> *S19: 我觉得可以在学生大三以及大四的时候。因为我觉得这可以当成一个辅助工具，但绝对不能是被依赖的一个翻译的道具。(I think students in their year three or year four can learn MT and PE. Because I think MT is more an assistive tool. It can never be a translation tool that is relied on for translation.)*
>
> *S18: I think when students reach grade 4. Before the introduction of MT and PE, students should have basic knowledge about translation.*
>
> *S12: 这样学生翻译出来的东西再好也好不过机器... (Students' translation can never be better than that of the machine.)*

After analysing students' responses, it could be seen that students did not want to receive MT and PE training at this stage because they considered MT to be a good and trusted tool, and they were afraid that they would overly rely on it. They expressed that such over-reliance on MT might limit their creativity and that they would not be able to produce better translations than MT in the future. Therefore, they preferred to learn to produce translations independently and to continue to only use MT as a reference at this stage.

> *S15: 我认为在学生了解了文化与翻译的关系后可以将这个介绍给学生，他们需要提前知道机器翻译的一些优缺点，以及在哪些场合不得使用，错误使用的一些负面影响。(I believe once students understand the relationship between culture and translation, MT can be introduced to students. They need to know the advantages and disadvantages of MT earlier, situations when MT shouldn't be used, and the negative impact of MT when it's wrongly used.)*

The other seven students were more open to integrating MT in the early stages of their studies and said that they would like to interact with MT more effectively.

Based on the above responses, all the students had positive attitudes towards MT, although some students wanted to engage with MT at a later stage after they could produce better translations than machines and would not be limited by them, while others wanted to make the best use of MT to continue to improve their translations.

4.5. Ethical concerns regarding MT

The survey asked the respondents if they thought that there were ethical concerns related to MT. The response was unexpected, as only five of the 20 students believed that there were ethical concerns associated with the use of MT.

The unethical behaviour mentioned by these five respondents included:

> S12, S14 and S19: Some private or confidential documents might be leaked.
>
> S16 and S19: Students gained an unfair advantage by referencing MT in translation assignments or competitions, which is regarded as cheating.
>
> S20: The translation quality might be compromised when using MT.
>
> S20: MT can assist scams in international and multilingual settings.

The other 15 respondents answered "no" to this question, as they did not consider ethical concerns to be involved in the use of MT.

> *S15: 我认为没有一些道德问题，它既没有威胁到集体利益也没有威胁到个人利益，它的出现为我们的翻译工作带来了很多便利。(I don't think there are some ethical problems. MT does not threaten collective benefits, nor does it threaten individual benefits. On the contrary, its advent has brought much convenience to our translation work.)*
>
> *S13: I don't think they (MT systems) are related to some ethical concerns. Indeed, it (MT) helps people who are not familiar with a foreign language.*
>
> *S18: No. Because technology is developing. We should take advantage of it and help humans to live more conveniently.*
>
> *S11: 我总认为这种事情，还是会阻碍社会的发展。(I always believe that such consideration [about ethics] is indeed an obstacle to the development of society.)*

Ethical behaviour in accessing MT was not of particular concern for translation students at this stage. The reasons that they gave indicated that they regarded MT as they would any other tool that has been developed throughout human history to aid translation, such as Microsoft Word; thus, it should not entail any unethical behaviour.

With MT systems being freely available online, preventing students from accessing them would be difficult. Given the lack of ethical awareness amongst the students, trainers and teachers should consider discussing the issue of MT ethics or even translation ethics earlier in translator education. Such discussions would benefit students in their interactions with MT.

5. Conclusion

This study solicited students' attitudes to and perceptions of MT via a qualitative questionnaire survey, the results of which were analysed with the assistance of NVivo.

It should be noted that the students did have a basic understanding of MT and even of PE. They were aware of the possible advantages and disadvantages of MT. Such knowledge means that their opinions could be of value in translator training. Trainers could spend time identifying their students' needs for MT training and involve students in making decisions about the integration of MT in translation classrooms.

In terms of the students' interactions with MT, they used MT more often as a reference than they did as a translation tool due to concerns about its impact on their creativity, their unfamiliarity with MT, and their lack of PE training. None of the respondents reported having post-edited the machine output of an entire text when using MT. As the students mainly only used MT as a reference, knowledge about MT, such as contexts in which MT functions most effectively, the text types for which MT produces the best translations, and the common error types that are often found in MT, might assist students in interacting with MT more effectively.

The students reported that they were generally more confident when translating and were more confident about the quality of their translations when using MT as a reference. They thought that MT would not negatively impact the quality of their translations. The students tended to have positive attitudes towards MT and PE and were not concerned about the negative impact of MT on the quality of their translations; in fact, some of the students believed that MT might have a positive impact on the quality of their translations.

Although the students thought highly of the quality of MT, curiously, they were reluctant to learn MT at their current stage of study. They were concerned about over-reliance on MT, which would affect their creativity. They thought that MT was good to a certain extent; however, they did not want to be limited by machines and wanted to produce better quality translations than those produced by machines.

What concerned the researcher was that students did not mention any potential negative impacts of MT on their language proficiency or translation competency in the survey. Even when they said that specialised PE training should only be provided at a later stage, their concern was not about the impact on translation quality but the impact on their creativity and critical thinking. More empirical studies of the impact of MT and the effect of PE training on the translation performances of undergraduate translation students in the early stages of translator training are needed. As it will become increasingly difficult to prevent students from accessing freely available MT online, it makes more sense to inform students about the positive and negative impacts of MT, which should be based on sound research findings.

Quite a few of the students believed that there were no ethical concerns associated with the use of MT. The students obviously lacked a clear understanding of translation ethics, particularly when including the use of MT and even artificial intelligence (AI). Ethics teaching should be an essential part of translator training in response to the challenges generated by MT.

This qualitative survey only solicited opinions from 20 respondents. In the future, a quantitative survey based on the current research could be developed to generalise the findings and to provide more evidence to inform MT and translator training.

References

Arenas, A. G., & Moorkens, J. (2019). Machine translation and post-editing training as part of a master's programme. *Journal of Specialised Translation*, 31, 217–238.

Bowker, L. (2015). Computer-aided translation: Translator training. In S. Chan (Ed.), *Routledge encyclopedia of translation technology* (pp. 126–142). Routledge.

Çetiner, C., & İşisağ, K. U. (2019). Undergraduate level translation students' attitudes towards machine translation post-editing training. *International Journal of Languages' Education and Teaching*, 7(1), 110–120. https://doi.org/10.18298/ijlet.3242

de Faria Pires, L. (2020). Master's students' post-editing perception and strategies: Exploratory study. *FORUM*, 18(1), 26–44. https://doi.org/10.1075/forum.19014.pir

Doherty, S., Kenny, D., & Way, A. (2012). Taking statistical machine translation to the student translator. *Proceedings of the 10th Conference of the Association for Machine Translation in the Americas: Commercial MT User Program*.

Gonzalez Pastor, D. (2021). Introducing Machine Translation in the Translation Classroom: A Survey on Students' Attitudes and Perceptions. *Tradumatica*, 19, 47–65. https://doi.org/10.5565/rev/tradumatica.273

Hutchins, W. J., & Somers, H. L. (1992). *An introduction to machine translation*. Academic Press.

Jia, Y. F., Carl, M., & Wang, X. L. (2019). How does the post-editing of neural machine translation compare with from-scratch translation? A product and process study. *Journal of Specialised Translation*, 31, 60–86.

Schmidhofer, A., & Mair, N. (2018). Machine translation in translator education. *CLINA*, 4(2), 163–180. https://doi.org/10.14201/clina201842163180

Wang, X., Wang, T., Muñoz Martín, R., & Jia, Y. (2021). Investigating usability in postediting neural machine translation: Evidence from translation trainees' self-perception and performance. *Across Languages and Cultures*, 22(1), 100–123. https://doi.org/10.1556/084.2021.00006

Yang, Y. X., & Wang, X. L. (2019). Modelling the intention to use machine translation for student translators: An extension of Technology Acceptance Model. *Computers & Education*, 133, 116–126. https://doi.org/10.1016/j.compedu.2019.01.015

Zaretskaya, A., Vela, M., Pastor, G. C., & Seghiri, M. (2016). Measuring post-editing time and effort for different types of machine translation errors. *New Voices in Translation Studies*, 15, 63–92.

MT and Legal Translation: applications in training

Suzana Noronha Cunha scunha@iscap.ipp.pt
CEOS.PP, ISCAP, Polytechnic of Porto, S. Mamede de Infesta, 4465-004, Portugal

Abstract

This paper investigates the introduction of machine translation (MT) in the legal translation class by means of a pilot study conducted with two groups of students. Both groups took courses in legal translation, but only one was familiarised with post-editing (PE). The groups post-edited an extract of a Portuguese company formation document, translated by an open-access neural machine translation (NMT) system and, subsequently, reflected on the assigned task. Although the scope of the study was limited, it was sufficient to confirm that prior exposure to machine translation post-editing (MTPE) did not significantly alter both groups' editing operations.

The pilot study is part of a broader investigation into how technology affects the decision-making process of trainee legal translators, and its results contributed to fine-tuning a methodological tool that aims to integrate MTPE procedures in an existing process-oriented legal translation approach developed by Prieto Ramos (2014). The study was repeated this year. This time both groups of trainees were introduced to and used the tool in class. A comparison of both studies' results is expected to provide insight onto the productive use of MTPE in other domain-specific texts.

1. Introduction

The advent of the World Wide Web and the emergence and evolution of computer-based tools has been changing the way translation is done for more than twenty years. More recently, machine translation (MT) and neural machine translation (NMT) brought about the second major technological shift in the translation industry (Doherty, 2016). These systems appeal to a wide range of users thanks to their ability to provide instant translation of large amounts of information with high-quality output in numerous language pairs. Furthermore, most major NMT providers now offer free versions of their systems that are accessed and used globally for translation of numerous types of texts, in numerous domains and for multiple purposes.

Translation trainees use open-access NMT systems, unaware of the systems' limitations and before acquiring competence in the particulars of in-domain translation. In legal translation, lack of familiarity with the subject matter, the textual genre, and intersystemic transfer barriers may cause them to miss errors or, conversely, overcorrect them. The increasing sophistication and "human-like qualities" of NMT make it even more difficult for trainees to flag errors (Yamada, 2019). In light of the above, the challenge for the translation trainer in the 2020s lies in providing guidance through the automated process of translating in-domain texts.

While the integration of technology in translation training is consensual, to our knowledge, not many studies focused on the integration of post-editing processes in domain-specific translation processes, which paved the way for investigating the specificities of implementing them in the legal translation class. The first step was to carry out a pilot study with 2 groups of participants, of which only one was formally trained in MTPE. The study and preliminary results are discussed in more detail in the present paper. In general, and although the

Proceedings of Machine Translation Summit XIX, Vol. 2: Users Track, pages 11–23
September 4–8, 2023, Macau SAR, China.

sample was not representative, editing operations were similar in both groups, both reveal special caution with terminology and no one is consistent when post-editing format, punctuation, or mechanic grammatical errors.

These results reinforced the conviction that a methodological tool could be useful to systematize the processes of post-editing the NMT output of legal documents. Prieto Ramos (2011, 2014) legal translation integrative methodology was the framework for the first proposal. This problem-solving model integrates the legal and linguistic dimensions in a 4-stage process comprising analysis of skopos and macro-contextualization; source text analysis; transfer and target text production; and revision (2014).

Our proposal reorganized the second and third stages of Prieto Ramos' model in an attempt to reflect a relevant shift in the translation workflow: that translators no longer work from decoding the source to transferring and recoding the same intent and information in the target text. Today, translators work with, at least, 3 texts simultaneously – the source, the MT output and the target - and, after considering the brief and the communicative situation, focus not on analyzing the source text but the NMT output, thus performing PE rather than producing a translation from scratch.

This shift needs to be addressed actively and openly in the specialised translation class, so as to make it very clear that, although MTPE apparently reduces the relevance of human intervention in the process by dislocating it to the end of the process, it entails as much competence in the legal domain and discourse as translation from scratch does. Post-editing skills are so critical in the process of comparing texts in different languages and assessing them for accuracy and naturalness, that it should be presented as a "validation" activity rather than a revision and proofreading procedure (Pym and Torres-Simon, 2021).

The following sections of the present paper discuss the relevant literature, describe and discuss the pilot study and preliminary results, and introduce future work on the development of the integrative methodological tool.

2. Related Work

Ten years ago, Pym alerted for the need to define new skill-sets for the translator in the MT age (2013). Traditionally, translation had been a "generative" activity consisting mostly in identifying solutions to translation problems, whereas today it requires selecting the adequate solution to a specific communicative situation among numerous possible candidates. This, in his words, is "a very simple and quite profound shift", unsettling for both trainers accustomed to the traditional process of transfer between source and target texts, and trainees provided with many ready-made solutions and not enough insight on how to address them.

More recently, Rodríguez de Céspedes discussing the implications for training of the shift of translation from human to machine, also warned that translator intervention at later stages of the process added a new dimension to the human cognitive act of translating (2019). Furthermore, although it is getting harder to distinguish between human and machine translation, because MT systems are trained and fed with human translations (Doherty, 2016), human translation remains the standard for quality evaluation of MT output, and the activity of editing and correcting MT output is carried out by humans (ISO 18587:2017).

Assuming that post-editing has become central in translation practice[1] and that it requires both specific competence and translation competence (Yamada, 2019), to prepare trainees for performing the roles of post-editor and translator interchangeably (Vieira, 2019) it is imperative that MTPE is openly integrated in the specialized translation class.

[1] For an overview of post-editing as an increasingly central practice in the translation field and of research on MTPE, see Koponen (2016).

Legal translation, as any other specialized language, requires knowledge of the domain and familiarity with its terminology (Wilss, 1996). However, unlike medicine or engineering, legal terminology is system-bound (Cao, 2007), which means that the concepts of source and target equivalents do not fully coincide, but rather overlap partially, leading to incongruity between what can be called legal functional equivalents. Incongruity is compensated by established translation strategies – e.g. borrowing, paraphrase, literal and functional equivalence – and constitutes a real challenge in legal translation: balancing accurate transfer of legal concepts with naturalness and target reader expectations. It also helps explain why legal translations are often "hybrid texts" that read like and look like translations: their purpose is not to replace but to reveal the source legal entity "through target language knowledge systems" (Biel, 2009).

Prieto Ramos' holistic model for legal translation competence (2014) systematizes the translation process workflow under the overarching procedural/methodological competence, combining legal and linguistic subcompetences. Such a model is flexible enough to accommodate specificities of legal translation and post-editing procedures. ISO 18587 requires that post-editors possess general knowledge of MT and the typical errors[2] it makes (2017), much in the same way as the European Master's in Translation framework recommends that translators know the basics of MT systems (2022).

To carry out the "observable operations performed by the translator over pre-existing text" – the 4 "editing actions" of inserting, deleting, replacing and moving (Carmo, 2017) –, post-editing usually involves error typology quality evaluation. The error typology approach is useful in identifying and fixing errors and it should be flexible to allow for the addition or deletion of error categories and sub-categories, according to the features of each text or the requirements of a translation task. The Language Service Provider (LSP) industry provides various guidelines for error evaluation, such as those of TAUS, the Translation Automation User Society (2017). TAUS and the German Research Center for Artificial Intelligence (DFKI) have harmonized their respective DQF (Dynamic Quality Framework) and MQM (Multidimensional Quality Metrics) into one DQF-MQM framework (Valli, 2015). A simplified adaptation of this harmonized framework was used to analyse the extracts post-edited by the participants in the pilot study.

3. The Pilot Study

As stated above, this paper investigates whether prior introduction to PE is enough for productive use of MTPE in the legal translation class. The pilot study is the initial stage of a larger project that aims to integrate adapted post-editing procedures and error categories in an existing problem-solving model for legal translation. The study tries to answer the following questions:

Q1. Do students with prior training in PE perform better in identifying or fixing MT errors?

Q2, Are there noticeable differences in students' lexical, grammatical or formatting edits?

Q3. Do students with PE training follow a different process or method?

The author evaluated the participants' post-edited texts using a simplified version of the Dynamic Quality Framework Knowledge Base (TAUS, 2017). First, the MT output was assessed and the author selected twenty-nine recommended edits covering 4 of the framework's high-level error types: Accuracy, Fluency, Style and Design. Each category was then divided into granular error types to facilitate tracking them in the edited texts of the

[2] Kenny (2022) enumerates 4 typical non-human errors: linguistic ambiguity, non-isomorphism, discontinuous dependencies and non-compositionality.

two groups. These were analysed to verify which errors were detected and fixed and whether there were relevant differences in each group's edits. Finally, the evaluated data were correlated with the answers to pre-questionnaire questions *7. Higher education studies in translation* and *8. Professional experience in translation*, and post-questionnaire questions *4. How do you rate the quality of the MT output?* and 5. *Your alterations to the MT text were...[few, some, many (in number and relevance)]* to compare participants' profiles with editing behavior. Questions 6 and 7 of the post-questionnaire, concerning error categories detected and MT output usefulness in fixing them, were also correlated with the evaluation results. The data was used to answer the first 2 questions,

Answers to question *9. Briefly describe the process you followed to carry out this post-editing task* (post-questionnaire) were analysed to check differences in the groups' PE procedures, and correlate participants' perceptions with the evaluator's analysis, to try and draw some insight for the third research question.

3.1. Participants' profile

Twenty-one students attending courses in legal translation at ISCAP, the Accounting and Business School of the Polytechnic Institute of Porto, participated in the pilot study on two consecutive days, in May 2022. The post-editing task was carried out by fourteen students of the Master's in Specialised Translation and Interpreting (MSTI), on day one, and by seven students from the Post-graduation in Specialised Translation and Translation Tools (PGSTTT), on day two. ISCAP's MSTI is a member of the EMT network and more than half the students take the master's following completion of the degree in Management Assistance and Translation at the same institution. The PGSTTT, in turn, is a lifelong learning, one-year course preferred by graduates wanting to start a career in translation and professional translators in search of updating.

The two groups (henceforward, the Master's – G1 and the Post-graduation – G2 groups) were not homogenous: G1 students were generally younger and less experienced. In the master's group, there were 5 males and 9 females, and all 7 G2 participants were females. English language proficiency was evenly distributed between C1 and C2 in G1; 70% of G2 participants indicated C2 as their level. As stated before, only G2 participants attended a module in PE.

3.2. Materials and procedures

The task consisted in post-editing a 330-word extract of the Articles of Association (AoA) of EDP, a Portuguese public limited company (*sociedade anónima*) from the energy sector. The extract consisting of the initial three articles had been previously translated into British English in the free version of DeepL[3], a German-based NMT system that used the existing dataset of the translation search engine Linguee[4]. Two reasons motivated the selection of the document: translation of company formation documents is frequent in Portugal and this type of text that can be easily accessed online, in both Portuguese and English. Participants were informed of and agreed with the content and purpose of the experiment.

British English was the preferred variant and participants were instructed to post-edit accordingly. Translation into L2 has been used for pedagogic purposes in countries with languages of limited diffusion (T. Pavlovic 2013; Fonseca, 2015) or where the hegemony of English creates a context where all other languages are *minority languages*. In these countries, such as Portugal, Germany, Spain and Brazil, professional translation into

[3] https://www.deepl.com/translator
[4] https://www.linguee.com/

English (L2) is an established reality that must somehow be dealt with in training (Kiraly, 2000; N. Pavlovic, 2007; Vigier, 2016; Ferreira et al., 2018). Post-editing in L2 is one of the exercises to address this issue[5].

The translation brief required post-editing for human translation quality (TAUS, 2016), since the purpose of the target text was the internationalisation of the company. In order to address the research questions, the brief did not include post-editing guidelines. In both groups, students were familiar with the extract's branch of law and text genre, and had translated examples of company AoA. They were also aware that documentary translation (Nord, 2016) is advisable when legal documents are translated for information of the target audience. At the time of the experiment, differences between the USA and the UK legal systems and how these reflect in legal discourse had been discussed in class.

On the days of the experiment, each group of participants filled in the pre-task questionnaire (9 questions) to collect data on educational and professional backgrounds and their perceptions of the benefits and limitations of MT. They then carried out the post-editing task followed by a post-task questionnaire, comprising 10 questions, in which they stated familiarity with NMT systems, perceptions on the quality and usefulness of the NMT output, degree of difficulty and satisfaction with the task and provided a brief description of how they carried out the post-editing task. There were no time constraints, and both groups took approximately the same time to complete the three tasks.

3.3. Analysis

On each day of the experiment, after completion of the post-questionnaire, participants emailed the post-edited texts to the author. The anonymised documents were downloaded and analysed using the MS Word Track Changes feature. Assessment of variation in the number and type of errors detected and fixed by each group[6] was supported in the Error Typology Best Practice Guidelines (TAUS, 2017).

TAUS recommends a limited number of error categories for quality evaluation and describes the four most commonly used: Language, Terminology, Accuracy and Style (2017). For evaluations that "seek to understand in detail the nature or cause of errors" (2017) a more detailed and flexible typology is advisable and the TAUS Dynamic Quality Framework Knowledge Base is referenced[7]. The quality error typology evaluation template sets 7 high-level error types, each divided into granular error types. From those, the author selected 4 high-level error types – Accuracy, Fluency, Design and Style – divided them in granular error types and used them to label the 29 recommended edits in the MT output. These were, then, tracked in G1 and G2 post-edited texts.

High-level error type	Granular error type	No. of edits
Accuracy	Mistranslation	5
	Under-translation	3
	Untranslated text	1
	Inconsistency	3
Fluency	Syntax	2

[5] Compiling small comparable corpora to compensate for lesser fluency, grammatical accuracy and phraseology, while providing context for analysis of incongruity in intersystemic translation into L2 (Scott, 2012; Vigier, 2016) are other exercises carried out in the legal translation class.

[6] In G2, there was 1 invalid contribution. Only 6 post-edited extracts were evaluated, although 7 answers to pre and post-questionnaires were validated.

[7] TAUS launched the first attempt at an industry-developed standard for translation quality evaluation in 2011, with a dynamic quality framework that lived up to today's translation quality requirements that change depending on content type, purpose and audience (Gorog, 2014).

	Grammar	2
Design	Formatting	5
	Conventions	1
Style	Awkward	3
	Unidiomatic	4
TOTAL		29

Table 1. TAUS Error Categories (adapted).

The 4 categories were selected taking into consideration the small size of the extract and the relevance of accurate representation of meaning in the translation of legal texts (Sarcevic, 2000; Prieto Ramos, 2014). Because "Legal terminology is the most visible, [.../...] and it is also one of the major sources of difficulty in translating legal documents" (Cao, 2007) all the examples included in the Accuracy category are terms. This is the most detailed category to which a granular error subcategory was added for Inconsistency in term usage. Fewer examples and sub-categories for Fluency are also due to the small size of the extract. Formatting illustrates the category's errors in NMT output. The Style category aims at highlighting content that, although grammatical, does not reflect the legal style of the target system. The category of Style is not analysed here.

Source text	NMT output	Recom. edit	PE text G1	PE text G2
1. Contrato de Sociedade	Memorandum and Articles of Association	Articles of Association	Error undetected:**7** Error fixed:**2** Error introduced:**5**	Error undetected:**4** Error fixed:**2** Error introduced:**0**
2. simples deliberação	simple resolution	ordinary resolution	Error undetected:**12** Error fixed: **0** Error introduced:**2**	Error undetected:**1** Error fixed:**5** Error introduced:**0**
3. agências	agencies	branches	Error undetected:**12** Error fixed:**0** Error introduced:**2**	Error undetected:**4** Error fixed:**0** Error introduced:**2**
4. proceder	proceed	define/ formulate	Error undetected:**13** Error fixed:**1** Error introduced: **0**	Error undetected:**6** Error fixed **0** Error introduced:**0**
5.c) assegurar... d) assegurar...	c) ensure... d) ensure...	c) ensure... d) undertake...	Error undetected:**14** Error fixed:**0** Error introduced:**0**	Error undetected:**5** Error fixed:**0** Error introduced:**1**

Table 2. Error Type evaluation of Accuracy (mistranslation).

In all five mistranslations over 70% of G1 and G2 participants fail to identify the error in the NMT output, probably because they lack domain competence (1 and 2) and efficient PE strategies (3 and 4). Apart from the slightly higher number of 'error introduced' by G1, there are no significant differences in PE procedures. In *deliberação simples*, an ellipsis, typical of expert communication, occurs. Undetected by the untrained NMT system, it is only identified and fixed by G2 participants. However, voting procedures in general meetings and the title of the incorporation document had been discussed in both groups' classes.

Literal translation of terms is another typical issue of online NMT output (3 to 5). A second ellipsis occurs in *agências*, short for *agências bancárias* (branches of banks), mistranslated by the cognate **agencies**. The term is followed by a synonym – *delegações* (**branches**, in the NMT output) which may explain why the 4 participants who identified the error failed in properly editing it, either replacing **branches** by **delegations** (literal mistranslation in the context) or by **subsidiaries** (a collocate of **branches**, though differing in meaning). The verbs *proceder* and *assegurar* (4 and 5) are also translated by cognates that do not represent the same meaning in the context of Article 3 of the AoA. The fact that the same verb is repeated at the beginning of consecutive sentences (5) may also contribute to failure in error identification.

Source text	NMT output	Recomm. edit	PE text G1	PE text G2
6. sede	head office	registered office	Error undetected:**10** Error fixed:**2** Error introduced:**2**	Error undetected:**6** Error fixed:**0** Error introduced:**0**
7. participações	participations	participating interests	Error undetected:**12** Error fixed:**1** Error introduced:**1**	Error undetected:**4** Error fixed:**1** Error introduced:**1**
8. suprimentos	loans	shareholders' loans	Error undetected:**9** Error fixed:**0** Error introduced: **5**	Error undetected:**4** Error fixed **0** Error introduced:**2**

Table 3. Error Type evaluation of Accuracy (under-translation).

As in the previous subcategory, between 70% to 80% of participants fail to spot errors. Differences in PE texts in G1 and G2 are limited to a slightly higher number of errors identified by G1. Consequently, G1 also introduce a higher number of errors. Procedures adopted to edit *suprimentos* – **loans** illustrate this: when the term **loans** is repeated in the following sentence in the NMT output: "4. The company may provide services and grant **loans** and other forms of **loans**…", participants would likely have consulted the ST to check the 2 different terms in Portuguese: *suprimentos* and *empréstimos*. When in doubt, G1 tend to try and fix the error, whereas most G2 participants prefer to accept the NMT suggestion.

Source text	NMT output	Recomm. edit	PE text G1	PE text G2
9. sociedade anónima	sociedade anónima	(public) limited liability company	Error undetected:**0** Error fixed:**12** Error introduced:**2**	Error undetected:**0** Error fixed:**5** Error introduced:**1**

Table 4. Error Type evaluation of Accuracy (untranslated text).

All participants identified the untranslated term, although both in G1 and G2 some chose to keep it in the SL between inverted commas and 3 fail to identify the type of company correctly.

Source text	NMT output	Recomm. edit	PE text G1	PE text G2
10. denominação denominação	name shall be known	name the Company's name is	Error undetected:**9** Error fixed:**4** Error introduced:**1**	Error undetected:**4** Error fixed:**2** Error introduced:**0**
(6). sede 11.sede social	head office registered office	registered office registered office	Error undetected:**10** Error fixed:**0** Error introduced:**4**	Error undetected:**6** Error fixed:**0** Error introduced:**0**
12. objecto objecto objecto social objecto social	object object corporate object corporate object	object object (Company's) object (Company's) object	Error undetected:**0** Error fixed:**0** Error introduced: **3**	Error undetected:**0** Error fixed **0** Error introduced:**2**

Table 5. Error Type evaluation of Accuracy (inconsistency).

Table 5 illustrates variation in the translation of the terms *denominação*, *sede* and *objecto*, occurring twice: in the Section's Title and in the text of the articles. Although there is no obvious reason not to repeat the term the second time it occurs, the majority in both groups fails to detect the inconsistency in the NMT text. The ellipsis referred to above – the omission of the adjective *social* in 11 and 12 – may account for the inconsistency in the NMT text, but does not explain why **name** is occasionally replaced by **denomination**, **registered office** by **head office** or **object** by **aim** or **purpose** in the PE texts. As with previous examples, these terms had been dealt with in class in the context of company law. A possible explanation is that some participants introduced error in the terms' second occurrences because they were concerned with terminological consistency, and thus repeated the mistranslated term of the first occurrences[8].

As regards the category of Accuracy as a whole, we observed that typical NMT errors, with the exception of inconsistency, are not detected by the majority of G1 and G2 participants. While G1 carry out more PE operations, G2 participants seem slightly better at handling terminology, thus not making it possible to state whether it is domain competence or prior training in PE to make a difference.

In the category of Fluency, two examples of syntax and two of grammar editing are analysed to illustrate how the groups handled post-editing long/complex sentences when compared with mechanical editing procedures. Numbers 1 and 2 of Article 3 were chosen as examples of a long sentence (n.1) and a syntactically complex one (n.2).

Article 3
1. The object of EDP is to promote, stimulate and manage, directly or indirectly, undertakings and activities in the energy sector, both at national and international level, with a view to increasing and improving the performance of all the companies of its group. 2. EDP, in the development of its corporate object, must, in relation to the companies of its group* a) proceed to the definition of the joint global strategy of those companies; b) coordinate their action, in order to guarantee compliance with the duties which at each moment are assigned to them; c) **to** ensure joint representation of the interests common to all of them* d) **to** ensure, globally, the functions common to all of them, namely in the financial area, with a view to obtaining group synergies.

Table 6. Error Type evaluation of Fluency (syntax).

In both groups and in the two sentences, PE operations were limited to minor changes, mainly, in conjunctions, prepositions and articles. In G1, some unnecessary alterations were made, and one error was introduced in n.1. Conversely, in n.2, alterations were more relevant, as both groups detected the awkward phrasing. Again, G1 participants made more alterations than G2, but were not more successful in improving fluency.

Fluency is also achieved through more mechanical operations, such as checking punctuation, spelling or enumerative structures[9]. A minority of participants in G1 and G2 fail to fix the two punctuation signs (see table 6*) missing in n. 2, Article 3. As for inconsistent use of preposition **to** in c) and d) of n.2, the majority in both groups does not restore the syntactic parallelism at the start of each item of the enumerative structure. Differences in each group PE behaviour are not noticeable.

In the design category, the aim was to verify editing behaviour in operations that did not require cognitive effort, nor any special domain or revision competences.

Source text	PE text G1	PE text G2
Title formatting	Error fixed:**13**	Error fixed:**3**
Title bold	Error fixed:**2**	Error fixed:**1**
Capital letters	Error fixed:**2**	Error fixed:**0**

[8] This explanation is corroborated by answers to question 9 (post-questionnaire), in which more than half the participants refer terminology as a major preoccupation when post-editing.

[9] According to Ho-Dac et al. (2012), enumerative structures are characterised by an internal organisation and involve several sub-segments: a trigger (optional), segments composing the enumeration, a closure (optional).

Typo error	Error fixed:2	Error fixed:0
Typo repetition	Error fixed:9	Error fixed:3
Address convention	Error fixed:2	Error fixed:0

Table 7. Error Type evaluation of Design

Interestingly, both groups do not carry out what can be considered simple revision operations. This behaviour is more noticeable in G2, who scored slightly better in the category of accuracy. The fact that both groups fail to carry out what can be considered simpler, more mechanical revision operations may indicate that explicit instructions on how to carry out MTPE of legal documents are needed.

4. Results and Discussion

The present study aimed at investigating whether prior introduction to MTPE reflected in the edited products of 2 groups of participants. Analysis of the edited extracts does not reveal significant differences in each group's results: the single noticeable evidence is that the majority of participants in both groups fail to identify many of the errors in the 3 categories analysed.

In pre and post-questionnaires, participants reveal a positive attitude towards MT recognizing time saving and cost-effective benefits of technology, stating its limits in translating of culturally-marked texts and emphasizing the need for human intervention. Most of them claim to be familiar with and use MT systems – especially DeepL and Google Translate –, they rate the quality of the MT output as generally good and around three-quarters are quite satisfied with their edited texts. This positive attitude seems to be in line with the way both groups approach the editing task: confidence in the MT output quality and affirmed usefulness of the MT output, especially for the fluency category, may help explain the few edits participants make. Accordingly, the only granular category that participants state requires relevant edits is terminology. Operations for the high-level Accuracy category are the most numerous, with G2 performing slightly better than G1 in fixing these errors. At the same time, G1 tend to make more edits that do not fix but introduce a new error. In the category of Fluency, both groups results are also quite similar. Correlating these results with participant profile – G2 are, on average, older and have professional experience in translation – may indicate that familiarity with the domain is responsible for G2 more efficient MTPE.

Conversely, when expected to carry out editing operations that did not require specific knowledge of domain or discourse, both groups failed to identify grammar, punctuation, spelling and formatting errors. In the post-questionnaire questions 7 and 8, the majority of participants perceived the MT output good linguistic quality as quite useful for the PE process, stating that it made the editing task easier and faster, an attitude that may have played a role in the seemingly careless way with which tasks requiring less cognitive effort were approached.

Answers to open question 9 of the post-questionnaire, in which participants described the process followed to PE the extract, further corroborate these results: over 80% of G1 mention verifying every term by resorting to dictionaries, glossaries and databases. About half mention using other tools – such as Grammarly – to revise language, while others refer that not translating from scratch allows them to focus on lexical errors and saves time because there is no need to formulate sentences. Most G2 participants mention the same preoccupation with accurate rendering of terminology. Sources used include EDP's site, glossaries and parallel texts. Only one participant refers the need to correct literal syntax.

As far as it is possible to answer the questions in 3., no noticeable differences in both groups' lexical, grammatical or formatting edits (Q. 2) were detected and G2 slightly better performance in fixing errors cannot be traced to prior PE training, due to participant age group and professional experience. Younger and less experienced G1 participants make a higher number of edits and mention using other tools to PE. Other than this, there are no significant differences in both groups' PE process description (Q. 3): more than half the participants explicitly say they compare source and MT texts, resort to external sources to check terminology, check language and do not mention design or style.

5. Conclusions and Future Work

As stated earlier, this was a small-scale, preliminary study, for which results have to be cautiously approached. The small number of participants, the reduced size of the edited extract, the heterogeneous profile of participants, and the experiment conditions (participants carried out the task as one more class exercise) do not favour the quantification of findings. From the trainer's point of view, though, variability is the rule: trainees change every six months and successful teaching strategies depend on factors that the trainer is not always able to control.

The decision not to control every variable in the study was due to its broader aim: to prepare the introduction of MTPE in the legal translation class. Preference was, therefore, given to detailed analysis of how each group edited each error (sub-)category and the categories selected covered the domain, discursive and stylistic components that need to be accounted for when training legal translators. It was possible to determine that, in general, participants focused their PE efforts on the category of accuracy, complying with the precision required to translate legal concepts. However, they relied too much on the perceived "fluency" of the MT output. The fast-growing linguistic quality of NMT output and a preference for literal solutions in legal translation, may account for participants' attitude, together with the fact that they post-edit into their L2. What these facts do not explain is why both groups failed in identifying and fixing error categories that are not cognitively demanding.

Legal translation is demanding for trainees and thus promoting the development of the methodological competence by proposing translation workflows to guide the translation process may reflect on more informed decision-making (Prieto Ramos, 2011). Although the addition of technological resources and tools to the process may add to the cognitive load, it is inevitable and, therefore, justifies further investigation on how to accommodate the shift from the traditional translation process to a process that is initiated with multiple texts, sources and tools from which the most adequate option has to be selected.

The study's preliminary results have led to fine-tuning the initial integrative methodology, specifically in the following: providing trainees with a brief introduction to MT's limits and typical error types and a simplified framework for error analysis, both adapted to the translation of legal texts; raising awareness to the abundance of incorrect literal options typical of legal translation and of automated systems output; redesigning steps 2 and 3 of the methodological tool by introducing a pre-documentation stage to edit the design and mechanic fluency categories and flag potential syntactic and terminological errors; promote guided documentation based on textual resources that efficiently provide insight on the legal and linguistic features that need to be catered for in PE; adding any sub-categories needed.

The fine-tuned model was presented in two legal translation classes that participated in the second version of the pilot study, in June of 2023. Comparison of both studies' results is expected to shed further light on the productive use of MTPE in domain-specific translation training. Professional post-editors of today may have been trained as translators, but present-day translation trainees will inevitably take up both activities simultaneously. It is not unlikely that PE is what trainees are now doing in translation classes, even if they and their trainers do not address it openly. It becomes imperative, therefore, to integrate MTPE in the specialised translation class.

This work is financed by portuguese national funds through FCT - Fundação para a Ciência e Tecnologia, under the project UIDB/05422/2020.

6. References

Albi, A. B. (2005): Es posible traducir realidades jurídicas? Restricciones y prioridades en la traducción de documentos de sucesiones británicos al español. In E. M. Nebot, A. B. Albi (Eds.), *La traducción y la interpretación en las relaciones jurídicas internacionales* (pp. 65-89). Publicacions de la Universitat Jaume I.

Alcaraz, E. & Hughes, B. (2002) *Legal Translation Explained.* St. Jerome.

Bestué, C. (2016) Translating law in the digital age. Translation problems or matters of legal interpretation?. *Perspectives, 24*:4, 576-590, DOI: 10.1080/0907676X.2015.1070884

Biel, Ł. (2008). Legal terminology in translation practice: Dictionaries, googling or discussion forums? *SKASE – Journal of Translation and Interpretation, 3*:1, 22-38. http://www.skase.sk/Volumes/JTI03/pdf.doc/3.pdf

Biel, Ł. (2009). Organization of background knowledge structures in legal language and related translation problems. *Comparative Legilinguistics, 1*, 176–189. https://doi.org/10.14746/cl.2009.01.13.

Cao, D. (2007). *Translating Law.* Multilingual Matters.

Carmo, F. E. M. (2017). *Post-editing: A Theoretical and Practical Challenge for Translation Studies and Machine Learning.* [Ph.D. thesis]. Universidade do Porto.

Directorate-General for Translation (2022). *EMT Competence Framework.* European Master's in Translation. https://commission.europa.eu/system/files/2022-11/emt_competence_fwk_2022_en.pdf.

Doherty, S. (2016). The impact of translation technologies on the process and product of translation. *International Journal of Communication, 10*, 947–969. https://ijoc.org/index.php/ijoc/article/viewFile/3499/1573

Ferreira, A., Gottardo, A. & Schwieter, J. (2018). Decision-making processes in direct and inverse translation through retrospective protocols. *Translation, Cognition & Behavior, 1*, 98-118. DOI:10.1075/tcb.00005.fer.

Fonseca, N. (2015). Directionality in translation: Investigating prototypical patterns in editing procedures. *Translation & Interpreting, 7*(1), 111-125 . DOI: ti.106201.2015.a08

Gorog, A. (2014). Quantifying and benchmarking quality: the TAUS Dynamic Quality Framework. *Revista Tradumàtica: tecnologies de la traducció, 12*, 443-454. DOI:10.5565/rev/tradumatica.66

Harvey, M. (2002). What's so Special about Legal Translation? *Meta, 47*(2), 177–185. https://doi.org/10.7202/008007ar

Ho-Dac, L., Fabre, C., Péry-Woodley, M., Rebeyrolle, J. & Tanguy, L. (2012). An Empirical Approach to the Signalling of Enumerative Structures, *Discours, 10.* http://journals.openedition.org/discours/8611. DOI: 10.4000/discours.8611.

Hu, K. & Cadwell, P. (2016). A comparative study of post-editing guidelines. *Baltic J. Modern Computing, 4*(2), 346-353. DOI: 10.13140/RG.2.1.2253.1446.

International Organization for Standardization (2017). *Translation services – Post-editing of machine translation output – Requirements* (ISO Standard No. 18587:2017).

Kenny, D. & Doherty, S. (2014) Statistical machine translation in the translation curriculum: overcoming obstacles and empowering translators, *The Interpreter and Translator Trainer, 8*(2), 276-294. DOI: 10.1080/1750399X.2014.936112.

Kenny, D. (2020). Technology in Translator Training. In M. O'Hagan (Ed.), *The Routledge Handbook of Translation and Technology* (pp. 498-515). Routledge.

Kenny, D. (2022). Human and machine translation. In D. Kenny (Ed.), *Machine translation for everyone: Empowering users in the age of artificial intelligence* (pp. 23-49). Language Science Press. DOI: 10.5281.

Kiraly, D. (2000). Translation into a non-mother tongue: From collaboration to competence. In M. Grosman, M. Kadric, I. Kovacic & M. Snell-Hornby (Eds.), *Translation into Non-mother Tongues* (pp.117-123). Stauffenburg Verlag.

Koponen, M. (2016). Is machine translation post-editing worth the effort? A survey of research into post-editing and effort. *The Journal of Specialised Translation, 25*, 131–148. http://www.jostrans.org/issue25/art_koponen.pdf.

Nord, C. (2016) Skopos and (Un)certainty: How Functional Translators Deal with Doubt. *Meta, 61*(1), 29-41. https://doi.org/10.7202/1036981ar.

O'Brien, S. (2022). How to deal with errors in machine translation: Postediting. In D. Kenny (Ed.), *Machine translation for everyone: Empowering users in the age of artificial intelligence* (pp. 105-120). Language Science Press. DOI: 10.5281.

Pavlović, N. (2007). Directionality in Translation and Interpreting Practice: Report on a questionnaire survey in Croatia. *FORUM Revue internationale d'interprétation et de traduction / International Journal of Interpretation and Translation*, 5(2), 79-99. DOI: 10.1075/forum.5.2.05pav.

Pavlovic, T. (2013). Exploring Directionality in Translation Studies. *ExELL (Explorations in English Language and Linguistics), 1*(2), 149-165. http://www.exell.ff.untz.ba/wp-content/uploads/2014/04/ExELL.1.149.Pavlovic.pdf.

Prieto Ramos, F. (2011). Developing Legal Translation Competence: An Integrative Process-Oriented Approach. *Comparative Legilinguistics, 5*, 7-22. https://doi.org/10.14746/cl.2011.5.01.

Prieto Ramos, F. (2014). Parameters for Problem-Solving in Legal Translation: Implications for Legal Lexicography and Institutional Terminology Management. In *The Ashgate Handbook of Legal Translation* (pp. 121-134). Routledge.

Pym, A. (2013). Translation Skill-Sets in a Machine-Translation Age. *Meta*, 58(3), 487–503. https://doi.org/10.7202/1025047ar

Pym, A., & Torres-Simon, E. (2021). Efectos de la automatización en las competencias básicas del traductor: la traducción automática neuronal. In A. V. Suñe, & A. A. Alarcón (Dirs.), *Ocupaciones y Lenguaje: Indicadores y Análisis De Competencias lingüísticas En El Ámbito Laboral*. Universitat Rovira i Virgili.

Rodríguez de Céspedes, B. (2019). Translator education at a crossroads: the impact of automation. *Lebende Sprachen, 64*(1). https://doi.org/10.1515/les-2019-0005.

Šarčević, S. (2000), Legal Translation and Translation Theory: a Receiver- oriented Approach, In *Legal translation: history, theory/ies and practice*. [Proceedings of the International colloquium University of Geneva], February 17-19, 2000 - Berne: ASTTI, cop. 2000. http://tradulex.org/Actes2000/sarcevic.pdf

Scott, J. (2012). Can Genre-Specific DIY Corpora, Compiled by Legal Translators Themselves, Assist Them in 'Learning the Lingo' of Legal Subgenres?. *Comparative Legilinguistics, 12*, 87–100. https://doi.org/10.14746/cl.2012.12.05

TAUS. (2016). *Post Editing Guidelines*. Isabella Massardo, Jaap van der Meer, Sharon O'Brien, Fred Hollowood, Nora Aranberri, Katrin Drescher. https://www.taus.net/resources/reports/mt-post-editing-guidelines

TAUS, (2017). *Quality Evaluation using an Error Typology Approach*. TAUS BV, De Rijp. https://cdn2.hubspot.net/hubfs/2734675/Reports,%20ebooks/Error%20Typology%20Best%20Practices%20Guidelines.pdf.

Valli, P. (2015). The TAUS Quality Dashboard (Review of The TAUS Quality Dashboard). *Proceedings of the 37th Conference Translating and the Computer* (pp. 127–136). AsLing. https://aclanthology.org/2015.tc-1.17.pdf.

Vieira, L.N. (2019). Post-Editing of Machine Translation. In M. O'Hagan (Ed.), *The Routledge Handbook of Translation and Technology* (pp. 319-335). Routledge.

Wilss, W. (1996). *Knowledge and skills in translator behaviour*. John Benjamins. DOI: https://doi.org/10.1075/btl.15.

Yamada, M. (2019). The impact of Google Neural Machine Translation on Post-editing by student translators. *The Journal of Specialised Translation*, 31. 87-106. https://jostrans.org/issue31/art_yamada.php.

Technology Preparedness and Translator Training: Implications for Pedagogy

Hari Venkatesan hariv@um.edu.mo

Abstract

With increasing acknowledgement of enhanced quality now achievable by Machine Translation, new possibilities have emerged in translation, both vis-à-vis division of labour between human and machine in the translation process and acceptability of lower quality of language in exchange for efficiency. This paper presents surveys of four cohorts of post-graduate students of translation from the University of Macau to see if perceived trainee awareness and preparedness has kept pace with these possibilities. It is found that trainees across the years generally lack confidence in their perceived awareness, are hesitant in employing MT, and show definite reservations when reconsidering issues such as quality and division of labour. While the size of respondents is small, it is interesting to note that the awareness and preparedness mentioned above are found to be similar across the four years. The implication for training is that technology be fully integrated into the translation process in order to provide trainees with a template/framework to handle diverse situations, particularly those that require offering translations of a lower quality with a short turnaround time. The focus here is on Chinese-English translation, but the discussion may find resonance with other language pairs.

1. Introduction

For much of its history the ultimate goal of achieving Fully Automatic High-Quality Translation remained out of reach for Machine Translation (Hutchins and Somers 1997, 148). However, with the emergence of Statistical Machine Translation (SMT) implementations around 2006, the quality of raw MT output became greatly enhanced compared to the former Rule Based Machine Translation (RBMT). University programmes in translation too began incorporating "Computer-Assisted Translation" (CAT, including TM and SBMT) in their curricula around this time (Kenny and Doherty 2014, 276).

In the case of English-Chinese translation, with the advent of SMT systems Cui predicted that Post-Editing (PE) was expected to play an increasingly important role in meeting the demands of the language services market efficiently (Cui 2014). This resonated with assessments elsewhere that reported gains in quality independent of factors such as language, text or translator ability (Garcia 2011). Cui also went on to suggest that PE, Human Translation (HT) and Project Management would have to come together to fully tap into the possibilities brought about by Machine Translation and meet the ever-increasing demand for translation (Cui 2014, 72–73). A study in Europe the same year echoed this by declaring that "the time is ripe to develop and publish an up-to-date holistic syllabus in SMT for trainee translators." (Kenny and Doherty 2014, 288). It also emphasized the need for integration of SMT in translation in order to ensure continued relevance of training, one that ensures

Proceedings of Machine Translation Summit XIX, Vol. 2: Users Track, pages 24–41
September 4–8, 2023, Macau SAR, China.

"ownership, critical understanding and a good deal of control" (Kenny and Doherty 2014, 290) on the part of translators. The statement is reflective of concerns both for continued relevance of training and also for the role of human translators.

With the emergence of Neural Machine Translation (NMT) systems that became available to users around 2016 (Y. Wu et al. 2016) it may be said that MT has come of age, where in case of language pairs such as English and Chinese there have even been bold claims of achieving parity with Human Translation (HT) (Hassan et al. 2018), though evidence to the contrary has also been provided (Läubli, Sennrich, and Volk 2018). Qin (2018) identifies persisting issues with Neural Machine Translation (NMT) between English and Chinese at lexical and syntactic and discourse levels and concludes that MT will not replace HT. Nevertheless, Qin yet calls for reconsidering division of labour, exploring possibilities brought about by PE and including MT, CAT and Translation Management Systems in teaching curricula (Qin 2018, 55–56). There has been increasing acknowledgement of the role that MT and post-editing MT output can play at least in certain domains of translation in case of other language pairs as well (Mellinger 2017; Massey and Ehrensberger-Dow 2017).

The higher quality of raw MT output has also brought about new possibilities, including that of variable efficiency and quality. There is much interest now in exploring post-editing and revision, and issues of variable quality in translation research (Drugan 2013; Way 2018; Bittner 2020; Konttinen, Salmi, and Koponen 2020). The quality achieved by raw MT output is such that there are even studies considering the role Machine Translation could play in making academic research in different languages globally available and enable global communication (Doherty 2016; Bowker and Ciro 2019; Escartín and Goulet 2020).

Citing an early survey of language service requirements in enterprises in China, Wang points out that 77.30% of enterprises prioritized familiarity with translation technology and aids in employees (H. Wang 2013, 23). Suggesting parallels in the case of language pairs in Europe, a study reports to have found that "only 10 % of all companies surveyed were operating without them" and that these competences were considered essential by employers (Rodríguez de Céspedes, 2019, p. 107, 111). Against this background it becomes pertinent to ask if trainees (at least at the postgraduate level) are prepared to respond to demands for higher efficiency in translation. This study examines perceived awareness towards technology among postgraduate trainees at one institution, and if it has changed over four years as use of MT becomes normalized. Importantly, it also explores if postgraduate students of translation find themselves prepared to offer lower quality in exchange for higher efficiency.

Accordingly, this study set out to explore the following questions:

- How do post-graduate trainees of translation perceive their awareness and preparedness towards MT, does this perception change over the years?
- Across the four years, how prepared are trainees to consider quality of translation as variable and a reduced or editing role for human translators in some contexts?
- What, if any, are the implications of the above for translator training.

2. The Surveys

Surveys were conducted over four consecutive years with four successive cohorts (2018-2021). The purpose behind this was to examine if there are significant temporal variations in perceptions of awareness and preparedness across the years. Given the increasingly widespread use of MT in translation, it may be reasonable to expect that more recent respondents might be more aware and likely to use MT, and also be more willing to consider modes of working that integrate MT in translation to achieve efficiency.

The respondents of these surveys were 2nd year postgraduate students of a two-year MA in Translation Studies (English-Chinese) programme at the University of Macau. Each cohort of students has roughly 25-30 students, of which 16-20 took the survey. The students of this programme include those from across the Greater China Region, of whom roughly half have Cantonese as their first language (hailing from Hong Kong, Macao and southern China), and slightly more than half have Modern Standard Chinese (*Putonghua*) as their first language (from various parts of China, including Taiwan). The students admitted to the programme include but are not limited to those who have majored in translation during their undergraduate studies. All candidates are subject to a rigorous assessment, including minimum IELTS / CET (College English Test) / TEM (Test for English Majors) scores and interviews to establish competence preparedness for a career in translation. In terms of age, all respondents reported themselves as falling between 20 and30 years of age, except 3 from the 2018 cohort, 1 from 2019 and 2 from 2021 who reported their age as 30-40 years.

The survey was conducted after the candidates had completed one year of study in translation but before taking any courses that specifically addressed translation technology. Given that these are students of translation with at least one year of formal training at the postgraduate level, it may be expected that they are generally aware of quality now achievable by MT and willing to employ it.

The questionnaire employed for the survey is reproduced in Appendix 1. The questionnaire was piloted in fall 2016 and 2017 with two cohorts of students (not included in the data presented herein) and the questions were adjusted for clarity based on feedback. In the data presented below 0-4 points are assigned in the order that the choices are presented in the questionnaire.

The questionnaire is divided into three sets, exploring two main questions identified above. The purpose of the first set (Q1-Q4) was to understand how trainees perceive their awareness of the quality now achievable by Machine Translation (Q1-Q2) and how willing they were to use Machine Translation in actual translation (Q3-Q4). The second set looks at how prepared trainees are towards reconsidering quality in certain contexts (Q5-Q6) and how they viewed the changing role of human beings in translation (Q7-8). Mean scores and standard deviations for responses to each question are presented below.

2.1 Results

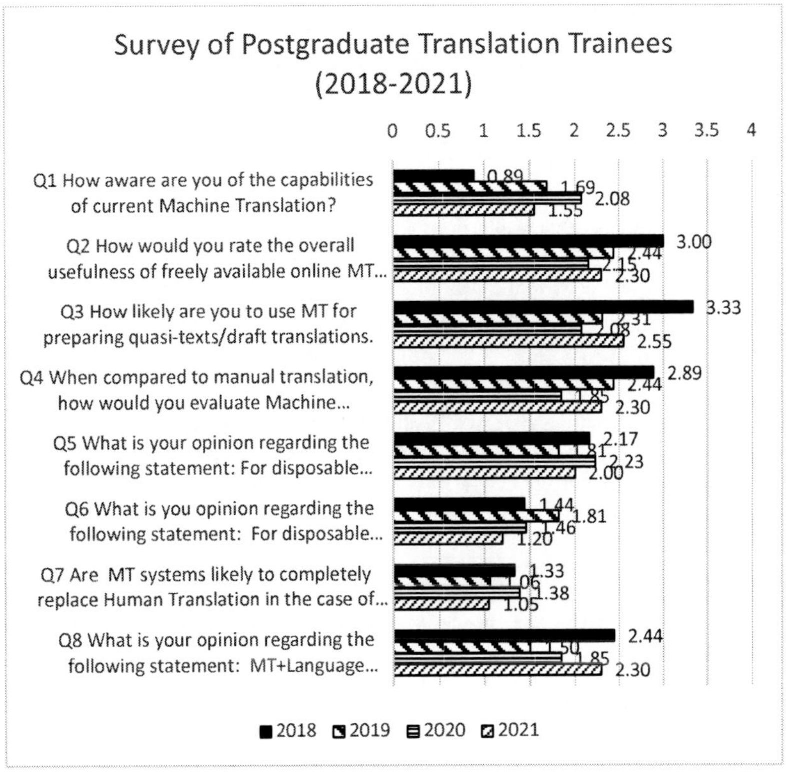

Fig. 1 Mean scores for each year (2018-2021)

	Q1	Q2	Q3	Q4	Q5	Q6	Q7	Q8
2018	0.758395	1.283378	0.840168	0.963382	1.043185	1.096638	1.283378	1.247219
2019	1.014479	0.963933	1.195478	1.093542	0.655108	0.910586	1.062623	1.21106
2020	0.954074	0.898717	1.497862	0.987096	0.83205	0.77625	1.043908	1.405119
2021	0.825578	0.656947	1.145931	1.031095	0.917663	0.767772	1.099043	0.864505

Fig. 2 Standard deviation in responses to each question (2018-21)

2.1.1 Awareness of Machine Translation:

In general respondents across the years seem modest in how they perceive their awareness towards current capabilities (quality) achieved by raw MT output in case of informative texts. Even respondents from 2020 who are the most confident in their awareness of MT reach a little over 2 points on average, which is equivalent to being ‘aware’ but not ‘quite aware’, leave alone ‘fully aware’, while the respondents from 2018 seem to be the most modest about their understanding (Q1) and paradoxically also the most positive towards integrating available it in translation (Q2, Q3).

Respondents from 2020 express most confidence in their awareness of current capabilities but are much more conservative when it comes to the usefulness of MT and likeliness of using it in translation ('likely' but not 'quite likely'). In each case respondents from 2019 and 2021 seem to fall roughly in the middle. The responses to Q2-Q4 show strong similarities of a decrease in favourable appraisal of technology between 2018-2020, which is contrary to what would be expected with passing years. The trend somewhat reverses in 2021 but does not reach the same level as 2018.

Fig. 2 shows the Standard Deviation in responses. The SD shows a variance of roughly 1 point in most cases and reaches a high of ±1.4-1.5 for Q3 and Q8 in case of the 2020 cohort. This indicates a variance that results in responses generally spanning three choices. For instance, in case of awareness the mean score of the 2018 cohort of 0.89 indicates that they are 'somewhat aware' of current capabilities of MT. However, a SD of ±0.75 reveals that responses ranged from 'not aware' to 'aware'. In case of 2019, 2020 and 2021 the responses similarly ranged from 'somewhat aware' to 'quite aware', 'somewhat aware' to 'quite aware' and 'somewhat aware' to 'aware' respectively.

In case of usefulness barring 2018 (1.28), all three cohorts show a deviation less than 1 point. This indicates that in case of the 2018 cohort responses varied from 'useful' to 'very useful'. Q3 asked respondents how likely they were to use MT and this question shows the most deviation among all, particularly with students from 2020 (1.49) who on average (2.15) seem 'likely' but given the deviation actually swing across the spectrum from 'somewhat likely' to 'very likely'. As for the comparison between HT and MT (Q4) the deviation observed was less than 1 in case of 2018 and 2020 and slightly more than 1 for others, who considered MT and HT to be 'roughly the same' on average ranged from 'somewhat fast and inferior' to 'fast and acceptable'.

Overall, it seems that between 2018 and 2020 awareness and appraisal increased and decreased respectively, while trending in the opposite direction starting 2021, yet not reaching the same level as 2018.

2.1.2 Preparedness in integrating MT into workflow and attitude towards future prospects:

Q5 and Q6 were intended to gauge how open respondents were to the idea that quality could be adjusted in exchange for higher efficiency (Q5) and if they believed that errors/inaccuracies may be tolerated in case of highly disposable content (Q6) (See Venkatesan 2021, 666 for a detailed discussion). On this question the 2019 cohort remained the most conservative, falling on an average between 'disagree' and 'neutral' while responses from 2020 ranged from 'neutral' to 'agree' and those from 2018 were similar but tilted even more towards 'neutral'. The respondents from 2021 on the other hand on an average disagreed (though tending towards being neutral) that high-quality is unnecessary and also generally disagreed on the following question (Q6) of allowing errors to remain. On Q6, respondents from 2018 and 2020 fell roughly between 'disagree' and 'neutral' with the 2019 cohort tending more towards being 'neutral'. As seen in Fig. 2 the responses for Q5 and Q6 show deviations less than 1 point except for 2018 that is slightly over 1, with most responses ranging between 'disagree' and 'agree'.

It is evident that respondents are generally uncomfortable with the idea of varying qualities of translation (Q5) and even more so with allowing errors in translation (Q6). However, it also shows that they are not strongly opposed to reconsidering the issue of quality based on considerations such as the nature of text being translated, purpose, efficiency etc. However, the general reticence shown in responses to Q5 in spite of responses to Q2 that seem to suggest that MT is viewed generally viewed as useful may indicate a potential site for training and scaffolding on the part of trainers.

With regard to future prospects, respondents from 2018 remained most positive on average in their attitude towards MT. However, based on the mean scores all four cohorts on average believe that MT is only 'somewhat likely' to completely replace Human Translation even in the case of non-literary texts (Q7). Respondents from 2020 were slightly more inclined to believe that this would be possible, in comparison to those from 2021 and 2018, while those from 2019 remained most conservative. When the question was modified to ask if MT+Language Editors (it was explained that this referred to monolingual TL editors) could replace Human Translation (Q8) respondents from all four years seem more likely to agree, with those 2019 expressing least optimism. Respondents from 2018 and 2021 on an average fell between 'neutral' and 'agree' while others fell between 'disagree' and 'neutral'.

Q7 showed deviations of more than 1 across the years, with responses ranging between 'unlikely' and 'neutral' indicating relatively strong reservations towards the idea. The responses to Q8 show deviations above 1.2 for 2018-2020, but there seems to be broad consensus in the cohort from2021 between 'neutral' and 'agree'. The responses from 2020 show maximum deviation of 1.4 with responses widely ranging from 'strongly disagree' to 'agree'. 2018 and 2019 on the other hand show deviations of 1.2 with responses ranging from 'disagree' to 'agree' and 'strongly disagree' to 'neutral'.

In summary, respondents are somewhat willing to view the issue of quality in translation as variable but have strong reservations towards any suggestion of permitting errors or believing that HT could be replaced even in case of non-creative texts. The response to Q8 however suggests that respondents are willing to consider the possibility that MT+PE could replace HT in case of non-creative texts.

2.2 Discussion

The results of the survey may seem paradoxical. With the advent of Neural Machine Translation in 2016 the quality of translation produced by MT has shown tremendous improvement. The annual report on the language service industry in China by the Translators Association of China in 2020 points out that there is increasing recognition by the industry of the role played by translation technology in enhancing efficiency, finding that 5.6% of respondents from language service providers reported that they always used MT while 36.8% reported frequent use. The numbers were 11.6% and 28.3% when it came to actual translators (Qu 2020).

Against such a background, it may be reasonable to expect at least postgraduate students of translation to be more aware of quality achievable by MT and open to using Machine Translation. However, it is seen that even the most positive respondents from 2018 are found to be quite modest in their awareness of current capabilities. On the other hand, students from 2019-2021 report being relatively more aware and yet appear less likely to use MT even for preparing draft translations, leave alone believing that MT or at least MT+Post-

Editing (PE) could replace human translation for non-creative/literary texts. This attitude contrasts with studies that demonstrate that post-editing output from NMT reduces technical and cognitive effort (Jia, Carl, and Wang 2019) even though productivity gains may vary across languages and domains (Sarti et al. 2022). This gap between respondents' appraisal of usefulness and willingness to use MT for draft translations may be indicative of lack of formal training in this mode of working.

The unwillingness to consider the possibility of allowing errors for disposable information (Q6) and even lower quality (Q5) seems to resonate with the traditional understanding of translation that "the human translator must always produce consistent high quality" (Pym, 2012, p. 146). The survey shows that while respondents are not entirely against the idea of concessions in quality in exchange for efficiency in the case of certain texts, there is much discomfort with any idea that involves not doing the "best". However, given the demands for rapid everyday exchange of information, particularly in multilingual communities, using MT to reduce effort when producing disposable texts would enable translators to adapt to the diverse requirements of the information age (Venkatesan 2021, 667) .

Respondents are generally unwilling to concede that human translation could ever be replaced (Q7), even for non-creative or purely technical/informative texts. Even when asked when such replacement could be conceivable in case of MT+Language Editors (Q8) the highest mean in all four years is 2.4 (between neutral and agree) while the lowest is 1.5 (between disagree and neutral). This reluctance could indicate a lack of awareness towards current developments and perhaps also some degree of insecurity as the possibility may be perceived as threatening the very purpose behind working towards a postgraduate degree in translation. This concern is shared by evaluations of MT as well, that frequently return to the theme of whether MT will replace HT (Qin 2018; Kenny and Doherty 2014). However, while the developments may threaten the traditional role of translators, they also point towards a new editing role that trainees must prepare for in order to remain relevant. This could be a direction for training by teachers in translation courses.

In summary, while there are variations in responses over the years, they do not lend credence to any suggestion that students are progressively more aware and/or willing to use technology with each passing year. The problem confronting translator training seems to be a tendency, even among trainers, to prioritize "bilingual and translation knowledge sub-competences" out of seven sub-competences that include the understanding of and ability to use technology (D. Wu, Zhang, and Wei 2019). Resonating with this, a survey of teachers covering 205 institutions and students from 143 students in China that was published in 2019 found the following:

> The objective of MTI [Masters in Translation and Interpreting] programs is narrowly focused on training "professional interpreters and translators," which does not meet the wider demand of the language service market for translators and interpreters, and skills in transcreation, transediting, localization, translation project management, technical communication, translation technology, and sales and marketing (Cui 2019b, 47).

The survey employed in the study also noted that teachers generally "do not understand technical communication, translation technology (such as machine translation, computer-assisted translation, etc.), translation project management, and other emerging areas of translation, which affects the quality of the MTI teaching they offer." (Cui 2019b, 48). Cui identifies lopsided emphasis on research over practice by employers in academic institutions in China as the primary cause behind this. This is also confirmed by Xu and You in a more recent study where they state that "most translation teachers in China have little or no experience working as full-time or even part-time translators in translation or language service companies. " (Xu and You 2021, 347). Parallels have been suggested in the case of European languages as well (Kornacki 2018)."

As studies show, the consequences of training that fails to integrate technology are that "among the 107 employers who were surveyed, 48 (44.86%) employers chose the response "lack of professional knowledge," and 35 (32.71%) chose "lack of internships and practice" to describe MTI graduates" (Cui 2019a, 63).

A gap between evolving technology and curricula is also reported in Taiwan where there were 7 research institutes 6 had courses that included translation technology, but 35 ordinary universities only 5 used Trados, Google Translate, corpora etc (Chang, Yang, and Wang 2019, 134).

In summary, studies show that while the industry requires translators to be able to work with new and evolving technologies, translator training remains largely traditional with more emphasis on linguistic proficiency. However, at least in the context of Chinese-English translation, a gap between curricular content and actual needs is highlighted.

Even where technology is introduced the standalone approach dominates translation curricula. Calling instead for curriculum-wide implementation of technology Mellinger says:

> By integrating and embedding machine translation across the curriculum, trainers can model expert behaviour and encourage students to engage in best practices, which will position them well for current industry practices (Mellinger 2017, 284).

By providing operational frameworks, standards and ethics for the use of technology, such a training would result in students being more willing to adopt and confident in using technology and also in employing it dynamically to respond to different requirements. This idea of integration resonates with the survey mentioned above that recommends that CAT tools be taught in a more practical manner rather than the predominant standalone treatment (Zhang and Nunes Vieira 2021, 119).

The general lack of training and standalone treatments may result in reluctance towards using MT and inability to respond to non-traditional contexts. An example here would be the ability to carry out post-editing of raw MT output that would be adequate for the purpose at hand. Drugan cites the predicament of a translator in this situation:

"This might seem standard practice in the industry already, but in research, translators recognized they struggled to produce different, particularly lower, quality levels. Those who accepted occasional jobs out of the mother tongue or agreed to post-edit MT output for less than their standard rate found such work 'really frustrating', even impossible: 'I ended up doing it to my usual standard. It took so long I was being paid less than the minimum wage (Drugan 2013, 180)."

The effect of absence of training that would allow the respondent above to do just what was required is notable. Training that integrates MT into translation could allow it to be seen as an opportunity to enhance both efficiency and quality, rather than a threat to what was exclusively the province of trained translators. With the maturing of Machine Translation, even where errors and deficiencies in MT output are found, the Post-Editing (PE) effort required is still justified given the overall savings in time and effort as would be required of Human Translation (HT) (X. Wang et al. 2021). This training may offer a hybrid model of working that goes beyond the either/or formulation of MT vs HT that has impeded wider integration of technology. This would in turn enable future translators to respond to varying requirements of efficiency and quality in translation.

3. Implications for Translator Training

1. There is a need for curricula to include increased interaction with available technology, with training in translation methods/techniques equally focused on enabling trainees to act as effective post-editors of raw MT output.
2. It is important to provide trainees with clear frameworks to adjust time/effort and offer varying qualities of translation that may be adequate for a given purpose.

In the following ideas for activities to integrate technology in translator training are discussed to address lacunae identified above.

3.1 Integrating Machine Translation into the Translation Process

Take the example of a course on translation of business writings. Such a course would be expected to include: a comparison of genre characteristics in the languages concerned; an introduction to appropriate register and style; a discussion of translation methods and oft employed techniques; and common errors observed in translation resulting from linguistic, stylistic or cultural differences. This could be followed and/or preceded by translation practice involving sample texts that allow students to gain experience in handling texts of the said genre.

In courses integrating Machine Translation, after foundational grounding in the above, students may be engaged in post-editing translations of sample business texts produced by available MT systems.

The training would have two learning outcomes: First, students would be able to apply the knowledge gained in the preceding part of the course to post-editing (MT output where it fails to conform with genre characteristics or contains errors in syntax and context); Second, Students will be enabled to achieve rapid production of translation by learning to devote time and effort to bringing texts to shape instead of producing initial drafts.

It may well be this "value-addition" that may serve to highlight the role of trained translators - who are capable of producing rapid yet high-quality translation, unlike amateur translators who may also use available technology to generate translations.

3.2 Customization (Varying Qualities)

It is imperative that students are trained in post-editing that attains different quality standards. In such cases, trainees need to be trained in a framework that defines minimum standards to be achieved in the case of each type of text. The ability to do this is identified as one among three sub-competences under revision and post-editing competence (Konttinen, Salmi, and Koponen 2020, 194). The TAUS guidelines for Post-Editing suggests building a "a clear matrix of post-editing productivity, quality, turnaround time and pricing discount expectations based on the results of your analysis" (Massardo et al. 2016, 12) and offers operational guidelines to achieve "Good Enough" Quality and "Human Translation Quality"(Massardo et al. 2016, 17–18). However, clearly defined standards and methods to attain and verify them would be crucial for training.

One framework that may help students identify the level of editing required and learn to do no more than required is examining disposability. Under this framework, translated texts may be classified as Disposable, Reusable and Documentary, each with pre-defined levels of translation to be attained and methods to be used (Venkatesan 2021, 670). In order to train students to offer varying qualities, informative texts may be taken up for translation and trainees may be asked to translate in groups collaboratively, treating the same text variously as a disposable, reusable and documentary and producing different qualities within time constraints. This may be followed by a discussion to examine if each translation attained the minimum requirements of quality based on the framework. The core aspect of the training here would be to guide trainees to do no more than required.

4. Summary

The surveys presented in this study show perceived lack of awareness and preparedness towards leveraging existing technology among respondents. The attitudes reported do not change significantly over the years, pointing towards possible causes such as absence of systematic training in integrating technology into the process of translation. Lack of training that integrates technology into the translation process and provides a framework by which variable qualities of translation may be attained may be among the reasons why trainees are hesitant to respond to such requirements.

Based on the above, it is suggested that translation technology be integrated across curricula in practical translation courses that provide a framework of reference for production of rapid and customized translation. The ability of translators to produce rapid, customized and localized translation through the use of technology may well be the key to the continued relevance of translator training and trained translators.

References:

Allen, Jeffrey. 2003. "Post-Editing." In *Computers and Translation: A Translator's Guide*, edited by Harold Somers, 297–317. Benjamins Translation Library 35. Amsterdam: Benjamins.

Bittner, Hansjörg. 2020. *Evaluating the Evaluator: A Novel Perspective on Translation Quality Assessment*. 1st ed. Routledge Advances on Translation and Interpreting Studies 44. New York: Routledge.

Bowker, Lynne. 2005. "What Does It Take to Work in the Translation Profession in Canada in the 21st Century?: Exploring a Database of Job Advertisements." *Meta* 49 (4): 960–72. https://doi.org/10.7202/009804ar.

Bowker, Lynne, and Jairo Buitrago Ciro. 2019. *Machine Translation and Global Research: Towards Improved Machine Translation Literacy in the Scholarly Community*. First edition. Bingley: Emerald Publishing.

Buysschaert, Joost, María Fernández-Parra, Koen Kerremans, Maarit Koponen, and Gys-Walt Van Egdom. 2018. "Embracing Digital Disruption in Translator Training: Technology Immersion in Simulated Translation Bureaus." *Tradumàtica: Tecnologies de La Traducció*, no. 16 (December): 125. https://doi.org/10.5565/rev/tradumatica.209.

Chang, Daphne Qi-rong, Samuel Ju-hsin Yang, and Tracy Jr-yun Wang. 2019. "動機！ 我需要動機！ 融合電腦輔助翻譯的大學翻譯課 [Motivation! I Need Motivation! Incorporation of CAT into University Translation Courses]." *翻譯學研究集刊 [Studies of Translation and Interpretation]*, no. 23 (November): 129–56.

Chung, Eun Seon. 2020. "The Effect of L2 Proficiency on Post-Editing Machine Translated Texts." *The Journal of AsiaTEFL* 17 (1): 182–93. https://doi.org/10.18823/asiatefl.2020.17.1.11.182.

Cui, Qiliang. 2014. "论机器翻译的译后编辑 [On Post-Editing of Machine Translation]." *中国翻译 Chinese Translators Journal*, no. 6: 68–73.

———. 2019a. "MTI Programs: Employment Investigation." In *Restructuring Translation Education: Implications from China for the Rest of the World*, edited by Feng Yue, 55–68. Singapore: Springer Singapore. https://doi.org/10.1007/978-981-13-3167-1.

———. 2019b. "MTI Programs: Teaching and Learning." In *Restructuring Translation Education: Implications from China for the Rest of the World*, edited by Feng Yue, 41–54. Singapore: Springer Singapore. https://doi.org/10.1007/978-981-13-3167-1.

Doherty, Stephen. 2016. "The Impact of Translation Technologies on the Process and Product of Translation." *International Journal of Communication* 10 (February): 969.

Drugan, Joanna. 2013. *Quality in Professional Translation: Assessment and Improvement*. Bloomsbury Advances in Translation. London ; New York: Bloomsbury.

"EMT Competence Framework 2017." 2017. European Master's in Translation (EMT). 2017. https://ec.europa.eu/info/sites/default/files/emt_competence_fwk_2017_en_web.pdf.

"EMT Competence Framework 2022." 2022. European Master's in Translation (EMT). 2022. https://commission.europa.eu/document/download/b482a2c0-42df-4291-8bf8-923922ddc6e1_en?filename=emt_competence_fwk_2022_en.pdf.

Escartín, Carla Parra, and Marie-Josée Goulet. 2020. "When the Post-Editor Is Not a Translator." In *Translation Revision and Post-Editing*, edited by Maarit Koponen,

Brian Mossop, Isabelle S. Robert, and Giovanna Scocchera, 1st ed., 89–106. London ; New York : Rutledge, 2020.: Routledge. https://doi.org/10.4324/9781003096962-8.

Flotow, Luise Von. 2017. "A Doctoral Program in Translation Studies." In *Teaching Translation: Programs, Courses, Pedagogies*, edited by Lawrence Venuti. London ; New York: Routledge, Taylor & Francis Group.

Garcia, Ignacio. 2011. "Translating by Post-Editing: Is It the Way Forward?" *Machine Translation* 25 (3): 217–37. https://doi.org/10.1007/s10590-011-9115-8.

Gaspari, Federico, Hala Almaghout, and Stephen Doherty. 2015. "A Survey of Machine Translation Competences: Insights for Translation Technology Educators and Practitioners." *Perspectives* 23 (3): 333–58. https://doi.org/10.1080/0907676X.2014.979842.

Grace, Katja, John Salvatier, Allan Dafoe, Baobao Zhang, and Owain Evans. 2018. "When Will AI Exceed Human Performance? Evidence from AI Experts." *ArXiv:1705.08807 [Cs]*, May. http://arxiv.org/abs/1705.08807.

Hassan, Hany, Anthony Aue, Chang Chen, Vishal Chowdhary, Jonathan Clark, Christian Federmann, Xuedong Huang, et al. 2018. "Achieving Human Parity on Automatic Chinese to English News Translation." https://doi.org/10.48550/ARXIV.1803.05567.

Hutchins, William John, and Harold L. Somers. 1997. *An Introduction to Machine Translation*. 2. printing. London: Academic Press.

"ISO 18587:2017 Translation Services — Post-Editing of Machine Translation Output — Requirements." 2017. International Organization for Standardization. 2017. https://www.iso.org/standard/62970.html.

Jia, Yanfang, Michael Carl, and Xiangling Wang. 2019. "Post-Editing Neural Machine Translation versus Phrase-Based Machine Translation for English–Chinese." *Machine Translation* 33 (1–2): 9–29. https://doi.org/10.1007/s10590-019-09229-6.

Kenny, Dorothy, and Stephen Doherty. 2014. "Statistical Machine Translation in the Translation Curriculum: Overcoming Obstacles and Empowering Translators." *The Interpreter and Translator Trainer* 8 (2): 276–94. https://doi.org/10.1080/1750399X.2014.936112.

Killman, Jeffrey. 2018. "A Context-Based Approach to Introducing Translation Memory in Translator Training." In *Translation, Globalization and Translocation*, edited by Concepción B. Godev, 137–59. Cham: Springer International Publishing. https://doi.org/10.1007/978-3-319-61818-0_8.

Konttinen, Kalle, Leena Salmi, and Maarit Koponen. 2020. "Revision and Post-Editing Competences in Translator Education." In *Translation Revision and Post-Editing*, edited by Maarit Koponen, Brian Mossop, Isabelle S. Robert, and Giovanna Scocchera, 1st ed., 187–202. London ; New York : Rutledge, 2020.: Routledge. https://doi.org/10.4324/9781003096962-15.

Kornacki, Michał. 2018. *Computer-Assisted Translation (CAT) Tools in the Translator Training Process*. Lódz Studies in Language 58. Berlin ; New York: Peter Lang GmbH, Internationaler Verlag der Wissenschaften.

Läubli, Samuel, Rico Sennrich, and Martin Volk. 2018. "Has Machine Translation Achieved Human Parity? A Case for Document-Level Evaluation." *ArXiv:1808.07048 [Cs]*, August. http://arxiv.org/abs/1808.07048.

Man, Deliang, Aiping Mo, Meng Huat Chau, John Mitchell O'Toole, and Charity Lee. 2020. "Translation Technology Adoption: Evidence from a Postgraduate Programme for

Student Translators in China." *Perspectives* 28 (2): 253–70. https://doi.org/10.1080/0907676X.2019.1677730.

Massardier-Kenney,Françoise. 2017. "An MA in Translation." In *Teaching Translation: Programs, Courses, Pedagogies*, edited by Lawrence Venuti. London ; New York: Routledge, Taylor & Francis Group.

Massardo, Isabella, Jap van der Meer, Sharon O'Brian, Fred Hollowood, Nora Aranberri, and Katrin Drescher. 2016. "TAUS Post-Editing Guidelines." TAUS. 2016. https://commission.europa.eu/document/download/b482a2c0-42df-4291-8bf8-923922ddc6e1_en?filename=emt_competence_fwk_2022_en.pdf.

Massey, Gary, and Maureen Ehrensberger-Dow. 2017. "Machine Learning: Implications for Translator Education." *Lebende Sprachen* 62 (2): 300–312. https://doi.org/10.1515/les-2017-0021.

Mellinger, Christopher D. 2017. "Translators and Machine Translation: Knowledge and Skills Gaps in Translator Pedagogy." *The Interpreter and Translator Trainer* 11 (4): 280–93. https://doi.org/10.1080/1750399X.2017.1359760.

———. 2018. "Problem-Based Learning in Computer-Assisted Translation Pedagogy." *HERMES - Journal of Language and Communication in Business*, no. 57 (June): 195–208. https://doi.org/10.7146/hjlcb.v0i57.106205.

Qin, Ying. 2018. "基于神经网络的机器翻译质量评析 及对翻译教学的影响* [An Analytical Study of Neural Network Machine Translation and Its Impacts on Translation Teaching]." *外语电化教学 [TEFLE]*, Translation Teaching & Research [翻译教学与 yanjiu], , no. 180 (April): 51–56.

Qu, Shaobing. 2020. *中国语言服务发展报告(2020) [Language Service Development in China 2020]*. Beijing: 商务印书馆 [The Commercial Press].

Rodríguez de Céspedes, Begoña. 2019. "Translator Education at a Crossroads:The Impact of Automation." *Lebende Sprachen* 64 (1): 103–21. https://doi.org/10.1515/les-2019-0005.

Sarti, Gabriele, Arianna Bisazza, Ana Guerberof Arenas, and Antonio Toral. 2022. "DivEMT: Neural Machine Translation Post-Editing Effort Across Typologically Diverse Languages." https://doi.org/10.48550/ARXIV.2205.12215.

Somers, Harold, ed. 2003. *Computers and Translation: A Translator's Guide*. Benjamins Translation Library 35. Amsterdam: Benjamins.

Venkatesan, Hari. 2009. "Teaching Translation Memory Systems: SDL Trados 2007." *Journal of Translation Studies* 13 (1 & 2): 71–81.

———. 2021. "The Fourth Dimension in Translation: Time and Disposability." *Perspectives*. https://doi.org/10.1080/0907676X.2021.1939739.

Wang, Huashu. 2013. "语言服务行业技术视域下的 MTI 技术课程体系构建 [A Constructive Technology Curriculum for MTI Education from the Perspective of Language Service Industry Technologies]." *中国翻译[Chinese Translator's Journal]*, no. 6: 23–28.

Wang, Xiangling, Tingting Wang, Ricardo Muñoz Martín, and Yanfang Jia. 2021. "Investigating Usability in Postediting Neural Machine Translation: Evidence from Translation Trainees' Self-Perception and Performance:" *Across Languages and Cultures* 22 (1): 100–123. https://doi.org/10.1556/084.2021.00006.

Way, Andy. 2018. "Quality Expectations of Machine Translation." In *Translation Quality Assessment*, edited by Joss Moorkens, Sheila Castilho, Federico Gaspari, and Stephen Doherty, 1:159–78. Machine Translation: Technologies and Applications.

Cham: Springer International Publishing. https://doi.org/10.1007/978-3-319-91241-7_8.

Wu, Di, Lawrence Jun Zhang, and Lan Wei. 2019. "Developing Translator Competence: Understanding Trainers' Beliefs and Training Practices." *The Interpreter and Translator Trainer* 13 (3): 233–54. https://doi.org/10.1080/1750399X.2019.1656406.

Wu, Yonghui, Mike Schuster, Zhifeng Chen, Quoc V. Le, Mohammad Norouzi, Wolfgang Macherey, Maxim Krikun, et al. 2016. "Google's Neural Machine Translation System: Bridging the Gap between Human and Machine Translation." *ArXiv:1609.08144 [Cs]*, October. http://arxiv.org/abs/1609.08144.

Wyke, Ben Van. 2017. "An Undergraduate Certificate in Translation Studies." In *Teaching Translation: Programs, Courses, Pedagogies*, edited by Lawrence Venuti. London ; New York: Routledge, Taylor & Francis Group.

Xu, Mianjun, and Xiaoye You. 2021. "Translation Practice of Master of Translation and Interpreting (MTI) Teachers in China: An Interview-Based Study." *The Interpreter and Translator Trainer* 15 (3): 343–59. https://doi.org/10.1080/1750399X.2021.1900711.

Zhang, Xiaochun, and Lucas Nunes Vieira. 2021. "CAT Teaching Practices: An International Survey." *JoSTrans: The Journal of Specialised Translation*, July.

Appendix 1

Computer-Assisted Translation

A survey of opinions on available technology .

* Required

1. How aware are you of the capabilities of current Machine Translation?

   * *Mark only one oval.*

   - Not aware
   - Somewhat aware
   - Aware
   - Quite aware
   - Fully aware

2. How would you rate the overall usefulness of freely available online MT systems?

   * *Mark only one oval.*

   - Useless
   - Somewhat useful
   - Useful
   - Quite useful
   - Very useful

3. How likely are you to use MT for preparing quasi-texts/draft translations in the future?

*Mark only one oval.

- ◯ Unlikely
- ◯ Somewhat likely
- ◯ Likely
- ◯ Quite likely
- ◯ Very likely

4. When compared to manual translation, how would you evaluate Machine Translation+Post Editing?

*Mark only one oval.

- ◯ Slow and inaccurate
- ◯ Somewhat faster but inferior
- ◯ Roughly the same
- ◯ Fast and acceptable
- ◯ Efficient and superior

5. What is your opinion regarding the following statement: For disposable information, spending much time to achieve high-quality is not required.

* *Mark only one oval.*

- Strongly disagree
- Disagree
- Neutral
- Agree
- Strongly agree

6. What is you opinion regarding the following statement: For disposable information, it is alright if the translation contains errors or inaccuracies.

* *Mark only one oval.*

- Strongly disagree
- Disagree
- Neutral
- Agree
- Strongly agree

7. Are MT systems likely to completely replace Human Translation in the case of non-creative/literary texts?

**Mark only one oval.*

- ⬭ Unlikely
- ⬭ Somewhat likely
- ⬭ Likely
- ⬭ Quite likely
- ⬭ Very likely

8. What is your opinion regarding the following statement: MT+Language Editors can replace Human Translation in the case of non-creative/literary texts

** Mark only one oval.*

- ⬭ Strongly Disagree
- ⬭ Disagree
- ⬭ Neutral
- ⬭ Agree
- ⬭ Strongly agree

Reception of Machine-Translated and Human-Translated Subtitles: A Case Study

Frederike Schierl frederike.schierl@tuni.fi
Tampere University, Finland

Abstract

Accessibility and inclusion have become key terms of the last decades, and this does not exclude linguistics. Machine-translated subtitling has become the new approach to overcome linguistic accessibility barriers since it has proven to be fast and thus cost-efficient for audiovisual media, as opposed to human translation, which is time-intensive and costly. Machine translation can be considered as a solution when a translation is urgently needed. Overall, studies researching benefits of subtitling yield different results, also always depending on the application context (see Chan et al., 2022; Hu et al., 2020). Still, the acceptance of machine-translated subtitles is limited (see Tuominen et al., 2023) and users are rather skeptical, especially regarding the quality of MT subtitles. In the presented project, I investigated the effects of machine-translated subtitling (raw machine translation) compared to human-translated subtitling on the consumer, presenting the results of a case study, knowing that HT as the gold standard for translation is more and more put into question and being aware of today's convincing output of NMT. The presented study investigates the use of (machine-translated) subtitles by the average consumer due to the current strong societal interest. I base my research project on the 3 R concept, i.e. response, reaction, and repercussion (Gambier, 2009), in which participants were asked to watch two video presentations on educational topics, one in German and another in Finnish, subtitled either with machine translation or by a human translator, or in a mixed condition (machine-translated and human-translated). Subtitle languages were English, German, and Finnish. Afterwards, they were asked to respond to questions on the video content (information retrieval) and evaluate the subtitles based on the User Experience Questionnaire (Laugwitz et al., 2008) and NASA Task Load Index (NASA, 2006). The case study shows that information retrieval in the HT conditions is higher, except for the direction Finnish-German. However, users generally report a better user experience for all languages, which indicates a higher immersion. Participants also report that long subtitles combined with a fast pace contribute to more stress and more distraction from the other visual elements. Generally, users recognise the potential of MT subtitles, but also state that a human-in-the-loop is still needed to ensure publishable quality.

1. Introduction

Accessible information is a pivotal element in today's society and audiovisual media have become a crucial channel of information, not only for everyday needs, but also, among others, in an educational context (Gernsbacher, 2015; Negi and Mitra, 2022, see also Zhang, 2005). Subtitles are nowadays one of the tools of choice to foster accessibility to information and knowledge, more and more also with the aid of machine translation (Castilho et al., 2017; Hu et al., 2020). Still, the overarching question remains how the consumer reacts to this rather new mode of subtitling (ST), compared to the 'traditional' human-translated subtitling (HTST). This can be particularly relevant when using machine-translated subtitles (MTST) in an educational context, in which language and topics can be ambiguous and complex; aspects, which can be still a challenge for the current state-of-the-art MT systems (see Bender, 2010; Bywood et al., 2017).

Proceedings of Machine Translation Summit XIX, Vol. 2: Users Track, pages 42–53
September 4–8, 2023, Macau SAR, China.

Reception studies have gained more and more attention over the last decades, especially regarding the investigation of the user's need facing audiovisual translation (Tuominen, 2013, 2018). The use of instruments for quantitative measurements, eye-tracking for instance, has also contributed to the growing interest in the topic and gives more insights into reading processes (cf. Orrego-Carmona, 2015; Lång, 2016; Hu et al., 2020). Investigating the reception of subtitles started in the late 80s and early 90s with studies by d'Ydewalle et al., (1987), d'Ydewalle et al. (1991), showing that reading subtitles cannot be avoided although the original audio language is known to the viewer.

With the evermore increasing use of videos as source of learning, not only as a complement but sometimes even a substitute to in-classroom teaching, the interest has grown in knowing how users (the viewers) perceive the material in terms of cognitive treatment, the cognitive load (cf. Paas et al., 2003; Sweller et al., 2011), redundancy effect (Kalyuga, 2012), and attention-split (Ayres and Sweller, 2005). This is especially of interest when adding the additional source of information that subtitling may offer and has been discussed whether it is an actual aid or a nuisance, considering the redundancy effect, which states that the same information given via various channels at the same time hinder the learning effect. Although a study by Diao and Sweller (2007) reports a concurrence between a written presentation and the verbatim spoken presentation in a study with first-year university students, other studies on the topic cannot confirm the findings, therefore subtitles do not pose a hindrance per se (see Perego et al., 2010; Kruger et al., 2014; Gernsbacher, 2015; Liao et al., 2020). For instance, a study investigating reception of subtitles in an educational context (Chan et al., 2022) has shown that watching subtitles in L1 improves comprehension, but subtitling in L2 also creates a higher cognitive load to the audience.

Studies investigating the reception of machine-translated subtitles are still scarce. In a study from 2023, Tuominen et al. (2023) researched users' perception of MT subtitles and concluded that those can be useful, but users are still rather skeptical and would not rely on machine translation alone but prefer human-translated subtitles or at least subtitles checked by a human translator.

2. Research interest and Methodological Framework

The presented study aims to build on previous research on subtitling reception in general and the comparison of MT and HT subtitles in particular, focusing on the perception of the subtitles (the act of paying and sharing attention) but also the cognitive processing (resulting in gaining information/learning from the material).

The research hypotheses are based on the 3 R concept (Gambier 2009): response, reaction, and repercussion. In this concept, response refers to the act of perceiving the subtitles visually (perceptual decoding), the reaction entails the cognitive treatment, how the subtitles are processed cognitively, and repercussion comprises a socio-cultural component, including expectations and attitudes. Therefore, the following hypotheses shall be investigated:

- H1 (for response): Informants in the conditions of MTST will pay more attention to the subtitles than to the image (compared to HTST) since they concentrate more on the written text when the subtitling quality is suspected to be low.
- H2 (for reaction): Informants in the conditions of MTST will report a lack of comprehension, which reflects in lower rating scores compared to HTST. The cognitive load will also be higher.
- H3 (for repercussion): Informants in the conditions of MTST report a less positive attitude towards subtitling than in the conditions of HTST.

3. Experimental Setup

3.1. Video Material

The corpus for the research experiment consisted of two videos recorded by teachers from the university in the native language of the respective speaker, i.e. German and Finnish. Both videos had an equal length of 6 to 7 minutes and were presented in a slide-show lecture format. The presentations contained information on a respective research/teaching topic of the speaker, in this case *professional listening in on-site interpreting* and *regional and culture studies in the German-speaking area.* The videos were recorded for the purpose of the experiment to avoid potential copyright issues that may appear when using prefabricated videos on the Internet. The videos were recorded in the video platform *Panopto*, which also supports generation of intralingual subtitling via automatic speech recognition (ASR). The generated speech transcripts were exported, light post-edited (only spelling errors, wrong punctuation and misrecognitions were corrected) and then machine-translated. Subtitling languages of the videos were English and German for the Finnish video and Finnish for the German video. It was considered to include also English subtitles for the German video, but soon was decided against due to the location of the research and the considered limited benefit for the outcomes.

For the machine-translated condition, the open-source software *SubtitleEdit* was chosen since it also has a built-in machine-translation function which operates with *Google Translate*, and this tool supports a direct export of the translated transcript with time codes.
The human-translated subtitles were done by a professional subtitler with 25 years of experience in both subtitling from scratch and with templates. The subtitler had no templates for this job, but created and translated the subtitles based on the provided videos.

3.2. Participants

36 participants took part in the experiment (27 female, 7 male, 1 other [non-binary], and 1 person did not want to give further information) with an age range from 20-69 (20-29: 16, 30-39: 11; 40-49: 6, 50-59: 2; 60-69: 1). They were recruited via the University's intranet and by contacting a German university through the network of the researcher. Participants were not asked directly about their native language, but the language(s) they are most proficient in ("considered native or near-native speaker"). The answers were as follows: 18x Finnish, 20x English, 16x German, 2x Swedish, 1x Spanish, 2x French, 1x Dutch (multiple answers were possible). Therefore, the general high language proficiency concentrates on Finnish, English, and German. Especially English was very often mentioned in addition to another (native) language. Since the videos were in Finnish and German, language proficiency in those languages was asked in particular, yielding the following distribution as seen in Table 1.

	No knowledge	Beginner	Intermediate	Advanced	Native Speaker
Finnish	13	3	1	0	19
German	6	8	5	3	14

Table 1 Distribution of language competencies in Finnish and German

Furthermore, participants were asked for their media consumption habits, especially how many hours they spent on a daily basis with audiovisual material and whether or how often they would consume subtitles when they watch audiovisual material. Five stated less than an hour, 9 participants 1-2 hours, 10 indicated 2-3 hours, and 12 participants said that they would watch more than 3 hours of audiovisual material per day. Asking for their habits of having subtitles on display while watching AV material, participants rated their consumption habits on a scale from 1 (never on display) to 7 (always on display) as shown in Table 2.

1	2	3	4	5	6	7
1x	4x	4x	7x	7x	5x	8x

Table 2 Frequency of subtitles display in AV consumption habits

Overall, the participant group was used to watch subtitles although it must be noted that this was partly to be expected due to the location of the study where the population is exposed to subtitles in the daily life. However, also the general young age of the participants might pose a factor since consumption habits have changed and there is a slight tendency, also in so-called "dubbing countries", to watch audiovisual material (shows on the Internet for example) in the original language with subtitles.

3.3. Methods

To investigate the reception of MT and HT subtitles in an educational context, the study comprised, on the one hand, ten (10) questions aiming at gaining insight into free recall of the video content, but this part also contained questions on perception of colours and shapes to gain insight of potential elements of attention of the participant. On the other hand, the surveys asked for information on subtitle use, in particular whether participants were dependent on the subtitles to understand the content or how they perceived the length of the subtitles. Furthermore, this part of the survey contained statements from the NASA Task Load Index (NASA, 2006) and User Experience Questionnaire (Laugwitz et al., 2008). The advantage of these questionnaires is their standardisation and their recognition and validation in the field of user experience research.

3.4. Procedure

The study was conducted online or also on-site at the University's facilities, depending on the availability of the participant. If participants chose to participate online, they were met in a one-to-one synchronous meeting in which the conducting researcher gave instructions on the procedure of the experiment and how to set it up from distance (how to display the subtitles if the participant was not familiar with the function). The study consisted of watching two videos and completing three surveys; two surveys were connected to the videos (video content, user experience evaluation), the last survey contained questions on attitudes and expectations towards subtitling in general and MT subtitles in particular. The general procedure of the experiment was watching the first video, completing the survey, watching the second video, completing the survey, and then completing the final survey. The participants saw the subtitles in a blinded condition, i.e. they did not know beforehand whether they were human-translated or machine-translated. Overall, the experiment duration was approximately one hour.

In the online participation, a link with access to the video material and to the surveys, which were also accessible online, were sent to them at the start of each meeting, also to avoid that the participant would be tempted to watch the videos beforehand. If participants chose to participate on-site, the experiment was set up for them in the right manner, so that they only had to watch the videos and fill in the surveys.

Before the experiment, in every case, participants were provided with an information sheet of the experiment, a privacy notice and an informed consent form, which they had to fill in and send back to the researcher before the beginning of the experiment. In the on-site condition, participants could fill in the form right before the experiment. Before the beginning of the experiment, the procedure of the experiment was explained again orally, what to do and what not to do during the experiment and participants were invited to ask questions if something remained unclear. After finishing the experiment, participants were furthermore invited to comment on the procedure, for instance how they felt while they were watching the videos and the subtitles.

4. Results

4.1. German – Finnish

36 participants saw the German video with the Finnish subtitles, of which 18 saw the MTST version (MT quality) and 18 the HTST version (HT quality). Out of the 36 participants, 18 stated that they have watched the subtitles all the time, 10 stated having them watched sometimes, and 8 stated not having watched them. Furthermore, on a scale from 'entirely' to 'not at all', (entirely, somewhat, a little, almost not, not at all), 12 participants had to rely entirely on the subtitles to understand the content (6 in the HTST condition and 6 in the MTST condition), 5 stated 'somewhat' (1 in HTST in 4 in MTST), 1 had to rely 'a little' (HTST) and 18 (10 in HTST and 8 in MTST) had not to rely on them at all.

Information Retrieval

In the first part of the survey, the section aiming at information retrieval and free recall from the video, 22 points could be reached in total. Table 3 shows a comparison between the two modes of presentation.

	MTST (Average [MD, SD])	HTST (Average [MD, SD])
Correct Response Rate (CRR)	13.41 [14, 2.9]	14.83 [14.75, 1.78]
In %	59.8	67.9

Table 3 Information Retrieval German video with Finnish subtitles

As the comparison shows, HTST outperforms MTST by 1.4 points on average (8.1% per cent) although it must be noted that the median score between MTST and HTST does differ significantly.

Task Load and User Experience

The initial design of the Task Load as well as the User Experience Questionnaire does not contain a direct numerical evaluation scale, but for unification and limits of the survey tool, it was chosen to modify the presentation into this scaling. Furthermore, the initial design of the Task Load Index comprises a 21-bar scale, divided into three main subscales, therefore it was decided to use a 7-point-scaling. Additionally, the UEQ contains a seven-bullet evaluation scale with two adjacent items (for instance good/bad). Due to the limits of the tools, it was chosen to keep the 7-point scaling, but to exclude the opposition due to non-feasibility. It is of note that participants were asked to complete the survey, the evaluation, to the best of their knowledge. There is a certain data loss due to missing data especially from those participants who were not proficient in Finnish.

NASA Task Load Index

	MTST (Average, [MD, SD])	HTST (Average, [MD, SD])
How mentally demanding was the task?	3.65 [4, 1.84]	2.94 [2, 1.47]
How insecure/stressed/annoyed were you during the task?	2.59 [2, 1.18]	1.67 [1, 0.97]

How much time pressure did you feel due to the rate at which the ST occurred?	3.57 [3.5, 1.79]	1.63 [1, 1.48]
How successful were you in accomplishing the task, i.e. understanding the content?	4.53 [5, 1.66]	4.75 [5.5, 2.05]

Table 4 NASA Task Load Index German video with Finnish subtitles

Task Load Index for the condition German video with Finnish subtitles shows overall better scores for HTST: Mental demand was perceived lower, participants reported being less stressed and insecure and they felt less time pressure. Task success was also perceived higher although only marginally.

User Experience Questionnaire

	MTST (Average, [MD, SD])	HTST (Average, [MD, SD])
enjoyable	3.77 [3, 1.24]	5.73 [6, 1.74]
understandable	4.69 [5, 1.65]	6.17 [7, 1.75]
supportive	4.33 [4.5, 1.37]	5.7 [6.5, 1.95]
bad	2.25 [1.5, 1.60]	1.08 [1, 0.29]
unpleasant	2.46 [2, 1.45]	1 [1, 0]
meet expectations	4.58 [4.5, 0.90]	5.92 [7, 1.83]
confusing	2.86 [2.5, 1.61]	1.67 [1, 1.73]
practical	4.5 [5, 1.45]	6.3 [7, 1.06]
efficient	4.09 [4, 1.44]	6 [6, 0.74]

Table 5 User Experience Questionnaire German video with Finnish subtitles

Participants reported a better user experience according to the user experience questionnaire in the HTST condition (Table 5). Of note are in particular the scores for HTST in 'understandability', 'practicality', and 'efficiency', which are close to perfect score. Also, the very low scores for 'unpleasure' and 'badness' are striking.

4.2. Finnish – German

Of the 36 participants, 20 were presented with a Finnish video and German subtitles. 10 watched the video with HT subtitles and 10 with MT subtitles. Overall, 10 stated having read the subtitles all the time, 4 read them sometimes and 6 stated not having read them. 10 participants stated that they were entirely dependent on the subtitles (4 in the HTST condition and 6 in the MTST condition) and 10 were not dependent on them at all (6 in the HTST and 4 in the MTST condition)

Information Retrieval

In the recall part of the survey, 21 points could be reached in total. Table 6 presents the results in the different modes of presentation.

	MTST (Average [MD, SD])	HTST (Average [MD, SD])
Correct Response Rate (CRR)	16.8 [17.25, 2.07]	14.9 [14.25, 1.91]
In %	80.00	70.96

Table 6 Information Retrieval Finnish video with German subtitles

Results show that there is a higher information retrieval (or free information recall) in the MTST condition.

NASA Task Load Index

	MTST (Average [MD, SD])	HTST (Average [MD, SD])
How mentally demanding was the task?	2.89 [2, 1.9]	3.9 [4, 1.20]
How insecure/stressed/annoyed were you during the task?	2.78 [2, 1.64]	2.3 [2, 0.95]
How much time pressure did you feel due to the rate at which the ST occurred?	3.5 [3, 1.93]	1.71 [1, 1.11]
How successful were you in accomplishing the task, i.e. understanding the content?	5.22 [6, 1.48]	4.6 [5, 1.58]

Table 7 NASA Task Load Index Finnish video with German subtitles

User Experience Questionnaire

	MTST (Average [MD, SD])	HTST (Average [MD, SD])
enjoyable	3.43 [3, 2.23]	5.67 [6, 1]
understandable	4.43 [4, 2.07]	6.38 [6, 0.52]
supportive	4.67 [4.5, 2.07]	6.25 [6, 0.71]
bad	2.14 [1, 1.57]	1.11 [1, 0.33]
unpleasant	2.57 [3, 1.40]	1.33 [1, 0.5]
meet expectations	4.8 [5, 1.64]	5.5 [5, 1.07]
confusing	2.2 [2, 1.30]	1.44 [1, 0.53]
practical	4.83 [4.5, 1.83]	5.5 [6, 1.41]
efficient	4.14 [5, 2.19]	5.75 [5.5, 0.87]

Table 8 User Experience Questionnaire Finnish video with German subtitles

The results (Table 7 and Table 8) indicate that mental demand is perceived lower in the MTST condition, and also that participants felt more successful in accomplishing the task. However, insecurity and stress as well as time pressure are lower in the HTST condition. Furthermore, the UEQ shows better results in all aspect compared to MTST.

4.3. Finnish – English

16 of the 36 participants were presented with the Finnish video and English subtitles: 8 with MTST and 8 with HTST. 8 stated having read the subtitles all the time, 4 sometimes and 4 said not having read them. In addition to the reading, 6 stated being entirely dependent on the ST to understand the content (3 in the HTST condition and 3 in the MTST condition), 1 participant indicated 'somewhat' dependent (MTST), 2 indicated 'almost not' (MTST), and 7 stated not being dependent on the subtitling at all (5 in the HTST condition and 2 in the MTST condition).

Information Retrieval

	MTST (Average [MD, SD])	HTST (Average [MD, SD])
Correct Response Rate (CRR)	14.63 [14.5, 1.79]	15.75 [16.25, 2.96]
In %	69.64	75

Table 9 Information Retrieval Finnish video with English subtitles

Regarding information retrieval, results show that HTST outperforms MTST by 1.12 points on average and higher information gain by approx. 5 per cent.

NASA Task Load Index

	MTST (Average [MD, SD])	HTST (Average [MD, SD])
How mentally demanding was the task?	4.25 [5, 1.58]	4.5 [4.5, 1.20]
How insecure/stressed/annoyed were you during the task?	3.25 [3, 1.67]	2.38 [2, 1.19]
How much time pressure did you feel due to the rate at which the ST occurred?	3.86 [4, 1.57]	2.75 [2.5, 2.05]
How successful were you in accomplishing the task, i.e. understanding the content?	4.38 [4, 1.51]	4.88 [5, 1.81]

Table 10 NASA Task Load Index Finnish video with English subtitles

The Task Load Index shows better results throughout HTST, however it is of note that mental demand and perception of task success are slightly higher. Insecurity or stress and time pressure are perceived lower in the HTST condition as well.

User Experience Questionnaire

	MTST (Average [MD, SD])	HTST (Average [MD, SD])
enjoyable	3.86 [4, 1.86]	4 [4, 2]
understandable	5.43 [6, 2.07]	5.43 [6, 1.51]
supportive	4.57 [4, 1.81]	4.83 [5, 2.31]
bad	2 [1, 1.53]	1.5 [1, 1.22]
unpleasant	2.29 [1, 1.89]	2.14 [1, 1.68]
meet expectations	4.43 [5, 1.51]	5.67 [6, 1.51]
confusing	4.14 [5, 1.86]	3.14 [3, 2.34]
practical	4.86 [4, 1.77]	5.29 [5, 1.50]
efficient	4.43 [5, 2.37]	4.71 [4, 1.70]

Table 11 User Experience Questionnaire Finnish video with English subtitles

Results for Task Load and User Experience show that mental demand was slightly lower in the MTST condition, but participants reported better scores for other aspects of the task load. Regarding user experience, HTST outperforms MTST in all items but for 'understandability', in which scores are equal.

4.4. Perception of Quality

Next to the evaluation of the subtitles, participants were asked to evaluate the quality on a scale from 1 – 7 (one being the lowest score, 7 the highest) and to comment on their perception of quality. The results are presented in Table 12.

	GE-FI	FI-GE	FI-EN
Machine Translation	4.3 [4, 0.67]	4 [4, 1.73]	5.29 [5, 1.50]
Human Translation	6 [6, 1.04]	6.17 [6, 0.41]	5.25 [5, 1.04]

Table 12 Evaluation of quality perception: Scale from 1-7

Further, participants were invited to comment on their perception of quality or how they define (high) quality, knowing that 'quality' is a highly subjective topic. Among the most often mentioned aspects were 'correctness' (spelling and grammar), 'shortness' and 'precision' (the message should be conveyed) and good subtitles should be well-timed.

4.5. Attitudes and expectations towards (machine-translated) subtitling

Generally, participants in the experiment stated that they have a positive attitude towards subtitling, stating that they pose an aid and are sometimes a crucial element in understanding the content of the AV material. Also, they recognise the potential of machine-translated subtitles (for example to have a gist of the content), however the informants very often stated that they would not trust the machine translation alone, but it needs a human-in-the-loop to reach good publishable quality.

5. Discussion

The presented study investigated differences in reception of MT and HT subtitles, based on quantitative (numeric evaluation scales) and qualitative (comments and open questions on atti-tutdes and expectations) research methods, which rely on the subjective percepetion of the participant. Each participant watched a video in German and Finnish and responded to a survey after each video. The ST language of the German video was only Finnish, the subtitle languages of the Finnish video were either German or English, depending on the assigned participant number. The research interest was based on Gambier's (2009) 3 R concept: response, reaction, repercussion. The results yielded a general difference in reception: For the combination German video and Finnish subtitle, HTST outperformed MTST in every measured aspect: information retrieval, task load, and user experience. For the combination Finnish video and German subtitle, results showed a better information retrieval in MTST, which was unexpected. Also, mental demand was perceived lower and task success was perceived higher with MT subtitles, for which a correlation cannot be excluded. There is no obvious explanation for this phenomenon, but an assumption is that Finnish-speaking participants did not read the ST consciously (at least they report for the majority that they did not read them) due to lacking language proficiency and speed of the ST, therefore they were less interested and focused more on the audio. At the same time, German-speaking participants (with no to little Finnish proficiency and therefore depending more on the ST) could gain enough information from the ST. This explanation, however, needs further investigation. User experience was again always perceived better in the HTST condition and clearly outperforms user experience with MTST. The experimental condition Finnish video and English subtitles yielded again mixed results: Participants reported a better information in the HTST condition and also in perception of task load. However, it is of note that mental demand and success rate were only perceived slightly higher in the HTST condition. Furthermore, investigating user experience, the aspect of 'understandability' reached equal scores in both conditions, and HTST is also perceived slightly better in the items of 'enjoyability', 'support', 'pleasure', and 'efficiency'.

Taking these results into account, there is no evidence in this study with the presented methods that participants will spend more time looking at the subtitles when they are machine-translated and will be therefore more distracted (H1). Furthermore, cognitive load was perceived higher in the conditions GE-FI and FI-EN, but not in FI-GE, therefore H2 could not be completely confirmed either. Of note is also that participants commented (either in written or oral form) that they felt stressed by the speed of the ST in the MT condition, especially when being dependent on the ST; therefore, they reported not being able to spend much time on other aspects of the video. User experience is, for one exception, always perceived better in the HT condition, which resulted in higher rating scores.

Participants were also asked to evaluate the quality, again based on personal perception. The results show a better score for the HT subtitles, except for MT, which scores marginally higher, which is therefore not significant. Lastly, it was assumed that participants watching MTST will report less satisfaction and lower expectations and attitudes (H3). This hypothesis could not be confirmed either since participants generally expressed a recognition for the potential of MT subtitles, with the condition that they still need improvement, that there should be a human-in-the-loop, and that the output of the MT, hence also the applicability, depends on the context. Some comments remarked, for example, that MT is unsuitable for a context with complex educational information.

6. Conclusion

The presented study aimed to contribute to the further research of user reception of HT and MT subtitles. The results of the study contributed to the potential of this mode of translation, especially in the context of accessibility at an efficient level (cost and time-efficient for an acceptable result), focussing among others on the aspect of pure information gain on the one hand and the overall perception (the whole entertainment) on the other. I would like to argue that the research results also contributed to a topic that might pose an easy question ('Are HT subtitles better than MT subtitles?') to which the answer is more complex than initially thought. The study has shown that MT subtitles can make AV content more accessible. Still there is a long way to go to reach an MT output that is qualitatively convincing and better applicable. Furthermore, there is still the average consumer who must be convinced but the study has also shown that expectations are not bad as long as the consumer is also aware that the ST was produced (mainly) by a machine. One may remember when MT entered the translation market in the early 2000s and everybody was rather skeptical about it and nowadays nobody can imagine a life without the aid of MT. After all, despite good results in information retrieval, the study does not answer the question of whether consumers would prefer the information gain alone or whether it must be seen as a whole entity in which user experience is part of the viewing process. The study had several limitations. Firstly, it must be noted that cognition and memory are highly individual, and some participants were maybe able to retain more information than others. The study had no baseline, i.e. they did not watch a video without subtitles (there was no control group in general) or it was not measured with a pre-test how well their working memory was. This was not considered in the initial planning of the experiment and would have been difficult to perform in the online setup of the experiment. The experiment also had no test round in which the participants could get familiar with the experimental setup, the video and the subtitling as well as potential questions. Since the overall duration of the main experiment was approximately one hour, a test round would have contributed to an extension in time and potentially less motivation and/or earlier fatigue, which could have had an influence of the results. Secondly, I am aware that the notion of quality is highly individualised and that there is no general definition. It was therefore important that participants could express their own understanding of quality next to the quantitative perception. It also must be taken into account that all participants had a background of higher education, which might have influenced their perception of quality as well. Thirdly, the experimental setup, which included always a combination of the Finnish video with the German one, limited data to this point: 36 participants watched the German video (18 HT/ 18 MT), but participants had to be split further due to the nature of two sets of subtitles for the Finnish video (German: 10 HT/10 MT; English 8 HT/8 MT), which leads to a stronger reliability for the German presentation with Finnish subtitles.

It is planned as further research to investigate more the perceptual decoding of the subtitles, which aims at a more detailed look into the first research hypothesis, particularly where the participants look when watching a video with subtitles. A further study will include eye-tracking, which intends also to have a closer look at results from the presented study.

References

Ayres, Paul, and John Sweller. 2005. 'The Split-Attention Principle in Multimedia Learning'. In *The Cambridge Handbook of Multimedia Learning*, edited by Richard Mayer, 1st ed., 135–46. Cambridge University Press. https://doi.org/10.1017/CBO9780511816819.009.

Bender, Oliver. 2010. 'Robust Machine Translation for Multi-Domain Tasks'. PhD Thesis, Aachen, Techn. Hochsch., Diss., 2010.

Bywood, Lindsay, Panayota Georgakopoulou, and Thierry Etchegoyhen. 2017. 'Embracing the Threat: Machine Translation as a Solution for Subtitling'. *Perspectives* 25 (3): 492–508. https://doi.org/10.1080/0907676X.2017.1291695.

Chan, Win Shan, Jan-Louis Kruger, and Stephen Doherty. 2022. 'An Investigation of Subtitles as Learning Support in University Education'. *Journal of Specialised Translation*, no. 38: 155–79.

Diao, Yali, and John Sweller. 2007. 'Redundancy in Foreign Language Reading Comprehension Instruction: Concurrent Written and Spoken Presentations'. *Learning and Instruction* 17 (1): 78–88. https://doi.org/10.1016/j.learninstruc.2006.11.007.

D'Ydewalle, Géry, Caroline Praet, Karl Verfaillie, and Johan Van Rensbergen. 1991. 'Watching Subtitled Television: Automatic Reading Behavior'. *Communication Research* 18 (5): 650–66. https://doi.org/10.1177/009365091018005005.

D'Ydewalle, Géry, Johan Van Rensbergen, and Joris Pollet. 1987. 'Reading a Message When the Same Message Is Available Auditorily in Another Language: The Case of Subtitling'. In *Eye Movements from Physiology to Cognition*, 313–21. Elsevier. https://doi.org/10.1016/B978-0-444-70113-8.50047-3.

Gambier, Yves. 2009. 'Challenges in Research on Audiovisual Translation'. In *Translation Research Projects 2*, edited by Pym, Anthony and Alexander Perekrestenko, 17–25. Tarragona: Intercultural Studies Group.

Gernsbacher, Morton Ann. 2015. 'Video Captions Benefit Everyone'. *Policy Insights from the Behavioral and Brain Sciences* 2 (1): 195–202. https://doi.org/10.1177/2372732215602130.

Hu, Ke, Sharon O'Brien, and Dorothy Kenny. 2020. 'A Reception Study of Machine Translated Subtitles for MOOCs'. *Perspectives* 28 (4): 521–38. https://doi.org/10.1080/0907676X.2019.1595069.

Kalyuga, Slava. 2012. 'Instructional Benefits of Spoken Words: A Review of Cognitive Load Factors'. *Educational Research Review* 7 (2): 145–59.

Kruger, Jan-Louis, Esté Hefer, and Gordon Matthew. 2014. 'Attention Distribution and Cognitive Load in a Subtitled Academic Lecture: L1 vs. L2'. *Journal of Eye Movement Research* 7 (5). https://doi.org/10.16910/jemr.7.5.4.

Lång, Juha. 2016. 'Subtitles vs. Narration: The Acquisition of Information from Visual-Verbal and Audio-Verbal Channels When Watching a Television Documentary'. In *Eye-Tracking and Applied Linguistics*, 59–81. Berlin: Language Science Press. http://langsci-press.org/catalog/book/108.

Laugwitz, Bettina, Theo Held, and Martin Schrepp. 2008. 'Construction and Evaluation of a User Experience Questionnaire'. In *Symposium of the Austrian HCI and Usability Engineering Group*, edited by Andreas Holzinger, 63–76. Springer.

Liao, Sixin, Jan-Louis Kruger, and Stephen Doherty. 2020. 'The Impact of Monolingual and Bilingual Subtitles on Visual Attention, Cognitive Load, and Comprehension'. *The Journal of Specialised Translation*, no. 33: 70–98.

NASA. 2006. 'NASA TLX: Task Load Index'.

Negi, Shivsevak, and Ritayan Mitra. 2022. 'Native Language Subtitling of Educational Videos: A Multimodal Analysis with Eye Tracking, EEG and Self-reports'. *British Journal of Educational Technology* 53 (6): 1793–1816. https://doi.org/10.1111/bjet.13214.

Orrego-Carmona, David. 2015. 'The Reception of (Non) Professional Subtitling.' PhD Thesis, Universitat Rovira i Virgili.

Paas, Fred, Juhani E. Tuovinen, Huib Tabbers, and Pascal W. M. Van Gerven. 2003. 'Cognitive Load Measurement as a Means to Advance Cognitive Load Theory'. *Educational Psychologist* 38 (1): 63–71. https://doi.org/10.1207/S15326985EP3801_8.

Perego, Elisa, Fabio Del Missier, Marco Porta, and Mauro Mosconi. 2010. 'The Cognitive Effectiveness of Subtitle Processing'. *Media Psychology* 13 (3): 243–72. https://doi.org/10.1080/15213269.2010.502873.

Sweller, John, Paul Ayres, and Slava Kalyuga. 2011. *Cognitive Load Theory*. New York, NY: Springer New York. https://doi.org/10.1007/978-1-4419-8126-4.

Tuominen, Tiina. 2013. *The Art of Accidental Reading and Incidental Listening. An Empirical Study on the Viewing of Subtitled Films*. Tampere University Press.

Tuominen, Tiina. 2018. 'Multi-Method Research: Reception in Context'. In *Benjamins Translation Library*, edited by Elena Di Giovanni and Yves Gambier, 141:69–90. Amsterdam: John Benjamins Publishing Company. https://doi.org/10.1075/btl.141.05tuo.

Tuominen, Tiina, Maarit Koponen, Kaisa Vitikainen, Umut Sulubacak, and Jörg Tiedemann. 2023. 'Exploring the Gaps in Linguistic Accessibility of Media: The Potential of Automated Subtitling as a Solution'. *Journal of Specialised Translation*, no. 39: 77–89.

Zhang, Dongsong. 2005. 'Interactive Multimedia-Based E-Learning: A Study of Effectiveness'. *American Journal of Distance Education* 19 (3): 149–62. https://doi.org/10.1207/s15389286ajde1903_3.

Machine Translation Implementation in Automatic Subtitling from a Subtitlers' Perspective

Bina Xie 21439095@life.hkbu.edu.hk
Department of Translation, Interpreting and Intercultural Studies, Hong Kong Baptist University, Hong Kong, China

Abstract

In recent years, automatic subtitling has gained considerable scholarly attention. Implementing machine translation in subtitling editors faces challenges, being a primary process in automatic subtitling. Therefore, there is still a significant research gap when it comes to machine translation implementation in automatic subtitling. This project compared different levels of non-verbal input videos from English to Chinese Simplified to examine post-editing efforts in automatic subtitling. The research collected the following data: process logs, which records the total time spent on the subtitles, keystrokes, and user experience questionnaire (UEQ). 12 subtitlers from a translation agency in Mainland China were invited to complete the task. The results show that there are no significant differences between videos with low and high levels of non-verbal input in terms of time spent. Furthermore, the subtitlers spent more effort on revising spotting and segmentation than translation when they post-edited texts with a high level of non-verbal input. While a majority of subtitlers show a positive attitude towards the application of machine translation, their apprehension lies in the potential overreliance on its usage.

1. Introduction

1.1. Automatic subtitling and machine translation implementation

The progress of technological advancements has led to the expansion of automation in subtitling, transitioning from machine translation (MT) to fully automatic subtitling. Automatic subtitling involves a complex workflow, including auto-transcription, automatic segmentation, auto-spotting and MT. Recently, the audiovisual industry has shown increasing interest in automatic subtitling. Prominent streaming platforms like YouTube and Bilibili have already adopted automatic subtitling. Moreover, several advanced subtitling platforms or software now incorporate automated tools to improve productivity.

Researchers also start to explore experimental research in MT and automatic subtitling. Georgakopoulou (2021) discusses machine translation implementation issues and future trends in MT research, such as intelligent text segmenters, MT quality estimation, and metadata usage. VARGA (2021) analysed machine translation quality from different online automatic subtitling platforms in audiovisual translation (AVT). Inconsistencies were reported, including literal translation, word order, language register, noun-adjective agreement, punctuation, and mistranslation. Karakanta (2022) introduces experimental methods from MT in subtitles to automatic subtitling and points out that automatic subtitling poses extra challenges for MT, such as segmentation and time stamps. Other research focuses on subtitler feedback. Karakanta et al. (2022b) collected subtitle post-editing data to investigate how subtitlers interact with automatic subtitling, through process logs, keystrokes and questionnaire. Karakanta et al. (2022a) analyse feedback from subtitlers on the use of automatic subtitling. Most subtitlers show a positive

Proceedings of Machine Translation Summit XIX, Vol. 2: Users Track, pages 54–64
September 4–8, 2023, Macau SAR, China.

attitude towards automatic subtitling. Besides, automatic subtitling helps subtitlers save time and effort on the tedious part of the work. In the end, they call for more automatic subtitling tests by the actual users and sufficient consideration of translators' views. Therefore, research in automatic subtitling still represents a significant research gap.

1.2. Non-verbal input of subtitle translation

Researchers have noticed non-verbal information in audiovisual translation for the last decade. Guillot (2018) proposes that non-verbal information in audiovisual materials is a unique feature of audiovisual translation because translators need to interact visual footage and audio tracks with written subtitles. This kind of information can affect the meaning of films and TV programs (e.g. Perego, 2009) and the decision-making process of subtitlers (e.g. Pérez-González, 2014). Díaz-Cintas and Remael (2014) discover that redundancy between "look, gestures, facial expressions and language" requires extra attention from translators. They expand non-verbal information in AVT that viewer obtains dialogue information from the images rather than from the verbal text, such as pronouns in audiovisual texts. They also introduce semiotic cohesion, the criteria to distinguish texts with different levels of non-verbal input, which are the interaction between images and words and the interaction between gestures and speech. Based on this theory proposed by Díaz-Cintas and Remael (2014), Huang and Wang (2022) compared low level of non-verbal input with high level one in two audiovisual texts. They use eye tracking and keystroke logging to compare post-editing and translation efforts from translation students. The results show that although non-verbal input affected post-editing effort, a higher level of non-verbal input required lower cognitive effort. Therefore, they conclude that the multimodal nature of audiovisual texts may not be an obstacle during the subtitle post-editing process since the texts with more non-verbal input are likely to help the translators.

Based on Huang and Wang's research, this study adopts a mixed method, combining process logs, keystrokes, and questionnaire to compare subtitlers' post-editing efforts. Unlike previous research, which has been focused on machine-translating human-generated source language subtitles, the experiment use machine-translating fully automatic subtitles (from English to Chinese Simplified), with a low or a high level of non-verbal input. This study aims to provide some suggestions for machine translation improvements in automatic subtitling.

2. Methods and materials

2.1. Methods

The research combines objective and subjective measures to help further triangulate the experiment results and provide further insight into the subtitling production process. Three measures were used in this experiment, process logs, keystrokes, and a user experience questionnaire (explained in Figure 1).

For process logs, this experiment analysed the total time spent on post-editing through logs documents generated by a professional subtitle software[1], which is also used by the participants.

Windows Problem Steps Recorder (PSR)[2] is used to record keystrokes during the post-editing process. It is a tool provided by Windows to automatically capture steps on a computer. It is convenient for subtitlers because the experiment was conducted online. These recorded steps include insertions and deletions, which show subtitlers' revision behaviours. This study also considers the purpose of insertions and deletion since machine translation is only part of

[1] The software is achieved from https://www.1sj.tv/

[2] See https://learn.microsoft.com/en-us/office/troubleshoot/settings/how-to-use-problem-steps-recorder

automatic subtitling. It shows how much effort the subtitlers spend on machine translation in automatic subtitling. Therefore, WinMerge[3], detecting and displaying differences within text files, is used to compare the differences between post-editing automatic subtitles and original automatic subtitles.

The questionnaire in this study was adapted from the User Experience Questionnaire (UEQ) developed by Karakanta et al. (2022a) for end-user evaluation of MT in automatic subtitling.

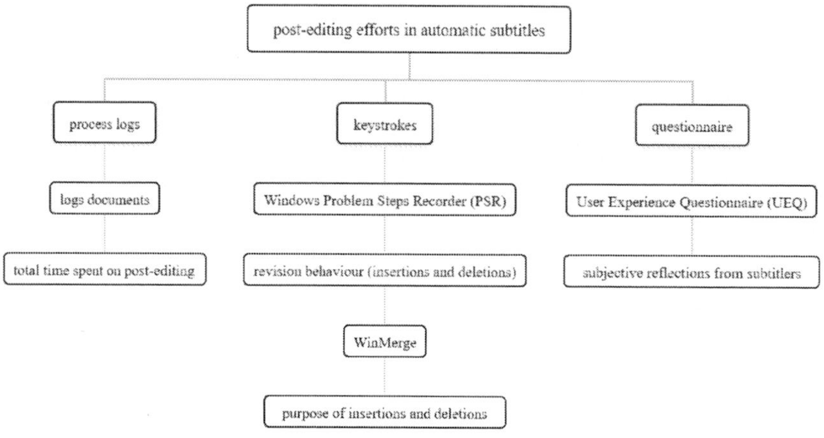

Figure 1. Three measures in this study.

2.2. Participants

12 subtitlers were recruited in the experiment. All are Chinese natives with English as their second language. All of them have passed the entry tests as a freelancer in a Mainland translation agency. According to the demographic data they provided, they have professional experience as subtitle translators in the relevant language pair, an average of 2.8 years (range 1-10 years). 75% of the participants have learned translation during their undergraduate or postgraduate study and 50% of them have passed the China Accreditation Test for Translators and Interpreters (CATTI) in the English-Chinese language pair. All of them have experience in using translation technologies such as machine translation. Over half of the subtitlers (58.3%) frequently use machine translation when they do translation projects, while just three participants seldom use it.

2.3. Materials

Video clips to be subtitled were selected based on the concept of "semiotic cohesion" (Díaz-Cintas & Remael, 2014, p. 51) and the research samples in Huang and Wang (2022). There are eight video clips in this experiment, four from a documentary film and four from TV series. All the video clips were cut from longer videos in English and each one lasts about one minute.

Table 1 shows the multimodal analysis of the image and speech information from the original materials to explain the selection.

[3] The software is achieved from https://winmerge.org/

	Description of the images	Description of the speech	Level of non-verbal input	Source material information
Documentary		Narration has no direct reference to image	Low (without subtitle-image and speech-gesture interaction)	<MINIMALISM: Official Netflix Documentary> by Netflix (2023)
Text 1	Moving shots of the minimalist going to work	Self-narration from a minimalist talking about his life		
Text 2	Moving shots of some houses	Narration from a third-person narrator talking about people's mistake of buying house		
Text 3	The screens when a minimalist faces the camera	Self-narration from a minimalist talking about his experience		
Text 4	Moving shots of a city	Narration from a third-person narrator talking about people's misunderstanding of buying		
TV series		Dialogues include pronouns that refer to the people in the images	High (with subtitle-image and speech-gesture interaction)	<Young Sheldon> Season 6 by CBS (2022)
Text 5	Static shots between six family members in the dining room	Diegetic dialogues between several people		Episode 2
Text 6	Static shots between four family members in their kitchen			Episode 3
Text 7	Static shots between six family members in the dining room			Episode 6
Text 8	Static shots between five family members in the dining room			Episode 12

Table 1. Multimodal analysis and selection criteria of the source materials.

	Total duration(s)	Number of sentences	Tokens
Text 1	72	18	115
Text 2	57	17	144
Text 3	65	15	116
Text 4	57	14	112
Text 5	60	37	174
Text 6	61	40	176
Text 7	62	33	189
Text 8	62	39	208

Table 2. Basic features of the source materials.

As shown in Table 1, Text 1-4 were selected from a documentary film, without subtitle-image and speech-gesture interaction. Therefore, they were evaluated as having a low level of non-verbal input because the images had no direct reference to the narration's content. Text 5-8, selected from a TV series, were considered to have a high level of non-verbal input. These videos contain character dialogues with facial expressions, pronouns, and gestures. The themes of all texts were based on the topic of life, especially daily life, to avoid any confounding results by different topics.

Each text has a similar duration and contains a complete scene to avoid any confusion. However, texts in the documentary and TV series were inevitably different in terms of their tokens and sentences (shown in Table 2).

All the subtitles were generated by the professional subtitle software through automatic transcription, spotting segmentation, and MT, without any human interruption. Besides, subtitlers received automatic subtitles in English for their references.

2.4. User experience questionnaire

An online questionnaire was used to collect subjective feedback from subtitlers. The objective of UEQ is to provide a user experience of post-editing and automatic subtitling. The questionnaire contained open and closed questions, which were delivered in English and were conducted through 问卷星 (www.wjx.cn). To obtain objective results, all responses were kept anonymous.

The questionnaire included three parts. The first part collected demographic data about the subtitlers, including gender, English proficiency, years of experience in subtitling and how often they use translation technologies, including machine translation. The second part focused on the user experience with the task of post-editing automatically generated subtitles. It contained 13 pairs of adjectives related to the post-editing experience for documentaries and TV series, in the form post-editing was... (difficult/easy, unpleasant/pleasant, etc.). Besides, it has evaluations on the quality of spotting and segmentation and the effort of editing them. For the second part, the author processed the scores using the formulae in the UEQ Data Analysis Tools (version 7)[4] to convert them to a scale of -3 to +3, with 0 representing a neutral mid-point. In the UEQ Data Analysis Tool, average scores between -0.8 and +0.8 are defined as neutral evaluations. Values below -0.8 correspond to negative and values above 0.8 to positive evaluations. The last part provided open questions on the quality and benefits of MT in automatic subtitling. Participants were also asked to provide their comments on machine translation and automatic subtitling.

[4] UEQ Data Analysis Tools: https://www.ueq-online.org/

2.5. Procedure

Before participating in the experiment, participants were asked to read the guidelines. The guidelines concern the task and the quality of subtitle production in the Code of Good Subtitling Practice (Ivarsson & Carroll, 1998). The quality guideline contains some major parts for subtitling, including grammar, spelling and punctuation, content and transfer, and readability. The guideline is accepted by researchers in AVT (Romero-Fresco & Pöchhacker, 2017; Huang & Wang, 2022), although it was released two decades ago. Besides, the participants were informed about the objective of the research, and the purposes of the data collection and gave their consent.

The subtitling tasks were carried out using the subtitling software and in one language pair: English to Chinese Simplified. Subtitlers had access to the internet as well as other resources normally used in their work. The participants were required to finish the tasks in one week. The experiment was conducted online.

The experiment includes two parts. In part one, the subtitlers were required to post-edit eight automatic subtitles. And they used the steps recorder when they were doing the post-editing tasks. In part two, the subtitlers were required to finish the user experience questionnaire and gave their comments on automatic subtitles and machine translation. All the subtitlers got their pay after finishing the task.

3. Data analysis

For each subtitler, the author collected the following data: 1) the final human post-edited subtitle files in SubRip.srt format; 2) logs documents from the subtitle tool, which records original and final timestamps; 3) keystrokes, using Windows Problem Steps Recorder (PSR), which automatically capture steps on a computer. At the end of the task, the subtitlers completed a questionnaire providing feedback on their user experience with automatic subtitling.

3.1. Process logs and keystroke logging

The time spent on post-editing was calculated based on the logging documents and steps recorder. Although each video clip lasts for about one minute, all clips have different tokens. Therefore, the average time spent on post-editing per token is calculated (see Figure 2). From Figure 2, subtitlers spent more time on just one text from TV series than texts from a documentary, while they spent less time on two texts from TV series than those from a documentary. Furthermore, in Text 1-4, the subtitlers spent about 8.75 seconds on post-editing per token. In Text 5-8, it takes about 8.60 seconds for the subtitlers to post-edit each token. Although Text 5-8 contain more non-verbal input, it seems that there are no significant differences (less than 0.5 seconds) between them and Text 1-4 in post-editing. This finding corroborates Huang and Wang's (2022) argument that non-verbal input from audiovisual texts was not an obstacle during post-editing.

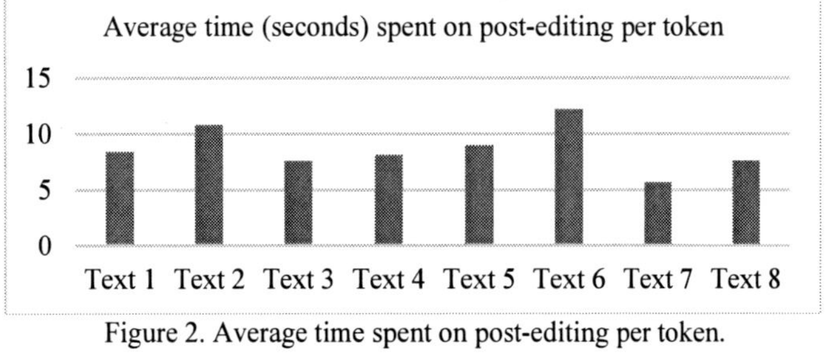

Figure 2. Average time spent on post-editing per token.

The number of keystrokes, insertions, and deletions were calculated by steps recorder (see Table 3). From Table 3, the deletions number of each text was much more than the number of insertions. Besides, when post-editing Text 5-8 from the TV series, the subtitlers used more insertions and deletions. Then, the subtitlers' revising behaviours were further analysed by WinMerge to get a full picture. WinMerge generated reports of differences between automatic subtitles and post-editing subtitles (samples are seen in Figure 3) and the reports showed the subtitlers revising efforts in translation, spotting, and segmentation. Considering that there are 12 subtitlers, the author calculated an average number of differences. Figure 4 shows the subtitlers' efforts on machine translation, spotting, and segmentation. It turns out that the subtitlers spent more effort on spotting and segmentation than on machine translation in Text 5-8. The reports also show how the subtitlers interact non-verbal information with verbal texts (samples are shown in Table 4). For instance, the subtitlers recognized characters through images and the audio in Text 6, so they revised the spotting, segmentation and translation. Without this interaction, the subtitles would make no sense.

	Average insertions	Average deletions
Text 1	44	111
Text 2	71	146
Text 3	45	109
Text 4	46	116
Text 5	76	205
Text 6	86	151
Text 7	69	135
Text 8	84	187

Table 3. Average insertions and deletions in different texts.

1 00:00:01,400 --> 00:00:03,200 哦，我想到了另一个我们可以先玩的游戏。	1 00:00:01,400 --> 00:00:03,133 我又想到了一个可以玩的游戏
2 00:00:03,200 --> 00:00:04,720 吃，融化巧克力和尿布。	2 00:00:03,133 --> 00:00:04,720 首先 把化了的巧克力涂到尿布上
3 00:00:04,800 --> 00:00:07,000 继续想，我们要想出游戏来玩、	3 00:00:04,800 --> 00:00:05,428 继续想
4 00:00:07,080 --> 00:00:08,080 因为我有一个好主意。	4 00:00:05,429 --> 00:00:07,000 要玩游戏吗
5 00:00:08,280 --> 00:00:09,960 智能动物技术。	5 00:00:07,080 --> 00:00:08,080 因为我有一个好主意

Figure 3. Screenshot of a WinMerge report from one subtitler in Text 8 post-editing.

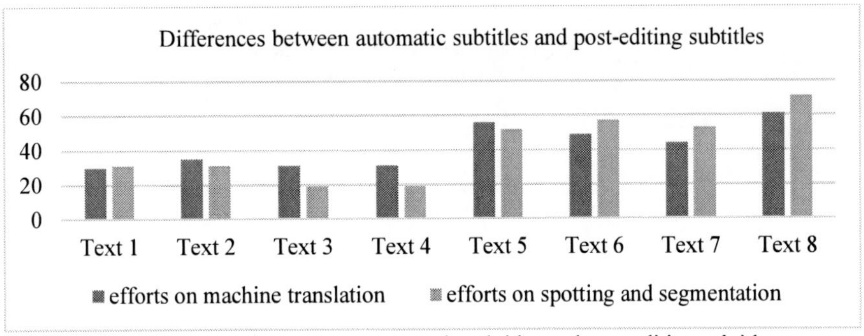

Figure 4. Differences between automatic subtitles and post-editing subtitles.

Text 6	Automatic subtitles	Post-editing subtitles
A multi-speaker event and pronouns in the text	13. 00:00:21,240 --> 00:00:**23,320**	13. 00:00:21,240--> 00:00:**22,333**
	只吃点吐司怎么样？**很好的吐司。**	只吃点吐司怎么样？
	14. 00:00:23,320 --> 00:00:23,560	14. 00:00:22,333 --> 00:00:23,560
	我可以的。	**好啊 吐司我会做**
	28. 00:00:42,070 --> 00:00:**43,630**	28. 00:00:42,070 --> 00:00:**43,333**
	我希望你能帮**我**解决**Sheldon的问题**。	我希望你能帮**我**解决
	29. 00:00:43,630 --> 00:00:44,470	29. 00:00:43,333 --> 00:00:44,470
	别管她了。	**谢尔顿** 别烦她了
	33. 00:00:49,190 --> 00:00:49,590	33. 00:00:49,190 --> 00:00:49,590
	我是什么？	**我**是什么来着？
	34. 00:00:49,790 --> 00:00:50,270	34. 00:00:49,790 --> 00:00:50,270
	没有盲文。	**侄辈母亲**

Table 4. Examples of the interaction between verbal and nonverbal information in a Win-Merge report.

3.2. Evaluation of user experience

The user experience (UX) scores are shown in Figure 5-6. Overall, the post-editing experience can be considered neutral to positive in Text 1-8 with different non-verbal input. The subtitlers found the post-editing process pleasant, enjoyable, and practical in all texts, with different levels of non-verbal input. When post-editing Text 5-8 with a high level of non-verbal input, the subtitlers found it more relaxed, exciting, fun, creative and motivating. When post-editing Text 1-4 with a low level of non-verbal input, the subtitlers felt less laborious, more efficient, simpler and faster, although there are no significant differences in average time spent on Text 1-4 and Text 5-8. In Figure 6, overall spotting and segmentation evaluations in all texts are neutral, except for the automatic segmentation evaluation. Compared with Text 1-4, the subtitlers considered automatic segmentation was poor in Text 5-8 from the TV series. The subtitlers found experience in spotting and segmentation much better when post-editing Text 1-4 with a low level of non-verbal input. These findings were in accord with the previous analysis of subtitlers' revising behaviours that they spent more effort in spotting and segmentation than translation.

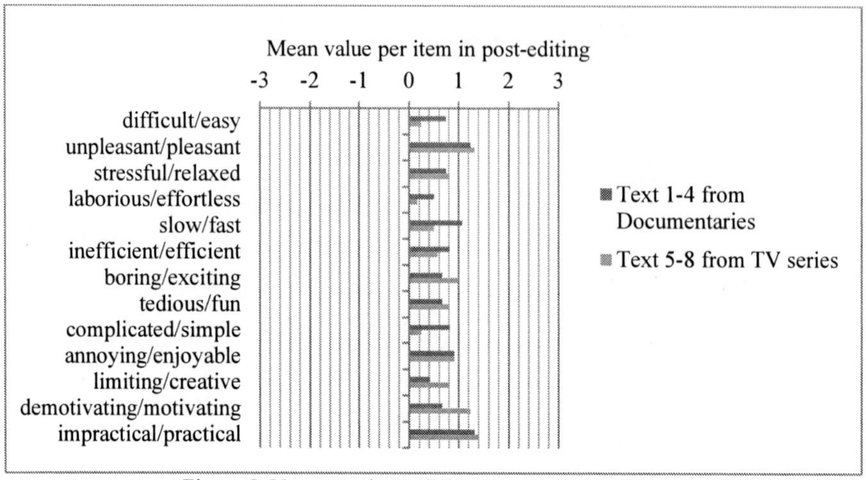

Figure 5. User experience (UX) scores in post-editing.

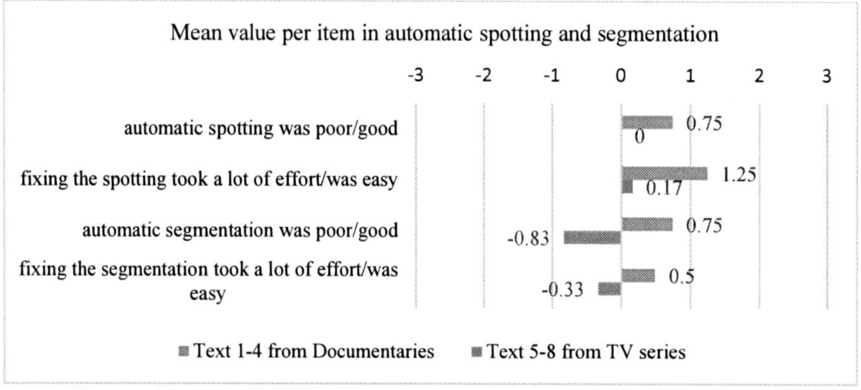

Figure 6. User experience (UX) scores in automatic spotting and segmentation.

3.3. Subtitlers' feedback

Main issues with the machine translation: For Text 1-4 from documentaries, some subtitlers found that for some sentences, the tense was wrong. Besides, some words were translated with the same meaning, although they occurred several times in one video. Two subtitlers thought that machine translation was not good at translating long sentences in subtitling. For Text 5-8 from the TV series, the subtitlers found more issues. For instance, the machine translation engine cannot recognize a multi-speaker event. The machine translations were literal and had problems with slang and new words created by the characters. At the same time, four subtitlers pointed out that the accuracy of machine translation was affected by the errors of automatic transcription. Most subtitlers responded that the translation style should be oral.

Main benefits of machine translation in subtitling: Most (67%) subtitlers mentioned that machine translation helps them to understand the main idea of the videos so that they can work efficiently. Some responded that machine translation helps them save time in typing. 91% of the participants thought that machine translation helps the work of subtitlers while just one participant held the neural opinion.

Impression of using machine translation in subtitling: The subtitlers gave feedback on the danger for the profession of the subtitler from using machine translation. Four participants said that there is no danger for the subtitlers. Half of the participants mentioned that they may rely on machine translation if they use it more frequently. They may lack initiative and think less when they become accustomed to using machine translation. Two participants predicted that the subtitlers who work with general texts may be replaced in the future.

4. Conclusions

This study examined post-editing efforts in automatic subtitling, with a focus on non-verbal input's effect on machine translation. In general, time spend is not significantly different between videos with low and high levels of non-verbal input, although subtitlers felt less laborious when translating texts with less non-verbal information. Furthermore, the subtitlers spent more effort on revising spotting and segmentation than translation when they post-edited texts with more non-verbal information. It may help to explain why the subtitlers felt faster when they translated texts with a low level of non-verbal input. The comparison between automatic subtitles and post-editing subtitles also shows that the subtitlers revised translation, spotting and segmentation to interact non-verbal information (images and audio) with verbal information (texts). Machine translation had more problems with texts containing non-verbal input, according to subtitler feedback. Most subtitlers hold a positive attitude towards machine translation usage. However, subtitlers may rely on it if they use it more frequently.

This experiment also offers valuable insights for MT improvements in automatic subtitling. For instance, pronoun detection in TV series and more high-quality training data with non-verbal information are needed to improve the machine translation engine. Additionally, it is crucial to provide more training to students or subtitlers to reduce reliance on machine translation during subtitle creation.

However, the study has certain limitations. The experiment was not conducted on a large scale, involving only 12 subtitlers, and the video clips were limited to one documentary and TV series. Further research, through eye tracking and interview, is necessary to explore how subtitlers interact non-verbal information with verbal text to help them post-edit machine translation in automatic subtitling.

Acknowledgement

The author kindly thanks all the subtitlers who took part in the experiment.

References

Bellés-Calvera, L., & Quintana, R. C. (2021). Audiovisual translation through NMT and subtitling in the Netflix series 'cable girls'. In R Mitkov et al. (Eds). *Proceedings of the Translation and Interpreting Technology Online Conference* (pp. 142-148). INCOMA Ltd.

Díaz-Cintas, J., & Remael, A. (2014). *Audiovisual translation: Subtitling*. Routledge.

Georgakopoulou, Y. (2021, March 22). Implementing Machine Translation in Subtitling. Multilingual. https://multilingual.com/implementing-machine-translation-in-subtitling/

Guillot, M.-N. (2018). Subtitling on the cusp of its futures. In L. Pérez-González (Ed.), *The Routledge handbook of audiovisual translation* (pp. 31–47). Routledge.

Huang, J., & Wang, J. (2022). Post-editing machine translated subtitles: examining the effects of non-verbal input on student translators' effort. *Perspectives, Studies in Translatology, ahead-of-print(ahead-of-print)*, 1–21.

Ivarsson, J., & Carroll, M. (1998). *Code of good subtitling practice.* European Association for Studies in Screen Translation.

Karakanta, A. (2022). Experimental research in automatic subtitling: At the crossroads between machine translation and audiovisual translation. *Translation Spaces, 11*(1), 89–112.

Karakanta, A., Bentivogli, L., Cettolo, M., Negri, M., & Turchi, M. (2022b). Towards a methodology for evaluating automatic subtitling. In H. Moniz et al. (Eds). *Proceedings of the 23rd Annual Conference of the European Association for Machine Translation* (pp. 333-334). European Association for Machine Translation.

Karakanta, A., Bentivogli, L., Cettolo, M., Negri, M., & Turchi, M. (2022a). Post-editing in Automatic Subtitling: A Subtitlers' Perspective. In H Moniz et al. (Eds). *Proceedings of the 23rd Annual Conference of the European Association for Machine Translation* (pp. 259-268). European Association for Machine Translation.

Koponen, M., Sulubacak, U., Vitikainen, K., & Tiedemann, J. (2020a). MT for Subtitling: MT for Subtitling: Investigating professional translators' user experience and feedback. In J. E. Ortega, M. Federico, C. Orasan, & M. Popovic (Eds), *Proceedings of 1st Workshop on Post-Editing in Modern-Day Translation* (pp. 79-92). Association for Machine Translation in the Americas.

Koponen, M., Sulubacak, U., Vitikainen, K., & Tiedemann, J. (2020b). MT for subtitling: User evaluation of post-editing productivity. In A. Martins et al. (Eds). *Proceedings of the 22nd Annual Conference of the European Association for Machine Translation* (pp. 115–124). European Association for Machine Translation.

Leijten, M., & Van Waes, L. (2013). Keystroke logging in writing research: Using Inputlog to analyze and visualize writing processes. *Written Communication, 30*(3), 358-392.

Pérez-González, L. (2014). Multimodality in translation and interpreting studies: Theoretical and methodological perspectives. In S. Bermann, & C. Porter (Eds.), *A companion to translation studies* (pp. 119–131). Wiley Blackwell.

Perego, E. (2009). The codification of nonverbal information in subtitled texts. *In New trends in audiovisual translation* (pp. 58–69). Cromwell.

Romero-Fresco, P., & Pöchhacker, F. (2017). Quality assessment in interlingual live subtitling: The NTR model. *Linguistica Antverpiensia, New Series: Themes in Translation Studies, 16*, 149–167.

Saarikoski, L., Van Rijsselbergen, D., Hirvonen, M., Koponen, M., Sulubacak, U., & Vitikainen, K. (2020). MEMAD Project: End User Feedback on AI in the Media Production Workflows. *Proceedings of IBC 2020*.

Varga, C. (2021). Online Automatic Subtitling Platforms and Machine Translation. An Analysis of Quality in AVT. *The Scientific Bulletin of the Politehnica University of Timişoara. Transactions on Modern Languages. 20* (1), 37-49.

Improving Standard German Captioning of Spoken Swiss German: Evaluating Multilingual Pre-trained Models

Jonathan Mutal Jonathan.Mutal@unige.ch
Pierrette Bouillon Pierrette.Bouillon@unige.ch
Johanna Gerlach Johanna.Gerlach@unige.ch
Marianne Starlander Marianne.Starlander@unige.ch

TIM, Faculty of translation and interpreting, University of Geneva, Geneva, Switzerland

Abstract

Multilingual pre-trained language models are often the best alternative in low-resource settings. In the context of a cascade architecture for automatic Standard German captioning of spoken Swiss German, we evaluate different models on the task of transforming normalised Swiss German ASR output into Standard German. Instead of training a large model from scratch, we fine-tuned publicly available pre-trained models, which reduces the cost of training high-quality neural machine translation models. Results show that pre-trained multilingual models achieve the highest scores, and that a higher number of languages included in pre-training improves the performance. We also observed that the type of source and target included in fine-tuning data impacts the results.

1 Introduction

In Switzerland, over 60% of the population speaks Swiss German, which is a collection of spoken dialects with many regional variations. Swiss German is widely used in daily life and in the media, both on the radio and on Swiss TV. As these dialects lack a standardised written form, Standard German is often used for written communication, captions and subtitles. Standard German is also used to make Swiss German content accessible to people who cannot understand the dialects.

The PASSAGE project (Bouillon et al., 2022), which is the product of a collaboration between SRF and recapp IT, aims at making Swiss TV shows more accessible by automatically generating Standard German captions for Spoken Swiss German using a cascade approach. Figure 1 illustrates the two main steps. In a first step, our project partner's ASR transcribes spoken Swiss German into *Normalised Swiss German*, maintaining the original syntax and expressions of Swiss German, but using German words (Arabskyy et al., 2021). A second step, using machine translation (MT) approaches, aims at transforming these normalised transcriptions into fully correct *Standard German*.

Our contribution to this pipeline focuses on the MT step. In this context, MT could be used to different ends (Buet and Yvon, 2021). In our case, the objective is a minimal trans-

Proceedings of Machine Translation Summit XIX, Vol. 2: Users Track, pages 65–76
September 4–8, 2023, Macau SAR, China.

formation to produce a correct Standard German transcription. This mainly involves resolving divergences between Swiss and Standard German by performing syntactical and lexical transformations, correcting speech recognition issues and removing spoken language phenomena such as dysfluencies. It would also be possible to condense and further transform content to achieve compliance with subtitling or captioning standards, which is not the aim of our task, but could be added as a subsequent step in the cascade approach. Since our input is not an actual language, but rather an artificial intermediate state between Swiss German and Standard German, the task is comparable to translation from low-resourced languages. We therefore propose to use multilingual pre-trained models which are often the best alternative in low-resource settings (Zanon Boito et al., 2022). In the absence of models for normalised Swiss German, we propose to use models trained on high-resource languages including German, that could generalise to normalised Swiss German (Kocmi and Bojar, 2018).

Some researchers have used multilingual pre-trained language models to generalise unseen languages – i.e. languages that are not covered in the pre-trained model (Wang et al., 2020; Pfeiffer et al., 2020; Muller et al., 2021). For example, (Muller et al., 2021) fine-tuned multilingual pre-trained models on 15 unseen languages to perform downstream tasks – POS (Part-of-Speech Tagging), NER (Named Entity Recognition) and DEP (Dependency Parsing). Their study shows that using multilingual pre-trained models increases the performance on these tasks for languages that have the same writing systems as the pre-trained languages. However, most of the researchers have applied these models to natural language understanding tasks from an unseen source language (Rust et al., 2021), but not many to machine translation. Multilingual models have already been applied to Swiss German, for example (Plüss et al., 2022) fine-tuned a multilingual pre-trained model to transcribe Swiss German and generate Standard German using an end-to-end approach. The model outperformed the transformer baseline by at least 8 BLEU points.

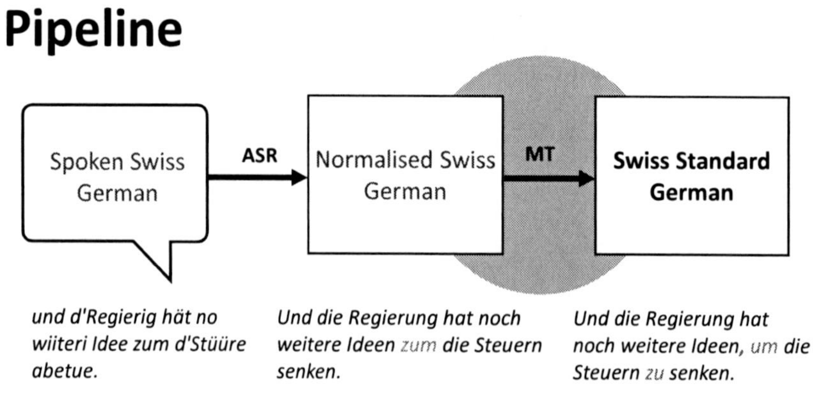

Figure 1: Overview of the pipeline from PASSAGE.

In this paper, we investigate different MT approaches for our task. Our first hypothesis is that in a low-resource setting such as this, pre-trained models will outperform a model trained from scratch with little data, as often shown in the literature. Our second hypothesis is that, in the absence of pre-trained models including our source language, models with a higher number of pre-trained languages will deliver better results. Finally, focusing only on fine-tuning of the best performing model, we will investigate the impact of different data characteristics, such as domain, provenance and quantity. The test data used in this study is available for research purposes.[1]

The remainder of this paper is organised as follows: Section 2 discusses the data, systems and evaluation methodology; Section 3 shows the results; and Section 4 presents the conclusion.

2 Methodology

In the following sections, we describe in more detail the data (Section 2.1), systems (Section 2.2) and evaluation methodology (Section 2.3).

2.1 Data

Due to the nature of the task, no large corpora were available. We therefore used data from two different sources: TV shows provided by our project partner SRF and the Swiss Parliaments Corpus, an automatically aligned Swiss German speech to Standard German text corpus, available for research purposes (Plüss et al., 2021). These data were processed in the following manner to produce aligned corpora:

Swiss German TV shows 1 This included data from a same set of talk shows and regional news, but in different unaligned forms, using different segmentation:

- GSW_NORM: normalised human transcriptions (using Standard German words). These data were originally created to train the Swiss German recogniser;
- DE_Subtitles: original Standard German subtitles. These data follow subtitling standards;
- ASR_NORM: automatic transcriptions produced by recapp IT ASR.

We combined the above to produce the following aligned data sets:

- **GSW_SubDE: Normalised Transcriptions to Subtitles** We used an algorithm proposed by (Plüss et al., 2021) to align GSW_NORM and DE_Subtitles. We then reduced the noise between the transcriptions and subtitles by removing blank lines, joining chunks of words together to create sentences, filtering out items based on length differences, and filtering sentences longer than 200 tokens. This filtered out 10% of the segments. Table 1 shows an extract of the automatic alignment.
- **GSW_PeDE: Normalised Transcriptions to Post-edited Standard German** We produced standard German by minimally post-editing the human transcriptions (GSW_NORM). The segments were provided to the post-editors in context. Table 2 shows examples of the transformations performed by the post-editors.
- **ASR_SubDE and ASR_PeDE: ASR output to Standard German** We manually aligned the automatic transcriptions (ASR_NORM) to the subtitles (ASR_SubDe) and the post-edited texts (ASR_PeDe).

Swiss Parliaments Corpus This corpus includes original Swiss German speech, automatically aligned with human transcription into Standard German. By processing the speech part of this corpus with recapp ASR, we produced a large aligned ASR output to Standard German corpus (**ASR_SwissPar**).

[1] https://doi.org/10/gr72xj

Transcription (GSW_NORM)	**Original Standard German Subtitle** (DE_Subtitles)
Weil	
dort steht eigentlich, was man mit dem, also	Dort steht, was man tun muss.
was	
man eigentlich muss machen. Also zum Beispiel, dass man ähm die neue Pensionskasse muss angeben.	Man muss z.B. seine neue Pensionskasse melden.
Oder	
wenn man jetzt zum Beispiel nicht gerade wieder geht gehen arbeiten, ähm in was für eine Freizügigkeitseinrichtung das Geld soll hin.	Wenn man nicht sofort wieder arbeiten geht, muss man angeben,an welche Freizügigkeitseinrichtung das Geld ausbezahlt werden soll.
Das ist ein so ein riesiges Volumen.	Das ist ein riesiges Volumen.

Table 1: Extract of the automatic alignment between the transcription (GSW_NORM) and the original subtitles (GSW_SubDE), (GSW_SubDE). The utterances with background colour were filtered out.

Transformation	**Normalised Human Transcriptions** (GSW_NORM)	**Post-edited Standard German** (GSW_PeDE)	**Literal Translation** (English)
Place modal after infinitive	Also, der einzige Ort, wo ich **würde gehen** ist Spanien.	Also, der einzige Ort, wo ich **hingehen würde**, ist Spanien.	The only place I would go to is Spain
Change subordinating conjunction	Wir haben es auch gesehen das letzte Jahr, **wo** ein Putschversuch [...]	Wir haben es auch im letzten Jahr gesehen, **als** ein Putschversuch [...]	We also observed it last year, when a coup attempt [...]
Disfluencies	die inländischen **produ- ähm** Produzenten geschützt sind	die inländischen Produzenten geschützt sind	the domestic producers are protected

Table 2: Extract of Normalised transcriptions and post-edited standard German (GSW_PeDe). Three examples of transformations performed by the post-editors on the transcriptions (GSW_NORM).

Swiss German TV shows 2 This second batch of more recent TV shows was also 1) transcribed automatically with the recapp ASR, 2) transcribed manually (normalised) and post-edited into Standard German. Part of the resulting aligned (ASR to Standard German) data was then put aside to be used as test data (cf. Section 2.3) and the remainder was used to constitute the **ASR_recent** data set.[2]

Table 3 summarises the data sets with the number of segments and words.

[2]The data set is available in `doi.org/10/gr72xj`

Data Set	#Segments	#Words		#Vocabulary	
		Source	Target	Source	Target
GSW_SubDE	59,932	910,597	649,039	47,846	65,918
GSW_PeDe	75,705	989,391	948,700	76,905	77,698
ASR_PeDe	9,223	213,185	201,328	24,899	27,216
ASR_SubDE	12,393	197,689	161,047	22,422	23,887
ASR_SwissPar	89,343	1,486,134	1,425,873	87,203	83,642
ASR_recent	979	20,358	19,660	4,639	5,024

Table 3: Number of segments, words and vocabulary (unique tokens) for each data set.

2.2 Systems and models

For our study, pre-trained models needed to fulfil several requirements 1) be available both in a monolingual German version and in a multilingual version including German in pre-training, 2) be adaptable to our particular task and 3) be computationally light-weight enough for use in production. Based on these criteria, we selected three different approaches: MT-based, which is trained to translate; Bert-based (Devlin et al., 2019), which is trained to predict words from a sentence; and Bart-based (Lewis et al., 2020), which is trained to reconstruct the original text and sentence order and exhibits increased robustness to language variation and noise.

We used a standard Transformer architecture for all the approaches (Vaswani et al., 2017). We carried out the training at FP16 precision. The models were trained and fine-tuned using the HuggingFace (Wolf et al., 2020) framework. We used default hyper-parameters for each approach.

MT-based We developed two neural machine translation models:

- **Monolingual** As no pre-trained model was available for normalised Swiss German, this model was trained using all our data (Normalised Swiss German to German).
- **Multilingual** We used a pre-trained machine translation model for Western Germanic languages, including Swiss German (Tiedemann, 2020).[3] We then fine-tuned it using all our data.

Bert-based We leveraged BERT for machine translation by initialising the Transformer architecture with BERT parameters as followed by (Rothe et al., 2020; Chen et al., 2022) and then fine-tuned with all our data:

- **Monolingual** The parameters of German BERT (Chan et al., 2020) were used to initialise the encoder and decoder of Transformer.
- **Multilingual** The parameters of Multilingual BERT – trained in 104 languages – were used to initialise the encoder and decoder of Transformer.[4]

Bart-based We used all our data to fine-tune two pre-trained models:

- **mBART25.** This model is pre-trained in 25 languages, including Standard German (Liu et al., 2020).
- **mBART50.** This model is an extension of mBART25 with 50 languages (Tang et al., 2020).

[3]https://huggingface.co/Helsinki-NLP/opus-mt-tc-big-gmw-gmw

[4]https://huggingface.co/bert-base-multilingual-cased

2.3 Evaluation methodology

To address our first hypothesis, we compare the MT-system trained from scratch with pre-trained models for the three approaches. To address the second hypothesis (higher number of languages on pre-trained models deliver better results), we assessed each model with different numbers of seen languages. To address our third research question, we compare the performance of systems fine-tuned with the different types of data.

Models were compared based on automatic metrics, using a test data set consisting of 1,542 segments of recent TV shows provided by our partners, SRF and recapp. The data come from four TV shows: *Der Club*, which consists of debates led by journalists in local dialects; *Eco Talk*, which consists of debates on economic and business topics led by journalists; *Gesichter und Geschichten*, which reports people's stories and often involves interviews of the public; *Schweiz Aktuell*, which reports daily news and often involves interviews of the public. Table 4 details the number of segments for each TV show.

TV Show	**#Segments**
Der Club	780
Eco Talk	356
Gesichter und Geschichten	205
Schweiz Aktuell	201
Total	1,542

Table 4: Number of segments for each TV show.

We used the human post-edited version as a reference to compute the following metrics using the open-source library SacreBLEU (Post, 2018): chrF (Popović, 2015), which allows us to quantify performance on the character level – good for Germanic languages, where small changes such as word endings are important; BLEU, which allows us to quantify the performance on the word level. We also calculated the Levenshtein distance between the system outputs and the raw ASR to quantify the number of changes made by each system.

In addition, to corroborate and verify that the changes made by the systems are perceived as useful by end-users, we have carried out a human evaluation comparing the raw ASR with the output of the best performing system according to the automatic metrics. Specifically, a subset of 400 sentences was randomly selected from the test data for the evaluation. Participants were asked to provide segment-level judgements on two aspects: language (including syntax, lexical choices, and punctuation) and meaning. The objective was to compare the outputs and indicate whether users perceived the systems to be equivalent or if one system was preferred over the other. To assess language, participants were presented with a five-point scale consisting of the following options: "A clearly better than B", "A slightly better than B", "A and B about the same", "B slightly better than A" and "B clearly better than A". For meaning, a four-point scale was used, including the options: "A better than B", "both ok", "both bad" and "B better than A". The Standard German transcription was provided to serve as a reference for the meaning evaluation.

All evaluations were carried out in spreadsheets that included all the segments of the shows in the original order to provide context, but judges were only required to evaluate the selected segments. To prevent bias, the position of the ASR and MT output was randomised. The spreadsheets were submitted to four native German speakers from Switzerland. Participants were compensated for the task.

3 Results

In this section, we present the results by hypothesis.

3.1 Usefulness of pre-trained models

Results for the automatic metrics are shown in Table 5. Overall, the scores show that adding a MT step improves the ASR output by at least 1 point chrF and BLEU. Regarding our first hypothesis, we observe the pre-trained models outperform the MT-based monolingual trained from scratch. The two monolingual systems achieve the lowest scores, with BERT outperforming the MT-based, which is unsurprising since the latter is trained on very little data.

Approach	Systems	#Lang	#Params	chrF	BLEU	Levenshtein
raw ASR	none	-	-	75.27	44.72	23.81
MT-based	Monolingual	1	215M	76.27	47.53	12.30
	Multilingual	104		78.95	52.37	9.61
Bert-based	Monolingual	1	384M	77.23	48.52	11.26
	Multilingual	104		78.90	51.98	10.20
Bart-based	mBART25	25	610M	77.70	51.36	10.50
	mBART50	50		79.82	54.68	9.63

Table 5: The table presents the details of each system, categorised by approach and system. It includes the number of languages, parameters, as well as the chrF, BLEU, and Levenshtein distance to the raw ASR. The number of parameters was calculated using the Huggingface library.

If we compare the various multilingual models, the results show that mBART50 outperforms the other approaches. These results concur with findings by (Lewis et al., 2020; Anastasopoulos et al., 2022), who showed that fine-tuned BART models often outperform other approaches on machine translation in low-resource settings. However, our results also show that the multilingual MT-based model, which is three times smaller than BART, achieved a competitive score.

Looking at the Levenshtein distance between system output and raw ASR, we observe that the best performing systems are also those that make the least changes.

3.2 Impact of Number of Languages

To verify our second hypothesis, regarding the number of languages in pre-training, we comparatively assessed the same models with different numbers of languages. The results show that models with more pre-trained languages, although they do not include normalised Swiss German, outperform the others on chrF and BLEU. However, further work would be necessary to explain what influence each individual pre-training language, and its distance to Swiss German, has on the task.

3.3 Impact of Fine-tuning Data

Since our data come from different sources and are constituted of different types, we wanted to see which source and type was the most useful for fine-tuning for the task. To assess this, we used mBART50 – the highest performing system from our approach comparison – which we fine-tuned individually with each of the different data sets described in Table 3. We compare performance with mBART50 without any fine-tuning. Since in our previous evaluation we observed the same pattern for both BLEU and chrF, we decided to solely calculate chrF for this evaluation.

The first aspect where our aligned data sets differ is the provenance of the Standard German target: post-edited, original subtitles or human transcriptions (Swiss Parliament). The results, reported in Table 6, show that fine-tuning improves performance on the task, with the exception of the two cases where the data consist of original subtitles (GSW_SubDE and ASR_SubDE). This can be explained by the fact that, contrary to the task, subtitles are shortened and often simplified. Using the post-edited data (GSW_PeDe and ASR_PeDE) produced the highest chrF scores. The model that was trained only with GSW_PeDe achieves a comparable chrF (79.15) score to the model trained with all the available data (79.82). We also observed that absolute performance varied between the four TV-shows, with "Der Club" obtaining the worst results. However, the different models have the same ranking for each show.

Data	Der Club	Ecotalk	Gesichter	Schweiz Aktuell	Total
None	**66.75**	**76.59**	**70.65**	**80.04**	**71.12**
GSW_SubDE	64.97	74.09	72.61	75.78	69.30
GSW_PeDe	75.92	83.74	77.31	84.20	79.15
ASR_PeDe	75.17	83.73	77.33	84.11	78.65
ASR_SubDE	63.37	72.90	70.30	74.56	67.99
ASR_SwissPar	73.08	80.56	76.74	81.37	76.40
ASR_recent	73.68	81.91	76.30	83.51	77.25

Table 6: chrF for each TV show, by fine-tuning data set.

The second aspect differentiating the data sets is the domain (TV shows vs Swiss Parliament). Results suggest that using a larger out-of-domain data set (the Swiss Parliament corpus, ASR_SwissPar, 89,343 segments) has almost the same impact as using a small number of in-domain segments (TV_recent, 979 segments). To confirm these results and make a comparable evaluation, we sampled 1,000 segments from the out-of-domain data (ASR_SwissPar) to reduce the size difference. Table 7 shows that using in-domain data results in a better performance on the task.

Type	Der Club	Ecotalk	Gesichter	Schweiz Aktuell	Total
Out-of-domain	72.26	80.60	75.49	81.71	75.77
In-domain	73.68	81.91	76.30	83.51	77.25

Table 7: chrF for each TV show, by domain of fine-tuning data.

The third aspect of interest is the provenance of the source side of the aligned data sets. Fine-tuning with data using human transcriptions (GSW_PeDE) obtained almost the same score as using automatic transcriptions (ASR_PeDE). However, these results might have been influenced by the difference in size between the two data sets (75,705 and 9,223 segments). We therefore performed an additional experiment, fine-tuning mBART using only a subset of the human transcription segments (GSW_PeDE), namely those corresponding to the segments included in the automatic transcription data set (ASR_PeDE). The results reported in Table 8 confirm that there is almost no difference in performance when using human transcriptions (GSW_PeDE) compared to automatic transcriptions (ASR_PeDE).

The results of these fine-tuning experiments show that the choice of data, particularly in

Transcription	Der Club	Ecotalk	Gesichter	Schweiz Aktuell	Total
Automatic	75.17	83.73	77.33	84.17	78.68
Human	75.88	83.39	77.10	84.18	78.52

Table 8: chrF for each TV show, by source of transcription of the fine-tuning data.

terms of domain and target-side data-type (post-edited vs. subtitles data), has a significant impact on performance. We also observe that adding less specialised data, available in larger quantities, does not improve the system for our particular task (refer to Table 5).

3.4 Human Evaluation

Table 9 shows the results of the comparative evaluation. In terms of language, with the original 5-point scale, 39% of segments did not receive a majority judgement (3 or 4 judges agree). We have therefore condensed the scale by combining the "slightly better" and "clearly better" assessments. On the resulting 3-point scale, agreement between judges is fair (Light's Kappa = 0.386) and 84% of segments received a majority judgement. For 71% of the segments, mBART's output was preferred to the raw ASR, which shows that the system succeeds at improving the language of the speech recognition output.

In terms of meaning, mBART improves on ASR for 32% of the segments, degrading 1%. Inter-annotator agreement on this task is moderate (Light's Kappa = 0.535), with 19% of segments left without majority judgement. For the remaining segments, which represent about half of the included data, the two system outputs were judged to be equivalent. For a high proportion of segments (29%), neither version was found to accurately convey the full meaning of the human transcription. Most of these cases can be attributed to incorrect lexical choices made by the ASR system, where the machine translation system was unable to generate the appropriate word. This finding highlights the need for improvement in accurately capturing the precise meaning of human transcriptions in these segments.

These evaluation results confirm that the improvements measured by the automatic metrics correspond to transformations perceived as useful by end users.

Language (5-point scale)		Language (3-point scale)		Meaning	
ASR clearly better	1 (0%)				
ASR slightly better	3 (1%)	ASR better	7 (2%)	ASR better	5 (1%)
Equivalent	45 (11%)	Equivalent	45 (11%)	Both ok	79 (20%)
mBART slightly better	97 (24%)	mBART better	284 (71%)	mBART better	127 (32%)
mBART clearly better	99 (25%)			Both bad	114 (29%)
No majority	155 (39%)	No majority	64 (16%)	No majority	75 (19%)
Light's Kappa	0.306	Light's Kappa	0.386	Light's Kappa	0.535

Table 9: mBART vs raw ASR output, majority comparative judgements for the 400 evaluated segments.

4 Conclusion

In this study we have applied different machine translation approaches to the task of improving ASR output for automatic Standard German captioning of Swiss German TV content in a cascade architecture. Overall, MT is able to improve the output, both according to automatic metrics and user perspective.

Our first hypothesis was confirmed by the better performance of all pre-trained models for this task. Among the tested approaches, Bart-based approach achieved the highest scores, possibly due to its ability to handle noisy text.

We also observed that a higher number of pre-trained languages improves performance on the task, meaning that more languages are useful to enable generalisation to an unseen language. However, we did not elucidate the influence of individual languages included in pre-training.

We also assessed the impact of fine-tuning data. In-domain data improved performance on the task, but there is no difference in performance when using as source side of the aligned data automatic or human transcriptions. Fine-tuning data for this task does not have to be clean human normalised transcriptions, which are more expensive to produce. Result shows that ASR output, despite being noisier, does not lead to significantly worse results. We also saw that target-side has a significant impact on performance. For the task as studied here, the subtitles, which contain many changes related to subtitling standards (shortening, simplification) are not ideal as training data.

The different systems described in this paper can be tested online at `https://passage-imi.unige.ch/demo/` and the test data is available at `https://doi.org/10/gr72xj`.

5 Acknowledgements

This project has received funding from the Initiative for Media Innovation, which is based at the EPFL's Media Center in Lausanne, Switzerland.

References

Anastasopoulos, A., Barrault, L., Bentivogli, L., Zanon Boito, M., Bojar, O., Cattoni, R., Currey, A., Dinu, G., Duh, K., Elbayad, M., Emmanuel, C., Estève, Y., Federico, M., Federmann, C., Gahbiche, S., Gong, H., Grundkiewicz, R., Haddow, B., Hsu, B., Javorský, D., Kloudová, V., Lakew, S., Ma, X., Mathur, P., McNamee, P., Murray, K., Nădejde, M., Nakamura, S., Negri, M., Niehues, J., Niu, X., Ortega, J., Pino, J., Salesky, E., Shi, J., Sperber, M., Stüker, S., Sudoh, K., Turchi, M., Virkar, Y., Waibel, A., Wang, C., and Watanabe, S. (2022). Findings of the IWSLT 2022 evaluation campaign. In *Proceedings of the 19th International Conference on Spoken Language Translation (IWSLT 2022)*, pages 98–157, Dublin, Ireland (in-person and online). Association for Computational Linguistics.

Arabskyy, Y., Agarwal, A., Dey, S., and Koller, O. (2021). Dialectal Speech Recognition and Translation of Swiss German Speech to Standard German Text: Microsoft's Submission to SwissText 2021. *arXiv:2106.08126 [cs, eess]*. arXiv: 2106.08126.

Bouillon, P., Gerlach, J., Mutal, J., and Starlander, M. (2022). The PASSAGE project : Standard German subtitling of Swiss German TV content. In *Proceedings of the 23rd Annual Conference of the European Association for Machine Translation*, pages 301–302, Ghent, Belgium. European Association for Machine Translation.

Buet, F. and Yvon, F. (2021). Vers la production automatique de sous-titres adaptés à l'affichage. In Denis, P., Grabar, N., Fraisse, A., Cardon, R., Jacquemin, B., Kergosien, E., and Balvet, A., editors, *Traitement Automatique des Langues Naturelles*, pages 91–104, Lille, France. ATALA.

Chan, B., Schweter, S., and Möller, T. (2020). German's next language model. In *Proceedings of the 28th International Conference on Computational Linguistics*, pages 6788–6796, Barcelona, Spain (Online). International Committee on Computational Linguistics.

Chen, C., Yin, Y., Shang, L., Jiang, X., Qin, Y., Wang, F., Wang, Z., Chen, X., Liu, Z., and Liu, Q. (2022). bert2bert: Towards reusable pretrained language models. In *Proceedings of the 60th Annual Meeting of the Association for Computational Linguistics (Volume 1: Long Papers)*, page 2134–2148, Dublin, Ireland. Association for Computational Linguistics.

Devlin, J., Chang, M.-W., Lee, K., and Toutanova, K. (2019). Bert: Pre-training of deep bidirectional transformers for language understanding. In *Proceedings of the 2019 Conference of the North*, page 4171–4186, Minneapolis, Minnesota. Association for Computational Linguistics.

Kocmi, T. and Bojar, O. (2018). Trivial transfer learning for low-resource neural machine translation. In *Proceedings of the Third Conference on Machine Translation: Research Papers*, pages 244–252, Brussels, Belgium. Association for Computational Linguistics.

Lewis, M., Liu, Y., Goyal, N., Ghazvininejad, M., Mohamed, A., Levy, O., Stoyanov, V., and Zettlemoyer, L. (2020). Bart: Denoising sequence-to-sequence pre-training for natural language generation, translation, and comprehension. In *Proceedings of the 58th Annual Meeting of the Association for Computational Linguistics*, page 7871–7880, Online. Association for Computational Linguistics.

Liu, Y., Gu, J., Goyal, N., Li, X., Edunov, S., Ghazvininejad, M., Lewis, M., and Zettlemoyer, L. (2020). Multilingual denoising pre-training for neural machine translation. *arXiv:2001.08210 [cs]*. arXiv: 2001.08210.

Muller, B., Anastasopoulos, A., Sagot, B., and Seddah, D. (2021). When being unseen from mBERT is just the beginning: Handling new languages with multilingual language models. In *Proceedings of the 2021 Conference of the North American Chapter of the Association for Computational Linguistics: Human Language Technologies*, pages 448–462, Online. Association for Computational Linguistics.

Pfeiffer, J., Vulić, I., Gurevych, I., and Ruder, S. (2020). MAD-X: An Adapter-Based Framework for Multi-Task Cross-Lingual Transfer. In *Proceedings of the 2020 Conference on Empirical Methods in Natural Language Processing (EMNLP)*, pages 7654–7673, Online. Association for Computational Linguistics.

Plüss, M., Hürlimann, M., Cuny, M., Stöckli, A., Kapotis, N., Hartmann, J., Ulasik, M. A., Scheller, C., Schraner, Y., Jain, A., Deriu, J., Cieliebak, M., and Vogel, M. (2022). SDS-200: A Swiss German speech to standard German text corpus. In *Proceedings of the Thirteenth Language Resources and Evaluation Conference*, pages 3250–3256, Marseille, France. European Language Resources Association.

Plüss, M., Neukom, L., Scheller, C., and Vogel, M. (2021). Swiss Parliaments Corpus, an Automatically Aligned Swiss German Speech to Standard German Text Corpus. *arXiv:2010.02810 [cs]*. arXiv: 2010.02810.

Popović, M. (2015). chrf: character n-gram f-score for automatic mt evaluation. In *Proceedings of the Tenth Workshop on Statistical Machine Translation*, page 392–395, Lisbon, Portugal. Association for Computational Linguistics.

Post, M. (2018). A call for clarity in reporting BLEU scores. In *Proceedings of the Third Conference on Machine Translation: Research Papers*, pages 186–191, Belgium, Brussels. Association for Computational Linguistics.

Rothe, S., Narayan, S., and Severyn, A. (2020). Leveraging pre-trained checkpoints for sequence generation tasks. *Transactions of the Association for Computational Linguistics*, 8:264–280.

Rust, P., Pfeiffer, J., Vulić, I., Ruder, S., and Gurevych, I. (2021). How good is your tokenizer? on the monolingual performance of multilingual language models. In *Proceedings of the 59th Annual Meeting of the Association for Computational Linguistics and the 11th International Joint Conference on Natural Language Processing (Volume 1: Long Papers)*, pages 3118–3135, Online. Association for Computational Linguistics.

Tang, Y., Tran, C., Li, X., Chen, P.-J., Goyal, N., Chaudhary, V., Gu, J., and Fan, A. (2020). Multilingual translation with extensible multilingual pretraining and finetuning.

Tiedemann, J. (2020). The tatoeba translation challenge – realistic data sets for low resource and multilingual MT. In *Proceedings of the Fifth Conference on Machine Translation*, pages 1174–1182, Online. Association for Computational Linguistics.

Vaswani, A., Shazeer, N., Parmar, N., Uszkoreit, J., Jones, L., Gomez, A. N., Kaiser, L., and Polosukhin, I. (2017). Attention is all you need. In Guyon, I., Luxburg, U. V., Bengio, S., Wallach, H., Fergus, R., Vishwanathan, S., and Garnett, R., editors, *Advances in Neural Information Processing Systems*, volume 30. Curran Associates, Inc.

Wang, Z., K, K., Mayhew, S., and Roth, D. (2020). Extending multilingual BERT to low-resource languages. In *Findings of the Association for Computational Linguistics: EMNLP 2020*, pages 2649–2656, Online. Association for Computational Linguistics.

Wolf, T., Debut, L., Sanh, V., Chaumond, J., Delangue, C., Moi, A., Cistac, P., Rault, T., Louf, R., Funtowicz, M., Davison, J., Shleifer, S., von Platen, P., Ma, C., Jernite, Y., Plu, J., Xu, C., Le Scao, T., Gugger, S., Drame, M., Lhoest, Q., and Rush, A. (2020). Transformers: State-of-the-art natural language processing. In *Proceedings of the 2020 Conference on Empirical Methods in Natural Language Processing: System Demonstrations*, page 38–45, Online. Association for Computational Linguistics.

Zanon Boito, M., Ortega, J., Riguidel, H., Laurent, A., Barrault, L., Bougares, F., Chaabani, F., Nguyen, H., Barbier, F., Gahbiche, S., and Estève, Y. (2022). ON-TRAC consortium systems for the IWSLT 2022 dialect and low-resource speech translation tasks. In *Proceedings of the 19th International Conference on Spoken Language Translation (IWSLT 2022)*, pages 308–318, Dublin, Ireland (in-person and online). Association for Computational Linguistics.

Leveraging Multilingual Knowledge Graph to Boost Domain-specific Entity Translation of ChatGPT

Min Zhang zhangmin186@huawei.com
Limin Liu cecilia.liulimin@huawei.com
Yanqing Zhao zhaoyanqing@huawei.com
Xiaosong Qiao qiaoxiaosong@huawei.com
Chang Su suchang8@huawei.com
Xiaofeng Zhao zhaoxiaofeng14@huawei.com
Junhao Zhu zhujunhao@huawei.com
Ming Zhu zhuming47@huawei.com
Song Peng pengsong2@huawei.com
Yinglu Li liyinglu@huawei.com
Yilun Liu liuyilun3@huawei.com
Wenbing Ma mawenbing@huawei.com
Mengyao Piao piaomengyao1@huawei.com
Shimin Tao taoshimin@huawei.com
Hao Yang yanghao30@huawei.com
Yanfei Jiang jiangyanfei@huawei.com
Huawei Translation Services Center, Beijing, 100095, China

Abstract

Recently, ChatGPT has shown promising results for Machine Translation (MT) in general domains and is becoming a new paradigm for translation. In this paper, we focus on how to apply ChatGPT to domain-specific translation and propose to leverage Multilingual Knowledge Graph (MKG) to help ChatGPT improve the domain entity translation quality. To achieve this, we extract the bilingual entity pairs from MKG for the domain entities that are recognized from source sentences. We then introduce these pairs into translation prompts, instructing ChatGPT to use the correct translations of the domain entities. To evaluate this novel MKG method for ChatGPT, we conduct comparative experiments on three Chinese-English (zh-en) test datasets constructed from three specific domains, of which one domain is from biomedical science, and the other two are from the Information and Communications Technology (ICT) industry — Visible Light Communication (VLC) and wireless domains. Experimental results show that both the overall translation quality of ChatGPT (+6.21, +3.13 and +11.25 in BLEU scores) and the translation accuracy of domain entities (+43.2%, +30.2% and +37.9% absolute points) are significantly improved with MKG on the three test datasets.

Proceedings of Machine Translation Summit XIX, Vol. 2: Users Track, pages 77–87
September 4–8, 2023, Macau SAR, China.

1 Introduction

Recently, the emergence of ChatGPT[1] has brought remarkable influence on Natural Language Processing (NLP) tasks. It is an intelligent chatbot developed by OpenAI, based on InstructGPT (Ouyang et al., 2022). ChatGPT is built on the top of GPT-3.5 and GPT-4 families of Large Language Models (LLMs) and has been fine-tuned using both supervised and reinforcement learning techniques. It possesses diverse abilities of NLP, including question answering, dialogue generation, code debugging, generation evaluation (Qin et al., 2023; Zhong et al., 2023; Wang et al., 2023; Kocmi and Federmann, 2023; Lu et al., 2023). We are particularly interested in ChatGPT for domain-specific Machine Translation (MT) tasks, especially how domain-specific knowledge can be introduced into ChatGPT to improve the translation accuracy of domain entities.

Source: 甚至光纤上去一照变成黑光纤了。

Prompt for ChatGPT: 请将下面的句子翻译成英文：甚至光纤上去一照变成黑光纤了。

MT by ChatGPT: Even the fiber optic cable turned into a black fiber optic cable when it was lit up.

Reference: Even the optical fiber is irradiated to become a dark fiber.

Figure 1: An MT example by ChatGPT in the VLC domain, where 光纤 and 黑光纤 are two domain entities and the corresponding English translations are *optical fiber* and *dark fiber* respectively, and the prompt "请将下面的句子翻译成英文: ..." means "Please translate the following sentence into English: ...".

Recent studies (Jiao et al., 2023; Hendy et al., 2023; Peng et al., 2023; Zhao et al., 2023) on translation tasks have found that ChatGPT performs competitively with commercial translation products (e.g., Google Translate and Microsoft Translate) in the general domain, but performs poorly in specific domains. According to the analysis by Jiao et al. (2023) and Zhao et al. (2023), it is a challenge for ChatGPT to correctly translate domain entities. Fig. 1 shows a Chinese sentence that contains two domain entities 光纤 and 黑光纤 in the Visible Light Communication (VLC) domain. We use the translation prompt in Fig. 1 for ChatGPT to translate this sentence into English. From Fig. 1, it could be seen that the two entities are wrongly translated as *fiber optic cable* and *black fiber optic cable* by ChatGPT, and the correct translations are *optical fiber* and *dark fiber*. Although ChatGPT shows strong translation capabilities in general domains, it is not so effective in specific domains, especially in domain entity translation.

In this paper, we propose to utilize Multilingual Knowledge Graph (MKG) to help ChatGPT address this issue. After we introduce bilingual entity pairs from MKG into translation prompts, ChatGPT can use the correct translations of domain entities. Experimental results in three specific domains (biomedical science, VLC, and wireless) demonstrate that the overall translation quality of ChatGPT is improved by +6.21, +3.13 and +11.25 respectively in terms of BLEU scores, and the translation accuracy of domain entities is improved by +43.2%, +30.2% and +37.9% absolute points respectively.

The main contributions of this paper are as follows:

- To the best of our knowledge, we are the first to propose to introduce MKG for ChatGPT to improve the translation accuracy of domain entities.

[1] `https://chat.openai.com`

- Experimental results in three specific domains demonstrate that the proposed method can significantly improve the translation quality of ChatGPT and the translation accuracy of domain entities.

2 Related Work

2.1 ChatGPT for MT

With ChatGPT showing remarkable capabilities in various NLP tasks, research on ChatGPT for MT has sprung up (Jiao et al., 2023; Hendy et al., 2023; Peng et al., 2023; Zhang et al., 2023).

Jiao et al. (2023) provided a preliminary evaluation of ChatGPT for MT, including translation prompt, multilingual translation, and translation robustness. Hendy et al. (2023) presented a comprehensive evaluation of ChatGPT for MT, covering various aspects such as quality of ChatGPT in comparison with state-of-the-art research and commercial systems, effect of prompting strategies, robustness towards domain shifts and document-level translation. These studies show that ChatGPT does not perform as well as commercial translation products in low-resource languages or specific domains.

Peng et al. (2023) proposed two simple yet effective prompts (task-specific and domain-specific prompts) to mitigate these issues. However, ChatGPT still faces great translation challenges if it is prompted only with the type name of an unfamiliar domain (i.e., ChatGPT knows little about the domain). In such case, domain-specific knowledge needs to be provided to ChatGPT (similar to the way by Zhang et al. (2023) for automatic post-editing). In this paper, we propose to introduce domain-specific MKG to ChatGPT.

2.2 Knowledge Graph for MT

Entity translation plays a particularly important role in determining the translation quality. Therefore, various methods (Shi et al., 2016; Lu et al., 2019; Moussallem et al., 2019; Zhao et al., 2020a,b; Zhang et al., 2022) are proposed to improve the entity translation quality with Knowledge Graph (KG).

With the help of KG, Shi et al. (2016) built and formulated a semantic space to connect the source and target languages, and applied it to the sequence-to-sequence framework to propose a Knowledge-Based Semantic Embedding method. Lu et al. (2019) utilized the entity relations in KG as constraints to enhance the connections between the source words and their translations. Under the hypothesis that KG could enhance the semantic feature extraction of neural models, Moussallem et al. (2019) proposed two strategies for incorporating KG into neural models without modifying the neural network architectures. Zhao et al. (2020a,b) not only proposed a multi-task learning method on sub-entity granularity for MT task and knowledge reasoning task, but also designed a novel KG enhanced Neural Machine Translation (NMT) method (i.e., transforming the source and target KGs into a unified semantic space). To apply the entity pairs of MKG, Zhang et al. (2022) proposed a data augmentation strategy for NMT.

In a word, all the above approaches are about how to introduce KG into neural networks for MT. In this paper, we utilize MKG to generate translation prompts for ChatGPT, which is very simple and effective.

3 Translation Prompt with MKG

The generation of MKG-based translation prompts for ChatGPT is described in Fig. 2, which consists of three steps:

(1) *Named Entity Recognition (NER)*: We extract domain entities from source sentences. In Fig. 2, two VLC domain entities 光纤 and 黑光纤 are extracted from the source sentence "甚至光纤上去一照变成黑光纤了。".

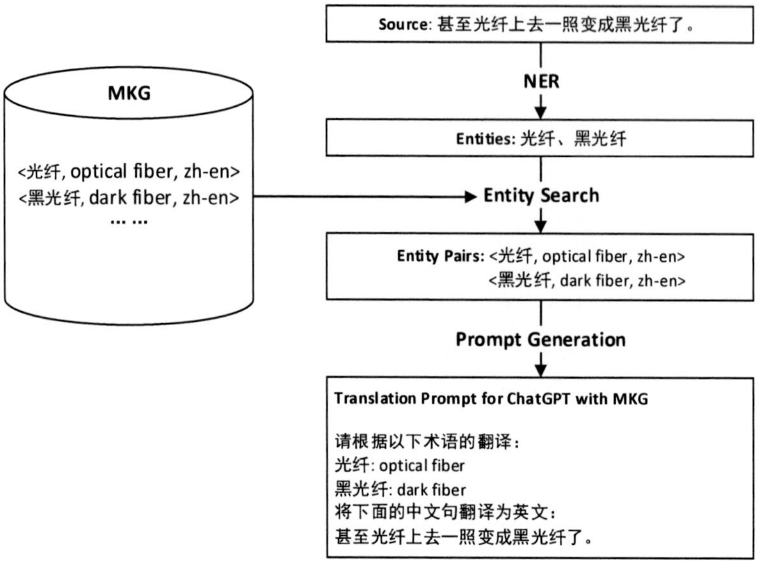

Figure 2: An example of translation prompt generation with MKG for ChatGPT.

(2) *Entity Search*: We search the MKG for the extracted entities to obtain bilingual entity pairs. In this paper, MKG is composed of triplets as <source entity, target entity, language pair>. In Fig. 2, by searching the MKG for 光纤 and 黑光纤, two entity pairs <光纤, optical fiber, zh-en> and <黑光纤, dark fiber, zh-en> are obtained.

(3) *Prompt Generation*: We introduce the obtained entity pairs into the translation prompt for ChatGPT, as the example illustrated in Fig. 2.

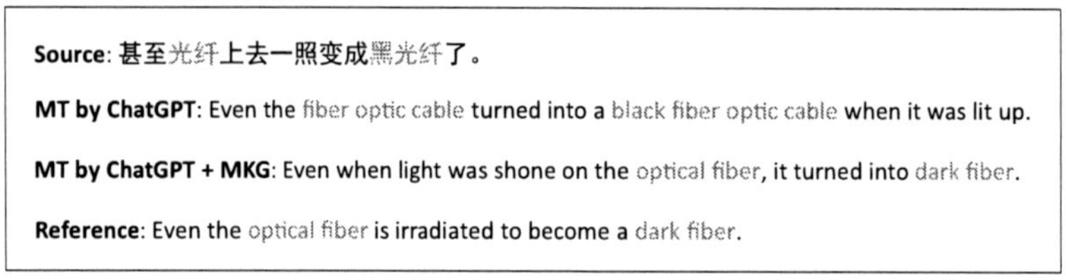

Figure 3: Translation results of ChatGPT with or without MKG for the sentence in Fig. 2.

Fig. 3 shows the translation results of ChatGPT with or without MKG for a sentence in the VLC domain (i.e., using the prompts in Fig. 2 and Fig. 1 for ChatGPT respectively). It could be seen that ChatGPT correctly translates the two domain entities 光纤 and 黑光纤 with MKG, but incorrectly without MKG. This means that introducing MKG to translation prompts does improve the entity translation accuracy of ChatGPT, thereby contributing to the translation quality of ChatGPT.

Domain	# Sent	# Ent	Precision	Recall	$F1$ Score
Biomedical	264	574	0.933	0.977	0.954
VLC	397	586	0.955	0.952	0.953
Wireless	200	855	0.956	0.988	0.972

Table 1: NER results on the three test datasets from the three specific domains, where "# Sent" and "# Ent" indicate the number of source sentences and the number of entities in these sentences respectively.

System	Biomedical (zh-en)			VLC (zh-en)			Wireless (zh-en)		
	BLEU	ACC	COMET	BLEU	ACC	COMET	BLEU	ACC	COMET
ChatGPT	29.37	0.500	81.2	22.10	0.563	81.6	21.08	0.507	80.5
ChatGPT+MKG	35.58	**0.932**	**82.8**	25.23	**0.865**	**82.6**	**32.33**	**0.886**	**82.6**
Google Translate	**37.06**	0.527	81.6	**29.80**	0.619	81.6	26.13	0.529	80.0

Table 2: BLEU scores, ACC values and COMET scores of ChatGPT with or without MKG and Google Translate on the three test datasets.

4 Experiments

4.1 Experiment Settings

We provide a brief description of the experiment settings, which mainly includes the used models, test datasets, MKG and evaluation metrics.

4.1.1 Models

We compare the translation results of ChatGPT with or without MKG in specific domains. The results in this paper come from the `gpt-3.5-turbo` models, which power the ChatGPT. In addition, the results of Google Translate[2] are used for reference. The NER models are fine-tuned on 1,000 annotated domain sentences with traditional BERT-LSTM-CRF Devlin et al. (2019) architecture for the three domains respectively.

4.1.2 Data

To evaluate the translation quality of ChatGPT with or without MKG, we construct three zh-en test datasets from three specific domains. The datasets consist of 264 parallel sentences from WMT22 biomedical science domain Neves et al. (2022), 397 parallel sentences from the VLC domain, and 200 parallel sentences from the wireless domain. It should be pointed out that data in the biomedical science domain is public, and the data in the other two domains is our own non-public data. And the MKGs for the three domains consist of about 2,000, 1,000,000 and 3,000,000 triplets respectively, which are automatically mined from domain parallel corpora (Zhang et al., 2022).

4.1.3 Metrics

We adopt the commonly used BLEU score (Papineni et al., 2002) as our primary metric, which is calculated by the toolkit `SacreBLEU` (Post, 2018). And we use the COMET (Rei et al., 2020) metric as reference. Specifically, we use the reference-based metric COMET-22 (`wmt22-COMET-da`) (Rei et al., 2022). Additionally, we report the translation accuracy of entities (ACC) in the translations.

4.2 Experimental Results

Our NER model achieves very good recognition results on all the three test datasets, which is helpful for domain entity translation correctness. The NER results of the source sentences in the

[2]`https://translate.google.com`

Item	Content
Source	现有的免疫功能定义如免疫过度、免疫抑制、免疫麻痹、免疫耐受均停留在描述性的概念，缺乏定量的诊断标准，结合临床表现及生物学指标将是未来最有效的量化方式。
Reference	The existing definitions of immune function, such as excessive immunity, immunosuppression, immune paralysis and immune tolerance, remain in descriptive concepts and lacks quantitative diagnostic criteria. Clinical manifestations combined with biological indicators will be the most effective quantitative method in the future.
Entities from MKG	<免疫过度, excessive immunity, zh-en> <免疫抑制, immunosuppression, zh-en> <免疫麻痹, immune paralysis, zh-en> <免疫耐受, immune tolerance, zh-en>
ChatGPT	The current definition of immune function, such as immune overreactivity, immune suppression, immune paralysis, and immune tolerance, remains descriptive and lacks quantitative diagnostic criteria. Combining clinical presentations and biological markers will be the most effective way of quantification in the future.
ChatGPT+ MKG	The existing definitions of immune functions, such as excessive immunity, immunosuppression, immune paralysis, and immune tolerance, are still descriptive concepts lacking quantitative diagnostic criteria. Combining clinical manifestations and biological indicators will be the most effective way to quantify these concepts in the future.
Google Translate	Existing definitions of immune function, such as immune hyperactivity, immunosuppression, immune paralysis, and immune tolerance, remain descriptive concepts and lack quantitative diagnostic criteria. Combining clinical manifestations and biological indicators will be the most effective quantitative method in the future.

Table 3: A case that contains four domain entities in the biomedical science domain.

Item	Content
Source	综述颈椎结核手术治疗中不同内植物材料的特点及使用方法，以及新型内植物的研究进展。
Reference	To review the characteristics and applications of different implantation in cervical tuberculosis surgery and the research progress of the new implantation.
Entities from MKG	<内植物, implantation, zh-en> <颈椎结核, cervical tuberculosis, zh-en>
ChatGPT	This article reviews the characteristics and usage of different internal implant materials in surgical treatment for cervical spine tuberculosis, as well as the research progress of new internal implants.
ChatGPT+ MKG	A review of the characteristics and usage methods of different implant materials in surgical treatment of cervical tuberculosis, as well as the research progress of new implants.
Google Translate	This paper reviews the characteristics and application methods of different implant materials in the surgical treatment of cervical tuberculosis, as well as the research progress of new implants.

Table 4: A case that contains three domain entities in the biomedical science domain.

three test datasets are shown in Table 1, where the precision, recall and $F1$ scores are included.

The three metrics (BLEU, ACC and COMET) of ChatGPT with or without MKG and Google Translate are illustrated in Table 2. It could be seen that MKG-based translation prompts not only improve the BLEU scores for ChatGPT, but also significantly improve the ACC values (improving 43.2%, 30.2% and 37.9% absolute points for the biomedical science, VLC and wireless domains respectively). Although the BLEU scores of ChatGPT with MKG are lower than those of Google Translate in the biomedical science and VLC domains, the ACC values of ChatGPT with MKG are significantly higher in all the three domains (40.5%, 24.6% and 35.7% absolute points higher in the biomedical science, VLC and wireless domains respectively). Due to the strong particularity of the wireless domain, ChatGPT with MKG has made the most

Item	Content
Source	那在可见光波段，它的衰减是非常非常大的，单模光纤很难传，那怎么能够传可见光?
Reference	In the visible light band, its attenuation is very, very large, and single-mode optical fiber is difficult to transmit, then how to transmit visible light?
Entities from MKG	<可见光波段, visible light band, zh-en> <单模光纤, single-mode optical fiber, zh-en> <可见光, visible light, zh-en>
ChatGPT	In the visible light wavelength, the attenuation is very, very large, and it is difficult for single-mode fibers to transmit. So, how can visible light be transmitted?
ChatGPT+ MKG	In the visible light band, the attenuation is very significant, and it is difficult for single-mode optical fiber to transmit. How can visible light be transmitted?
Google Translate	In the visible light band, its attenuation is very, very large, and single-mode fiber is difficult to transmit, so how can it transmit visible light?

Table 5: A case that contains three domain entities in the VLC domain.

Type	Content
Source	电源线与空开连接器接触不良，如电源线剥线过短导致压绝缘皮等。
Reference	The connection between the power cable and circuit breaker connector is poor. For example, the insulation sheath is pressed because the stripped length is too short for the power cable.
Entities from MKG	<空开连接器, circuit breaker connector, zh-en> <绝缘皮, insulation sheath, zh-en> <电源线, power cable, zh-en>
ChatGPT	Poor contact between power cord and circuit breaker connector, such as insufficiently stripped wires of the power cord causing pressure on the insulation.
ChatGPT+ MKG	The power cable has poor contact with the circuit breaker connector, which may be caused by the stripping of the power cable being too short and pressing against the insulation sheath.
Google Translate	The power cord is in poor contact with the circuit breaker connector, for example, the stripping of the power cord is too short and the insulation is pressed.

Table 6: A case from the wireless domain, which contains four domain entities.

significant improvement in translation quality (+11.25 BLEU), scoring even 6.2 BLEU points higher than Google Translate. In addition, ChatGPT with MKG gets the best COMET scores in all the three domains (82.8, 82.6 and 82.6 in biomedical science, VLC and wireless domains respectively).

4.3 Case Study

In this section, we provide four cases from three specific domains, which are illustrated in Tables 3 to 6. For each case, the source sentence, its reference, the entities from MKG, and the translations from ChatGPT, ChatGPT+MKG and Google Translate are provided.

In Table 3, four domain entities are highlighted in blue in the source sentence and its reference. ChatGPT (without MKG) can only correctly translate two entities (免疫麻痹 and 免疫耐受), and the translations of the other two entities (免疫过度 and 免疫抑制) are wrong (in red). With the MKG-based translation prompt, ChatGPT can correctly translate all the four entities (in blue). Google Translate has one entity mistranslation in this sentence.

In Table 4, there are three domain entities in the source sentence and ChatGPT (without MKG) cannot correctly translate these entities. Although the correct translations of these entities from MKG are provided in the prompt, ChatGPT still cannot translate the entity "内植物" correctly. This suggests that better prompts need to be designed for ChatGPT.

From Table 5 and Table 6, ChatGPT with MKG can correctly translate all the domain entities, while ChatGPT without MKG and Google Translate cannot. This shows the effectiveness

Dataset	# Sentence	# Entity
WMT19 en-zh	1,997	5,492
WMT19 en-de	1,997	5,045

Table 7: Statistics of the en-zh and en-de datasets from WMT19, where "# Sentence" and "# Entity" denote the number of source sentences and the number of entities in these sentences respectively.

En-Zh translation prompt with MKG:
Based on the following translations for these entities:
Lifeguard: 救生员
Shark: 鲨鱼
Please translate the following sentence to Chinese:
Lifeguard Capt. Larry Giles said at a media briefing that a shark had been spotted in the area a few weeks earlier, but it was determined not to be a dangerous species of shark.

En-Zh translation prompt without MKG:
Please translate the following sentence to Chinese:
Lifeguard Capt. Larry Giles said at a media briefing that a shark had been spotted in the area a few weeks earlier, but it was determined not to be a dangerous species of shark.

En-De translation prompt with MKG:
Based on the following translations for these entities:
Lifeguard: Rettungsschwimmer
Shark: Hai
Please translate the following sentence into German:
Lifeguard Capt. Larry Giles said at a media briefing that a shark had been spotted in the area a few weeks earlier, but it was determined not to be a dangerous species of shark.

En-De translation prompt without MKG:
Please translate the following sentence into German:
Lifeguard Capt. Larry Giles said at a media briefing that a shark had been spotted in the area a few weeks earlier, but it was determined not to be a dangerous species of shark.

Figure 4: Examples of translation prompts with or without MKG for en-zh and en-de datasets from WMT19.

System	WMT19 (en-zh)			WMT19 (en-de)		
	BLEU	ACC	COMET	BLEU	ACC	COMET
ChatGPT	33.02	0.737	84.8	38.70	0.785	**86.2**
ChatGPT+MKG	34.24	**0.905**	84.5	39.72	**0.869**	85.6
Google Translate	**37.68**	0.810	**85.4**	**42.85**	0.805	84.5

Table 8: BLEU scores, ACC values and COMET scores of ChatGPT with or without MKG on the en-zh and en-de datasets from WMT19.

of MKG-based translation prompts.

It is should be pointed out that the entities pairs provided for ChatGPT prompts must be correct, otherwise it is likely to deteriorate the translation results.

4.4 Effects on the News Domain

Since our domain-specific data (parallel sentences and MKG) for experiments is not yet publicly available, we further evaluate the MKG-based translation prompts for ChatGPT on public domain data. To the best of our knowledge, only in the annotated WMT19 news translation task data by Gekhman et al. Gekhman et al. (2020), both the parallel sentences and MKG are publicly available. In this section, we choose the English-Chinese (en-zh) and English-German (en-de) datasets from WMT19 to evaluate the translation performance of ChatGPT with or without MKG. It should be noted that the translation prompts used for ChatGPT are the English versions as illusatrated in Fig. 4. The statistics of the two datasets are shown in Table 7.

The BLEU scores, ACC values and COMET scores of ChatGPT with or without MKG are illustrated in Table 8. It could be clearly seen that both the BLEU scores and the ACC values are improved by the MKG-based translation prompts for ChatGPT. However, because the news domain is not so particular as the above three specific domains (biomedical science, VLC and wireless domains), the BLEU scores and ACC values are improved modestly (+1.22 BLEU and +16.8 absolute points of ACC for en-zh, and +1.02 BLEU and +8.4 absolute points of ACC for en-de). Nevertheless, the MKG-based translation prompts proposed in this paper are very effective in improving the translation quality of ChatGPT and the translation accuracy of domain entities.

5 Conclusion

In this paper, a novel MKG-based translation prompt is designed for ChatGPT to improve the domain-specific translation quality, especially the translation accuracy of domain entities. Domain entities are first recognized from the source sentences and are used to extract corresponding bilingual entity pairs from MKG. Then MKG-based translation prompts are generated for ChatGPT with the bilingual entity pairs. Experimental results in the three specific domains demonstrate that the ChatGPT empowered by MKG-based translation prompts greatly improves the translation accuracy of the domain entities, even outperforming Google Translate. However, the BLEU scores of ChatGPT with the MKG-based translation prompts in two of the three domains are still lower than those of Google Translate, although they are greatly higher than those of the ChatGPT without MKG. This suggests that better prompt engineering needs to be developed for ChatGPT to further unlock its potential in translation. In addition, the performance of the MKG-based translation prompts for ChatGPT in the general domain (news domain) is also investigated.

References

Devlin, J., Chang, M.-W., Lee, K., and Toutanova, K. (2019). BERT: Pre-training of deep bidirectional transformers for language understanding. In *Proceedings of the 2019 Conference of the North American Chapter of the Association for Computational Linguistics: Human Language Technologies, Volume 1 (Long and Short Papers)*, pages 4171–4186, Minneapolis, Minnesota. Association for Computational Linguistics.

Gekhman, Z., Aharoni, R., Beryozkin, G., Freitag, M., and Macherey, W. (2020). KoBE: Knowledge-based machine translation evaluation. In *Findings of the Association for Computational Linguistics: EMNLP 2020*, Online. Association for Computational Linguistics.

Hendy, A., Abdelrehim, M., Sharaf, A., Raunak, V., Gabr, M., Matsushita, H., Kim, Y. J., Afify, M., and Awadalla, H. H. (2023). How good are gpt models at machine translation? a comprehensive evaluation. *arXiv preprint arXiv:2302.09210*.

Jiao, W., Wang, W., tse Huang, J., Wang, X., and Tu, Z. (2023). Is chatgpt a good translator? a preliminary study. In *ArXiv*.

Kocmi, T. and Federmann, C. (2023). Large language models are state-of-the-art evaluators of translation quality. *ArXiv*, abs/2302.14520.

Lu, Q., Qiu, B., Ding, L., Xie, L., and Tao, D. (2023). Error analysis prompting enables human-like translation evaluation in large language models: A case study on chatgpt. *arXiv preprint*.

Lu, Y., Zhang, J., and Zong, C. (2019). Exploiting knowledge graph in neural machine translation. In Chen, J. and Zhang, J., editors, *Machine Translation*, pages 27–38, Singapore. Springer Singapore.

Moussallem, D., Ngonga Ngomo, A.-C., Buitelaar, P., and Arcan, M. (2019). Utilizing knowledge graphs for neural machine translation augmentation. In *Proceedings of the 10th International Conference on Knowledge Capture*, K-CAP '19, page 139–146, New York, NY, USA. Association for Computing Machinery.

Neves, M., Jimeno Yepes, A., Siu, A., Roller, R., Thomas, P., Vicente Navarro, M., Yeganova, L., Wiemann, D., Di Nunzio, G. M., Vezzani, F., Gerardin, C., Bawden, R., Estrada, D. J., Lima-Lopez, S., Farre-Maduel, E., Krallinger, M., Grozea, C., and Neveol, A. (2022). Findings of the wmt 2022 biomedical translation shared task: Monolingual clinical case reports. In *Proceedings of the Seventh Conference on Machine Translation*, pages 694–723, Abu Dhabi. Association for Computational Linguistics.

Ouyang, L., Wu, J., Jiang, X., Almeida, D., Wainwright, C., Mishkin, P., Zhang, C., Agarwal, S., Slama, K., Ray, A., Schulman, J., Hilton, J., Kelton, F., Miller, L., Simens, M., Askell, A., Welinder, P., Christiano, P. F., Leike, J., and Lowe, R. (2022). Training language models to follow instructions with human feedback. In Koyejo, S., Mohamed, S., Agarwal, A., Belgrave, D., Cho, K., and Oh, A., editors, *Advances in Neural Information Processing Systems*, volume 35, pages 27730–27744. Curran Associates, Inc.

Papineni, K., Roukos, S., Ward, T., and Zhu, W.-J. (2002). Bleu: a method for automatic evaluation of machine translation. In *Proceedings of the 40th Annual Meeting of the Association for Computational Linguistics*, pages 311–318, Philadelphia, Pennsylvania, USA. Association for Computational Linguistics.

Peng, K., Ding, L., Zhong, Q., Shen, L., Liu, X., Zhang, M., Ouyang, Y., and Tao, D. (2023). Towards making the most of chatgpt for machine translation. *arxiv preprint*.

Post, M. (2018). A call for clarity in reporting BLEU scores. In *Proceedings of the Third Conference on Machine Translation: Research Papers*, pages 186–191, Belgium, Brussels. Association for Computational Linguistics.

Qin, C., Zhang, A., Zhang, Z., Chen, J., Yasunaga, M., and Yang, D. (2023). Is chatgpt a general-purpose natural language processing task solver? *ArXiv*, abs/2302.06476.

Rei, R., Stewart, C., Farinha, A. C., and Lavie, A. (2020). COMET: A neural framework for MT evaluation. In *Proceedings of the 2020 Conference on Empirical Methods in Natural Language Processing (EMNLP)*, pages 2685–2702, Online. Association for Computational Linguistics.

Rei, R., Treviso, M., Guerreiro, N. M., Zerva, C., Farinha, A. C., Maroti, C., C. de Souza, J. G., Glushkova, T., Alves, D., Coheur, L., Lavie, A., and Martins, A. F. T. (2022). CometKiwi: IST-unbabel 2022 submission for the quality estimation shared task. In *Proceedings of the Seventh Conference on Machine Translation (WMT)*, pages 634–645, Abu Dhabi, United Arab Emirates (Hybrid). Association for Computational Linguistics.

Shi, C., Liu, S., Ren, S., Feng, S., Li, M., Zhou, M., Sun, X., and Wang, H. (2016). Knowledge-based semantic embedding for machine translation. In *Proceedings of the 54th Annual Meeting of the Association for Computational Linguistics (Volume 1: Long Papers)*, pages 2245–2254, Berlin, Germany. Association for Computational Linguistics.

Wang, J., Liang, Y., Meng, F., Li, Z., Qu, J., and Zhou, J. (2023). Cross-Lingual Summarization via ChatGPT. *arXiv.org*.

Zhang, M., Peng, S., Yang, H., Zhao, Y., Qiao, X., Zhu, J., Tao, S., Qin, Y., and Jiang, Y. (2022). Entityrank: Unsupervised mining of bilingual named entity pairs from parallel corpora for neural machine translation. In *2022 IEEE International Conference on Big Data (Big Data)*, pages 3708–3713.

Zhang, M., Zhao, X., Yanqing, Z., Yang, H., Qiao, X., Zhu, J., Ma, W., Chang, S., Liu, Y., Li, Y., Wang, M., Peng, S., Tao, S., and Jiang, Y. (2023). Leveraging chatgpt and multilingual knowledge graph for automatic post-editing. In *International Conference on Human-Informed Translation and Interpreting Technology (HiT-IT 2023)*. accepted for publication.

Zhao, Y., Xiang, L., Zhu, J., Zhang, J., Zhou, Y., and Zong, C. (2020a). Knowledge graph enhanced neural machine translation via multi-task learning on sub-entity granularity. In *Proceedings of the 28th International Conference on Computational Linguistics*, pages 4495–4505, Barcelona, Spain (Online). International Committee on Computational Linguistics.

Zhao, Y., Zhang, J., Zhou, Y., and Zong, C. (2020b). Knowledge graphs enhanced neural machine translation. In Bessiere, C., editor, *Proceedings of the Twenty-Ninth International Joint Conference on Artificial Intelligence, IJCAI-20*, pages 4039–4045. International Joint Conferences on Artificial Intelligence Organization. Main track.

Zhao, Y., Zhang, M., Chen, X., Deng, Y., Geng, A., Liu, L., Liu, X., Li, W., Jiang, Y., Yang, H., Han, Y., Tao, S., Li, X., Ma, M., Zhang, Z., and Xie, N. (2023). Human evaluation for translation quality of chatgpt: A preliminary study. In *International Conference on Human-Informed Translation and Interpreting Technology (HiT-IT 2023)*. accepted for publication.

Zhong, Q., Ding, L., Liu, J., Du, B., and Tao, D. (2023). Can chatgpt understand too? a comparative study on chatgpt and fine-tuned bert. *arXiv preprint*.

Human-in-the-loop Machine Translation with Large Language Model

Xinyi Yang* nlp2ct.xinyi@gmail.com
Runzhe Zhan* nlp2ct.runzhe@gmail.com
Derek F. Wong † derekfw@um.edu.mo
Junchao Wu nlp2ct.junchao@gmail.com
Lidia S. Chao lidiasc@um.edu.mo
NLP^{2}CT Lab, Department of Computer and Information Science, University of Macau

Abstract

The large language model (LLM) has garnered significant attention due to its in-context learning mechanisms and emergent capabilities. The research community has conducted several pilot studies to apply LLMs to machine translation tasks and evaluate their performance from diverse perspectives. However, previous research has primarily focused on the LLM itself and has not explored human intervention in the inference process of LLM. The characteristics of LLM, such as in-context learning and prompt engineering, closely mirror human cognitive abilities in language tasks, offering an intuitive solution for human-in-the-loop generation. In this study, we propose a human-in-the-loop pipeline that guides LLMs to produce customized outputs with revision instructions. The pipeline initiates by prompting the LLM to produce a draft translation, followed by the utilization of automatic retrieval or human feedback as supervision signals to enhance the LLM's translation through in-context learning. The human-machine interactions generated in this pipeline are also stored in an external database to expand the in-context retrieval database, enabling us to leverage human supervision in an offline setting. We evaluate the proposed pipeline using the GPT-3.5-turbo API on five domain-specific benchmarks for German-English translation. The results demonstrate the effectiveness of the pipeline in tailoring in-domain translations and improving translation performance compared to direct translation instructions. Additionally, we discuss the experimental results from the following perspectives: 1) the effectiveness of different in-context retrieval methods; 2) the construction of a retrieval database under low-resource scenarios; 3) the observed differences across selected domains; 4) the quantitative analysis of sentence-level and word-level statistics; and 5) the qualitative analysis of representative translation cases.

Keywords: Machine Translation, Large Language Model, Human-in-the-loop, In-context Learning, Prompt Engineering, Natural Language Processing

1 Introduction

Large language models (LLMs) have exhibited remarkable proficiency in comprehending natural language prompts (OpenAI, 2023; Touvron et al., 2023), enabling them to execute vari-

*Equal Contribution. Xinyi Yang contributes to the experiments, data curation, and analysis. Runzhe Zhan contributes to the methodology, code skeleton, and paper drafting.
†Corresponding Author.

Proceedings of Machine Translation Summit XIX, Vol. 2: Users Track, pages 88–98
September 4–8, 2023, Macau SAR, China.

ous controllable generation tasks based on human instructions. Furthermore, LLMs can acquire knowledge from limited demonstrations that are relevant to the input data and generate desired outputs through analogy. This paradigm, known as in-context learning (ICL) (Dong et al., 2023), represents a significant advancement in prompt engineering and offers insights into adapting LLMs to downstream tasks without the need for fine-tuning the models.

Machine translation (MT) serves as a representative sequence-to-sequence task that also requires tailoring models to produce domain-specific translations. Traditional approaches to building domain-specific MT models involve fine-tuning pre-trained models with domain data or utilizing domain adaptation techniques to transfer in-domain MT models to out-of-domain requirements. However, these methods are suited for accessible, medium-scale MT models, which may not be suitable for LLMs. Notably, certain LLMs available through application programming interfaces (API) lack accessible weight matrices. Furthermore, optimizing LLM parameters with domain data can be expensive under resource-limited scenarios. Consequently, current research on LLM-based MT predominantly focuses on ICL, including in-context selection methods (Agrawal et al., 2022), in-context prompt engineering (Zhang et al., 2023), and the systematic evaluation of LLM-based MT (Hendy et al., 2023; Jiao et al., 2023). While these lines of research present empirical studies investigating ICL in the MT task, they still exhibit a dearth of exploration in customizing LLMs for domain-specific needs. Given the representative capabilities of LLMs, which rely on generating outputs based on provided instructions, it is intuitive to leverage LLMs to refine general MT outputs for different domains.

Nevertheless, there remain challenges and issues when utilizing ICL to adapt LLMs for domain-specific needs. Firstly, ICL demonstrations for MT typically comprise source input and target reference, lacking domain features. Secondly, the ICL retrieval database is usually constructed using separate labeled data, and the retrieved demonstrations fail to capture LLMs' translation preferences. Last but not least, the adaptation of black-box LLMs does not benefit from parameter optimization, thereby limiting adaptation methods to modifying ICL inputs alone. In response to these challenges, we propose integrating LLM-specific translation feedback into ICL inputs, enabling the model to learn from both relevant input-output pairs and domain preferences.

Specifically, the proposed pipeline consists of two essential parts: feedback collection, and in-context refinement. To collect LLM-specific feedback associated with domains, we first request the LLM to produce domain-specific translations and obtain feedback by comparing its translation with a reference translation. The feedback takes the form of a sequence of revision instructions, indicating the necessary edits to transform the LLM's translation into the reference translation. Ideally, these revision instructions originate from human feedback sources. However, due to resource limitations, we simulate this process and generate synthetic human feedback in this study. Subsequently, these translation texts and feedback are stored together in the ICL retrieval database. For in-context refinement, when faced with new in-domain translation requests, the pipeline initially prompts the LLM to generate a draft translation. It then retrieves similar translation pairs and their revision histories as in-context demonstrations tied to the specific domain. Finally, the model refines the draft translation based on the retrieved domain-specific demonstrations. Any new human-machine interactions generated within this pipeline are incorporated to expand the in-context retrieval database. Overall, the primary concept revolves around enabling the LLM to revise its outputs by learning from relevant domain-specific revision feedback.

We conduct experiments using the proposed pipeline in the German-English translation direction across five domains, utilizing the GPT-3.5 Turbo API as a testbed for the black-box LLM. The results demonstrate that the proposed pipeline enhances domain translation performance in selected domains, as indicated by four automated evaluation metrics. To further elu-

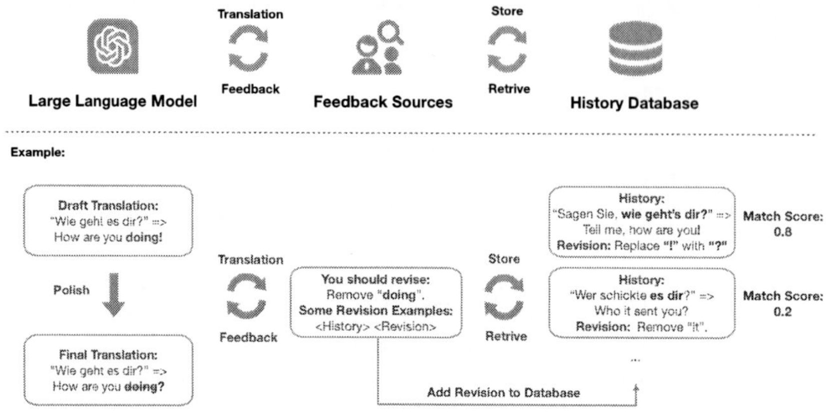

Figure 1: Illustration of the proposed human-in-the-loop translation method in the context of the large language model.

cidate the effectiveness of our approach, we discuss the pipeline and results through an ablation study, quantitative analysis, and qualitative analysis.

2 Methodology

We leave the discussion of related work in the Appendix A due to page limitation. The overall pipeline is illustrated in Figure 1. The feedback retrieved from a data store aims to provide domain-specific revision demonstrations to LLM. Furthermore, it can also be jointly used with external human supervision in real-world applications. In addition to the feedback that exists in the database, any newly produced feedback for current text will be also recorded into the database to be used as a candidate for ICL retrieval in the future.

2.1 Feedback Collection

To correct LLM's bias in domain translation through the ICL paradigm, we must first construct an ICL retrieval database that reflects the gap between LLM's translation preferences and domain preferences. To do this, we ask LLM to translate several domain texts first, and then use automated methods or human intervention to generate feedback on LLM's translation. To simulate the process of human feedback, we use an automated evaluation method based on edit distance theory to generate feedback for the translations. Computing edit distance is a dynamic programming problem, where the cost matrix reflects what editing operations are needed to transform from the machine translation to the reference translation. Specifically, bottom-up recursion yields the minimum cost of editing the translation, so we can generate human-like feedback by back-tracing the optimal alignment of the cost matrix and converting it to natural language. There are three kinds of editing operations are considered in our case: deletion, insertion, and substitution. Given an LLM's translation h and reference translation r, the cost matrix $D(i, j)$ indicates the edit distance between $h_{<i}$ and $r_{<j}$. Let the cost of deletion, insertion, and

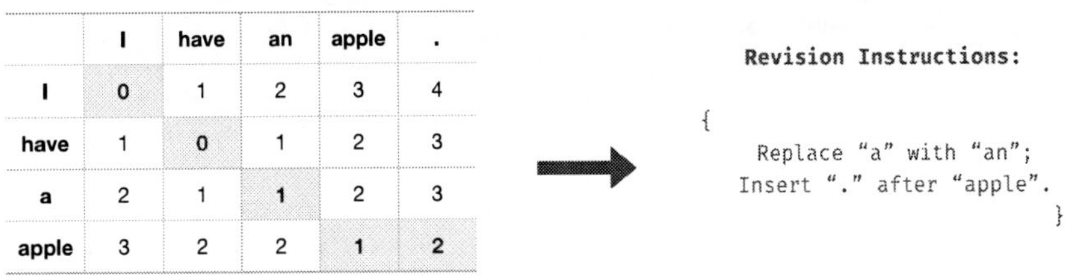

Figure 2: An example of describing the optimal path of minimum edit distance.

substitution be 1, the cost matrix $D(i,j)$ can be calculated as:

$$\begin{aligned} &D(i,0) = i \\ &D(0,j) = j \\ &D(i,j) = \begin{cases} D(i-1,j-1) & \text{if } h_i = r_j \\ \min \begin{cases} D(i-1,j)+1 \\ D(i,j-1)+1 \\ D(i-1,j-1)+1 \end{cases} & \text{if } h_i \neq r_j \end{cases} \end{aligned} \tag{1}$$

We can obtain an optimal path of minimum edit distance by back-tracing the cost matrix D and then convert this path to the natural language instruction as shown in Figure 2. Once the feedback of a specific test instance is produced, we combine it with the source text, LLM's translation, and reference translation to form the new ICL demonstration instance. This enables LLM to learn from its deviations from in-domain reference translations and how to polish the draft translation.

2.2 In-context refinement

We construct a database for ICL retrieval using the automatic feedback generation method mentioned in the previous section. In this section, we will describe how to retrieve and utilize these ICL demonstrations as well as feedback records for conducting a two-stage translation.

Demonstration Retrieval We retrieve the relevant ICL demonstrations by evaluating the relevance between test instances and examples stored in the database. Specifically, we follow the previous exploratory work on ICL for MT and use two retrieval metrics: the BM25 score (Robertson et al., 1995) and the BM25-rerank score (Agrawal et al., 2022). BM25 is a common retrieval metric that evaluates the relevance between the query and the documents. Here we consider each source sentence in the ICL database as a document and calculate the BM25 score. BM25-Rerank, as a post-screening method for BM25, first selects the N samples with the highest BM25 scores and re-scores these samples based on the n-gram recall score R to select the top-K samples as ICL demonstrations. Let the input in source language be s, and a demonstration candidate stored in the database be c, then the recall score can be calculated as:

$$R = \exp \frac{1}{n} \sum_{i=1}^{n} \log \frac{\text{Count}(i\text{-gram} \in s \cap c)}{\text{Count}(i\text{-gram} \in s)} \tag{2}$$

Two-stage Translation As mentioned in the previous section, we first ask the LLM to generate a draft translation, and then polish the draft translation by providing the ICL demonstrations, resulting in a two-stage translation process. In practice, we implement the two-stage translation through the multi-turn dialog feature of the GPT-3.5 API. In addition, we empirically found that the LLM may incorrectly modify the draft translation after observing the ICL demonstrations. We attribute this phenomenon to the fact that the scale limitation of the retrieval database, which may lead to the inclusion of some irrelevant samples. Therefore, we asked the LLM further compare the polished translations with the draft translations at the second stage, and finally select the higher quality one. It is worth noting that the LLM did not observe the reference translation of the test instance during the whole process but only compared the translation quality by means of self-reflection.

3 Experiments

3.1 Data and Evaluation

We verify the effectiveness of the proposed pipeline on a multi-domain German-English translation benchmark (Aharoni and Goldberg, 2020). The test data keeps the same setting as the same benchmark, which involves five domains including IT, Koran, Law, Medical, and Subtitles. We randomly sample 2,000 samples from the training set of each domain as the source of constructing the ICL retrieval database. To complete this process, we use GPT-3.5 API to generate the translation and employ the edit-distance-based method mentioned in Section 2.1 to produce human-like feedback. We use several automated metrics to evaluate the translation quality, including BLEU (Papineni et al., 2002), TER (Snover et al., 2006), BERTScore (Zhang et al., 2020), and COMET (Rei et al., 2020). BLEU and TER are the traditional metrics that evaluate the text overlap whereas the others can evaluate the semantic overlap based on neural networks. We also found that APIs sometimes produce hallucinations or refuse to translate some sentences. To make a fair comparison, we manually check the translation results and remove the invalid results, and only evaluate the performance of the sentences that are successfully translated by all the methods.

3.2 Settings

The experiments were conducted using GPT-3.5 API. The decoding temperature and the top_p parameters are set to 1 by default. When evaluating the relevance of demonstrations, we first retrieve the top K=200 demonstrations with the highest BM25 scores and then select top-N demonstrations with the highest 4-gram re-rank scores as the finalized ICL demonstrations.

3.3 Main Results

Table 1 presents the automated evaluation results of the baseline methods. The experimental findings demonstrate that the proposed approach effectively enhances the performance of GPT-3.5-Turbo baseline. Importantly, we observe that the impact of the proposed HIL method varies across different domains, a topic that will be thoroughly examined in Section 4.2. In addition, we were limited to varying the number of ICL demonstrations from 1 to 3 due to constraints on request tokens. Nonetheless, the results strongly indicate that providing more ICL demonstrations leads to improved performance. Moreover, when evaluating the performance with neural metrics, the differences in scores are not substantial compared to the traditional metrics. We postulate that the process of refining the draft translation may not deviate significantly from the original semantic content but rather brings it closer to specific translation preferences in certain domains. These findings will be elucidated through a detailed case study in the subsequent section.

	IT				Koran			
	BLEU	TER	BERT-F	COMET	BLEU	TER	BERT-F	COMET
GPT-3.5-Turbo	34.4	62.3	93.2	82.5	16.2	**74.1**	90.6	73.4
+*1-shot HIL*	29.0	77.3	92.5	81.1	15.7	80.8	90.5	72.8
+*2-shot HIL*	33.9	64.7	92.9	82.3	15.8	77.7	90.6	73.2
+*3-shot HIL*	32.6	68.8	93.0	82.2	16.5	76.0	90.7	73.6
+*Compare HIL*	**35.2**	**61.3**	**93.3**	**82.8**	**16.6**	74.6	**90.7**	**73.8**
	Law				Medical			
GPT-3.5-Turbo	37.6	54.7	93.7	83.8	40.0	**59.4**	**93.9**	83.4
+*1-shot HIL*	36.2	59.6	93.5	83.1	36.6	67.9	93.3	82.1
+*2-shot HIL*	37.0	56.6	93.6	83.5	39.2	63.0	93.6	83.0
+*3-shot HIL*	36.7	56.5	93.6	83.7	38.4	63.0	93.7	83.2
+*Compare HIL*	**37.7**	**54.5**	**93.8**	**83.9**	**40.9**	60.1	**93.9**	**83.6**
	Subtitles							
GPT-3.5-Turbo	27.9	64.8	93.0	80.0				
+*1-shot HIL*	26.3	69.4	92.5	78.8				
+*2-shot HIL*	26.4	67.1	92.6	79.4				
+*3-shot HIL*	27.4	64.6	93.0	79.8				
+*Compare HIL*	**28.0**	**64.1**	**93.1**	**80.1**				

Table 1: Automated evaluation results of different translation strategies. "K-shot HIL" indicates the proposed HIL method with K demonstrations used. "Compare HIL" indicates using the comparison strategy to finalize the two-stage translation.

4 Analysis

4.1 Effects of ICL Retrieval Methods

To explore the potential impact of different demonstration retrieval methods on our proposed HIL translation workflow, we conducted experiments using two strategies: BM25 and BM25 Re-rank, in a 3-shot translation scenario. The comparative results are summarized in Table 2. Based on the automated metrics, both BM25 and BM25 Re-Rank methods exhibited strengths and weaknesses in various domains. Specifically, BM25 Re-Rank slightly outperformed BM25 in terms of the BLEU metric. The advantage of BM25 Re-Rank was particularly evident in the IT domain, as it achieved higher scores than BM25 across all metrics. However, this conclusion was reversed in the Law domain. The advantage of the BM25 Re-Rank strategy lies in its ability to filter out repetitive context with identical queries. Consequently, this approach selects more relevant examples related to the IT domain, leading to an improvement in the quality of the translation output within this domain. The BM25 method for demonstration retrieval focuses on document frequency and keyword matching, making it more effective in ensuring proper usage of legal terminology. This observation underscores the necessity of adopting different strategies for demonstration retrieval across different domains to ensure the selection of contextually relevant and domain-specific examples for the target sentences.

4.2 Domain Differences

In general, the HIL approach exhibits superior performance compared to the GPT-3.5 API baseline across all five domains, with particularly notable advantages in the IT and Medical domains. However, the differences in performance are relatively smaller in Law and Subtitles domains. These variations can be attributed to the distinct sentence styles and structures prevalent in each

Method	BM25				BM25 Re-Rank			
	BLEU	TER	BERT-F	COMET	BLEU	TER	BERT-F	COMET
IT	34.9	62.3	93.1	82.5	**35.2**	**61.3**	**93.3**	**82.8**
Koran	16.2	**74.3**	90.7	73.7	**16.6**	74.6	90.7	**73.8**
Law	**38.0**	**54.2**	**93.8**	**84.2**	37.7	54.5	93.8	83.9
Medical	40.6	**58.8**	94.0	**83.8**	**40.9**	60.1	94.0	83.6
Subtitles	**28.2**	64.5	93.0	**80.2**	28.0	**64.1**	**93.1**	80.1

Table 2: Automated evaluation results for *3*-shot HIL with different ICL retrieval strategies.

domain. Upon analyzing the translation results, it becomes evident that HIL excels in IT and Medical domains by effectively aligning terminology with the reference translations. For example, consider the phrase "Returns a character string" in the IT domain, HIL correctly recognizes the need to use the third-person singular form of the word "returns" and avoids translating "character string" simply as "string". While these words may not be technical terms, their specific usage preferences in the IT domain are crucial, and such nuances cannot be captured by the GPT-3.5 API baseline. Conversely, in domains such as Law and Subtitles, where HIL's performance is comparatively lower, the sentences tend to adhere to specific legal clauses or follow a more colloquial and concise style. As GPT-3.5 is a multi-domain language model, it already possesses substantial knowledge related to these domains, leading to satisfactory draft translations in the initial output, thereby reducing the necessity for extensive corrections through demonstrations. Furthermore, it is worth noting that the quality of the data within the demonstration pool may not be very high, as they were randomly sampled from the training set. This behavior could also have a negative impact on the final results.

4.3 Quantitative Analysis

We conducted quantitative analysis on the translation results with the help of `compare-mt`[1] (Neubig et al., 2019) toolkit.

Part of Speech (POS) We applied Stanford's POS tagging toolkit (Toutanova et al., 2003) to label the target-side text and subsequently examined the translation outcomes of both the baselines and HIL method across different POS categories. The results are presented in Figure 3. Overall, HIL outperforms the baselines in all noun categories, including singular or mass nouns (NN), plural nouns (NNS), and singular proper nouns (NNP). Additionally, among the three verb types, HIL exhibited superior performance to the baseline in base form verbs (VB) and third person singular present verbs (VBZ), with the most noticeable advantage observed in base form verbs (VB). Furthermore, the advantage of HIL is particularly evident in POS categories where the baseline exhibits lower translation accuracy. These findings underscore the effectiveness of the HIL approach in handling various parts of speech and its ability to deliver improved translation outputs, especially in challenging linguistic contexts.

Sentence Length Figure 4 presents the translation performance of both the baseline and HIL models for sentences of varying lengths. HIL exhibits a clear advantage over the baseline for sentences that are shorter than 10 words as well as those longer than 60 words. Unfortunately, HIL performs less effectively for medium-length sentences compared to the baseline's initial draft. This observation indicates that there might be challenges specific to this sentence length range that warrant further investigation and potential refinement of the HIL approach.

[1]https://github.com/neulab/compare-mt

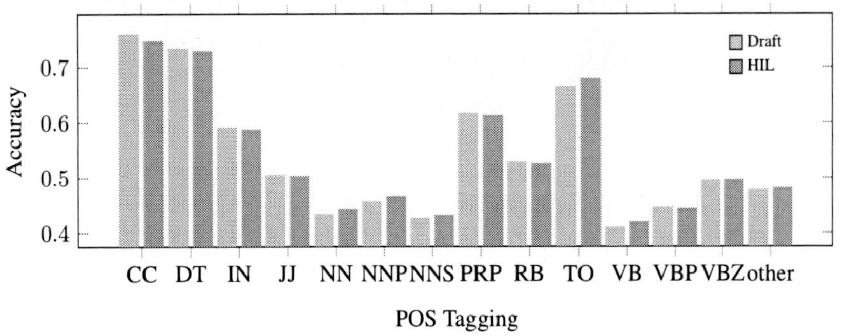

Figure 3: The translation comparison in terms of different POS tags.

In conclusion, our analysis of translation performance across different POS categories and sentence lengths reveals that HIL exhibits exceptional proficiency in translating both nouns and verbs, particularly excelling in extreme-short and extreme-long sentences.

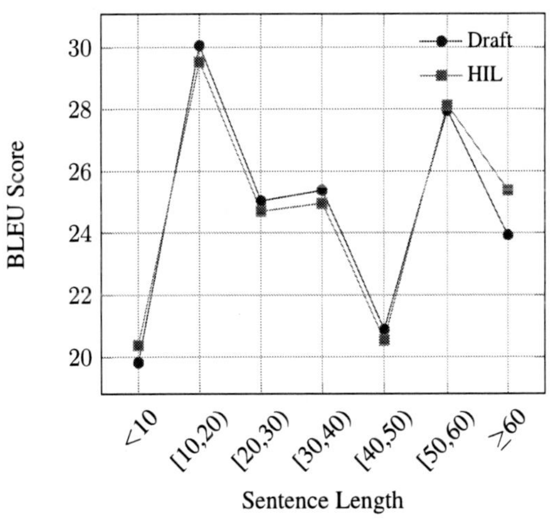

Figure 4: The translation comparison across various sentence lengths.

4.4 Case Study

Below, we present an illustrative example from the IT domain to showcase the advantages of HIL in terms of terminology translation. Additionally, we compare the proposed HIL method with the ordinary ICL method without revision feedback. The results are shown in Table 3. In the given example, while the German word "Handbuch" was translated as "manual" in both the draft and ICL translations, the reference and retrieved demonstration suggest that "Handbook" is a more accurate translation. Regarding the terminology usage of the IT domain, "Handbook" precisely describes a professional document type, whereas "manual" might be more generic and provide less specific information. Among the three translation methods, the HIL translation successfully captures this crucial information based on the provided demonstrations. On the

IT Domain	
Source	Das **Handbuch** zu **& ksnapshot**;
Reference	The **& ksnapshot; Handbook**
Demonstrations	1. <input>Das **Handbuch zu & kontact;** <hypothesis>The manual for & kontact; <reference>& kontact; Handbook <revision>"the" should be deleted. "manual" should be deleted. "for" should be deleted.", "handbook" should be inserted after "kontact;" 2. <input>Das **Handbuch** zu & kanagram; <hypothesis>The **manual for & kanagram;** <reference>& kanagram; Handbook <revision>"the" should be deleted. "manual" should be deleted. "for" should be deleted. "handbook" should be inserted after "kanagramt;" 3. ...
Draft	The manual **for & ksnapshot;**
ICL	The manual **for &ksnapshot;**
HIL	The **& ksnapshot; Handbook**

Table 3: An example result of three different translation strategies. "Draft" represents the preliminary translation results obtained at the initial turn in our HIL pipeline. "ICL" presents the translation results achieved using ordinary ICL demonstrations without revision feedback.

other hand, HIL also learns from revisions in the demonstration and opts to translate the original sentence as "The &ksnapshot; Handbook", aligning more accurately with the word order of the original text. This demonstrates how HIL can effectively incorporate valuable revision feedback to produce more contextually appropriate and accurate translations.

5 Conclusions and Future Work

In this paper, we present an empirical study focused on enhancing the translation capabilities of the LLM by integrating concrete feedback within the translation process. Our objective is to establish a human-in-the-loop machine translation pipeline, where human feedback plays a pivotal role. To simulate this concept, we utilize an automated feedback method, leveraging the GPT-3.5 API as our testbed, which yields effective results. In the future, our plan is to collect human feedback to create a novel dataset and conduct experiments on the proposed pipeline using this dataset. This approach will enable us to further validate and implement our human-in-the-loop machine translation system in the context of LLM, enhancing its practical applicability and performance.

Acknowledgement

This work was supported in part by the Science and Technology Development Fund, Macau SAR (Grant Nos. FDCT/0070/2022/AMJ, FDCT/060/2022/AFJ), the Multi-year Research Grant from the University of Macau (Grant No. MYRG2020-00054-FST), and the Research Program of Guangdong Province (Grant No. 2220004002576). This work was performed in part at SICC which is supported by SKL-IOTSC, and HPCC supported by ICTO of the University of Macau.

References

Agrawal, S., Zhou, C., Lewis, M., Zettlemoyer, L., and Ghazvininejad, M. (2022). In-context examples selection for machine translation. *ArXiv preprint*, abs/2212.02437.

Aharoni, R. and Goldberg, Y. (2020). Unsupervised domain clusters in pretrained language models. In *Proceedings of the 58th Annual Meeting of the Association for Computational Linguistics*, pages 7747–7763. Association for Computational Linguistics.

Dong, Q., Li, L., Dai, D., Zheng, C., Wu, Z., Chang, B., Sun, X., Xu, J., and Sui, Z. (2023). A survey for in-context learning. *ArXiv preprint*, abs/2301.00234.

Hendy, A., Abdelrehim, M. G., Sharaf, A., Raunak, V., Gabr, M., Matsushita, H., Kim, Y. J., Afify, M., and Awadalla, H. H. (2023). How good are gpt models at machine translation? a comprehensive evaluation. *ArXiv preprint*, abs/2302.09210.

Jiao, W., Wang, W., tse Huang, J., Wang, X., and Tu, Z. (2023). Is chatgpt a good translator? yes with gpt-4 as the engine. volume abs/2301.08745.

Neubig, G., Dou, Z.-Y., Hu, J., Michel, P., Pruthi, D., and Wang, X. (2019). compare-mt: A tool for holistic comparison of language generation systems. In *Proceedings of the 2019 Conference of the North American Chapter of the Association for Computational Linguistics (Demonstrations)*, pages 35–41. Association for Computational Linguistics.

OpenAI (2023). Gpt-4 technical report. *ArXiv preprint*, abs/2303.08774.

Papineni, K., Roukos, S., Ward, T., and Zhu, W.-J. (2002). Bleu: a method for automatic evaluation of machine translation. In *Proceedings of the 40th Annual Meeting of the Association for Computational Linguistics*, pages 311–318. Association for Computational Linguistics.

Rei, R., Stewart, C., Farinha, A. C., and Lavie, A. (2020). COMET: A neural framework for MT evaluation. In *Proceedings of the 2020 Conference on Empirical Methods in Natural Language Processing (EMNLP)*, pages 2685–2702. Association for Computational Linguistics.

Robertson, S. E., Walker, S., Jones, S., Hancock-Beaulieu, M. M., Gatford, M., et al. (1995). Okapi at trec-3. *Nist Special Publication Sp*, 109:109.

Snover, M., Dorr, B., Schwartz, R., Micciulla, L., and Makhoul, J. (2006). A study of translation edit rate with targeted human annotation. In *Proceedings of the 7th Conference of the Association for Machine Translation in the Americas: Technical Papers*, pages 223–231. Association for Machine Translation in the Americas.

Toutanova, K., Klein, D., Manning, C. D., and Singer, Y. (2003). Feature-rich part-of-speech tagging with a cyclic dependency network. In *Proceedings of the 2003 Human Language Technology Conference of the North American Chapter of the Association for Computational Linguistics*, pages 252–259.

Touvron, H., Lavril, T., Izacard, G., Martinet, X., Lachaux, M.-A., Lacroix, T., Rozière, B., Goyal, N., Hambro, E., Azhar, F., Rodriguez, A., Joulin, A., Grave, E., and Lample, G. (2023). Llama: Open and efficient foundation language models. *ArXiv preprint*, abs/2302.13971.

Wang, D., Wei, H., Zhang, Z., Huang, S., Xie, J., and Chen, J. (2022). Non-parametric online learning from human feedback for neural machine translation. In *Thirty-Sixth AAAI Conference on Artificial Intelligence, AAAI 2022, Thirty-Fourth Conference on Innovative Applications of Artificial Intelligence, IAAI 2022, The Twelveth Symposium on Educational Advances in Artificial Intelligence, EAAI 2022 Virtual Event, February 22 - March 1, 2022*, pages 11431–11439. AAAI Press.

Wu, X., Xiao, L., Sun, Y., Zhang, J., Ma, T., and He, L. (2022). A survey of human-in-the-loop for machine learning. *Future Generation Computer Systems*, 135:364–381.

Zhang, B., Haddow, B., and Birch, A. (2023). Prompting large language model for machine translation: A case study. *ArXiv preprint*, abs/2301.07069.

Zhang, T., Kishore, V., Wu, F., Weinberger, K. Q., and Artzi, Y. (2020). Bertscore: Evaluating text generation with BERT. In *8th International Conference on Learning Representations, ICLR 2020, Addis Ababa, Ethiopia, April 26-30, 2020*. OpenReview.net.

A Appendix: Related Work

A.1 ICL-based MT

Agrawal et al. (2022) proposed an ICL example selection method for machine translation, aiming to explore the impact of ICL examples on translation output quality. To address the issues in existing BM25 retrieval methods, the proposed approach re-ranks the top 100 candidate sentences selected by the BM25 score and introduces a re-ranking score, thereby maximizing the coverage of input words. Zhang et al. (2023) aims to explore different prompts in the context of LLM-based machine translation. In comparison to previous related research, the main innovation of this study lies in exploring how to design prompts for LLMs to enhance their translation capabilities from three different perspectives. Specifically, the research investigates different prompting strategies, the utilization of unlabeled data, and the flexibility of transfer learning. These research achievements demonstrate the significant value of ICL in improving the quality of machine translation systems.

A.2 Human-in-the-Loop MT

The concept of Human-in-the-Loop (HIL) (Wu et al., 2022) aims to leverage user feedback for optimizing the model. Building on this idea, Wang et al. (2022) proposes a novel non-parametric online learning method called kNN-over-kNN (KoK) that does not alter the model structure. KoK is a plug-and-play non-parametric approach that learns online based on human feedback, reducing the number of user interactions and improving machine translation model performance. The online learning process of KoK involves three steps: decoding, correcting, and adapting. In the decoding phase, the MT system translates the source sentence, and the output is obtained by weighting the KoK method and kNN-MT. In the correcting phase, users provide corrections of the machine-translated text, resulting in the post-edited translation. Finally, in the adapting phase, post-edited and source sentences are jointly used to expand the data repositories of token-kNN and policy-kNN, thereby optimizing the model. Through these three steps, the KoK framework can promptly influence the kNN translation model's decision-making. It is worth noting that, as of now, the HIL method has not been applied to LLM translation. Our paper focuses on exploring the potential integration of HIL into LLM translation to further enhance its performance and capabilities.

The impact of machine translation on the translation quality of undergraduate translation students

Jia Zhang jia.zhang2@unsw.edu.au
School of Humanities and Languages
University of New South Wales, Sydney, 2052, Australia
Hong Qian hongqian@uic.edu.cn
Department of Languages and Cultures
BNU-HKBU United International College, Zhuhai, 519087, China

Abstract

The importance of machine translation (MT) and post-editing (PE), as well as the importance of MT and PE training, has been widely acknowledged, and specialised courses have recently been introduced at universities worldwide. However, MT courses are usually offered to students at the postgraduate level or in the last year of an undergraduate programme. In addition, existing empirical studies have mainly investigated the impact of MT on postgraduate students or undergraduate students in the last year of their studies. The present paper reports on a study that aimed to determine the possible effects of MT and PE on the translation quality of undergraduate students in the early stages of translator training. Methodologically, an experiment was conducted to compare the students' (n = 10) post-editing machine translation (PEMT)-based translations and from-scratch translations. Several methods of translation quality assessment were adopted, including rubric-based scoring and error analysis. It was found that the quality of students' PE translations was compromised in comparison to the quality of their from-scratch translations. In addition, errors were more homogenised in the PEMT-based translations. It is hoped that this study can shed light on the role of PEMT in translator training and contribute to the curricula and course designs of PE for translator education.

1. Machine translation and translator training

Following several decades of development, machine translation (MT) systems can now translate more accurately than ever before. However, due to the complexity of human languages, MT cannot yet truly or fully convey the meaning of a text in the target language; thus, post-editing machine translation (PEMT) has become necessary. Post-editing (PE) refers to the process of improving machine-generated translations. House (2017, p. 20) pointed out that, in the future, translators would 'have to devote considerably more time to pre- and post-editing of texts'. Therefore, PE should be an essential skill for all translators.

In recent years, PEMT has been introduced at universities with the aim of training would-be translators with this skill. Since translators are destined to become post-editors (Pym, 2013), training programmes for translators should be redesigned. Some universities offer specialised courses, while others incorporate PEMT as an essential module in courses on translation technology. For example, a PEMT course was introduced for students in the Localisation Master's programme at Universitat Autònoma de Barcelona in Spain in 2009 and in 2017 (Arenas & Moorkens, 2019), while the University of Helsinki in Finland provided a course on PE for

Proceedings of Machine Translation Summit XIX, Vol. 2: Users Track, pages 99–108
September 4–8, 2023, Macau SAR, China.

undergraduate students and postgraduate students (Koponen, 2015); furthermore, the University of Exeter in Britain offers a course in machine-assisted translation at the final-year undergraduate level, including a PE workshop (Belam, 2003). Trainers appear to have reached a consensus that these specialised courses should be offered at the postgraduate level or towards the end of an undergraduate programme and that undergraduate students in the early stages of translator training should not be introduced to the knowledge or skills pertaining to MT and PE.

There have always been concerns about whether teachers should allow novice translation students to use and post-edit MT because novice translators do not have the confidence or experience to critically evaluate the output of a technology (Bowker, 2015) nor the linguistic competence to identify errors in machine-suggested translations in the early stages of translator training; thus, the quality of their translations may be affected. One may even suspect that their reliance on machine-suggested translations might affect the development of their translation competencies, such as critical thinking and creativity. In addition, some technologies, such as MT, are regarded as being more complex tools and are thus difficult for undergraduate students to master, which is why they are often integrated into translation curricula later in the programme. As a result, translation programmes may forbid undergraduate students from resorting to MT before a specialised course is offered.

However, it has been observed that undergraduate translation students may use MT as a reference in their translation assignments even without having received any appropriate training in PEMT.

Empirical evidence suggesting the negative impact of MT and PE on undergraduate translation students' translation performances in previous studies is insufficient. Empirical studies often recruit postgraduate or undergraduate students in the last year of their programmes (e.g., Jia et al., 2019; Wang et al., 2021; Zaretskaya et al., 2016). Less attention has been paid to the possible effects of PEMT on the quality of students' translations if they are introduced to PEMT at an early stage in their translator training. Even when attempts to compare undergraduate students' PE results and from-scratch translations are made, such comparisons are usually based on an overall quality assessment with a score being assigned to each translation product. There is a lack of detailed and closer examinations of the quality of students' translation products with or without MT assistance.

If MT and PE are proven to be beneficial for novice translation students to a certain extent, teachers might consider ways of integrating PEMT as a course component in translator training for students in an earlier stage at the undergraduate level. Nonetheless, novice translation students should be informed about the possible negative impacts of PEMT in order to interact with it more effectively.

2. Research questions

In light of the above discussion, the current research aimed to explore the impact of MT and PE on the quality of undergraduate translation students' translations in the early stages of their translator training by comparing their from-scratch translations and their PEMT-assisted translations. The research questions (RQs) for the study were as follows:

1) How do undergraduate translation students' from-scratch translations differ from their PEMT-based translations?

2) What are these students' perceptions of the use of PEMT in translation?

3) What are the pedagogical implications of the use of PEMT in translator training at the undergraduate level?

An experiment was designed to compare novice translation students' PEMT and from-scratch translations in an attempt to answer the first RQ. Students' perceptions of MT and PE were also solicited to understand the analysis of the experimental results. It is hoped that this study can shed light on the role of PEMT in translator training and contribute to the curricula and course design of PE for undergraduate education.

3. Methodology

3.1. Experimental design

An experiment was conducted amongst novice translation students to compare PEMT-assisted translations and from-scratch translations. Before the implementation of the experiment, ethical approval was obtained from the ethics committee of the university. Once the project had been approved, the participants were recruited quickly. In the experiment, the participants

(1) were briefed about the tasks,

(2) signed the informed consent form,

(4) translated the first text from scratch,

(5) post-edited the machine-generated translation of the second text (the order of the two translation tasks was randomised), and

(6) completed a survey.

The participants were second-year undergraduates who were enrolled in a translation programme at a university based in Zhuhai, China, at the time of the experiment. Their educational backgrounds were comparable, as the students were native Chinese speakers who had been learning English for more than ten years from primary school onwards. At the time of the experiment, all the students have taken at least three fundamental translation courses in which they obtained grades higher than B+; according to the university's grading system, a B+ indicates good competence in the performance in a course. In addition, the students had not taken any other translation courses on or off campus prior to the experiment. They had little translation experience and no knowledge of PEMT.

The participants were asked to translate two texts of around 300 words each from English into Chinese. One of the texts was translated from scratch, while the other was translated by post-editing machine-generated output. The direction of English-to-Chinese translation was chosen in our study in consideration of the commonly accepted belief that translation into the native tongue is easier than translation into a non-native language.

Several methods were adopted to guarantee that the textual difficulty of the two texts was similar. Firstly, the sources of the two texts were controlled. The texts were selected from the Accreditation Test for Translators and Interpreters in China (CATTI). As the national qualification test for translators in China, the level III exam questions must be controlled to maintain consistent levels of difficulty over the years. Two texts with a similar topic were chosen from the level III exam of December 2017 and were adapted by the researchers. The texts, adapted from two news reports, involved few or no professional terms from a specific field. No professional knowledge was needed to understand or translate the texts.

Secondly, some linguistic features were referred to as markers of text difficulty. The type-token ratio, the number of sentences, the average sentence length, the number of different sentence types and the level of the words in each text were calculated using the corpus tools AntConc and AntWordProfiler. The texts were rewritten to ensure that the markers were comparable.

Thirdly, the number of problem triggers, which were annotated by three raters, was comparable in both texts: Problem triggers were defined as words, phrases or sentences in the source texts that might cause translation errors. According to the three raters, there were 15, 21 and 20 problem triggers in text 1 and 17, 21 and 21 in text 2. The author then further edited the texts based on the results of the annotations.

The texts were edited to control the overall difficulty at the lexical, syntactic, semantic and pragmatic levels. The researchers rewrote the texts, and a native speaker was invited to assist with the editing and proofreading once all the preparatory work mentioned above was complete. The texts were comparable in terms of difficulty and were also clear and accurate.

The environment in which the experiment was conducted was a laboratory for translator training in which the students had attended classes for one semester. The lighting, room temperature and noise level were maintained at the same level. The participants could choose to sit in the same seat in which they sat in the class and adjust the height of their chairs and the positions of their computer monitors. They could use the computers in the room or bring their personal computers. All of the above requirements guaranteed that the students completed the translations in a safe, quiet and comfortable setting. Each participant went through all the steps individually in the laboratory at a time slot that they had chosen to avoid possible stress created by the presence of peer participants.

The participants were provided with the same hard-copy dictionary and had no access to an internet connection. As this research intended to explore the quality of the students' translations, the students' decisions in the translation process should be based on their knowledge of and thoughts about translation instead of drawing on online resources.

The participants were also briefed about the translation standards of achieving accuracy and fluency, which are two basic requirements for novice translation students. These requirements were essentially the same as those in the students' translation assignments in the previous year of learning to translate.

The students recorded their translation time on the document for each text and were told to submit their translations when they had decided that their translations had met the quality standards. The expected time for the translation of a 300-word text is approximately 45 to 60 minutes, but no specific time limit was set for the translation tasks.

Immediately after they had completed both translation tasks, the participants were instructed to complete a questionnaire survey inquiring about their attitudes to and perceptions of MT and PE. The survey included several open-ended questions. The students could answer the questions in either Chinese or English according to their preferences. The researcher, who is also an experienced translator with over 15 years of experience, translated the answers that were in Chinese for further analysis.

3.2. Data collection

The translation products, including the from-scratch translations and the PEMT-assisted translations, were first rated by three raters who assessed the translations and scored each translation based on the rubrics provided by the researchers. The three raters were experienced translator trainers based in China who had taught foundational translation courses for at least three years.

The rubrics that were used were divided into translation accuracy and language quality. Therefore, each translation product was given a total score, an accuracy sub-score and a fluency sub-score. Inter-rater agreement was tested before the scores for each translation were finalised by averaging the scores given by the three raters. Paired-sample *t*-tests were conducted to explore the relationships between the scores for the from-scratch translations and those for the PEMT-assisted translations.

A paired-sample *t*-test was also conducted to reveal the relationship between the time spent translating from scratch and the time for the PEMT to reveal the students' translation efficiency in both tasks.

The error analysis of the translation products was implemented in two ways. Firstly, with reference to the TAUS Harmonised DQF-MQM Error Typology, errors in the translations were first annotated independently by the two researchers; the results revealed that both researchers agreed about most of the errors. When a discrepancy occurred, the two researchers engaged in discussions to reach an agreement. The errors were divided into four types: The count for each type of error and the total error count in each translation product were then calculated. The paired-sample t-tests revealed the relationship between error counts in the from-scratch translations and those in the PEMT-assisted translations. Secondly, the errors in the translation products were observed and examined further in a qualitative manner to identify other issues related to translations with or without MT.

The survey of the students' attitudes to and perceptions of MT and PE was analysed manually with the assistance of NVivo to identify significant arguments, which would help to understand the results of the experiment in more depth.

4. Analysis and discussion

4.1. Rubric-based scoring

After the three raters had completed the grading, each translation product was given an overall score, which was divided into an accuracy sub-score and a fluency sub-score. Inter-rater agreement was verified by calculating the intraclass correlation coefficient (ICC). ICC estimates and 95% confidence intervals were calculated using the SPSS statistical package version 27 based on a mean-rating (k = 3), absolute-agreement, 2-way mixed-effects model. The value was .69. The scores were thus deemed to be reliable.

The score for each translation was then obtained by averaging the three scores given by the three raters. Paired-sample t-tests were conducted to understand the relationship between the scores for the from-scratch translations and those for the PEMT-assisted translations. Table 1 presents the results of the t-tests, and Figure 1 shows the corresponding boxplots. The from-scratch translations are indicated by "H", while the PEMT-assisted translations are marked as "M".

	MEAN	STD. DEVIATION	STD. ERROR MEAN	95% CONFIDENCE INTERVAL OF THE DIFFERENCE		T	DF	SIG. (2-TAILED)
				Lower	Upper			
SCORE H – SCORE M	5.93	6.23	1.97	1.48	10.39	3.01	9.00	0.01
ACCURACY H – ACCURACY M	2.97	2.82	0.89	0.95	4.98	3.33	9.00	0.01
FLUENCY H – FLUENCY M	2.97	3.77	1.19	0.27	5.66	2.49	9.00	0.03

Table 1 *T*-test results for the rubric-based scores

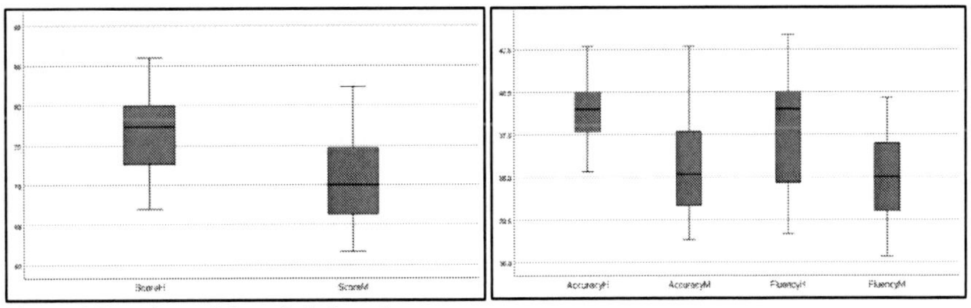

Figure 1 Boxplots of the rubric-based scores

The scores for the from-scratch translations (M = 76.7, SD = 5.34) were significantly higher than those for the PEMT-assisted translations (M = 70.77, SD = 5.88), with $t(9) = 3.01$, $p = .01$.

Similarly, the accuracy scores (M = 38.8, SD = 1.98) for the from-scratch translations were significantly higher than those (M = 35.83, SD = 3.19) for the PEMT-assisted translations, with $t(9) = 3.33$, $p = .01$.

The fluency scores (M = 37.9, SD = 3.47) for the from-scratch translations were significantly higher than those (M = 34.93, SD = 2.77) for the PEMT-assisted translations, with $t(9) = 2.49$, $p = .03$.

This result shows that the students' performances in the PEMT-assisted translations were not as good as they were in the from-scratch translations. The quality of the PE results decreased.

4.2. Translation time

The students were instructed to record the start time and the end time for the two tasks. The researchers then calculated the translation time needed for each task. Again, a paired-sample *t*-test revealed the relationship between the time spent translating from scratch and the PE time. In Table 2 and Figure 2, TIME H refers to the time needed for from-scratch translations, while TIME M indicates the time required for PE.

	MEAN	STD. DEVIATION	STD. ERROR MEAN	95% CONFIDENCE INTERVAL OF THE DIFFERENCE		T	DF	SIG. (2-TAILED)
				Lower	Upper			
TIME H – TIME M	7.20	18.17	5.75	-5.80	20.20	1.25	9.00	0.24

Table 2 *T*-test result for translation time

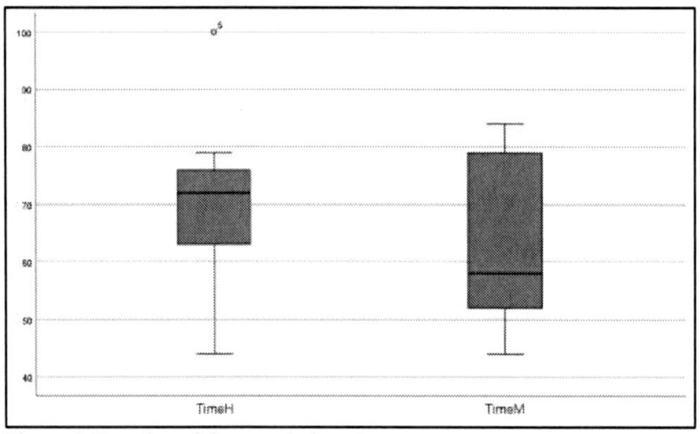

Figure 2 Boxplot of the translation time

The translation time for the from-scratch translations (M = 70.50, SD = 14.79) was not significantly different from that for the PEMT-assisted translations (M = 63.30, SD = 14.59), with $t(9) = 1.25$, $p = .25$. The PEMT output did not increase the translation efficiency of the participants in general.

When each student's translation time was examined closely, it was found that only half of the participants reported a subtle decrease in the time needed for the PE task, while three other participants spent the same amount of time on both tasks. It is worth noting that two participants spent significantly more time on the PE task.

4.3. Error counts

TAUS Harmonised DQF-MQM Error Typology is an internationally recognised framework for the assessment of translation quality. It is not only used to assess automated translations but also to assess post-edited machine translation and human translations. As the texts chosen for the translations only involved certain types of translation errors, the typology was adapted to suit the purposes of the annotations, as displayed in Table 3.

ID	Error type	Definition
1	Accuracy	The target text does not accurately reflect the source text, allowing for any differences authorised by the specifications.
2	Fluency	Issues related to the form or content of a text, irrespective of whether it is a translation or not.
4	Style	The text has stylistic problems.
7	Verity	The text makes statements that contradict the world of the text.

Table 3 Adapted TAUS Harmonised DQF-MQM Error Typology

Both researchers identified the errors in the students' translations by referring to the error types. The annotation results were compared, and the two researchers engaged in discussions when they had different opinions about some translation errors. The errors in each translation product were thus confirmed. The errors in each type were counted, and a total error count was calculated. Paired-sample *t*-tests revealed the relationships amongst the error counts, as shown in Table 4 and Figure 3.

	MEAN	STD. DEVIATION	STD. ERROR MEAN	95% CONFIDENCE INTERVAL OF THE DIFFERENCE Lower	Upper	T	DF	SIG. (2-TAILED)
ERROR H - ERROR M	-2.50	4.17	1.32	-5.48	0.48	-1.90	9.00	0.09
ERROR TYPE I H - ERROR TYPE I M	-3.50	4.09	1.29	-6.43	-0.57	-2.71	9.00	0.02
ERROR TYPE II H - ERROR TYPE II M	0.20	0.79	0.25	-0.36	0.76	0.80	9.00	0.44
ERROR TYPE III H - ERROR TYPE III M	0.50	3.63	1.15	-2.10	3.10	0.44	9.00	0.67
ERROR TYPE IV H - ERROR TYPE IV M	0.30	0.48	0.15	-0.05	0.65	1.96	9.00	0.08

Table 4 *T*-test results for the error counts

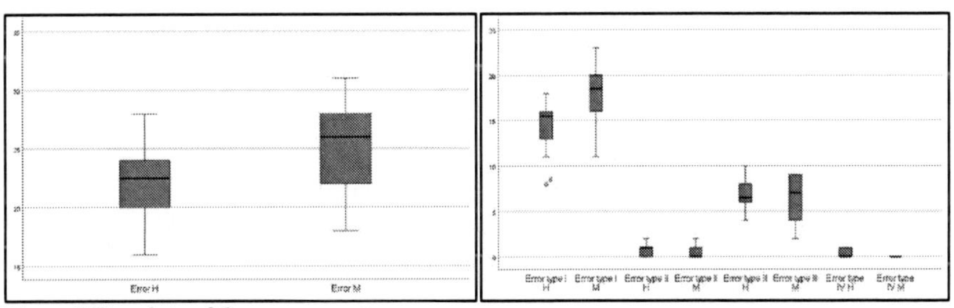

Figure 3 Boxplots of the error counts

The total error count in the from-scratch translations (M = 22.30, SD = 3.368) was lower than it was in the PEMT-assisted translations (M = 24.80, SD = 4.341), but not significantly so, with $t(9) = -1.90$, $p = .09$. Of the four types of errors, only type I accuracy errors in the from-scratch translations (M = 14.4, SD = 3.169) were significantly lower than they were in the PEMT-assisted translations (M = 17.90, SD = 3.725), with $t(9) = -2.71$, $p = .02$.

The number of errors might have increased when the students were engaged in PE, but a definite conclusion based on our data could not be drawn. This result may have been affected by the small number of participants who were recruited and the small number of error counts for each error type given that the length of each text was only 300 words. Further studies must be conducted to determine the impact of MT and PE on students' error counts.

4.4. Error observation

The errors in the students' translation products were observed closely. It could clearly be seen that, in the from-scratch translations, the errors triggered by the same point were very different. However, when the students engaged in PEMT, the errors tended to be homogenised. The error types and words used to translate a certain point were exactly the same.

An example is the phrase "native English speaker" in the text translated from scratch, which was translated using different renderings. Some students made errors when translating this phrase, but the error types differed. These students intended to be more creative in their translations but still made various errors, as shown in Table 5.

Source text	Target text	Error
native English speaker	土生土长的英语母语者[back translation: English native speaker born and raised in an English-speaking country]	Over-translation
	那些英语母语者（英语可能并不是他们所在国的唯一语言）[back translation: English native speaker (English might not be the only language in their country)]	Addition
	以英语为主要语言的人[back translation: People who use English as the main language]	Mistranslation
	天生就讲英语的人[back translation: people who speak English after they were born]	Unidiomatic

Table 5 Examples of errors in the from-scratch translations

The translation errors in the PEMT-based translations were identical. The two phrases in Table 6 were translated as identical Chinese versions in the PE task by most of the participants. Seven out of 10 students mistranslated "English speakers with no other language" as "英语使用者" (English users). Similarly, seven students translated the phrase "simple but standard grammar" word for word, which resulted in awkwardness in the target text. It can be inferred that the students could not improve on the unidiomatic or awkward expressions provided by the MT. The students may not have been able to identify all the errors in the machine-generated output, and their critical thinking was also impacted.

Source text	Target text	Error	Frequency
English speakers with no other language	英语使用者[back translation: English users]	Mistranslation	7/10
Globish -- a distilled form of English, stripped down to 1,500 words and simple but standard grammar	1500 个单词和简单但标准的语法[1500 words and simple but standard grammar]	Awkward	7/10

Table 6 Examples of errors in PEMT-based translations

4.5. Students' perceptions

Contrary to the experimental results, eight out of 10 participants stated in the survey that they felt more confident when post-editing the MT output. As a result, they also felt more confident about the quality of their PEMT-assisted translations. Even though some of the students doubted the quality of the MT, they did trust MT to a certain extent, as they clearly expressed that MT helped them to understand the source text better, particularly with regard to the text structure and complicated sentences. In addition, they believed that the MTs provided good references that decreased their efforts to find the correct words.

Of note, all ten students also said that they invested more effort in the PEMT tasks and made more judgement about the quality of and adjustments to the MT output. This echoed the analysis of the time spent on the translation tasks to some extent. According to the survey, such efforts were mainly aimed at improving awkwardness in the machine-generated translations.

One point worth noting is that none of the students mentioned that such an increase in effort was the result of their insufficient translation competence or language proficiency. Instead, they believed that the main reasons were their unfamiliarity with MT and their lack of PE training.

5. Concluding remarks

This research required students to perform from-scratch translations and PEMT-assisted translations and compared the quality of the products with the aim of exploring the impact of MT and PE on the translation performances of undergraduate students in the early stages of translator training.

The quality of the students' PEMT-assisted translations was compromised in comparison to that of their from-scratch translations. The overall score, the accuracy sub-score and the fluency sub-score for the PEMT-assisted translations were significantly lower than those for the from-scratch translations. The total error counts and accuracy error counts in the PEMT tasks were higher than those in the from-scratch translation tasks.

The students' perceptions of translation quality were the opposite. The students felt more confident when having a pre-translated version to hand and thus had more confidence in the outcomes of the translations.

The students' translation efficiency was not improved via MT assistance. The time spent on PE was reduced, but not significantly from that spent on the from-scratch translations. Two students obviously spent more time on the PEMT-assisted translation. This result is consistent with the students' perceptions. Most students expressed feeling annoyed and burdened because correcting "weird" expressions took them more time. The students attributed the increase in effort to a lack of MT knowledge and PE training rather than to their translation competence or language proficiency.

The students' translation errors in the PEMT tasks were homogenous. A closer examination of their translation products revealed that they could not identify an error made by a machine and tended to retain these errors in their final translation products.

It is thus probably concluded that MT may not benefit undergraduate students in the early stages of translator training in the absence of specialised MT and PE training. Without any training, MT impacted negatively on their translation quality and possibly on their critical thinking. If students rely too extensively on MT too early in their translator training, one might be concerned that MT might have a negative impact on the development of their translation competence. However, since the students raised the issue of training, the next step could be to test the effectiveness of MT and PE training on the translation performances of undergraduate translation students.

Even if PE training is not to be incorporated at an early stage in translator training, it is strongly suggested that trainers and teachers should provide lectures about basic MT knowledge. The students obviously trusted MT to a certain degree, particularly with regard to understanding the source text. Although they were not engaged in PEMT directly, they were willing to use MT as a helpful reference in their translations. As many MT systems are freely available online, preventing students from accessing them would be difficult. Therefore, specific guidance should be provided to students to make them aware of the best practices when interacting with MT at this stage. For example, students should be aware that, although technology is overwhelming the industry and education sectors, the fundamental factor for translation learners, language proficiency, must still be prioritised.

As this was a small-scale experiment with only ten participants and two texts of 300 words each, we understand that there is a limitation in terms of generalising the results of the experiment. Our findings prove that this topic requires further exploration. Experiments involving more participants and longer texts could be conducted to provide more empirical evidence in this regard.

Acknowledgement

This work is supported by the FHSS Teaching and Learning Grant (FHSS TLSE Committee) of BNU-HKBU United International College.

References

Arenas, A. G., & Moorkens, J. (2019). Machine translation and post-editing training as part of a master's programme. *Journal of Specialised Translation*, 31, 217–238.

Belam, J. (2003). Buying up to falling down: A deductive approach to teaching post-editing. *Proceedings of MT Summit IX Workshop on Teaching Translation Technologies and Tools*, 1–10.

Bowker, L. (2015). Computer-aided translation: Translator training. In S. Chan (Ed.), *Routledge encyclopedia of translation technology* (pp. 126–142). Routledge.

House, J. (2017). *Translation: The basics*. Routledge.

Jia, Y. F., Carl, M., & Wang, X. L. (2019). How does the post-editing of neural machine translation compare with from-scratch translation? A product and process study. *Journal of Specialised Translation*, 31, 60–86.

Koponen, M. (2015). How to teach machine translation post-editing? Experiences from a post-editing course. *Proceedings of the 4th Workshop on Post-editing Technology and Practice*.

Pym, A. (2013). Translation Skill-Sets in a Machine-Translation Age. *Meta*, 58(3), 487–503. https://doi.org/10.7202/1025047ar

Wang, X., Wang, T., Muñoz Martín, R., & Jia, Y. (2021). Investigating usability in postediting neural machine translation: Evidence from translation trainees' self-perception and performance. *Across Languages and Cultures*, 22(1), 100–123. https://doi.org/10.1556/084.2021.00006

Zaretskaya, A., Vela, M., Pastor, G. C., & Seghiri, M. (2016). Measuring post-editing time and effort for different types of machine translation errors. *New Voices in Translation Studies*, 15, 63–92.

Leveraging Latent Topic Information to Improve Product Machine Translation

Bryan Zhang bryzhang@amazon.com
Stephan Walter sstwa@amazon.com
Liling Tan lilingt@amazon.com
Amita Misra misrami@amazon.com
Amazon.com, USA

Abstract

Meeting the expectations of e-commerce customers involves offering a seamless online shopping experience in their preferred language. To achieve this, modern e-commerce platforms rely on machine translation systems to provide multilingual product information on a large scale. However, maintaining high-quality machine translation that can keep up with the ever-expanding volume of product data remains an open challenge for industrial machine translation systems. In this context, topical clustering emerges as a valuable approach, leveraging latent signals and interpretable textual patterns to potentially enhance translation quality and facilitate industry-scale translation data discovery. This paper proposes two innovative methods: topic-based data selection and topic-signal augmentation, both utilizing latent topic clusters to improve the quality of machine translation in e-commerce. Furthermore, we present a data discovery workflow that utilizes topic clusters to effectively manage the growing multilingual product catalogs, addressing the challenges posed by their expansion.

Keywords: *product information translation, topic signal augmentation, topic-based data selection, textual pattern extraction, topical clustering, data discovery*

1 Introduction

With the advent of localized e-commerce sites, customers can now shop in their preferred language. Modern e-commerce platforms provide multi-lingual product discovery (Rücklé et al., 2019; Nie, 2010; Saleh and Pecina, 2020; Bi et al., 2020; Jiang et al., 2020; Lowndes and Vasudevan, 2021) with machine translated product information, titles, descriptions, and bullet points (Way, 2013; Guha and Heger, 2014; Zhou et al., 2018; Wang et al., 2021).

As e-commerce product catalogs continue to expand, the task of maintaining up-to-date machine translation systems poses significant challenges. When the vast amount of product information is sourced from various sellers or suppliers, each can present the data differently. Consequently, this can lead to inconsistencies in the source data and, in turn, translation inaccuracies. Validating such a substantial volume of data for MT training at scale becomes increasingly difficult and time-consuming, demanding significant resources for manual review and error correction to guarantee the accurate interpretation of product information.

From data usage perspective, topic words extracted from the latent topic clusters in the training data can be mapped to topics that can help with word sense disambiguation and improve

Proceedings of Machine Translation Summit XIX, Vol. 2: Users Track, pages 109–118
September 4–8, 2023, Macau SAR, China.

overall performance of MT. Therefore, in this study, we propose two approaches to leverage latent topical clusters to improve machine translation quality: (i) **topic-based data selection** and (ii) **topic-signal augmentation**. Both approaches use Dirichlet Mixture Model (DMM) (Nigam et al., 2000) with Collapsed Gibbs Sampling (CoGS) (Yin and Wang, 2014) to cluster large volumes of data efficiently, and the number of the clusters can be inferred automatically. The topic-based data selection approach first distinguishes between clusters of clean desirable data and those of noisy undesirable data based on the inspection of textual patterns, then selects training data from the desirable clusters for MT training. The topic-signal augmentation approach extends training data with extracted latent topic words prefixed to the source input and augments MT training with additional contextual information. Additionally, we propose a **data discovery workflow** to cluster training data and generates cluster summary and data visualization to uncover the latent topics and textual patterns, it can also identify new noisy data patterns so that strategies can be devised to prevent the occurrence of such data in the future.

2 Related Work

Previous studies have successfully used topic models to improve statistical machine translation (Eidelman et al., 2012; Hu et al., 2013; Xiong et al., 2015; Mathur et al., 2015) and neural machine translation (Zhang et al., 2016; Chen et al., 2019). Mathur et al. (2015) integrates topic models as feature functions in the phrase-tables to improve statistical machine translation for e-commerce domain adaption. Zhang et al. (2016) presents an approach using topic models to increase the likelihood of word selection from the same topic as the source context. Instead of explicitly affecting the parameters or vocabulary selection, in this paper, we utilize a topical cluster model for data selection, and context augmentation implicitly adapting the MT model to the latent topic information.

3 Topical clustering

We use Dirichlet Multinomial Mixture (DMM) (Nigam et al., 2000) and Collapsed Gibbs Sampling (CoGS) (Yin and Wang, 2014) for topical clustering. DMM and CoGS are efficient clustering algorithms capitalizing on symbolic text representation, making them ideal to cluster industry scale e-commerce data based on textual patterns. Moreover, the number of topic clusters is automatically inferred to adequately capture both frequent and rare textual patterns.

We use the DMM model to label each document (input text) with one topic tag. DMM is a probabilistic generative model for documents and embodies two assumptions about the generative process: first, the documents are generated by a mixture model; second, there is one-to-one correspondence between mixture components and clusters. When generating document d, DMM first selects a mixture component (topic cluster) k according to the mixture weights (weights of clusters) $P(z = k)$. Then document d is generated by the selected mixture component (cluster) from distribution $P(d|z = k)$. We can characterize the likelihood of document d with the sum of the total probability over all mixture components:

$$P(d) = \sum_{k=1}^{K} P(d|z = k)P(z = k) \tag{1}$$

where, K is the number of mixture components (topic clusters). DMM assumes that each mixture component (topic cluster) is a multinomial distribution over words and each mixture component (topic cluster) has a Dirichlet distribution prior:

$$P(w|z = k) = P(w|z = k, \Phi) = \phi_{k,w} \tag{2}$$

$$P(z = k) = P(z = k|\Theta) = \theta_k \tag{3}$$

where[1] $\sum_{w}^{V} \phi_{w,k} = 1$ and $P(\Phi|\beta) = Dir(\theta|\beta)$ and $\sum_{k}^{K} \theta_k = 1$ and $P(\Theta|\alpha) = Dir(\theta|\alpha)$.

The collapsed Gibbs sampling is used to estimate DMM parameters, documents are randomly assigned to K clusters initially and the following information is recorded:

z is the cluster labels of each document
m_z is number of documents in each cluster z
n_z^w is the number of occurrences of word w in each cluster z
N_d is the number of words in document d
N_d^w is the number of occurrence of word w in the document d

The documents are traversed for a number of iterations. In each iteration, each document is reassigned to a cluster according to the conditional distribution of $P(Z_d = z|z_{\neg d}, d)$, $\neg d$ means d is not contained:

$$P(Z_d = z|z_{\neg d}, d) \propto \frac{m_{z,\neg d} + \alpha}{D - 1 + K\alpha} \frac{\prod_{w \in d} \prod_{j=1}^{N_d^w} (n_{z,\neg d}^w + \beta + j - 1)}{\prod_{i=1}^{N_d} (n_{z,\neg d} + V\beta + i - 1)} \tag{4}$$

where, hyper-parameter α controls the popularity of the clusters, hyper-parameter β emphasizes on the similar words between a document and clusters.

4 Topic-based data selection

As Figure 1 shown, the data selection approach first clusters large volume of the training data. Empirically, larger clusters can capture the major topical and textual patterns so they are usually the clean desirable data whereas the smaller clusters can capture smaller and rare textual patterns so they are likely to be the noisy undesirable data. Additionally, we can also distinguish between desirable and undesirable data based on the data inspection of the clusters, we will further discuss the data discovery and inspection process in section 8. Finally, only clusters of desirable data are chosen for training to improve MT. Data providers are also informed of the undesirable data patterns for future data quality control.

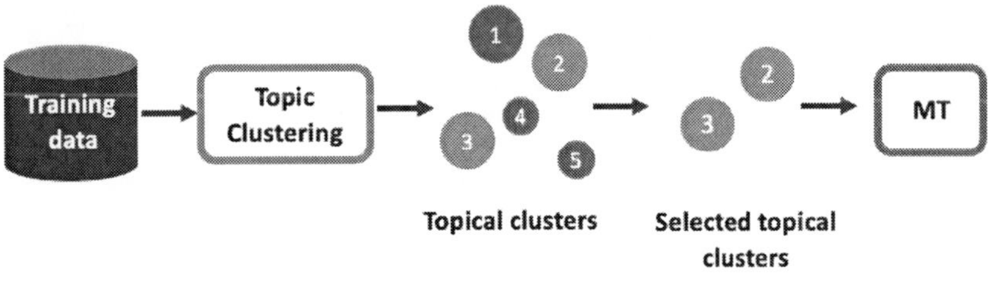

Figure 1: Choosing desirable data for MT training

5 Topic-signal augmentation

Figure 2 presents the topic-signal augmentation approach. We first cluster the data, then extract the most frequent top-k content words as the topic words for each cluster. Then, we choose the

[1]The weight of each mixture component (cluster) is sampled from a multinomial distribution which has a Dirichlet prior

larger clusters and prefix the source texts with the top-k topic words as topic signal as shown in Figure 4, we choose larger clusters are usually have more clear and interpret-able topic words, which can provide clear topic signals. Finally we extend the original training data with the training data with topic signal before training the MT model in Figure 3.

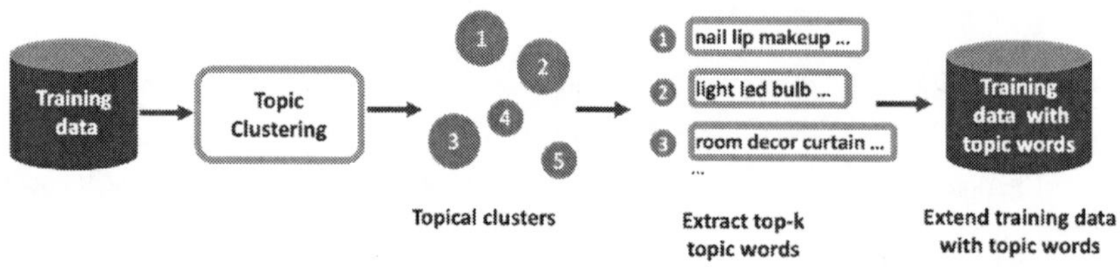

Figure 2: Topic signal approach to improve MT for product information

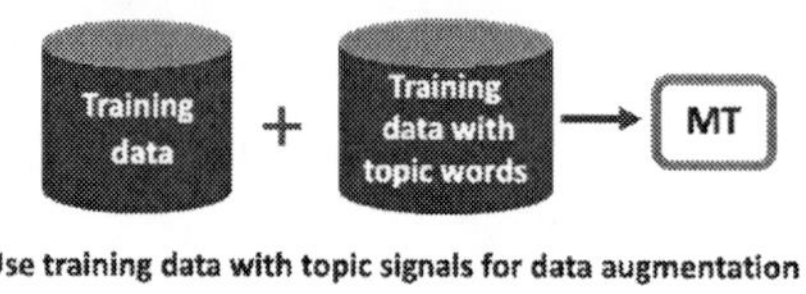

Figure 3: Use training data extended with topic words to further augment the MT training

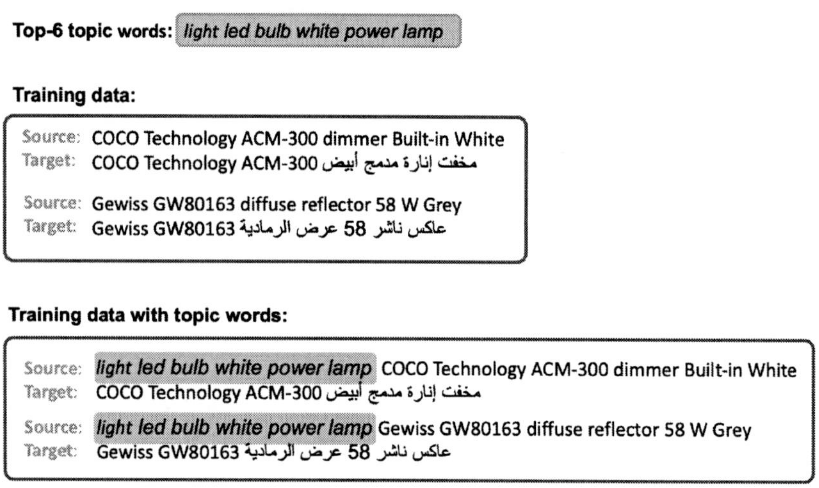

Figure 4: Extend the source text of the training data with top-k (k=6) topic words as topic signal

6 Experiment Setup

We experiment on four language pairs, English-Chinese (ENUS-ZHCN), English-Arabic (ENUS-ARAE), English-German (ENGB-DEDE), Spanish-English (ESES-ENGB). We train the models on a large volume of in-house generic training data and a subset of product-information data (product titles, descriptions and bulletpoints) for domain adaptation. We use the transformer-based architecture (Vaswani et al., 2017) with 20 encoder and 2 decoder layers with the Sockeye MT toolkit (Domhan et al., 2020) to train a generic MT using generic data and domain-specific data, then fine-tune the model on the domain-specific product information data for domain adaptation. For each language pair, we have three test data sets for product titles, descriptions and bulletpoints respectively. Each test data set has 2000 test segments and evaluate the models using BLEU[2] and chrF (Popović, 2015) to assess the translation quality.

For the topic clusters, the source text is lower-cased, tokenized and stemmed using NLTK ToolKit (Bird et al., 2009), stemmed tokens with document frequency less than or equals to 2 are removed in the preprocessing steps. For all 4 language pairs, the initial upper-bound number of topical clusters is set to 500 for ENUS-ZHCN and ENUS-ARAE, and 1000 for ENGB-DEDE and ESES-ENGB. The number of the topic clusters is inferred automatically during the collapsed Gibbs sampling process. The number of iterations is set to 30, and both hyper-parameters α and β are set to 0.1. We create 2-D plots using Jensen-Shannon distance (Fuglede and Topsoe, 2004) and multi-dimensional scaling technique (Borg and Groenen, 2005) with *LDAvis* (Sievert and Shirley, 2014) to easily visualize the size and relations of the topic clusters returned from the algorithm, and to inspect the topic words extracted from the clusters.

7 Experiment Results

7.1 Results: clustering results for four language pairs

	Num of total clusters	Num of major clusters	Num of minor clusters	% of data from the minor clusters	Major cluster threshold
ENUS-ZHCN	329	194	135	0.07%	50
ENUS-ARAE	374	110	264	1.32%	1000
ENGB-DEDE	536	117	419	0.09%	1000
ESES-ENGB	546	139	407	0.09%	1000

Table 1: Statistics of the Resulting Topic Clusters

Table 1 shows the statistics of the resulting clusters for each language pair. The number of the total clusters is automatically inferred by the algorithm. Each segments in the training data is assigned cluster IDs, and data selection uses a surprisingly simple heuristic-based human inspection of the data clusters.

We distinguish between major and minor clusters by the number of segments assigned to each cluster. For example, ENUS-ARAE clusters that contain more than 1000 segments are considered as major and selected as the training data for the model training; 1.32% of the training data with less than 1000 segments per cluster were dropped from the training data after the selection process. To yield a similar size data to the other three language pairs, we lower the major cluster threshold to 50 for the ENUS-ZHCN. The other language pairs have their major cluster threshold set at 1000. By removing minor clusters, 0.07%-1.32% data from the training data are removed.

Based on our inspection, we observe that the major clusters contain mostly the desirable data that captures the e-commerce themes, and the top-k words in the major clusters are intuitively good topic signals to improve machine translation. Meanwhile, we observe that the minor clusters capture undesirable various textual patterns that include noisy data. Therefore,

[2]SacreBLEU version 2.0.0 (Post, 2018)

we select only the data from the major clusters for our experiments. Section 8 will discuss further details on the data inspection process with an analysis for ENUS-ARAE translations.

7.2 Experiment Results: Improving MT with Topic Signals Augmentation and Topic-based Data Selection

As the described in Section 5, we extract the *top-6 most frequent content words*[3] from the major topic clusters and extend the source text to augment the original domain specific data to train the model. We refer to the models trained with augmented topic words as `Model Topi6`, and the models trained with the selected data from the major cluster as `Model Cluney`. We compare both `Model Topi6` and `Model Cluney` against the baseline models trained with the full in-domain dataset.

	Models	**Model Cluney**		**Model TOPI-6**	
	Domain	**BLEU**	**chrF**	**BLEU**	**chrF**
ENUS-ZHCN	Title	+1.40%	+2.87%	+1.77%	+3.56%
	Description	+0.58%	+1.63%	+2.85%	+4.12%
	Bulletpoints	+0.38%	+0.69%	+1.76%	+1.96%
ENUS-ARAE	Title	+7.20%	+2.79%	+3.03%	+0.09%
	Description	+1.45%	+0.87%	+2.14%	+0.32%
	Bulletpoints	+0.57%	+0.41%	+0.14%	0.00
ENGB-DEDE	Title	-0.11%	+1.23%	+1.70%	+0.55%
	Description	-0.43%	-0.17%	+0.80%	+0.46%
	Bulletpoints	+0.08%	+0.11%	+1.48%	+0.72%
ESES-ENGB	Title	+1.41%	+0.31%	+0.69%	+0.28%
	Description	-0.98%	-0.50%	+0.18%	-0.16%
	Bulletpoints	-0.58%	-0.31%	+0.51%	+0.04%

Table 2: Model Cluney and Model TOPI-6 Quality Improvement % over the Baseline Models

Table 2 presents the improved machine translation quality of the `Cluney` and `Topi6` model across language pairs and product information types. The `Topi6` model for ENUS-ZHCN reported the best improvements against the baseline with +2.85% BLEU and +4.12% chrF for description while the best `Cluney` improvements come from ENUS-ARAE with +7.20% BLEU and +2.79% chrF. The ESES-ENGB and ENGB-DEDE models have less improvement compared to the ENUS-ZHCN and ENUS-ARAE. It is possible that language pairs with similar source and target languages benefit less from the `Topi6` approaches.

Source	*100 GSM Comforter, Quality California* ***Queen*** *400 Thread Count, 100% Egyptian Cotton*
Baseline MT	100 GSM 棉被,加州女王 400 支,100% 埃及棉
Topi6 MT	100 GSM 棉被,加州大号双人床 400 支,100% 埃及棉
Source	*Foot Fashion Lace Women's Dress Shoes,* ***Platform****, High Heel, Peep Toe (7.5, Rose Red)*
Baseline MT	Charm Foot 尚蕾女式正装鞋,高跟,露趾(7.5,玫瑰)
Topi6 MT	Charm Foot 尚蕾女式正装鞋,防水台,高跟鞋,露趾(7.5,玫瑰)

Table 3: Translation examples with improved word sense disambiguation

[3] $k = 6$ is chosen arbitrarily for this study, we will further investigate the impact of the span of the topic signal on the MT improvement in future work.

Anecdotally, we also observe some word sense disambiguation improvement in the translation especially in language pairs which the source and target languages are much different such as ENUS-ZHCN. Table 3 shows two translation examples of improved lexical disambiguation. In the first example, the word ***queen*** can refer to both a person and size semantically. In this case, it refers to the size of the comforter. The baseline MT incorrectly translates *the queen* to the person (女王) whereas the Topi6 MT successfully translates it to the size (大号双人床). In the second example, the word *platform* has a specific term in Mandarin when it refers to the platform of women's high-heel shoes. The baseline model conveniently ommits the translation for ***platform*** whereas Topi6 model translates it into the correct terminology 防水台.

8 Data discovery workflow and cluster inspection

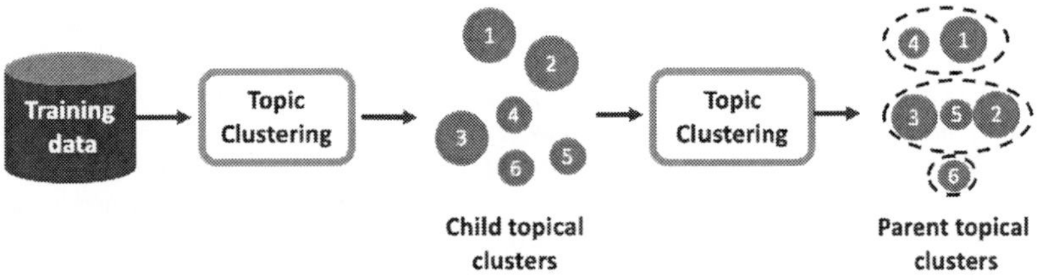

Figure 5: Data topic clustering workflow

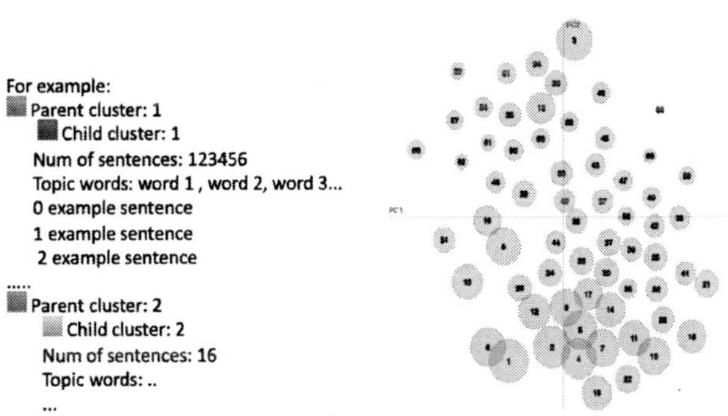

Figure 6: Left: Topic cluster summary for manual inspection. Right: 2-D plot for cluster visualization

Data quality management at scale for industry machine translation systems for an ever-expanding e-commerce product catalog is an open challenge. In this section, we describe a data discover workflow that clusters large volumes of data to allow human-computer interactive data inspection based on latent topic textual patterns. The process first cluster the texts into child clusters then optionally a second-stage clustering to create parent clusters as shown in Figure 6 on the left. Every cluster contains the segment IDs that fall within the cluster and a list of topic words that represent the textual patterns of the cluster.

This is particularly useful when acquiring training data from multiple sources on a regular basis or working with new language pairs, where unforeseen patterns may exist in the data. For each child cluster, we label its size with a color-coded square, where red is for large clusters (e.g., $\geq$ 1K data points) and yellow is for smaller clusters. We sample a few sentences from each child cluster for manual inspection, along with the top-K most frequent content words to indicate the thematic information of the cluster. If child clusters are further clustered into parent clusters, we group them into a green square-labeled group cluster. We also generate 2-D data visualization with projected child clusters to understand the relations of clusters as Figure 6 on the right. These 2-D data plot can be generated using Jensen-Shannon distance (Fuglede and Topsoe, 2004) and multi-dimensional scaling technique such as Principle Coordinate Analysis (PCoA) (Borg and Groenen, 2005) .

We use ENUS-ARAE language pair to illustrate of our data inspection findings. For this language pair, there are total of 374 child clusters and 155 parent clusters returned from the data discovery workflow. Figure 7 displays the plots of all the 374 child clusters, where the size of the child clusters in the plot corresponds to the number of segments labeled for the clusters. Upon plotting all the 374 clusters, we observe a long tail of small clusters that deviated from the major clusters.

To gain further insight into the latent patterns of each cluster, we generate a cluster summary with sample sentences and parent clusters. We observe there are 110 major clusters, each containing >= 1000 segments. The topic words and sample sentences in the cluster summary making it easy to infer the themes of these clusters. For instance, there are clusters having clear themes such as beauty and toiletry products or author names in European languages.

Meanwhile, many smaller clusters indicate undesirable textual patterns. For instance, there are clusters containing source texts in mixed English and Arabic, which also appears on the target side. Some clusters comprise source texts entirely in Arabic, with only some of the data appearing on the target side. There are also several clusters in which the source texts are in other languages besides the target side. Some clusters exhibit different noise patterns, which also appeared on the target side. Therefore, we use the major clusters in both experiments of the proposed MT improvement approaches.

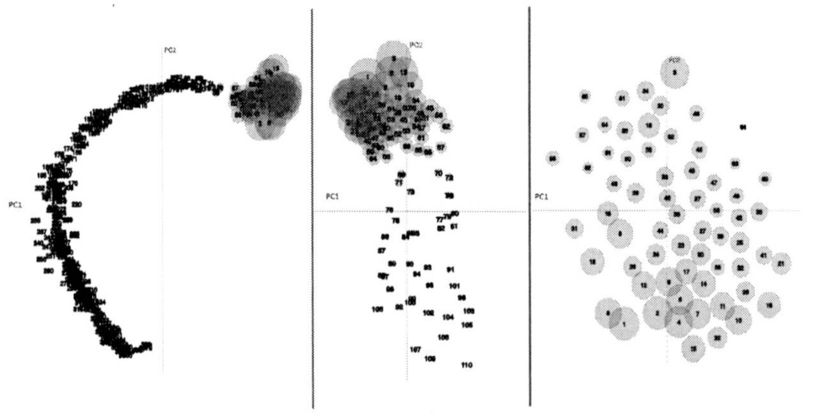

Figure 7: Data clusters of the English data (source text) from the ENUS-ARAE training Data using PCoA. The plot on the left is the visualization of all 374 clusters. The plot in the middle is for the top 110 clusters which size is >= 1K sentences. The plot on the right is for the top 64 clusters which size is >= 100 K sentences.

9 Conclusion

In this paper, we propose topic-based data selection and topic-signal augmentation approaches which leverage latent topic information to improve machine translation quality. Our experiments show that topic-based data selection and topic-signal augmentation approaches work better on source and target languages that are more dissimilar (ENUS-ARAE and ENUS-ZHCN) than translations between similar languages (ENGB-DEDE and ESES-ENGB). Additionally, the latent topic words and clusters creates a data discovery workflow that allows manual data inspection and translation data quality control.

References

Bi, T., Yao, L., Yang, B., Zhang, H., Luo, W., and Chen, B. (2020). Constraint translation candidates: A bridge between neural query translation and cross-lingual information retrieval.

Bird, S., Klein, E., and Loper, E. (2009). *Natural language processing with Python: analyzing text with the natural language toolkit.* " O'Reilly Media, Inc.".

Borg, I. and Groenen, P. J. (2005). *Modern multidimensional scaling: Theory and applications.* Springer Science & Business Media.

Chen, K., Wang, R., Utiyama, M., Sumita, E., and Zhao, T. (2019). Neural machine translation with sentence-level topic context. *IEEE/ACM Transactions on Audio, Speech, and Language Processing*, 27(12):1970–1984.

Domhan, T., Denkowski, M., Vilar, D., Niu, X., Hieber, F., and Heafield, K. (2020). The sockeye 2 neural machine translation toolkit at AMTA 2020. In *Proceedings of the 14th Conference of the Association for Machine Translation in the Americas (Volume 1: Research Track)*, pages 110–115, Virtual. Association for Machine Translation in the Americas.

Eidelman, V., Boyd-Graber, J., and Resnik, P. (2012). Topic models for dynamic translation model adaptation. In *Proceedings of the 50th Annual Meeting of the Association for Computational Linguistics (Volume 2: Short Papers)*, pages 115–119, Jeju Island, Korea. Association for Computational Linguistics.

Fuglede, B. and Topsoe, F. (2004). Jensen-shannon divergence and hilbert space embedding. In *International Symposium onInformation Theory, 2004. ISIT 2004. Proceedings.*, pages 31–.

Guha, J. and Heger, C. (2014). Machine translation for global e-commerce on ebay. In *Proceedings of the AMTA*, volume 2, pages 31–37.

Hu, Y., Zhai, K., Edelman, V., and Boyd-Graber, J. (2013). Topic models for translation domain adaptation. In *Topic Models: Computation, Application, and Evaluation. NIPS Workshop.*

Jiang, Z., El-Jaroudi, A., Hartmann, W., Karakos, D., and Zhao, L. (2020). Cross-lingual information retrieval with BERT. In *Proceedings of the workshop on Cross-Language Search and Summarization of Text and Speech (CLSSTS2020)*, pages 26–31, Marseille, France. European Language Resources Association.

Lowndes, M. and Vasudevan, A. (2021). Market guide for digital commerce search.

Mathur, P., Federico, M., Köprü, S., Khadivi, S., and Sawaf, H. (2015). Topic adaptation for machine translation of e-commerce content. In *Proceedings of Machine Translation Summit XV: Papers*, Miami, USA.

Nie, J.-Y. (2010). Cross-language information retrieval. *Synthesis Lectures on Human Language Technologies*, 3(1):1–125.

Nigam, K., McCallum, A. K., Thrun, S., and Mitchell, T. (2000). Text classification from labeled and unlabeled documents using em. *Machine learning*, 39(2-3):103–134.

Popović, M. (2015). chrF: character n-gram F-score for automatic MT evaluation. In *Proceedings of the Tenth Workshop on Statistical Machine Translation*, pages 392–395, Lisbon, Portugal. Association for Computational Linguistics.

Post, M. (2018). A call for clarity in reporting BLEU scores. In *Proceedings of the Third Conference on Machine Translation: Research Papers*, pages 186–191, Brussels, Belgium. Association for Computational Linguistics.

Rücklé, A., Swarnkar, K., and Gurevych, I. (2019). Improved cross-lingual question retrieval for community question answering. In *The World Wide Web Conference*, WWW '19, page 3179–3186, New York, NY, USA. Association for Computing Machinery.

Saleh, S. and Pecina, P. (2020). Document translation vs. query translation for cross-lingual information retrieval in the medical domain. In *Proceedings of the 58th Annual Meeting of the Association for Computational Linguistics*, pages 6849–6860, Online. Association for Computational Linguistics.

Sievert, C. and Shirley, K. (2014). LDAvis: A method for visualizing and interpreting topics. In *Proceedings of the Workshop on Interactive Language Learning, Visualization, and Interfaces*, pages 63–70, Baltimore, Maryland, USA. Association for Computational Linguistics.

Vaswani, A., Shazeer, N., Parmar, N., Uszkoreit, J., Jones, L., Gomez, A. N., Kaiser, L., and Polosukhin, I. (2017). Attention is all you need.

Wang, H., Wu, H., He, Z., Huang, L., and Church, K. W. (2021). Progress in machine translation. *Engineering*.

Way, A. (2013). Traditional and emerging use-cases for machine translation. *Proceedings of Translating and the Computer*, 35:12.

Xiong, D., Zhang, M., and Wang, X. (2015). Topic-based coherence modeling for statistical machine translation. *IEEE/ACM Transactions on Audio, Speech, and Language Processing*, 23(3):483–493.

Yin, J. and Wang, J. (2014). A dirichlet multinomial mixture model-based approach for short text clustering. In *SIGKDD*, pages 233–242. ACM.

Zhang, J., Li, L., Way, A., and Liu, Q. (2016). Topic-informed neural machine translation. In *Proceedings of COLING 2016, the 26th International Conference on Computational Linguistics: Technical Papers*, pages 1807–1817, Osaka, Japan. The COLING 2016 Organizing Committee.

Zhou, M., Cheng, R., Lee, Y. J., and Yu, Z. (2018). A visual attention grounding neural model for multimodal machine translation. *CoRR*, abs/1808.08266.

Translating Dislocations or Parentheticals: Investigating the Role of Prosodic Boundaries for Spoken Language Translation from French into English

Nicolas Ballier nicolas.ballier@u-paris.fr
Laboratoire de linguistique formelle/ CLILLAC-ARP, Université Paris Cité, Paris, F-75013, France

Behnoosh Namdarzadeh behnoosh.namdar@gmail.com
Maria Zimina-Poirot maria.zimina-poirot@u-paris.fr
CLILLAC-ARP, Université Paris Cité, Paris, F-75013, France

Jean-Baptiste Yunès jean-baptiste.yunes@u-paris.fr
IRIT, Department of Computational Science, Université Paris Cité, Paris, F-75013, France

Abstract

This paper examines some of the effects of prosodic boundaries on ASR outputs and Spoken Language Translations into English for two competing French structures (*"c'est"* dislocation vs. *"c'est"* parentheticals). One native speaker of French read 104 test sentences that were then submitted to two systems. We compared the outputs of two toolkits, SYSTRAN Pure Neural Server (SPNS9) (Crego et al., 2016) and Whisper. For SPNS9, we compared the translation of the text file used for the reading with the translation of the transcription generated through Vocapia ASR. We also tested the transcription engine for speech recognition uploading an MP3 file and used the same procedure for AI Whisper's Web-scale Supervised Pretraining for Speech Recognition system (Radford et al., 2022).
We reported WER for the transcription tasks and the BLEU scores for the different models. We evidenced the variability of the punctuation in the ASR outputs and discussed it in relation to the duration of the utterance. We discussed the effects of the prosodic boundaries. We described the status of the boundary in the speech-to-text systems, discussing the consequence for the neural machine translation of the rendering of the prosodic boundary by a comma, a full stop, or any other punctuation symbol. We used the reference transcript of the reading phase to compute the edit distance between the reference transcript and the ASR output. We also used textometric analyses with iTrameur (Fleury and Zimina, 2014) for insights into the errors that can be attributed to ASR or to Neural Machine translation.

Keywords: MT with speech recognition, quality estimation, toolkit comparison, prosodic boundaries, parentheticals, dislocations

Proceedings of Machine Translation Summit XIX, Vol. 2: Users Track, pages 119–131
September 4–8, 2023, Macau SAR, China.

1 Introduction

In French (Fagyal, 2002), as in different languages (Dehé and Kavalova, 2007), parentheticals have specific prosodic patterns. Several papers have shown the crucial role of prosodic boundaries for dislocations in French (Ashby, 1994; Buthke et al., 2010; Avanzi, 2012). We aimed to investigate the effect of prosodic boundaries and analyse whether the second prosodic boundary of the parenthetical was accurately translated and distinguished from the final rise of the left periphery dislocations. Our small-scale analysis compares a successive pipeline including VOCAPIA and SYSTRAN automated speech translation generated by SYSTRAN Pure Neural Server (SPNS9)[1] and a multitask multilingual pipeline using Whisper, an Automatic Speech Recognition (ASR) system trained on audio data for transcription and translation.

Speech technologies such as Automatic Speech Recognition were already coupled with automatic translation within Phrase-Based statistical Machine Translation (PBMT) (Reddy et al., 2007). As part of a more general project on error evaluation of ASR systems, ERA project (adVanced ERrors Analysis for speech recognition), ASR systems have been analysed in (Santiago et al., 2015). In a more pragmatically oriented paper, eight ASR platforms were assessed for accuracy and time-saving purposes on five documents from different fields of research in humanities (Tancoigne et al., 2022).

Preliminary investigations of chatGPT-3 for translation suggest a better performance (Hendy et al. (2023) and Jiao et al. (2023); other audio Large Language models have been built for speech recognition such as LXSR-53 large model Grosman (2021)). The Whisper paper describes its performance in relation to other systems such as mSLAM (Bapna et al. (2022)), a multilingual Speech and Language Model that learns cross-lingual cross-modal representations of speech, trained on LibriSpeech and other resources like a thousand hours of speech from Babel.

The rest of the paper is organised as follows: Section 2 details our experiments; Section 3 presents the results; Section 4 discusses them and outlines further research.

2 Materials and Methods

2.1 Challenge Set Recording

We adopted a challenge set approach (Isabelle et al., 2017), by recording challenging examples compiled and adapted from attested data. We used adapted data from the CFPP corpus, ie *le Corpus de Français Parlé Parisien* (Branca-Rosoff and Lefeuvre, 2016). Our dataset also includes examples from (Tellier and Valois, 2006) and (Blasco-Dulbecco, 1999) for reported examples of dislocations in spoken French. Our challenge test is aimed at evaluating whether the systems correctly process the dislocation or the parenthetical structures and the punctuation symbols used in their transcripts. Our challenge set is much more modest than previous work in the field, such as (Besacier et al., 2014). We have centered our analysis on the potential ambiguity between parentheticals and dislocations, having noticed that dislocation is a troublesome construction for neural machine translation systems Namdarzadeh and Ballier (2022) and that when the dislocation was properly translated in the DeepL outputs, it nevertheless could entail potential ambiguities with parentheticals. We also wanted to analyze the ability of the models to translate right and left dislocations, so that we replicated textbook examples using the same constituent either in right or left periphery. The overall assumption is in spoken data constructions that structure is even more used and may be consequently troublesome for neural machine translation, given its rarity in the training data. We did not resort to an anechoic chamber for our recordings but used a standard headset when recording over Zoom in a quiet office. We

[1]The service is available via the platform *Pure Neural Server – CLILLAC-ARP:* `https://plateformes.u-paris.fr`

Size	Parameters	Required VRAM	Relative speed
tiny	39 M	1 GB	32x
base	74 M	1 GB	16x
small	244 M	2 GB	6x
medium	769 M	5 GB	2x
large	1550 M	10 GB	1x
large-v2	1550 M	10? GB	1?x

Table 1: Whisper models tested for this experiment

voluntarily used a Zoom recording facility for a more ecologically valid acoustic environment. We included several types of ambiguities to gauge the impact of the detection of silent pauses.

Our dataset also includes examples from Tellier and Valois (2006) and (Blasco-Dulbecco, 1999) for reported examples of dislocations in spoken French. We did not test the sound file with the best sampling rates. We converted the mp4 file generated by Zoom into an mp3 file that was compatible with the Vocapia SPNS9 system. It should be noted that Whisper down-converts to lower sampling rates.

2.2 Parameters

We used the Huggging Face distribution of the models trained on multilingual data.[2] Table 1 sums up the number of parameters for each model size from `tiny` to `large` models. As indicated in Radford et al. (2022), the distinction between the `large` model and the largest model (`large-v2`) is not based on a difference in the number of parameters but rather on a fine-tuning of the large model. As reported in the appendix of the Whisper paper, French is the fifth language for hours of speech in the training data for speech recognition with 9,752 hours and the eighth for translation (4,481 hours of audio).

The data was processed on a server using an NVIDIA A100 GPU.[3] We measured our carbon fooootprint using the codecarbon **?**library (version 2.4.4), we used the 8 CPUs of an A100. 79s were required for the processing of our experiments and we reckon that it corresponds to an estimated total emission of 0.0002048757071268 g of CO_2.

2.3 Evaluation Metrics

We resorted to quantitative and qualitative analyses. With the Natural Language Toolkit (NLTK) library (Bird, 2006), we used BLEU score (Papineni et al., 2002) for the comparison based on our in-house translation dataset and Word Error Rate (WER) for the analysis of the discrepancies between the original script and the ASR transcriptions. As is well-known, WER is computed by adding substitutions (S), insertions (I), and deletions (D), divided by the N total words in the reference transcription, and multiplied by 100 as expressed in the formula (1).

$$WER = \frac{I + D + S}{N} X100(1)$$

We did not normalise the outputs in terms of capitals and punctuation, whereas Whisper has been tested using a normalisation procedure described in the appendix of the Whisper paper (Radford et al., 2022). To distinguish "innocuous differences in wording and genuine mistranscriptions", they used text normalisation to minimise the difference between strings like "ten thousand dollars" and "$10000".

[2]`https://huggingface.co/models?search=openai/whisper`
[3]`https://u-paris.fr/plateforme-paptan/`

3 Experiments and Results

Our analysis compares two translation pipelines for spoken data: ASR (Vocapia) then translation (SPNS9 MT engine) and audio LLM translation output from the speech signal with Whisper. In the Whisper output, the numbers of segments produced by the different models do not match for translation and transcription tasks, so that we can reasonably assume that the translation is not based on the transcription. We both resort to quantitative and to qualitative analyses. We report WER and BLEU scores for the different systems, analyse vocabulary growth curves for the data sets produced by different models and then discuss some characteristic phenomena, such as the use of punctuation marks ("." and ",") more qualitatively.

3.1 Quantitative Analysis of Translations and Transcriptions

Figure 1a sums up the results for the BLEU score and the effect of ASR errors that can be revealed when comparing the Vocapia ASR output to the SPNS9 translation which is based on the original transcript. The performance on translations for Whisper outputs needs to be related to the performance on the transcription task. It should be noted that not all the utterances we read were actually transcribed. This is why we realigned the translation outputs and, in the case of repetitions, we assumed the first occurrence was actually translated.

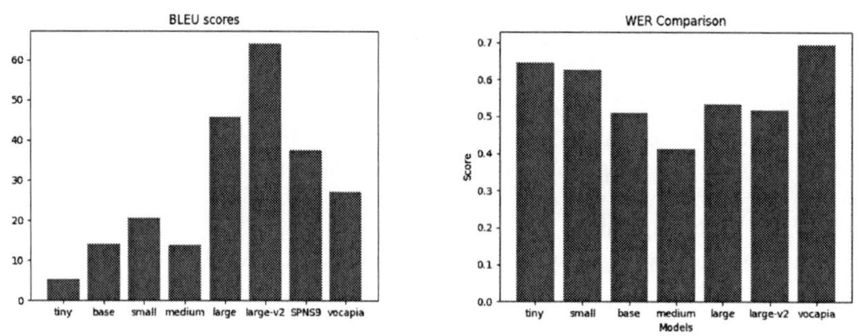

(a) BLEU scores (realigned output)

(b) WER scores (raw outputs)

Figure 1: Performance on translation (BLEU) and on transcription (WER)

We used the Python JIWER library to compute WER as shown in Figure 1b. The striking difference is the `medium` model does much better for transcription but not for translation.

3.2 Textometric Analysis

We used textometric analyses with iTrameur (Fleury and Zimina, 2014)[4] to compare raw translations of test models. Repeated segments computation (Lebart et al., 1997) might shed light on the automatic chunking produced by the machine to recognise text patterns and insert punctuation marks in translated output, as in the following lines produced by `small` model (segments with 10 or more repetitions in the test set output are underlined): *Comedian, he will always remain. Comedian, he will always remain. He was still a comedian. He was still a comedian. He was still a comedian.* One way to give an account of the textual production is to surmise that the machine tries to generate text chunks that are compatible with training data. It may as well be that the presence of these repeated segments is only the artefact of the somewhat artificial character of the textbook examples that are used in our data.

[4] `https://itrameur.clillac-arp.univ-paris-diderot.fr`

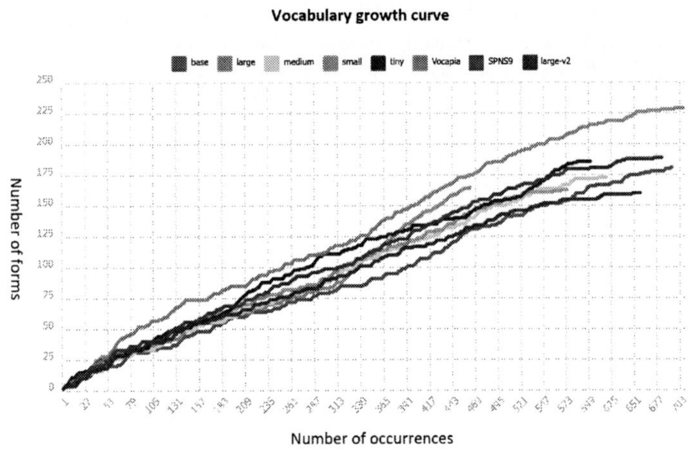

Figure 2: Vocabulary Growth Curves of the different models

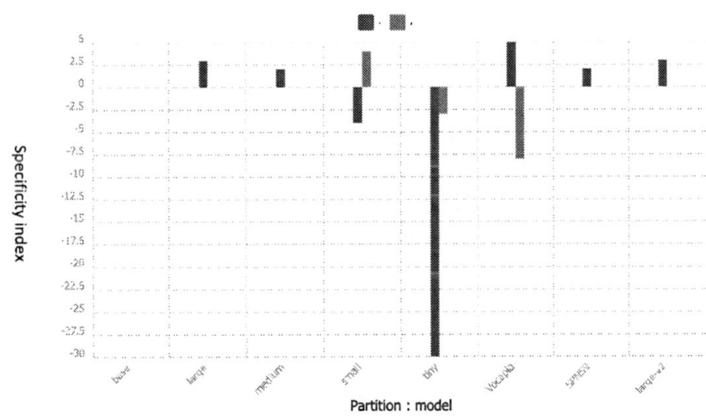

Figure 3: Characteristic elements: specificity of a full stop and a comma in raw translations

Exploring Vocabulary growth curves in Figure 2, one can notice that both output length (number of occurrences) and lexical diversity (number of different forms) are greater in the case of more "mature" models, such as `Vocapia`. The discrepancy shows that some tokens were misrecognised by "weaker" ASR models, such as `tiny`, hence the variability that can be observed here. From that point of view, the vocabulary growth analysis is a potential reflection of the errors that can be attributed to a specific ASR system: the difference between the Vocapia curve and the SPNS9 one corresponds to ASR-generated artefacts.

Figure 3 shows the results of characteristic elements computation of two punctuation marks (a comma "," and a full stop "."). For each model, the specificity index (Lebart et al. (1997)) reveals characteristic presence or absence of the two punctuation marks in the raw translations. For example, one can easily notice the absence of ``.") in the output of the `tiny` model (specificity index: -30), suggesting that the next token prediction on the basis of the transcribed data does not allow the model to identify the final stop. Conversely, the results presented on Figure 3 show that sentence boundaries are better transcribed by the `Vocapia`, `large` and `large-v2` models. At the same time, while the full stop is over-represented in the translation generated on the basis of the `Vocapia` transcription (specificity index: +5), clause boundaries isolated by commas are under-represented in this output (specificity idex: -8) revealing the presence of over-segmentation, for example: *I stayed there for a long time. In there. Do you know what he's doing.*

Thus, by studying the presence and absence of punctuation marks, it is possible to see the trough of the models, as for instance in the case of `tiny` and `small`, which often fail to produce translations in chunks of sentences.

3.3 Qualitative Insights

This sub-section attempts to characterise the observed behaviour of transcriptions/translations in particular the number of segments produced by each Whisper model. [5]

For the `large` model, it looks like some of the sentences that are repeated are not perceived as such, and a certain number of spoken utterances are reduced to only one sentence in the output. It remains to be seen whether a certain form of threshold for the duration between the different utterances can be observed. It may be the case that the distinction is not so much about pauses but about models. For example, the `small` model produces *"[...], free I never follow it at all[...]"* for *"libre, je ne le suis à peu près jamais"*, where the homonymous *"suis"* has been translated by *"follow it"* (in French: *"je le suis"*), which means that the sequence *"I am not"* was not related to the dislocated item *"libre"*. The absence of translation of the dislocation and the re-analysis of the sequence *"suis"* as being *"followed"* seems to prove that the dislocation was not perceived, perhaps due to the duration of the pause between the dislocated item *"libre"* and the corresponding predicate *"je ne le suis"*.

We then had to manually realign the different utterances to the corresponding sentences. We tried to keep the original punctuation of the model output so that many sentences ended with a comma where the original signal would have a full stop and a pause, a major boundary pause. The realignment process was not easy and guided with the original text that was used for the realisation of the sentences. For the `medium` model, the discrepancy between the transcription model output and the translation output is the most striking. The translation has 48 segments and the transcriptions have 102 segments. From the point of view of AI faithfulness, the `medium` model is pretty accurate in the translation of *libre, je ne le suis pratiquement jamais, free I'm almost never*, but the erasure or absence of reproduction of repetitions is also very striking. 56 sentences were omitted and the BLEU score would have been more degraded if the sentences were longer. We need to investigate whether the transcription output can duplicate the copied or repeated segments from the sound file, but do not include them in the translation output. It may be the case that the `medium` model might be the most efficient to suppress disfluencies, with the very unfortunate consequence that repeated segments get to be omitted in the transcription or at least in the translation. The `base` model gives examples of some absurd translations: with the use of Chinese character 465 and the translation "I asked him who's that pomm, he asked his poms you and asked the poms". Using a detached structure in the left periphery with a pause may trigger a phonological reanalysis in the left periphery of the dislocated constituent, this could account for the transcription of the sequence *danser,* as *dans ses* in the translation *In (=dans?) them (=ses??), she will do all her life.*

As reported in the Whisper paper, Named entity recognition (NER) still remains an issue: In French, the initial consonant for 'Chomsky' is realised as a voiceless fricative and not as an affricate, so that the closest transcription 'Jomski' (`large` model) fails to recognise the

[5]Data to be found on `https://github.com/nballier/NMT/tree/master/MTS2023`.

named entity. Interestingly enough, models have different transcriptions for this named entity: *je me skie* (`tiny`) *j'aime ce qui* (`base`), *James Key* (`medium`), *Jomski* (`large`) and *Jamsky* (`small/largev-2`). The tokens predicted for the translation of this named entity by the smaller models seem to correspond to a grammatical sequence, and models beyond the `small` one correspond to plausible proper nouns.

3.4 Punctuation and Prosodic Boundaries

Reference transcripts for the evaluation of Automatic Speech Recognition (ASR) usually imply removing punctuation (Matassoni et al., 2013) except apostrophes when normalising data before computing Word Error Rate (WER), sometimes reported as case-insensitive word error rates (Despres et al., 2013). For neural machine translation, a change in punctuation may entail on-the-fly modifications of the translation outputs on available on-line systems. Properly assigning punctuation symbols proves crucial for ASR systems and spoken language translation. Errors may entail linguistic ambiguity when prosodic boundaries help to recognise sentence structures such as dislocation (source: *"La traduction automatique neuronale, c'est impressionnant"* target: *"neural machine translation is impressive"*) and parentheticals (source: *"la traduction automatique neuronale, c'est vrai, est impressionnante"*, target: *"True, neural machine translation is impressive"*). In this context, when the autonomous parenthetical accent phrase is not perceived as parenthetical, the translation is *"neural machine translation is true"*.

4 Discussion

This experiment is really intended as a pilot study, we did not control for the effect of speech rate nor did we rely on inter-annotator agreement for the reference transcription TextGrid of the time stamps represented Figure 5.

4.1 Contextualisation

For a strict parentheticals versus dislocations comparison, as one of the reviewers suggested, we would need to report more information about the frequency of dislocations and parentheticals in the source language to judge impact more reliably. Taking reference treebanks as a proxy for integral corpus queries, we found that dislocations are more frequent than parentheticals : if we take the example of the CFPP Treebank, only 14 occurrences of parataxis (a more general label than just parentheticals) to be compared to 264 dislocations.

4.2 Time-Stamps in the Transcription Task

As described in the corresponding reference paper (Radford et al., 2022) Whisper uses text normalisation but little is known about the punctuation restoration task and how it fares on test datasets (Lerner et al., 2022): semi-columns are absent in the translation output dataset.

It may be an effect of the training data, and another feature of the training probably takes its toll, the segmentation into 30s windows. As described in the methodology of the Whisper systems "when a final transcript segment is only partially included in the current 30-second audio chunk, we predict only its start time token for the segment when in timestamp mode, to indicate that the subsequent decoding should be performed on an audio window aligned with that time, otherwise we truncate the audio to not include the segment." (Radford et al., 2022) That decision may explain why some of the timestamp boundaries in the SLT format often correspond to speech and not to pauses. In the figure describing the overview of the approach, the multitask training format does mention the timestamp tokens and their operationalizations as time-aligned transcription. Nevertheless, the variability across models of this time-aligned transcription is not reported in the Whisper paper. Admittedly, the emphasis of these generative pre-trained models is on generating texts but the generation of time stamps does not seem to have not been monitored so closely. Speech alignment is acknowledged to be potentially problematical above the 30 second window the models were trained with. The result is also a variability in the segmentation of speech. The same sound file produces different segmentations (and corresponding time stamps) across models for the translation and transcription task. Figure 4 recaps the effect of the size of the model on the number of segments for our data. Above the medium model, the intervals get bigger and segments are arbitrarily cut off as 2,3 or 5 second intervals, sometimes in the middle of the speech signal.

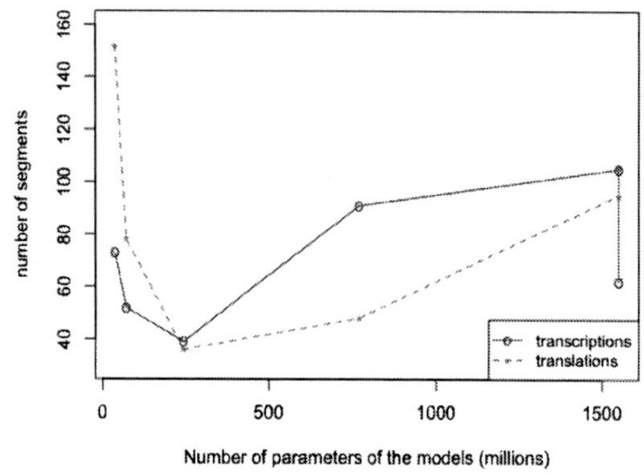

Figure 4: Variability of whisper segmentation across model size

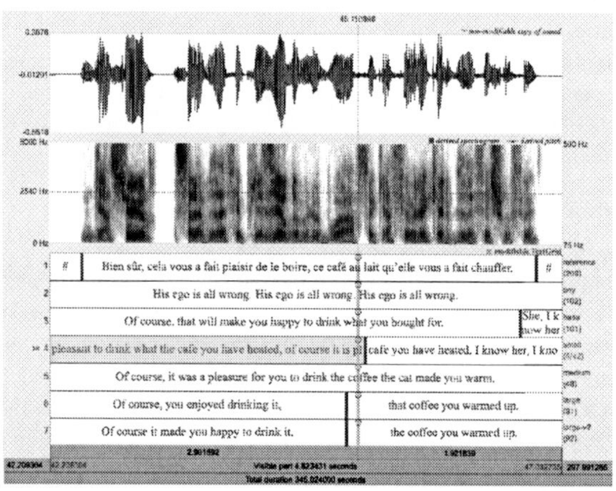

Figure 5: Variability of whisper segmentation of time intervals across models

Silence portions are sometimes used as left initial boundary signals. In other terms, the chunk speech is represented as beginning with a pause. We have used the SRT output of the whisper models to convert them into a Praat (Boersma and Weenink, 2023) TextGrid (the standard tool for phonetic analysis) and we have realigned the original sound file onto a Praat transcription. Figure 4 displays the waveform, the spectrogram of the speech signal and the corresponding read speech (reference) and the tiers below it represent the different segmentations of the same speech utterance contained in the time stamps in the .SRT file outputs of the different models. The reference tier shows the presence of boundaries corresponding to the speech pauses represented by hashtags and the absolute absence of them in the different time representation of the translations. One can see that a single French sentence might potentially correspond to several segments in the base transcription. The second interval in the `small` tier includes an overlap of two utterances, while the `large` tier splits the reference into two intervals/segments. The vertical lines correspond to the segments/intervals and, interestingly enough, one can see that for the `large` and `large-v2` models the dislocated item almost corresponds to the phonetic boundary in the original sound file (represented by the vertical lines that crosses tiers). The beginning of the phrase is actually beginning on the vertical line following the acoustic cues. The interval boundary proposed for the `small` model somewhat reflects the beginning of the signal whereas the `base` model has almost the initial silence as a cue for the beginning of the following intervals. This Praat representation is very representative of the mismatches between the different intervals produced with the different models for the translation task (but this is also true for the Whisper transcriptions). For each tier, under each name of the model is the number of intervals. For the upper reference tier, we have 104 utterances and 105 silent intervals. One can see the variability of the different numbers of segments that are produced to supposedly align with the signal. It is striking that a unique sound file should have so many different time representations of the corresponding speech, especially for the transcription task.

4.3 Further Research and Generalisability

More experiments are needed to address the same phenomenon and perform testing with variable phonological environments in order to determine for example whether the liaison as a cue is really taken by the model. It is also important to note that the sentences of the test set were read successively but were realised in isolation, no co-referential cues were available in the data, contrary to what would be found in continuous speech.

It may be the case that some Whisper models eliminate disfluencies, hence the absence of repeated segments. Again, disfluencies and repairs are much less frequent in the training data based on read books. We segmented the sound file into smaller sound files using `ffmpeg`. We investigated whether we obtained more consistent intervals on these re-cut files. We did not systematically investigate the role of the variability of the speech rate on the cut-off points for full stops or commas but we represent the variability of the speech rate (number of syllables duration) in our data as calculated by de Jong and Wempe algorithm (De Jong and Wempe, 2009). Figure 6 shows the variability of the speed of the different segments.

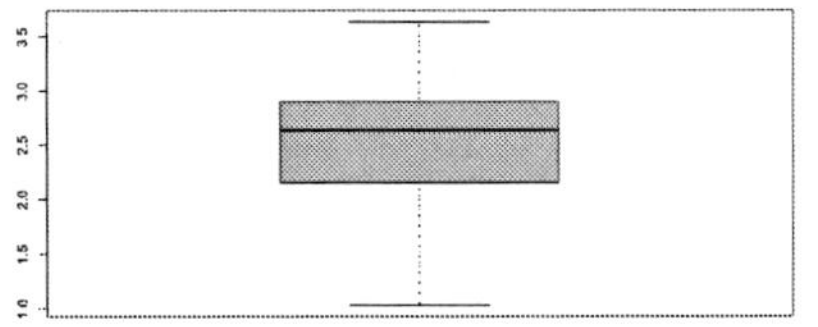

Figure 6: Variability of the speech rate (number of syllables per second) across utterances

As one of the reviewers wondered how portable the findings are to other language combinations, we replicated the experiments with a prototype dataset we designed for Persian (Namdarzadeh et al., 2022). We read it in the same recording conditions, but it should be noted that our test for Persian did not include repeated utterances with shorter pauses between the dislocated items and the predicate. We also read aloud the number of the utterance. From the point of view of transcriptions, we observed inconsistencies among different models of Whisper. In the case of `tiny`, `small`, and `medium` models, transcriptions are incomplete and they encountered difficulties in accurately identifying the correct graphic representation of a given phoneme in Persian, considering the possibility of several letters for the same sound. Furthermore, it should be noted that in the `tiny` model of Whisper, we observe a few Chinese and Spanish words. However, when it comes to `large` and `largev2` models, there are significant improvements. Although there may still be some instances of incorrect alphabet detection, these models outperform the previously mentioned models in terms of word detection. Regarding translations, the `tiny` and `small` models do not produce meaningful outputs as most of the lines are empty or lack proper translation. The `medium` model, while showing some progress, stops translating after a few translations that are not very accurate and then only focuses on translating the numbers recorded by the Persian speaker at the beginning of each sentence. In the case of the `large` and `largev2` models, there are notable improvements. However, there are still instances where the translated outputs failed to properly incorporate the dislocated item from the Persian source text. This suggests that there are some limitations in capturing the specific linguistic phenomenon of dislocation or understanding the intended meaning behind it.

Another generalisable aspect is the discrepancy between the time stamps reported in the .SRT files and the sound file. The use of linebreaks and commas can probably be generalised across languages but we will need to recode the end of line with or without punctuation symbols to analyze the frequency of the carrier return in transcriptions to investigate how it could be analysed to better understand how prosodic chunking is repressented in the whisper outputs.

5 Conclusion

In this paper, we compared the performance of different Whisper models for the translation task from French into English. We compared these multilingual models trained on multimodal data with SYSTRAN Pure Neural Server translations, generated from the transcribed text and from the Vocapia ASR output, and analysed the different translation outputs. Whisper large models and Vocapia fared better, but for Whisper some translations generated by smaller size models were more accurate for some sentences, including a better containment of the gender bias effect. For translations, the main finding is that the medium model does much better on the transcription task than for the translation task, probably because in our data the translation segment often corresponds to two utterances on the sound files. For the transcription task, the key finding is the apparent anarchic distribution of time stamps across models for the same speech signal.

More research is needed to better understand the time interval (mis)management of the Whisper transcriptions and translations encoded in the SRT file outputs. Should Whisper be used for the translations of subtitles, one may wonder about the absence of pauses in the time stamps. More research is needed to evaluate the potential architectural effect of the training of Whisper on 30s windows of speech.

Author contributions

Nicolas Ballier designed the study, developed the validation procedures with the speech signal and wrote the first draft of the manuscript. Behnoosh Namdarzadeh and Nicolas Ballier designed the test set and Nicolas Ballier recorded it. Maria Zimina-Poirot managed the test settings for Vocapia-SPNS9 translations and conducted textometric analysis of raw translation outputs for all test models. Jean-Baptiste Yunès implemented the JupyterHub, supervised some of the experiments and conducted impact measurements. All authors contributed to the analysis of the outputs.

Acknowledgements

We thank the four anonymous reviewers for their input on a preliminary version of this paper.

This publication has emanated from research supported in part by a 2021 research equipment grant (PAPTAN project)[6] from the Scientific Platforms and Equipment Committee, under the ANR grant (ANR-18-IDEX-0001, Financement IdEx Université de Paris).

Nicolas Ballier benefited from a CNRS research leave at LLF (Laboratoire de Linguistique Formelle), which is gratefully acknowledged.

References

Ashby, W. J. (1994). An acoustic profile of right-dislocations in French. *Journal of French Language Studies*, 4(2):127–145.

Avanzi, M. (2012). *L'Interface Prosodie Syntaxe en français : Dislocations, Incises et Asyndètes*. Peter Lang, Bruxelles.

Bapna, A., Cherry, C., Zhang, Y., Jia, Y., Johnson, M., Cheng, Y., Khanuja, S., Riesa, J., and Conneau, A. (2022). mSLAM: Massively multilingual joint pre-training for speech and text.

Besacier, L., Lecouteux, B., Luong, N. Q., Hour, K., and Hadjsalah, M. (2014). Word confidence estimation for speech translation. In *Proceedings of The International Workshop on Spoken Language Translation (IWSLT)*, Lake Tahoe, USA.

Bird, S. (2006). Nltk: the natural language toolkit. In *Proceedings of the COLING/ACL 2006 Interactive Presentation Sessions*, pages 69–72.

Blasco-Dulbecco, M. (1999). *Les dislocations en français contemporain. Etude syntaxique.* Honoré Champion, Paris.

Boersma, P. and Weenink, D. (2023). Praat: doing phonetics by computer [computer program]. version 6.3.10. *Retrieved May*, 3:2023.

Branca-Rosoff, S. and Lefeuvre, F. (2016). Le corpus de français parlé parisien des années 2000: Constitution, outils et analyses. le cas des interrogatives indirectes. *Corpus*, 15:265–284.

Buthke, C., Sichel-Bazin, R., and Meisenburg, T. (2010). Sujets disloqués vs. sujets doublés: À la recherche de la frontière prosodique. In *Journées PFC (Phonologie du Français Contemporain) Paris (Des normes à la périphérie). Journées PFC Paris, décembre 2010 :des normes à la périphérie.*

Crego, J., Kim, J., Klein, G., Rebollo, A., Yang, K., Senellart, J., Akhanov, E., Brunelle, P., Coquard, A., Deng, Y., et al. (2016). Systran's pure neural machine translation systems. *arXiv preprint arXiv:1610.05540*.

[6]Plateforme pour l'apprentissage profond pour la traduction automatique neuronale, in English: Deep Learning for Machine Translation at Universite Paris Cité. See the description of the platform on the project website: `https://u-paris.fr/plateforme-paptan`

De Jong, N. H. and Wempe, T. (2009). Praat script to detect syllable nuclei and measure speech rate automatically. *Behavior research methods*, 41(2):385–390.

Dehé, N. and Kavalova, Y. (2007). *Parentheticals*, volume 106. John Benjamins Publishing.

Despres, J., Lamel, L., Gauvain, J.-L., Vieru, B., Woehrling, C., Le, V. B., and Oparin, I. (2013). The vocapia research asr systems for evalita 2011. In *Evaluation of Natural Language and Speech Tools for Italian: International Workshop, EVALITA 2011, Rome, January 24-25, 2012, Revised Selected Papers*, pages 286–294. Springer.

Fagyal, Z. (2002). Prosodic boundaries in the vicinity of utterance-medial parentheticals in French. *Probus*, 14(1):93–111.

Fleury, S. and Zimina, M. (2014). Trameur: A framework for annotated text corpora exploration. In *Proceedings of COLING 2014, the 25th International Conference on Computational Linguistics: System Demonstrations*, pages 57–61.

Grosman, J. (2021). Fine-tuned XLSR-53 large model for speech recognition in English. `https://huggingface.co/jonatasgrosman/wav2vec2-large-xlsr-53-english`.

Hendy, A., Abdelrehim, M., Sharaf, A., Raunak, V., Gabr, M., Matsushita, H., Kim, Y. J., Afify, M., and Awadalla, H. H. (2023). How good are GPT models at machine translation? a comprehensive evaluation. *arXiv preprint arXiv:2302.09210*.

Isabelle, P., Cherry, C., and Foster, G. (2017). A challenge set approach to evaluating machine translation. *Proceedings of the 2017 Conference on Empirical Methods in Natural Language Processing*, pages 2486—-2496.

Jiao, W., Wang, W., Huang, J.-t., Wang, X., and Tu, Z. (2023). Is ChatGPT a good translator? a preliminary study. *arXiv preprint arXiv:2301.08745*.

Lebart, L., Salem, A., and Berry, L. (1997). *Exploring textual data*, volume 4. Springer Science & Business Media.

Lerner, P., Bergoënd, J., Guinaudeau, C., Bredin, H., Maurice, B., Lefevre, S., Bouteiller, M., Berhe, A., Galmant, L., Yin, R., and Barras, C. (2022). Bazinga! A Dataset for Multi-Party Dialogues Structuring. In *13th Conference on Language Resources and Evaluation (LREC 2022)*, pages 3434–3441, Marseille, France. European Language Resources Association (ELRA).

Matassoni, M., Brugnara, F., and Gretter, R. (2013). Evalita 2011: Automatic speech recognition large vocabulary transcription. In *Evaluation of Natural Language and Speech Tools for Italian: International Workshop, EVALITA 2011, Rome, January 24-25, 2012, Revised Selected Papers*, pages 274–285. Springer.

Namdarzadeh, B. and Ballier, N. (2022). The neural machine translation of dislocations. *ExLing 2022*, 28:127–131.

Namdarzadeh, B., Ballier, N., Wisniewski, G., Zhu, L., and Yunès, J.-B. (2022). Toward a test set of dislocations in persian for neural machine translation. In *The Third International Workshop on NLP Solutions for Under Resourced Languages (NSURL 2022)*, pages 14–21.

Papineni, K., Roukos, S., Ward, T., and Zhu, W.-J. (2002). Bleu: a method for automatic evaluation of machine translation. In *Proceedings of the 40th annual meeting of the Association for Computational Linguistics*, pages 311–318.

Radford, A., Kim, J. W., Xu, T., Brockman, G., McLeavey, C., and Sutskever, I. (2022). Robust speech recognition via large-scale weak supervision. *arXiv preprint arXiv:2212.04356*.

Reddy, A. M., Rose, R. C., and Désilets, A. (2007). Integration of ASR and machine translation models in a document translation task. In *INTERSPEECH*, pages 2457–2460.

Santiago, F., Dutrey, C., and Adda-Decker, M. (2015). Towards a typology of ASR errors via syntax-prosody mapping. In Adda, G., Mititelu, V. B., Mariani, J., and Vasilescu, D. T. . I., editors, *Errors by Humans and Machines in Multimedia, Multimodal and Multilingual Data Processing. Proceedings of ERRARE 2015*, pages 175–192. Editura Academiei Române.

Tancoigne, E., Corbellini, J. P., Deletraz, G., Gayraud, L., Ollinger, S., and Valero, D. (2022). Un mot pour un autre ? Analyse et comparaison de huit plateformes de transcription automatique. *Bulletin de Méthodologie Sociologique / Bulletin of Sociological Methodology*, 155(1):45 – 81.

Tellier, C. and Valois, D. (2006). *Constructions méconnues du français*. Presses Universitaires de Montréal.

Exploring Multilingual Pretrained Machine Translation Models for Interactive Translation

Ángel Navarro[1] annamar8@prhlt.upv.es
Francisco Casacuberta [1,2] fcn@prhlt.upv.es
[1]PRHLT, Universitat Politècnica de València, Spain,
[2]ValgrAI - Valencian Graduate School and Research Network for Artificial Intelligence, Camí de Vera s/n, 46022 Valencia, Spain

Abstract

Pre-trained large language models (LLM) constitute very important tools in many artificial intelligence applications. In this work, we explore the use of these models in interactive machine translation environments. In particular, we have chosen mBART (multilingual Bidirectional and Auto-Regressive Transformer) as one of these LLMs. The system enables users to refine the translation output interactively by providing feedback. The system utilizes a two-step process, where the NMT (Neural Machine Translation) model generates a preliminary translation in the first step, and the user performs one correction in the second step–repeating the process until the sentence is correctly translated. We assessed the performance of both mBART and the fine-tuned version by comparing them to a state-of-the-art machine translation model on a benchmark dataset regarding user effort, WSR (Word Stroke Ratio), and MAR (Mouse Action Ratio). The experimental results indicate that all the models performed comparably, suggesting that mBART is a viable option for an interactive machine translation environment, as it eliminates the need to train a model from scratch for this particular task. The implications of this finding extend to the development of new machine translation models for interactive environments, as it indicates that novel pre-trained models exhibit state-of-the-art performance in this domain, highlighting the potential benefits of adapting these models to specific needs.

1 Introduction

Machine translation (MT) has become an integral part of modern communication, facilitating cross-border communication and interaction among people from different linguistic backgrounds. However, the effectiveness of MT depends heavily on the quality of the translation models and the techniques used for training them. Recently, pre-trained multilingual MT models such as mBART (multilingual Bidirectional Auto-Regressive Transformer) (Liu et al., 2020), mT5 (Xue et al., 2020), and XLM (Lample and Conneau, 2019) have emerged as powerful tools that can achieve state-of-the-art performance on various benchmark datasets. Now, we can obtain high-quality translations for a specific task or domain by fine-tuning them with a not large training data, which is very effective in using them in low-resource settings.

However, even with the high performance of these pre-trained models, there are still challenges in achieving accurate and fluent translations for all languages and domains (Toral, 2020). Interactive machine translation (IMT), which combines human intelligence with MT, has been proposed as a potential solution to address these challenges and ensure consistently

Proceedings of Machine Translation Summit XIX, Vol. 2: Users Track, pages 132–142
September 4–8, 2023, Macau SAR, China.

high-quality translations (Peris et al., 2017). IMT systems allow users to actively participate in the translation process by providing feedback to the machine, which generates a new translation that corrects the previous error. This process repeats until the machine generates a perfect translation, and the user validates it.

In this paper, we explore the use of mBART in an IMT environment. We aim to investigate and compare the effectiveness of using a pre-trained model like mBART, which assesses state-of-the-art results in a large set of translation tasks, with models we train from scratch for a specific domain using the OpenNMT-py toolkit (Klein et al., 2017). To achieve this, we design and implement an IMT system with a prefix-based protocol (Foster et al., 1997) that integrates mBART. In this protocol, firstly described by Foster et al. (1997), further developed by Alabau et al. (2013); Barrachina et al. (2009); Langlais et al. (2000), the user only corrects at each iteration the first error that he finds from left to right. This process repeats until the user validates the machine-generated translation. We also fine-tune mBART to compare our results with the two versions of it, with and without the fine-tuning. To compare the different models, we use different evaluation metrics that help us evaluate the effort the user has to perform during the translation session. Our results showed that although the mBART models obtained higher quality translation than ours, the user effort results are similar. We need to fine-tune the mBART model on the specific domain to achieve a better effort reduction. In order to achieve optimal translation quality, our models should produce the most accurate translations possible on the initial attempt. However, when operating in an IMT environment, the model must adapt to user feedback. Based on our findings, it can be concluded that while pre-trained models generally achieve better translation quality, training a MT model from scratch for a specific domain can lead to better generalization, which produces significant benefits in this field.

Our work presents several contributions to the field of IMT. Specifically, our contributions are as follows:

- **Creation of an IMT system with mBART**: We have implemented an IMT system that uses as the principal MT model mBART. It uses a prefix-based protocol and forces the decoder to use the prefix that the user has validated.
- **Fine-Tune mBART**: The primary objective of our study is to investigate whether pre-trained models, known for achieving state-of-the-art results in translation tasks, can also perform well in the context of IMT. To conduct a more comprehensive experiment, we fine-tuned the model on a specific domain.
- **Compare IMT results with traditional techniques**: We compare and analyze the results obtained with the mBART models with ours, which have been trained from scratch. Our study evaluates the quality of translations and the level of user effort required during translation sessions.

The rest of the paper is organized as follows. In Section 2, we provide a brief overview of related work in pre-trained language models and IMT. Section 3 describes our proposed approach in detail, including the architecture of the IMT system and the feedback mechanism. In Section 4, we present the experimental framework, and in Section 5, we discuss the results obtained. Finally, we conclude the paper in Section 6 and discuss potential future directions for this research.

2 Related Work

In this work, our primary focus is to investigate whether pre-trained models, which have shown significant success in various tasks such as translation, can also be used effectively for IMT. Training a MT model from scratch for a specific domain can be time-consuming and challenging to obtain a suitable dataset. Therefore, evaluating whether pre-trained models can achieve similar results in this field as in MT tasks would be beneficial. Although MT and IMT tasks are similar, the goal of the first is to obtain the most accurate translation, while the second tries to obtain a perfect translation with minimal user interaction, so we need a model that can generalize well more than one that performs better translations.

This paper uses the multilingual pre-trained model mBART to compare its performance with our models trained from scratch for the specific task. There are other pre-trained multilingual models, such as mT5 (Xue et al., 2020), XLM, (Lample and Conneau, 2019) DeltaLM (Ma et al., 2021), or XGLM (Lin et al., 2021), that we could have used for our purpose. As we have used, other people are trying to use these models for new tasks that were not initially thought. Shen et al. (2021) used to resolve math word problems, Farahani et al. (2021) to summarize Persian texts, Chakrabarty et al. (2021) generated poetry with them, and Li et al. (2020) implemented it in the speech translation field.

Apart from pre-trained multilingual models, the advent of Large Language Models has prompted research into their utilization for specific tasks, including translation. These models have undergone extensive training on large-scale multilingual datasets, enabling them to capture linguistic patterns and translations across multiple languages (Scao et al., 2022; Hoffmann et al., 2022; Brown et al., 2020). In some scenarios, the translations produced by these models exhibit such remarkable quality that they pose a competitive challenge to the existing state-of-the-art translation models (Hendy et al., 2023; Zhang et al., 2023).

The task in which we have employed and compared mBART is that of IMT. This field has been under investigation since Foster et al. (1997), with the first appearance of the prefix approach, and has continued to evolve ever since. Numerous research branches have emerged, exploring different techniques to reduce human effort in translation. Domingo et al. (2017) proposed a fresh approach to the behavior of translators, transitioning from correcting at the prefix level to enabling the validation of multiple segments within a single translation. Other techniques aim to minimize human effort more directly, such as optimizing the utilization of user mouse actions (Navarro and Casacuberta, 2021b; Sanchis-Trilles et al., 2008) or implementing a confidence measurement system to provide an initial evaluation of the translation (Navarro and Casacuberta, 2021a; González-Rubio et al., 2010). Additional techniques take advantage of the ability of the IMT system to guarantee perfect translations, utilizing them to enhance the translation model through active and online learning techniques (Peris and Casacuberta, 2019, 2018; Rubio and Casacuberta, 2014). Some frameworks like Casmacat (Alabau et al., 2013) and TransType (Cubel et al., 2003) add a large set of these innovations in the same workplace. Commercial environments like *Lilt* and *Unbabel* can also use interactive machine translation.

In the upcoming section, we will explore the framework of prefix-based IMT, which will provide a deeper understanding of how we have tailored the mBART model for this specific task.

3 IMT Framework

First, it is essential to examine the neural machine translation (NMT) framework to elucidate the modifications undertaken to adapt it for IMT systems. The NMT framework, introduced by Castaño and Casacuberta (1997), has demonstrated its efficacy and power in recent years. Its impact and effectiveness have been widely recognized in the field of MT (Stahlberg, 2020; Klein et al., 2017). Given the sentence $x_1^J = x_1, ..., x_J$ from the source language X, to get the translation with the highest probability $\hat{y}_1^{\hat{I}} = \hat{y}_1, ..., \hat{y}_{\hat{I}}$ from the target language Y, the fundamental equation of the statistical approach to NMT would be:

$$\hat{y}_1^{\hat{I}} = \underset{I,y_1^I}{\arg\max}\ \Pr(y_1^I \mid x_1^J) = \underset{I,y_1^I}{\arg\max} \prod_{i=1}^{I} \Pr(y_i \mid y_1^{i-1}, x_1^J) \tag{1}$$

where $\Pr(y_i \mid y_1^{i-1}, x_1^J)$ is the probability distribution of the next word given the source sentence and the previous words. The distinguishing feature of the IMT framework lies in its utilization of human feedback as valuable information for determining the translation with the highest probability. In this framework, the professional users provide feedback when encountering the first error reviewing from left to right. When an error is identified at position p, the user moves the cursor to that position, producing the feedback $f_1^p = f_1, ..., f_p$, where f_1^{p-1} is the validated prefix, and f_p is the word that the user has typed to correct the error. The following equation adds this feedback to Equation 1 with two constraints that apply for the range of words $1 \leq i < p$:

$$\begin{aligned} \hat{y}_1^{\hat{I}} &= \underset{I,y_1^I}{\arg\max}\ \Pr(y_1^I \mid x_1^J, \bar{y}_1^{\bar{I}}, f_1^p) = \underset{I,y_1^I}{\arg\max} \prod_{i=1}^{I} \Pr(y_i \mid y_1^{i-1}, x_1^J, \bar{y}_1^{\bar{I}}, f_1^p) \\ \text{subject to} \quad & 1 \leq i < p \\ & f_i = y_i = \bar{y}_i \\ & f_p = y_p \neq \bar{y}_p \end{aligned} \tag{2}$$

where $\bar{y}_1^{\bar{I}} = \bar{y}_1, ..., \bar{y}_{\bar{I}}$ is the previous translation, f_1^p is the feedback provided by the user, which corresponds with the validated prefix with the new word typed, and p is the length of the feedback. With constrain $f_i = y_i = \bar{y}_i$, we assure that all the words before the error position, the validated prefix, are in the new translation, and with constrain $f_p = y_p \neq \bar{y}_p$, we force to use the new word typed by the user. As the user corrects and validates the translation from left to right, in a more general way, this equation generates the most probable suffix for the prefix provided.

We have implemented this framework to be compatible with models from both *OpenNMT-py* toolkit (Klein et al., 2017), which we trained from scratch, and HuggingFace library (Wolf et al., 2020), from where we obtained the mBART model checkpoint. We have developed an IMT system in which the translation model interacts with a simulated user to generate translations. The simulated user detects the first error by comparing the generated translation with the reference word-by-word. Section 4.4 of the paper describes the simulation process in more detail.

4 Experimental Framework

This section provides a comprehensive account of our experimental procedures, beginning with an overview of the evaluation metrics used to assess our proposal. We then describe the corpora utilized to train and test our models and outline the specific training procedures employed for our machine translation systems. Finally, we describe the user simulation process in detail.

4.1 Evaluation metrics

We made use of the following well-known metrics in order to assess our proposal:

Word stroke ratio (WSR) Tomás and Casacuberta (2006): measures the number of words typed by the user, normalized by the number of words in the final translation.

Mouse action ratio (MAR) Barrachina et al. (2009): measures the number of mouse actions made by the user, normalized by the number of characters in the final translation.

		Europarl		
		De–En	Es–En	Fr–En
Train	$\|S\|$	1.9M	2.0M	2.0M
	$\|T\|$	49.8M/52.3M	51.6M/49.2M	60.5M/54.5M
	$\|V\|$	394.6K/129.1K	422.6K/309.0K	160.0K/131.2K
Val.	$\|S\|$	3000	3003	3000
	$\|T\|$	63.5K/64.8K	69.5K/63.8K	73.7K/64.8K
	$\|V\|$	12.7K/9.7K	16.5K/14.3K	11.5K/9.7K
Test	$\|S\|$	2169	3000	1500
	$\|T\|$	44.1K/46.8K	62.0K/56.1K	29.9K/27.2K
	$\|V\|$	10.0K/8.1K	15.2K/13.3K	6.3K/5.6K

Table 1: Corpora statistics. K denotes thousands and M millions. $|S|$ stands for number of sentences, $|T|$ for number of tokens and $|V|$ for size of the vocabulary. **Fr** denotes French; **En**, English; **De**, German; and **Es**, Spanish.

Additionally, we assessed the initial translation quality of each system using:

Bilingual evaluation understudy (BLEU) Papineni et al. (2002): computes the geometric average of the modified n-gram precision, multiplied by a brevity factor that penalizes short sentences. In order to ensure consistent BLEU scores, we used *sacreBLEU* Post (2018) for computing this metric.

Translation error rate (TER) Snover et al. (2006): computes the number of word edit operations (insertion, substitution, deletion and swapping), normalized by the number of words in the final translation. It can be seen as a simplification of the user effort of correcting a translation hypothesis on a classical post-editing scenario.

4.2 Corpora

For our experiments, we utilized the Europarl corpus, which is a collection of proceedings from the Europarl Parliament. We used the training set to train our MT model and to fine-tune mBART. To validate and test the De–En and Fr–En models, we used WMT[1 2]'s's *news-test2013* and *news-test2015* datasets, respectively. For the Es–En models, we used *news-test2012* and *news-test2013* for validation and test purposes. It is worth noting that these datasets are commonly used in machine translation research and provide a benchmark for evaluating the performance of the models.

Table 1 shows the main features of the corpora.

4.3 Systems

Our system was built using the *OpenNMT-py* toolkit (Klein et al., 2017) and employed a Transformer architecture (Vaswani et al., 2017) that consisted of 6 layers, with all dimensions set to 512 except for the hidden Transformer feed-forward layer, which was set to 2048. We utilized 8 heads of Transformer self-attention, with 2 batches of words in a sequence to run the generator in parallel. A dropout of 0.1 was applied, and the optimization was carried out using Adam (Kingma and Ba, 2017) with a beta2 of 0.998, a learning rate of 2, and Noam learning rate decay with 8000 warm-up steps. We implemented label smoothing of 0.1 (Szegedy et al.,

[1]`http://www.statmt.org/wmt12/translation-task.html.`

[2]`http://www.statmt.org/wmt15/translation-task.html.`

SOURCE: El Estado de Indiana fue el primero en exigirlo.
TARGET: Indiana was the first State to impose such a requirement.

ITER-0	Translation hypothesis	Indiana was the sooner State to impose that condition.
ITER-1	Feedback	*Indiana was the* **first**
	Translation hypothesis	*Indiana was the first* State to impose such a condition.
ITER-2	Feedback	*State to impose such a* **requirement**
	Translation hypothesis	*Indiana was the first State to impose such a requirement.*
END	Final translation	*Indiana was the first State to impose such a requirement.*

Figure 1: Prefix-based IMT session to translate a sentence from Spanish to English. The process starts with the system offering an initial hypothesis. Then, at iteration 1, the user makes a word correction (**first**), validating the prefix *Indiana was the*. The system reacts to this feedback by generating a new translation hypothesis. Once more, the user reviews the hypothesis, making the word correction **requirement**, and updating the validated prefix *Indiana was the first State to impose such a*. Finally, since the next hypothesis is the desired translation, the process ends with the user accepting the translation. Overall, this process has a post-editing effort of 2 wordstrokes and 3 mouse actions.

2015) and used beam search with a beam size of 6. Finally, we applied joint byte pair encoding to all corpora, merging them using 32, 000 operations.

We utilized the *facebook/mbart-large-50-many-to-many-mmt*[3] checkpoint (Tang et al., 2020) from the Hugging Face library (Wolf et al., 2020), which employs a Seq2Seq Transformer architecture (Vaswani et al., 2017). The model consists of 12 encoder layers and 12 decoder layers, with a model dimension of 1024 and 16 heads. For customizing the mBART model to a specific pair of languages of our domain, we fine-tuned it on a single bi-text dataset from the training set of the corpora, calling this models mBART FT. During training, we inputted the source language into the encoder and used the decoder to decode the target language, resulting in a new model for each language pair. We conducted 100K training updates with a learning rate of $2e-5$ and a weight decay of 0.01 for training each model.

4.4 Simulation

To minimize the high time and economic costs associated with frequent human evaluations during the development stage, we opted to use simulated users to conduct the evaluations. Additionally, due to the novelty of our work, as it represents the first integration of mBART with an IMT system, we decided to perform the experiments in a more controlled environment with the simulation. These simulated users were tasked with generating translations from a given reference.

To conduct these evaluations, we utilized the prefix-based protocol described by Foster et al. (1997), in which the user identifies and corrects the leftmost incorrect word, validating all the previous words in the prefix up to the point of correction. In other words, the validated prefix consists of all the words before and including the corrected word.

We have opted for this prefix-based protocol to assess the effectiveness of the LLMs in an IMT system by its simplicity. The post-edition work is more in line with the segment-based protocol in which the corrections are made throughout the translation, focusing on the most incorrect words first. This protocol may introduce additional variables that may alter the intended demonstration of this paper, gauge the ability to recover from errors and generate a correct translation of the LLM, thereby examining their effectiveness in the context of interactive

[3] https://huggingface.co/facebook/mbart-large-50-many-to-many-mmt

translation. For this reason, as it helps us to isolate and evaluate the generative capacity of the LLMs, we have opted for the prefix-based protocol.

When the simulation begins, the system generates an initial hypothesis for the translation, which the simulated user then reviews. The user searches for the first error in the translation by comparing the words and their positions in the hypothesis with those in the reference. If the user identifies an error, they consult the reference to determine the correct word and provide it as feedback to the system. This feedback is entered into the system by performing a word stroke, and if the error position is not adjacent to the previous correction, a mouse action is also required. This process is repeated until the simulated user has successfully translated the entire sentence without any errors. The user performs a mouse action to validate the translation, indicating that the entire sentence has been correctly translated.

Figure 1 presents an example of the simulation performed to translate a source sentence. The translation session starts with the system generating an initial hypothesis that needs to be reviewed and corrected. Then, at iteration 1, the simulated user corrects the word *first* at the fourth position, validating all the previous words. With the feedback provided, the system generates a new hypothesis. At iteration 2, the simulated user corrects the word *requirement*, updating the validated prefix. This time the translation hypothesis that the system generates with the new feedback is correct, and the simulated user validates at the next iteration.

5 Results

In order to perform our comparison, we evaluated the three different models in a prefix-based IMT system. We aim to see a reduction in human effort when using the mBART models. In this case, we evaluate the human effort with two different metrics, the WSR, and the MAR, each evaluating a different kind of effort—the effort performed by typing the words and the one by moving the mouse. In order to achieve a more precise evaluation of the models, we will consider that the effort required to type a word exceeds that of moving the mouse. Furthermore, in a professional setting with real translators, there may be instances where mouse actions are performed using the keyboard, diminishing their implication.

Table 2 shows the experimental results, where the *OpenNMT-py* model trained from scratch is compared with mBART and mBART FT. The quality of the models in terms of TER and BLEU is included for each experiment to get a grasp of the quality of the initial hypothesis that the simulated users will translate interactively with the IMT system. The first observation that can be made when looking at the results is that the best MAR values were obtained in all experiments using the *OpenNMT-py* model. However, it is important to note that this happens while not consistently achieving the lowest WSR values due to the fact that the errors identified by the simulated user are contiguous, thereby eliminating the need for mouse movement to correct each subsequent error. This hypothesis is supported by the TER values obtained, which despite not producing translations of the highest quality in terms of BLEU, indicate that the translations generated need a lower number of word editing operations, suggesting that errors within a translation are grouped. This fact also means that the translations generated with the mBART models, while producing higher-quality translations, have their errors more distributed.

Regarding the effort derived from keyboard usage, evaluated through the WSR and assumed to be more important than mouse usage, the mBART models achieve the best results. Except for the En–De language pair experiment, the mBART FT model has successfully reduced the effort compared to our baseline model, suggesting that proper fine-tuning of mBART can yield better results in the field of interactive machine translation than training a model from scratch. It is also worth noting that when comparing the *OpenNMT-py* model with mBART, in cases where the target language was English, mBART achieved superior results without requiring fine-tuning. This fact aligns with the findings reported in Tang et al. (2020), where the best results were

Model	Language Pair	Translation Quality		User Effort	
		TER [↓]	BLEU [↑]	WSR [↓]	MAR [↓]
OpenNMT-py	De–En	60.91	20.67	38.5	**4.6**
	En–De	66.31	17.35	**34.9**	**4.2**
	Es–En	70.56	15.90	48.3	**4.8**
	En–Es	**57.05**	23.88	37.4	**4.3**
	Fr–En	**54.94**	25.83	37.3	**4.6**
	En–Fr	**55.33**	32.16	35.5	**4.1**
mBART	De–En	**58.55**	**31.69**	**35.2**	7.0
	En–De	65.50	27.56	37.6	6.5
	Es–En	65.82	**31.09**	38.5	6.8
	En–Es	64.27	**29.66**	39.3	6.8
	Fr–En	57.56	**34.17**	34.9	7.4
	En–Fr	62.40	24.90	40.2	8.1
mBART FT	De–En	60.49	30.49	36.7	5.8
	En–De	**64.94**	**27.92**	36.8	5.2
	Es–En	**61.14**	31.03	**36.3**	5.8
	En–Es	58.86	33.47	**35.3**	5.3
	Fr–En	57.67	34.00	**34.7**	5.8
	En–Fr	57.87	**40.07**	**30.7**	5.4

Table 2: Results of the *OpenNMT-py*, mBART, and mBART FT models in a prefix-based IMT system. All values are reported as percentages. Best results are denoted in bold.

achieved in the Many-to-One configuration when translating into English.

In summary, the best results in terms of WSR for reducing the human effort during interactive machine translation sessions in a prefix-based environment have been achieved using the mBART FT model, which has shown reductions in WSR of up to 5 points. This indicates that if maximum effort reduction is desired, fine-tuning the model to our specific domain is necessary. For tasks targeting the English language, the base mBART model has already demonstrated a reduction in human effort, suggesting that for such tasks, using the base mBART model may be more beneficial and efficient than training a model from scratch.

6 Conclusions and future work

In this study, we have compared the effectiveness of pretrained multilingual machine translation models with those we can train from scratch in the IMT field. Both models have achieved similar results, although mBART has excelled in language pairs where the target language is English. Furthermore, by fine-tuning the pretrained models in the specific domain, the reduction in human effort is further improved, surpassing our baseline model. This confirms that pretrained models can also yield good results in this field after adjusting the model for the specific domain. By performing fine-tuning instead of training a translation model from scratch, we can significantly reduce the computational cost associated with training. This approach allows us to achieve a competent model while minimizing computational resources.

Based on the obtained results, we can conclude that mBART with fine-tuning achieves better results in the field of IMT compared to training a model from scratch. As future work, it would be interesting to investigate whether other pretrained models, such as mT5, exhibit similar characteristics. Additionally, conducting a comparative analysis among these pretrained models would provide valuable insights.

Acknowledgements

This work received funding from *Generalitat Valencia* under the program *CIACIF/2021/292* and from *ValgrAI (Valencian Graduate School and Research Network for Artificial Intelligence)*. Work partially supported by grant PID2021-124719OB-I00 funded by MCIN/AEI/10.13039/501100011033 and by *European Regional Development Fund (ERDF)*.

References

Alabau, V., Bonk, R., Buck, C., Carl, M., Casacuberta, F., García-Martínez, M., González-Rubio, J., Koehn, P., Leiva, L., Mesa-Lao, B., et al. (2013). Casmacat: An open source workbench for advanced computer aided translation. *The Prague Bulletin of Mathematical Linguistics*, 100(1):101–112.

Barrachina, S., Bender, O., Casacuberta, F., Civera, J., Cubel, E., Khadivi, S., Lagarda, A., Ney, H., Tomás, J., Vidal, E., and Vilar, J.-M. (2009). Statistical approaches to computer-assisted translation. *Computational Linguistics*, 35(1):3–28.

Brown, T., Mann, B., Ryder, N., Subbiah, M., Kaplan, J. D., Dhariwal, P., Neelakantan, A., Shyam, P., Sastry, G., Askell, A., et al. (2020). Language models are few-shot learners. *Advances in neural information processing systems*, 33:1877–1901.

Castaño, A. and Casacuberta, F. (1997). A connectionist approach to machine translation. In *Fifth European Conference on Speech Communication and Technology*, pages 91–94.

Chakrabarty, T., Saakyan, A., and Muresan, S. (2021). Don't go far off: An empirical study on neural poetry translation. *arXiv preprint arXiv:2109.02972*.

Cubel, E., González, J., Lagarda, A., Casacuberta, F., Juan, A., and Vidal, E. (2003). Adapting finite-state translation to the transtype2 project. In *EAMT Workshop: Improving MT through other language technology tools: resources and tools for building MT*, pages 15–17, Budapest, Hungary. European Association for Machine Translation.

Domingo, M., Peris, Á., and Casacuberta, F. (2017). Segment-based interactive-predictive machine translation. *Machine Translation*, 31(4):163–185.

Farahani, M., Gharachorloo, M., and Manthouri, M. (2021). Leveraging parsbert and pretrained mt5 for persian abstractive text summarization. In *2021 26th International Computer Conference, Computer Society of Iran (CSICC)*, pages 1–6. IEEE.

Foster, G., Isabelle, P., and Plamondon, P. (1997). Target-text mediated interactive machine translation. *Machine Translation*, 12(1):175–194.

González-Rubio, J., Ortíz-Martínez, D., and Casacuberta, F. (2010). Balancing user effort and translation error in interactive machine translation via confidence measures. In *Proceedings of the Association for Computational Linguistics 2010 Conference Short Papers*, pages 173–177, Uppsala, Sweden. ACL.

Hendy, A., Abdelrehim, M., Sharaf, A., Raunak, V., Gabr, M., Matsushita, H., Kim, Y. J., Afify, M., and Awadalla, H. H. (2023). How good are gpt models at machine translation? a comprehensive evaluation. *arXiv preprint arXiv:2302.09210*.

Hoffmann, J., Borgeaud, S., Mensch, A., Buchatskaya, E., Cai, T., Rutherford, E., Casas, D. d. L., Hendricks, L. A., Welbl, J., Clark, A., et al. (2022). Training compute-optimal large language models. *arXiv preprint arXiv:2203.15556*.

Kingma, D. P. and Ba, J. (2017). Adam: A method for stochastic optimization. *arXiv preprint arXiv:1412.6980.*

Klein, G., Kim, Y., Deng, Y., Senellart, J., and Rush, A. (2017). OpenNMT: Open-source toolkit for neural machine translation. In *Proceedings of the Association for Computational Linguistics 2017, System Demonstrations*, pages 67–72, Vancouver, Canada. Association for Computational Linguistics.

Lample, G. and Conneau, A. (2019). Cross-lingual language model pretraining. *arXiv preprint arXiv:1901.07291.*

Langlais, P., Foster, G., and Lapalme, G. (2000). TransType: a computer-aided translation typing system. In *ANLP-NAACL 2000 Workshop: Embedded Machine Translation Systems*, pages 46–51.

Li, X., Wang, C., Tang, Y., Tran, C., Tang, Y., Pino, J., Baevski, A., Conneau, A., and Auli, M. (2020). Multilingual speech translation with efficient finetuning of pretrained models. *arXiv preprint arXiv:2010.12829.*

Lin, X. V., Mihaylov, T., Artetxe, M., Wang, T., Chen, S., Simig, D., Ott, M., Goyal, N., Bhosale, S., Du, J., et al. (2021). Few-shot learning with multilingual language models. *arXiv preprint arXiv:2112.10668.*

Liu, Y., Gu, J., Goyal, N., Li, X., Edunov, S., Ghazvininejad, M., Lewis, M., and Zettlemoyer, L. (2020). Multilingual denoising pre-training for neural machine translation. *Transactions of the Association for Computational Linguistics*, 8:726–742.

Ma, S., Dong, L., Huang, S., Zhang, D., Muzio, A., Singhal, S., Awadalla, H. H., Song, X., and Wei, F. (2021). Deltalm: Encoder-decoder pre-training for language generation and translation by augmenting pretrained multilingual encoders. *arXiv preprint arXiv:2106.13736.*

Navarro, Á. and Casacuberta, F. (2021a). Confidence Measures for Interactive Neural Machine Translation. In *Proceedings of the IberSPEECH 2021*, pages 195–199. IberSPEECH.

Navarro, Á. and Casacuberta, F. (2021b). Introducing mouse actions into interactive-predictive neural machine translation. In *Proceedings of the 18th Biennial Machine Translation Summit (Volume 1: Research Track)*, pages 270–281.

Papineni, K., Roukos, S., Ward, T., and Zhu, W.-J. (2002). Bleu: a method for automatic evaluation of machine translation. In *Proceedings of the 40th Annual Meeting of the Association for Computational Linguistics*, pages 311–318, Philadelphia, Pennsylvania, USA. ACL.

Peris, Á. and Casacuberta, F. (2018). Active learning for interactive neural machine translation of data streams. In *Proceedings of the 22nd Conference on Computational Natural Language Learning*, pages 151–160, Brussels, Belgium. ACL.

Peris, Á. and Casacuberta, F. (2019). Online learning for effort reduction in interactive neural machine translation. *Computer Speech & Language*, 58:98–126.

Peris, Á., Domingo, M., and Casacuberta, F. (2017). Interactive neural machine translation. *Computer Speech & Language*, 45:201–220.

Post, M. (2018). A call for clarity in reporting bleu scores. In *Proceedings of the Third Conference on Machine Translation*, pages 186–191.

Rubio, J. G. and Casacuberta, F. (2014). Cost-sensitive active learning for computer-assisted translation. *Pattern Recognition Letters*, 37:124–134. Partially Supervised Learning for Pattern Recognition.

Sanchis-Trilles, G., Ortíz-Martínez, D., Civera, J., Casacuberta, F., Vidal, E., and Hoang, H. (2008). Improving interactive machine translation via mouse actions. In *Proceedings of the 2008 Conference on Empirical Methods in Natural Language Processing*, pages 485–494, Honolulu, Hawaii. Association for Computational Linguistics.

Scao, T. L., Fan, A., Akiki, C., Pavlick, E., Ilić, S., Hesslow, D., Castagné, R., Luccioni, A. S., Yvon, F., Gallé, M., et al. (2022). Bloom: A 176b-parameter open-access multilingual language model. *arXiv preprint arXiv:2211.05100*.

Shen, J., Yin, Y., Li, L., Shang, L., Jiang, X., Zhang, M., and Liu, Q. (2021). Generate & rank: A multi-task framework for math word problems. *arXiv preprint arXiv:2109.03034*.

Snover, M., Dorr, B., Schwartz, R., Micciulla, L., and Makhoul, J. (2006). A study of translation edit rate with targeted human annotation. In *Proceedings of the 7th Conference of the Association for Machine Translation in the Americas: Technical Papers*, pages 223–231, Cambridge, Massachusetts, USA. AMTA.

Stahlberg, F. (2020). Neural machine translation: A review. *Journal of Artificial Intelligence Research*, 69:343–418.

Szegedy, C., Liu, W., Jia, Y., Sermanet, P., Reed, S., Anguelov, D., Erhan, D., Vanhoucke, V., and Rabinovich, A. (2015). Going deeper with convolutions. In *Proceedings of the IEEE Conference on Computer Vision and Pattern Recognition*, pages 1–9.

Tang, Y., Tran, C., Li, X., Chen, P.-J., Goyal, N., Chaudhary, V., Gu, J., and Fan, A. (2020). Multilingual translation with extensible multilingual pretraining and finetuning. *arXiv preprint arXiv:2008.00401*.

Tomás, J. and Casacuberta, F. (2006). Statistical phrase-based models for interactive computer-assisted translation. In *Proceedings of the COLING/ACL 2006 Main Conference Poster Sessions*, pages 835–841, Sydney, Australia. ACL.

Toral, A. (2020). Reassessing claims of human parity and super-human performance in machine translation at wmt 2019. In *Proceedings of the 22nd Annual Conference of the European Association for Machine Translation*, pages 185–194, Lisboa, Portugal. EAMT.

Vaswani, A., Shazeer, N., Parmar, N., Uszkoreit, J., Jones, L., Gomez, A. N., Kaiser, L., and Polosukhin, I. (2017). Attention is all you need. *arXiv preprint arXiv:1706.03762*.

Wolf, T., Debut, L., Sanh, V., Chaumond, J., Delangue, C., Moi, A., Cistac, P., Rault, T., Louf, R., Funtowicz, M., Davison, J., Shleifer, S., von Platen, P., Ma, C., Jernite, Y., Plu, J., Xu, C., Scao, T. L., Gugger, S., Drame, M., Lhoest, Q., and Rush, A. M. (2020). Transformers: State-of-the-art natural language processing. In *Proceedings of the 2020 Conference on Empirical Methods in Natural Language Processing: System Demonstrations*, pages 38–45, Online. Association for Computational Linguistics.

Xue, L., Constant, N., Roberts, A., Kale, M., Al-Rfou, R., Siddhant, A., Barua, A., and Raffel, C. (2020). mt5: A massively multilingual pre-trained text-to-text transformer. *arXiv preprint arXiv:2010.11934*.

Zhang, B., Haddow, B., and Birch, A. (2023). Prompting large language model for machine translation: A case study. *arXiv preprint arXiv:2301.07069*.

Machine Translation of Korean Statutes Examined from the Perspective of Quality and Productivity

jieun.lee@ewha.ac.kr
hyoeun.choi@ewha.ac.kr
Graduate School of Translation & Interpretation, Ewha Womans University, Seoul, 03760, ROK

Abstract

Because machine translation (MT) still falls short of human parity, human intervention is needed to ensure quality translation. The existing literature indicates that machine translation post-editing (MTPE) generally enhances translation productivity, but the question of quality remains for domain-specific texts (e.g. Aranberri et al., 2014; Jia et al., 2022; Kim et al., 2019; Lee, 2021a,b). Although legal translation is considered as one of the most complex specialist translation domains, because of the demand surge for legal translation, MT has been utilized to some extent for documents of less importance (Roberts, 2022). Given that little research has examined the productivity and quality of MT and MTPE in Korean-English legal translation, we sought to examine the productivity and quality of MT and MTPE of Korean of statutes, using DeepL, a neural machine translation engine which has recently started the Korean language service. This paper presents the preliminary findings from a research project that investigated DeepL MT quality and the quality and productivity of MTPE outputs and human translations by seven professional translators.

1. Introduction

Human intervention, namely post-editing, is needed to ensure quality translation when machine translation (MT) is used. The existing literature indicates that compared to from-scratch translation, namely human translation (HT), machine translation post-editing (MTPE) enhances translation productivity, but the question of domain-specific MT and MTPE quality still remains to be answered (Aranberri et al., 2014; Jia et al., 2022; Kim et al., 2019; Lee, 2021a). In the case of patent translation, MT quality is still less than adequate (Choi et al., 2023; Lee and Choi, 2022; Tsai 2017) and MTPE may not be efficient to produce HT quality output. Legal translation is also considered as a specialist domain, but facing the demand surge for legal translation, the translation industry and the language service providers have resorted to MT for documents of less importance (Roberts, 2022). However, translation of legal texts, such as statutes and contracts, requires accuracy and generally been reserved for HT. Therefore, MTPE can be effective only when MT quality is good enough, thus not needing heavy post-editing. Otherwise, it would be simply more time-consuming and inefficient to post-edit

Proceedings of Machine Translation Summit XIX, Vol. 2: Users Track, pages 143–151
September 4–8, 2023, Macau SAR, China.

inadequate MT than translate from scratch. Given that little research has examined the productivity and quality of legal translation via MTPE, this paper aims to examine the performance of a general use neural machine translation (NMT) engine, DeepL, and MTPE productivity and quality of Korean statutes in comparison with HT.

The quality of post-editing results may vary depending on the ability, text type, and difficulty level, such as post-editor's experience in translation and post-editing training, native language, and subject knowledge (Kim, 2022b; Lee, 2021a; Seo and Kim, 2020). As such, it may be argued that translation competence is a necessary condition for post-editing competence (Lee, 2021b: 190). Because previous research on MTPE often engaged student translators rather than professional translators or post-editors, who were likely to lack translation and post-editing experiences and skills, we will examine professional translators' HT and MTPE products from the perspective of productivity and quality to find out if legal translation based on MTPE can be a productive alternative without sacrificing quality.

Productivity is not just a matter of time, and the effort required for post-editing can be analyzed in terms of technical, temporal, and cognitive efforts (Krings, 2001; Snover et al., 2006). Technical effort refers to the frequency and amount of correction, whereas temporal effort refers to the time required for task completion, and cognitive effort means the effort required to identify and correct errors in MT (Krings, 2001). Translation Edit Rate (TER) is often used to measure technical effort, such as inserting, deleting, replacing, and moving. However, it can only infer productivity through the modification rate, and thus not an absolute indicator of productivity. Further, because HT cannot calculate TER, it cannot be directly compared with HT (Snover et al., 2006). Although MTPE appears to have similar quality and improved productivity compared to HT, some studies suggest that it requires more cognitive effort than from-scratch translation (Guerberof Arenas, 2020: 347; Krings, 2001: 320; O'Brien, 2017). It is said that the cognitive load is large in correcting syntax problems, word order, mistranslation, and idiomatic mistranslations (Daems et al., 2015, 2017; Teminkova, 2010; Popović et al., 2014). In the following section, we will review the relevant literature, focusing on MT and MTPE involving the Korean language and legal texts.

2. Literature Review

2.1. MTPE studies

Recent MTPE studies generally indicate that MTPE is superior to HT in terms of speed while maintaining similar translation quality (Cadwell et al., 2016; Guerberof Arenas, 2009; Kim et al., 2019; Kim, 2022a,b; Lee and Kim, 2022; Seo and Kim, 2020). Jia et al. (2019) compared and analyzed the results of HT and Google NMT post-editing for two types of text in the English-Chinese direction. They investigated 30 postgraduate translation students' translation and MTPE processes and output quality, using two types of texts— two in specific fields such as patient description materials and dishwasher manuals, and the other two general texts (beverage brand promotion brochures). They noted that for the domain-specific texts, the participants completed MTPE a little faster than HT, and that cognitive efforts decreased in MTPE of both domain-specific and general text types. As for quality, MTPE output quality showed an equal level of accuracy and fluency as HT. In Jia et al. (2019), four evaluators—two professional translators and two Ph.D. students majoring in translation—evaluated a total of 154 sentences. The quality in terms of accuracy was as follows: The average score of the domain-specific text MT was 2.76, 3.2 for MTPE results, and 3.29 for HT, revealing statistically significant differences between the different modes of translation (Jia et al., 2019: 74). In the case of general texts, the difference in evaluation scores was narrower, with post-editing averaging at 3.19 and HT at 3.16, slightly lower than MTPE. Regarding fluency, the domain-specific text MT result scored an average of 2.88, MTPE result was significantly higher at 3.25, and HT was the highest at 3.31. On the other hand, in the case of general texts, the results of HT and PE were 3.19 and 3.33, respectively, showing no statistically significant difference.

MTPE studies involving Korean also demonstrated that MTPE was productive compared to HT. Kim et al. (2019) looked at the time effort required for correction along with the correction rate as an index of productivity. They examined the productivity of light post-editing of the English-Korean MT generated by three general-use NMT engines, namely Google Translate, Papago and Kakao*i*. The participants translated and post-edited without a time limit, and worked on IT manuals, which apparently has contributed to the enhancement of productivity. Based on the number of processed words per minute in HT and MTPE, MTPE productivity increased at least 78% higher than HT, and the Translation Edit Rate (TER) was 3% for Google NMT, 5.9% for Papago, and 5.4% for Kakao*i* (Kim et al., 2019: 65). Except for Kim et al. (2019), the other Korean MTPE studies investigated full post-editing.

Lee and Lee (2021) compared the quality of Korean-English news text MTPE and HT by undergraduate translation students, and found that the productivity as well as the quality of MTPE was better than those of HT. Lee (2021a) examined the difference between HT and MTPE productivity and cognitive processes by having five professional translators translate and post-edit technical texts (IT manuals) in the Korean-English direction. The participants translated around 100 word-long texts in two ways, HT and MTPE, in 10-minute-time frames, respectively, which were subject to evaluation by two experts. He noted that MTPE productivity was higher than HT productivity in terms of task completion time, and that despite individual variations, MTPE quality was not inferior to that of HT. Another study by Lee (2021b), which was based on nine translators' HT and MTPE, confirmed approximately 34% increase of MTPE productivity measured in terms of time, compared to HT. Both Lee (2021a,b) also demonstrated that the MTPE output quality was not inferior to HT in the case of technical texts.

Kim (2022a) also confirmed MTPE's productivity by analyzing Korean-English HT and MTPE outputs provided by 13 postgraduate translation students, comparing technical effort and search effort. She analyzed the English translation of Korean economic text of 76 words for HT and MTPE of 360 word-long economic text generated by Google NMT.

Lee and Kim (2022) analyzed the quality and productivity of English-Korean MTPE based on TER, word throughput, and output quality evaluation. Fourteen undergraduate and graduate students, who had received PE training through regular university courses or special lectures, participated in their research. The task completion time for HT or post-editing was set to 20 minutes (Lee and Kim, 2022: 128-129). Similarly, MTPE demonstrated a productivity advantage of nearly 70% compared to HT, comparable to the productivity of light post-editing in their earlier work (Kim et al., 2019). In addition, the quality of the post-editing results was not inferior to that of HT (Lee and Kim, 2022: 134, 140).

In summary, the existing Korean MTPE productivity-related research pointed to an average of more than 30% productivity enhancement compared to HT. However, the texts used in the previous research were mainly manuals, news and economic texts. Few Korean researchers investigated MT or MTPE of legal texts. In this paper, we will present the preliminary findings from our research on the Korean-English MT and MTPE, focusing on the temporal and technical efforts as productivity indicators, and the output quality relative to HT.

2.2. Legal Text MTPE

There is a lacuna in the literature on MTPE of legal texts, particularly in Korean and English language combinations. When it comes to English and Spanish, Killman and Rodríguez-Castro

(2022) analyzed 26 translators' from-scratch translations of English-Spanish legal texts and their Google Translate (SMT) post-editing. They reported that post-editing was superior in quality and productivity. The found that MTPE reduced time by 16%, with an average of 56.6 minutes for MTPE and 67.1 minutes for HT. Human evaluations revealed that MTPE contained fewer translation errors, with an average of 14.5 errors, whereas HT contained an average of 22.9 errors (Killman and Rodríguez-Castro, 2022: 63). The results did not indicate that the participants' translation experience and translation training made any significant difference in quality and time.

There are few studies that investigated MT or MTPE of Korean legal texts. For instance, Lee (2022) undertook an evaluation of Korean-English contract MTs produced by Google NMT and a legal domain-specific NMT. He found that the domain-specific NMT produced a better quality output than the generic NMT. While Lee (2022) examined MT quality of Korean-English contract translation, Lee and Choi (2023) examined the quality of English translations of Korean statutes generated by three NMT engines. They analyzed the output quality of two general-use NMT engines, Papago and Google Translate, and a legal domain-specific NTM engine, Otran, drawing on human and automatic evaluations. Four experienced legal translators evaluated the output quality, using a five-point rating scale—0 to 4—based the criteria of accuracy, fluency, and terminology. The human evaluation resulted in an average of 2.8 for Google NMT and Papago, and 3.5 for Otran (Lee and Choi, 2023:83). BLEU score for each NMT recorded 0.421, 0.395 and 0.585 (Lee and Choi, 2023: 82). As the figures suggest, the legal domain-specific NMT outperformed the other two generic NMT engines in both human and automatic evaluations. However, there was still a substantial gap between HT and MT, requiring human intervention in order to produce legal translation of publishable quality.

Considering that the largest Korean government-funded legal translation service provider, Korean Legal Research Institute's Translation Center, has sought to improve the efficiency and quality of its legal translation services by introducing computer-assisted-translation and translation automation (Lee, 2021), the current research is expected to throw some light on the prospect of MTPE in the legal translation domain from the perspective of productivity and quality. Further, DeepL recently launched its Korean language services in 2023, and merits scholarly investigation of its performance in the legal domain. Against this backdrop, this paper aims to investigate the DeepL Korean-English legal MT quality and the MTPE productivity and quality in comparison with HT.

3. The Study

The current research was designed to answer the folllowing research questions:

1. What is the quality of DeepL Korean-English legal translation according to human and automatic evaluations?
2. What is the quality of DeepL MTPE and HT according to human evaluation?
3. What is the productivity of MTPE in comparison with HT in terms of temporal and technical efforts?

3.1. Research Methods

For this study, we used extracts from two Korean statutes for source texts. Text 1 (241 Korean words/21 segments) was extracted from the Act on the Punishment of Stalking Crimes and was used for HT. Text 2 (242 Korean words/24 segnents) from the Act on Registration and Inspection of Water Leisure Devices was translated by DeepL and the MT output was post-edited by seven professional translators. The text difficulty was about the same in terms of readability (Flesch Kincaid Score was 31.04 and 24.42 respectively) and lexical density (52.33 and 57.93 respectively).

We recruited seven professional translators who had at least three years' experience in legal translation after a MA in Translation. The participants were requested to translate one text from scratch and post-edit the other to produce a HT quality output referring to the translation and post-editing guidelines we had provided. They were given 90 minutes each for HT and MTPE with 10 minutes' break in between. We measured their translation and post-editing time and calculated the words per minute for productivity analysis, and analysed the evaluation results and errors analyses provided by evaluators, who had assessed the MTPE and HT outputs according to the evaluation criteria of accuracy, fluency, and terminology.

We engaged three evaluators, two veteran professional legal translators and a translator trainer who are familiar with MTPE. They were requested to evaluate not only the raw MT output but also the seven HT outputs of Text 1 and seven MTPE outputs of Text 2, using a five-point rating scale (zero to four points), and also annotate errors.

To assess the MT quality through automatic evaluation, we checked the BLEU score of DeepL MT output.

3.2. Results

Both human and automatic evaluations revealed that DeepL MT quality was not bad. The raw MT output received an average of 3.15 points (segment average scores) in human evaluation, and the BLEU score recorded 29.92.[1] As requested, the evaluators identified errors in MT, MTPE and HT outputs. Twenty six errors were identified in the raw MT output by at least two of the three evaluators (68 out of 450 English words), giving a TER score of 15.1%.

Regarding the text difficulty level, the translator participants considered both texts not too easy nor too difficult for legal translation. There was a consensus among the participants. However, there was some disagreement among the evaluators because they agreed on the medium difficulty level of Text 1, but they were divided in their opinion on Text 2, each selecting high, medium, and low difficulty.

Participant	HT (min.)	MTPE (min.)	HT word/min.	MTPE word/min.	Productivity growth (%)
P1	90	90	2.7	2.7	0
P2	80	74	3.0	3.3	9
P3	80	53	3.0	4.6	52
P4	59	47	4.1	5.2	26
P5	65	65	3.7	3.7	0
P6	83	52	2.9	4.7	60
P7	90	90	2.7	2.7	0
Average	**78.1**	**57.3**	**3.2**	**3.8**	**21**

Table 1. Comparison of HT and MTPE productivity

In terms of temporal productivity, as Table 1 shows, the seven participants (P1 to P7) tended to spend less time on post-editing than on from scratch translation, HT. The average time they spent on MTPE recorded 57.3 minutes whereas the average time spent on HT was 78.1 minutes. A t-test revealed a statistically significant differences at the 90% confidence level ($p<0.1$). As shown in Table 1, the number of words processed during MTPE was higher

[1] The results indicated that DeepL outperformed other general-use NMTs, such as Google Translate and Papago, but its performance was inferior to that of a domain-specific NMT, Otran in Korean-English legal translations (see Lee and Choi, 2023).

than that of HT, confirming enhanced productivity observed in the MTPE research discussed in this paper (e.g. Kim, 2022a,b; Kim et al., 2019; Lee and Kim, 2022). The average productivity growth of 21% in legal MTPE is smaller than the average productivity of MTPE of non-legal texts in these previous studies involving non-legal texts, which hovered above 30% on average. Therefore, it may be argued that MTPE productivity is better than HT in general, but legal MTPE productivity may not be as good as other text types'. Further, individual differences were quite large as shown in Table 1. It may be partly due to the fact that the participants were allowed to spend up to 90 minutes for each task and were encouraged to work at a normal speed to avoid affecting participants' translating and post-editing behaviour. Therefore, individual differences might have affected the temporal aspect of task completion. Some participants were observed to have completed the task early and spend the rest of the time reviewing their work, spending 90 minutes for each task to the full extent.

Participant	Number of edited words	TER
P1	128	0.28
P2	100	0.22
P3	132	0.29
P4	105	0.23
P5	84	0.19
P6	76	0.17
P7	125	0.28
Average	**107.14**	**0.24**

Table 2. TER of MTPE Results

As for MTPE technical productivity, TER of each MTPE output was calculated. Based on Snover et al. (2006), we counted insertion, deletion, substitution, and shift in each of the seven MTPE results by using JavaScript. As shown in Table 2, the average TER was 0.237, which means that 23.7% of MT were edited on average. According to Kim et al. (2019: 65), TER of light post-editing was recorded 3% whereas the average TER of full post-editing involing Korean was 0.230 (Lee and Kim, 2002 : 135). As such, our TER results suggest that the seven participants' MTPE was carried out on a full post-editing scale. However, TER and MTPE time did not tend to correlate. For example, P3 edited the largest number of words, while spending only 53 minutes in MTPE. In other words, more editing does not always mean more post-editing time, which was also observed in Lee and Kim (2022 : 135). Meanwhile, P3's correction rate was lower than the other participants' as shown in Table 5, so processed words may not always be considered as an indicator of MTPE quality either.

In addition to productivity, we compared the quality of HT and MTPE products through human evaluation by three evaluators (E1 to E3). The evaluation results and the average scores for each participant are presented below (see Table 3 and Table 4). In summary, MTPE quality measured in terms of the segment average scores surpassed HT quality. As shown in Table 4, the MTPE scores for each participant exceeded HT scores except on two occasions (E3-P2 & E1-P5). The average MTPE evaluation scores also indicated superior quality (see Table 4).

	E1		**E2**		**E3**	
	HT	**MTPE**	**HT**	**MTPE**	**HT**	**MTPE**
P1	2.52	3.50	3.04	3.88	3.62	3.79
P2	3.57	3.79	3.29	3.88	3.81	3.38
P3	3.05	3.25	3.17	3.79	3.57	3.83

P4	3.76	3.75	3.33	3.83	3.48	3.88
P5	3.67	3.54	3.46	3.79	3.48	3.71
P6	3.29	3.63	3.29	3.88	3.67	3.75
P7	3.05	3.67	3.00	3.71	3.67	3.58

Table 3. HT and MT Quality (Segment Average Scores)

AVE	**P1**	**P2**	**P3**	**P4**	**P5**	**P6**	**P7**
HT	3.06	3.56	3.26	3.52	3.54	3.42	3.24
MTPE	3.72	3.68	3.62	3.82	3.68	3.75	3.65

Table 4. HT and MT Average Scores

The inter-rater agreement in HT quality evaluation was stronger than MT quality evaluation. 95% confidence interval (CI) of interclass correlation coefficient (ICC) for HT evaluation was 0.289 to 0.907 (ICC = 0.720) with a p-value of 0.004. The results suggest that the quality of the post-edited legal texts was not inferior to that of HT, but there was a lack of consensus on the MTPE output quality among the three evaluators.

In terms of the average segment scores, the raw MT output was rated 3.15. Compared with the seven participants' HT and MTPE average scores, MT quality was perceived to be worse than HT except for P1, whereas all the seven MTPE outputs got much higher average points than the raw MT output (see Table 4). That means, DeepL's Korean-English statute MT was inferior to HT, and MTPE could improve the result, largely better than HT, in a time-efficient manner.

Correction rates[2] also demonstrated MTPE quality improvement over the MT output. As shown in Table 5, most of the 26 errors identified by the evaluators were corrected by the seven participants. Except for P3, the other six participants corrected 23-26 out of the total 26 errors, which resulted in an average correction rate of 89.61%. The high correction rate led to higher MTPE average segment scores than the raw MT average segment scores, meaning that post-editing did enhance MT quality.

	P1	**P2**	**P3**	**P4**	**P5**	**P6**	**P7**	**AVE**
Number of errors corrected	26	24	18	24	24	24	23	23.28
Correction rate (%)	100	92.30	69.23	92.30	92.30	92.30	88.46	89.61

Table 5. Number of Corrected Errors and Correction Rates

4. Conclusion

This paper investigated the quality and productivity of MT of legal texts based on DeepL Korean-English MT of statutes. In addition to raw MT output quality, we examined the productivity and quality of HT and MTPE outputs produced by seven professional translators. The BLEU score indicated 29.92, which was not that high, but the MTPE results suggested that the raw MT was good enough to produce publishable quality through post-editing.

[2] In this study, the correction rate refers to the ratio of post-editors' corrections to the errors identified in the raw MT (Kim 2022b).

To examine the productivity of MTPE, we analyzed temporal productivity and technical productivity (TER). The participants tended to spend significantly less time post-editing (57.29 minutes) than translating from scratch (78.14 minutes). The average productivity growth of 21% appears to be smaller than the average productivity of MTPE of non-legal texts in the previous studies. Still, it may be argued that MTPE productivity is better than HT in legal texts, too. As for technical productivity, the average TER was 0.237, which means that an average of 23.7% of MT were edited. However, TER and MTPE time did not tend to correlate.

The overall MTPE quality measured in terms of the segment average scores was superior to HT quality evaluation scores. Regarding the correction rate, most of the errors identified by the evaluators were corrected during MTPE with an average correction rate of 89.61%. As a result, the MTPE outputs got higher points than the original MT output.

Based on the results, it may be argued that for statute translation, MTPE tends to be more productive than HT in terms of task time and number of processed words, and that professionals' MTPE process enhanced MT quality to human parity. All of the seven participants got higher points for MTPE than HT, which pointed to the better quality of MTPE than HT. Nonetheless, the two texts used for this study were not identical, and due to the small sample size, it is impossible to generalize the current research findings. Despite its limitations, however, the findings suggest that in Korean-English legal statute translation, MTPE by professional translators may be more productive and of better quality than translation from scratch. Further research is needed to investigate the merits of MTPE of legal texts in comparison with HT and to explore the cognitive effort involved in MTPE of legal texts.

References

Aranberri, N., Labaka, G., Diaz de Illaraza, A. and Sarasola, K. (2014). Comparison of post-editing productivity between professional translators and lay users. In *Proceedings of the 11th Conference of the Association for Machine Translation in the Americas,* 20-30, Vancouver, Canada.

Cadwell, P., Castilho, S., O'Brien, S. and Michell, L. (2016). Human factors in machine translation and post-editing among institutional translators. *Translation Spaces*, *5*(2): 222–243.

Choi, H., Lee, C. and Lee, J.-H. (2023). 자동화된 기계학습(AutoML)을 활용한 특허 특화 번역엔진의 영한번역 성능(Evaluation of Patent English-Korean Machine Translations by a Patent-Specific NMT Engine Using AutoML). *The Journal of Translation Studies*, 23(5): 101-130.

Daems, J., Vandepitte, S., Hartsuiker, R. and Macken, L. (2015). The impact of machine translation error types on post-editing effort indicators. In S. O'Brien and M. Simard (eds) *Proceedings of the 4th Workshop on Post-Editing Technology and Practice*, 31-45, location, country.

Dames, J., De Clercq, O. and Macken, L. (2017). Translationsese and post-editese: How comparable is comparable quality? *Linguistica Antverpiensia,* 16: 89-103.

Guerberof Arenas, A. (2009). Productivity and quality in MT post-editing. *XII MT Summit Workshop: Beyond Translation Memories*, 26-30.

Guerberof Arenas, A. (2020). Pre-editing and post-editing. In E. Angelone, M. Ehrensberger-Dow and Gary Massey (eds) *The Bloomsbury Companion to Language Industry Studies.* London: Bloomsbury Academic, 333-360.

Jia, Y., Carl, M., and Wang, X. (2019). How does the post-editing of neural machine translation compare with from-scratch translation? A product and process study. *The Journal of Specialised Translation,* 31: 60-86.

Killman, J. and Rodriguez-Castro, M. (2022). PE vs Translating in the legal context: Quality and time effects from English to Spanish. *Revista de Llengua I Diret/Journal of Language and Law,* 78: 56-72.

Kim, J. (2022a). 한영 포스트에디팅 과정에서의 노력 탐색 - 시간, 기술적 노력, 검색을 중심으로(An investigation into temporal, technical, and web-searching efforts during Korean-to-

English post-editing process compared with from-scratch translation). *Interpreting and Translation Studies*, 26(2): 1-24.

Kim, J. (2022b). 한영 포스트에디팅에서 정확성 오류의 수정 양상 고찰 (An investigation into correction of accuracy errors in post-editing). *The Journal of Translation Studies*, 23(5): 91-116.

Kim, S. M., Lee, J. H. and Shin, H. S. (2019). 번역학계와 언어서비스업체(LSP)간 산학협력연구: '포스트에디팅 생산성'과 '기계번역 엔진 성능 비교' (A university-industry joint study on machine translation post-editing productivity and MT engine error rate). *The Journal of Translation Studies*, 20(1): 41-76.

Krings, H. (2001). *Repairing texts: Empirical investigations of machine translation post-editing processes*. Kent, Ohio: Kent State University Press.

Lee, J. and Choi, H. (2023). A case study on the evaluation of Korean-English legal translations by generic and custom neural machine translation engines. *Interpretation and Translation*, 25(1): 75-98.

Lee, J. and Choi, H. (2022). 인공신경망 특허 기계번역 성능에 관한 연구: Patent Translate 와 WIPO Translate 한영 번역 결과물의 누락과 통사 오류 분석을 중심으로 (A study on the quality of patent neural machine translation: A comparison of omission and syntactic errors in the Korean-English translations by patent-specialized Patent Translate and WIPO Translate). *T&I Review*, 12(2): 129-154.

Lee, J.-H. (2021a). 한영 포스트에디팅 노력 예비연구: 트랜스로그 II 를 활용한 한영 인간번역과 포스트에디팅의 차이 분석 (A pilot investigation into Korean to English post-editing efforts). *The Journal of Translation Studies*. 22(5): 271-298.

Lee, J.-H. (2021b). 한영 포스트에디팅, 누구나 수행할 수 있는가? 포스트에디팅 수업 설계를 위한 예비 연구 (Can anybody perform Korean to English post-editing tasks? A pilot study for mtpe module design). *The journal of Translation Studies*. 22(1):171:197.

Lee, J.-H. (2022). 법률 특화 번역엔진 성능 평가-한영 계약서 번역을 중심으로 (A study on performance evaluation of a specialized machine translation engine in the legal domain: Focusing on the Korean-to-English translation of legal contracts). *T&I Review*, 12(1): 162-192.

Lee, J.-H. and Kim, S. M. (2022). 풀 포스트에디팅에 대한 고찰—풀 포스트에디팅 생산성에 영향을 주는 요소를 중심으로 (An investigation into English to Korean full post-editing: Factors affecting productivity of full post-editing). *The Journal of Translation Studies*, 23(5): 119-146.

Lee, S. M. (2021). 기계번역을 활용한 법령번역의 실제와 과제 (Practices and challenges in translating statutes using machine translation). *T& I Review*, 11(1): 35–56.

Lee, S.W. and Lee, S. B. (2021). 학부번역전공자의 인간번역과 기계번역 포스트에디팅 품질 비교 (Comparing human translation and post-edited machine translation: A case study of Korean undergraduate students). *T&I Review*, 11(2):101-123.

O'Brien, S. (2017). Machine translation and cognition. In J. W. Schwieter and A. Ferreira (eds) *The Handbook of Translation and Cognition*, 311-331. Wiley-Blackwell.

Popović, M., Lommel, A., Burchardt, A., Avramidis, E. and Uszkoreit, H. (2014). Relations between different types of post-editing operations, cognitive effort and temporal effort. In *Proceedings of the Seventeenth Annual Conference of the European Association for Machine Translation*, 191-198, Dubrovnik, Croatia.

Roberts, B. (2022). Machine vs. Human translation: When to use which for legal translation. Retrieved July 10, 2023, from https://www.attorneyatwork.com/machine-translation-vs-human-translation-when-to-use-which-for-legal-translation/

Seo, B. H. and Kim, S, (2020). A case study on the influence of translator's experience in translation education on the quality of post-editing results. *The Journal of Translation Studies*, 21(3): 63-91.

Snover, M., Dorr, B., Schwartz, R., Micciulla, L. and Makhoul, J. (2006). A study of translation edit rate with targeted human annotation. In *Proceedings of the Association for Machine Translation in the Americas*, 223-231, Boston: AMTA.

Temnikova, I. (2010). Cognitive evaluation approach for a controlled language post-editing experiment. In *Proceedings of the 7th International Conference on Language Resources and Evaluation*. European Language Resources, 3485-3490, Valletta, Malta.

Tsai, Y. (2017). Linguistic evaluation of translation errors in Chinese–English machine translations of patent titles. *Forum*, 15(1): 142-156.

Fine-tuning mBART50 with French and Farsi data to improve the translation of Farsi dislocations into English and French.

Behnoosh Namdarzadeh behnoosh.namdar@gmail.com
CLILLAC-ARP, Université Paris Cité, Paris, F-75013, France

Sadaf Mohseni sadafmohseni@gmail.com
CLILLAC-ARP, Université Paris Cité, Paris,F-75013, France

Lichao Zhu lichao.zhu@u-paris.fr
CLILLAC-ARP, Université Paris Cité, Paris, F-75013, France

Guillaume Wisniewski guillaume.wisniewski@u-paris.fr
Laboratoire de Linguistique formelle, Department of Linguistics, Université Paris Cité, Paris,F-75013, France

Nicolas Ballier nicolas.ballier@u-paris.fr
Laboratoire de linguistique formelle/ CLILLAC-ARP, Université Paris Cité, Paris, F-75013, France

Abstract

In this paper, we discuss the improvements brought by the fine-tuning of mBART50 for the translation of a specific Farsi dataset of dislocations. Given our BLEU scores, our evaluation is mostly qualitative: we assess the improvements of our fine-tuning in the translations into French of our test dataset of Farsi. We describe the fine-tuning procedure and discuss the quality of the results in the translations from Farsi. We assess the sentences in the French translations that contain English tokens and for the English translations, we examine the ability of the fine-tuned system to translate Farsi dislocations into English without replicating the dislocated item as a double subject. We scrutinized the Farsi training data used to train for mBART50 (Tang et al., 2021). We fine-tuned mBART50 with samples from an in-house French-Farsi aligned translation of a short story. In spite of the scarcity of available resources, we found that fine-tuning with aligned French-Farsi data dramatically improved the grammatical well-formedness of the predictions for French, even if serious semantic issues remained. We replicated the experiment with the English translation of the same Farsi short story for a Farsi-English fine-tuning and found out that similar semantic inadequacies cropped up, and that some translations were worse than our mBART50 baseline. We showcased the fine-tuning of mBART50 with supplementary data and discussed the asymmetry of the situation, adding little data in the fine-tuning is sufficient to improve morpho-syntax for one language pair but seems to degrade translation to English.

Keywords: mBART50, Farsi-French, Farsi-English, fine-tuning multilingual models

Proceedings of Machine Translation Summit XIX, Vol. 2: Users Track, pages 152–161
September 4–8, 2023, Macau SAR, China.

1 Introduction

Farsi (Persian) is shown to be the language having least datasets in a survey of Neural Machine Translation for low-resource languages (Ranathunga et al., 2023). [1] Previous research on Neural Machine translation for Farsi shows clear limitations of existing systems (Ghasemi and Hashemian, 2016) and highlights the scarcity of NLP resources (Namdarzadeh et al., 2022) for Farsi, as shown in the contributions of the Proceedings of the Workshop on NLP Solutions for Under-Resourced Languages (Freihat and Abbas, 2021).Moreover, previous research on using mBART50 (Liu et al., 2020), a multilingual model trained on 50 languages, has shown its limitations for the translations of Farsi into English and even more so for the translations into French where hallucinations (Raunak et al., 2021) and English words were observed in the translated texts (Namdarzadeh et al., 2022). This paper is a follow-up on this initial series of observations and reports our first series of experiments to fine-tune mBART50 for the translation of Farsi into English and French. Farsi being an under-resourced language, we found that the translation into French gave way to hallucinations and English words, whereas most of the challenge set created for the occasion was translated into grammatical sentences from Farsi into English, but nevertheless failed to capture what we called 'pragmatic adequacy'. The translations into English like '*I hate the heat*' followed the English SVO canonical order and lost the pragmatic intention ('*as to the heat, I hate it*').

Focusing on a specific syntactic phenomenon, dislocation, may provide us with a better perspective on the nature of pragmatic inadequacies. Dislocation is a syntactic phenomenon that is productive in Farsi. Left dislocation constructions, like in French and, less frequently, in English, can have specific semantic and pragmatic functions . They can be used to promote a topic (Azizian et al., 2015) or to focus on a specific constituent of the sentence. Several constructions are available for dislocations in Farsi. Azizian et al. (2015) studied left dislocated construction as a marked construction in the framework of Construction Grammar (Goldberg, 1995). They suggest that "a syntactic two-place construction is responsible for preposing the oblique to the sentence-initial position by leaving a pronominal enclitic coreferential with it in its original place", show that it may apply to monovalent, divalent and trivalent verbs. In the construction they identify, almost all participant roles can be left-dislocated except agents and experiencers. The left-dislocated element can be marked with "-ra." In this example, the object (*Garma*) is initially stated, and it can transfer a semantic effect based on the context.

Garma ro azash motenaferam.

Heat- RA-OBJ of-OBJ hate-1SG-PRE

Reference translation: *As for the heat, I hate it* (Azizian et al., 2015: 104). Google Translation and Microsoft Bing: I hate the heat.

Ketab o Saman ferestad.

book RA-OBJ S send-1SG-PST

Reference translation: *The book, Saman sent.* (Azizian et al., 2015) Google: Saman sent the book.

To answer one of the reviewers' concerns on the centrality of dislocations in our study, the reason we focused our analysis on this construction is we first noticed in a previous paper that this structure was difficult to translate into French and into English for the mBART50 model (Namdarzadeh et al., 2022) and because this syntactic phenomenon is frequent in spoken data (Dabir-Moghaddam, 1992), and can manifest in various forms and functions. In other words, left dislocated constituents can co-occur with several types of markers such as reflexives, making their translations by NMT toolkits challenging. According to discourse configurations, dis-

[1]The use of Persian is more common in formal and academic settings, while Farsi is commonly used in informal and everyday conversations among native speakers.

location constructions can serve different functions, and capturing the corresponding pragmatic intention can be challenging. This is the reason why we assign such importance to investigating this construction.

The rest of the paper is structured as follows: Section 2 sums up previous research, Section 3 presents our testing set, our additional data used for fine-tuning and the parameters we used to fine-tune mBART50. Section 4 presents our results, we both discuss the Farsi to French and French to Farsi translations. Section 5 discusses them and outlines our future research.

2 Previous Research

To improve multilingual models, previous methods include adding data with back-translation from monolingual data (Sennrich et al., 2016), data from multimodal input (see for instance pictures and their descriptions for Bengali (Parida et al., 2021), data from languages of the same language family (Chronopoulou et al., 2022), using denoisers to add other languages incrementally (Üstün et al., 2021) or fine-tuning on small datasets (Smirnov et al., 2022). While other researchers have worked on more "massively multilingual NMT" (Aharoni et al., 2019) adding data to an initial subset of the TED talks for no less than 103 languages (including one million examples in Farsi), we have focused on controlling parallel data for Farsi to English and Farsi to French translations.

Among the research questions we had is the effect of language interference or at least the fact that we found English tokens in the translation of Farsi into French, probably because of this bootstrapping effect of the co-presence of the different languages. We were more interested in the change in one language, namely potentially English, when we added more data in French and especially we wanted to see if adding more French data would change the number of English tokens that we found in the translations into French.

3 Materials and Methods

For mBART50, the system does not include bilingual French and Farsi data, but the 25 and then 50 language pairs of languages with English as a pivot so that the system manages to learn from the different language pairs including English and another language and enable translation from one language to the other even if there are no training data for a specific language pair outside English. As indicated in (Tang et al., 2021), in mBART50, French belongs to the first group of training data, containing more than 10 Millions of training data in bitext pairs and Farsi corresponds to the middle tier (100k to 1M tokens). The appendix mentions 14,4895 sentences for Farsi (TED 58) used for training and 3,930 for validation and 4,490 for test. The training data for French is made up of the WMT14 training data, resulting in 36,797,950 (train), 3,000 (validation) and 3,003 (test) sentences.

3.1 Testing Set

As a testing set, we used a simple data set that suggested the research question in the first place (Namdarzadeh et al., 2022). The existence of English tokens in the translations into French by mBART50 and a discrepancy in the quality of the translation into English and into French triggered the investigation of fine-tuning with French and Farsi aligned data. For the translation into French, we had observed issues in syntactic adequacy, namely some sentences were incomplete and from the translation into English we analysed, we had observed syntactic adequacy, the sentences were grammatical, but we evidenced a form of pragmatic inadequacy: the order of the constituents was too close to the English canonical order (subject verb object), so that we regretted the lack of pragmatic adequacy to account for the focalisation effects in the Farsi original. For a sentence like, "as to the heat, I hate it", a "focus construction", as Huddleston and Pullum call them (Huddleston and Pullum, 2002), would be more suitable than the simple, plain and somewhat inexpressive "I hate the heat". The data set is comprised of 57 sentences comprising a dislocation and has been compiled using several sources from typical textbooks to more elaborate grammars of Farsi.

3.2 Fine-tuning parameters for mBART50

For the fine-tuning, we followed the instructions from the scripts available from the HuggingFace implementation. [2] We retrained the model with three epochs, using gelu as an activation function. The process took 25 seconds on an NVIDIA A100 GPU and consumed 152.544 W for the GPU and 77.5 W for the CPU (we used the codecarbon library [3] (Schmidt et al., 2021) to measure our carbon footprint). For the data, we first use the translation of a short story from Farsi into French. We privileged literary material because we expected rarer structures to be relevant for the translation of the translation into French. We used the short story 'Zayandeh Roud's wounds', which is one of the short stories in a short story collection called 'Angel Cake Recipe', consisting of fifteen short stories written by Pooya Monshizadeh, an Iranian writer currently living in the Netherlands. This short story won several national literary awards in Iran. The short story was translated into French by the second author. For the translation into English, we found a translation by Sajedeh Asna'ashari published online in the "*Stockholm Review*". [4] Since we used the HuggingFace scripts for the fine-tuning as a starting point, this had a consequence on the output language after the fine-tuning. No possible predictions in another language than the one provided in the fine-tuning is then possible. As a consequence, we first fine-tuned with Farsi and French and then fine-tuned from scratch from the same mBART50 model with Farsi and English.

4 Results

This section summarises some of our findings in terms of the quality of the translations.[5] By paying attention to our distinction between pragmatic adequacy and syntactic adequacy, we discuss the differences in translation that were more satisfactory from a pragmatic standpoint.

4.1 Impact on the translation into French

Compared to the baseline of our initial mBART translation from Farsi into French, dramatic improvements were noted from a morpho-syntactic standpoint: the translation contained only one English token (suppressing English in the translations was our main expectation) and the subject/verbs agreements were correct except for two first plural person verbal agreements for a second singular person subject in a cleft sentence *C'est toi qui me connaissons mieux que lui. / Ce n'est pas toi qui l'avons vu, mais nous.* In spite of an error for gender (*ton lèvre*), this change was spectacular, given the small size of the fine-tuning data (116 sentences). Nevertheless, semantic issues were not resolved and other cropped up. For named entities, a regional football team was translated as *l'équipe de Napoléon [Napoleon's team]* and some sentences did not make sense at all. Dislocations tended to be more often translated by cleft sentences, which sounds like a relevant strategy for topic promotion. A case of catastrophic forgetting has been noticed: the NMT system lost its ability to translate towards any other language than the one it was fine-tuned with. As a consequence, we first tried to test the backtranslation abilities if the fine-tuning was operated with Farsi as the target language and French as the source Language. We report our main observations in the following subsection.

---

[2] https://github.com/huggingface/transformers/blob/main/examples/pytorch/translation/run_translation.py

[3] https://pypi.org/project/codecarbon/

[4] https://thestockholmreview.org/the-wounds-of-zayanderud-fiction-by-pooya-monshizadeh

[5] Data is available on https://github.com/Behnooshn/Summit2023

4.2 Impact on Back-translation

When using back-translation from French into Farsi, the following phenomena were observed: for some sentences where the reflexive is part of the dislocation construction, the translation hallucinated and repeated a reflexive pronoun. This seems to suggest that this construction is rarer in mBART50 training data. Some sentences were translated into English and some objects tended to be suppressed as well as reflexive pronouns. Lexical errors were spotted in the choice of verbs NER issues appeared, for example, confusions between family name (*Iradji*) and country (*Irak*). Analysing the fine-tuned back-translation output, from French to Farsi, we noted that, even though the fine-tuning bore on a very limited set of sentences, the number of tokens in English in the Farsi translation was limited to proper nouns, so that NER remains an issue. There are less hallucinations but more omissions could be noted: several phrases were not translated. Some translations were still impaired semantically, some verbs being translated by their very opposite ("*hate the heat*" becomes "*love the heat*"). Severe misunderstandings were spotted, sometimes leading to contradictions (ie the believer that does not believe).

4.3 BLEU scores

We compared with a reference translation before and after our fine-tuning with mBART50. Once more, the BLEU score is not a satisfactory instrument to measure progress in the textual output of the translation. Even though the difference in BLEU score is not really meaningful below five, the difference between and after fine-tuning is striking in terms of morphosyntactic quality and spectacularly so with so little data. The result is not necessarily more satisfying from a semantic point of view and definitely not from a pragmatic point of view, but the grammatical well-formedness has dramatically improved with fine-tuning with so few differences and so small BLEU scores. It is likely that for our BLEU scores below 5, the unigram matches can probably be attributed to punctuation or function words. The BLEU scores are inferior to five and show the mBART50 predictions are very different from our proposed translations. Named entities remain a crucial issue with first names in the reference translations often not being recognised in the translation.

4.4 Qualitative Analysis

Contrary to our findings for the baseline of the mBART50 translation from Farsi into French, no English tokens were found. Two cases of hallucination were observed, for one of the most complex sentences of the dataset and with the same token repeated over and over (*vieille*). The changes are quite dramatic for syntactic adequacy: contrary to our baseline all the agreements in person, number gender and even mode (for an imperative form) are correct and predictions for French are consistent with well-formedness constraints, even if some averbal sentences are debatable. Semantically, many issues remain unsolved, such as *"by bus"* translated by *"by train"* or self-contradictory sentences such as *"Je n'aime pas la chaleur, mais je l'aime"*, meaning *"I don't like the heat, but I like it"* instead of something like *"as to the heat, I hate it"*). Pragmatically, richer topic/focus constructions were observed with several *c'est* cleft constructions.

Regarding the English outputs after fine-tuning mBART50, we have observed critical points related to the translation of Farsi dislocation constructions into English. For instance, named entities have not been translated accurately, as they may not be (sufficiently) present in the training data. Additionally, there are instances where the English translations contain more information compared to the original Farsi source text, indicating over-translation (Wang, 2012).

Another frequent issue in NLP is gender bias, which involves a preference towards one gender over the other. This bias is prevalent in the outputs of the systems (Wisniewski et al., 2022a; Matthews et al., 2021). We have also noticed the same bias in the English outputs of mBART50, where the system seems to prefer masculine genitives over feminine ones.

As Azizian et al. (2015) pointed out, some dislocations entail a complex interaction with argument structure, which may account for the introduction of unnecessary arguments in the mistranslation of reflexives. The use of reflexives holds high importance in Farsi, since they carry a pragmatic effect based on the discourse and the prosody effect applied by the speaker.

Man khodam yadam hast.

I-SUB-SG REF-SG remember-SG be-SG

Reference translation: *I myself remember.* mBART50: I remember you.

As shown in the above example, not only is the use of reflexive ignored, but mBART50 also adds the object **you** in its translation, which undermines the entire meaning of the Farsi source text. There are different examples of this kind in our test set for which the mBART50 outputs are not semantically and pragmatically adequate translations.

This failure may be due to the fact that such structures are often under-represented in the training data (Hovy and Prabhumoye, 2021) and more generally, in available reference data such as treebanks in Farsi (Namdarzadeh et al., 2022). In the next section, we will discuss the available data and materials, and integrate another model for transcription and translation of this low-resourced language.

5 Discussion

5.1 Asymmetry of Data

Contrary to expectations, our fine-tuning experiment with the same Farsi short story proved to be more efficient with French than for English, giving an edge to the lower resource for the initial training of mBART50, which contradicts the adage that NMT results in "worse quality in low-resource settings, but better performance in high-resource settings" Koehn and Knowles (2017). Such a discrepancy in the initial training data for mBART50 should be replicated for another language pair involving a lesser-resource language. We should also try to replicate the fine-tuning on a bigger scale, to see whether English needs more data than the other languages when fine-tuning mBART50.

An alternative strategy would be to fine-tune for English with the whole Farsi-English data available on OPUS. We have retrieved aligned Farsi-English TED Talks raw corpus from OPUS which is tokenized with Stanza NLP Pipeline and sub-tokenized by SentencePiece with a language model trained with CC-aligned Farsi data (5 million lines) for our future experiments with English and Farsi. The French-Farsi Opus data is available but a 2017 extraction from the most translated TED talks exists with their French and English translations. [6] We also aim to analyse the initial mBART50 training data, reported in the reference paper as being based on TED talks, but the source of the bilingual corpus is not mentioned (Farsi subtitles of American TED talks or English subtitles of Farsi talks).

5.2 Language Direction of the translated material

In our experiment, we have used data originally in Farsi translated into French. It should be noted that the mBART50 system is trained for Farsi with TED Talks. It is not clear whether the talks are in English and subtitled into Farsi, so that the direction of the language was also of interest to us. In our next experiments, we plan to control language direction for the fine-tuning data and use data from a translation of a French novel into Farsi, the translation of Simone de Beauvoir's *Journal de Guerre, septembre 1939-janvier 1941*. Because of its occasionally more informal style, we would expect the data to potentially include more dislocations in French.

[6] `https://github.com/neulab/word-embeddings-for-nmt`

5.3 Further Research

For Farsi, we have identified three types that we would like to translate better. And for French, we have identified the construction as being of paramount importance in the translation. We intend to search existing data using universal dependency annotation, making the most of the dislocated dependency relation label, see our previous paper that described the methodology. We intend to potentially observe a threshold of data that may enable a better translation of the dislocation construction. Possibly realised by using synthetic data, namely transforming, updating current authentic sentences by changing the noun, for example, by synonymous, so that we would easily expand our data sets by reduplicating the structure.

By investigating such challenging cases of dislocation, we aim to enhance the multilingual translation toolkits' accuracy and overall performance, especially for languages that exhibit similar characteristics (ie dislocation) and possess limited training data. Through a thorough analysis of the toolkits' errors, we can develop more robust models capable of effectively handling various types of dislocation.

The incorporation of the different typologies of dislocation and corresponding markers can help us expand our test sets, especially when it comes to less-resourced languages. To achieve this for Farsi, we will investigate three types of dislocation, including object markers *sh* and *râ*, and reflexive pronouns. For example, commercial toolkits still misfire when translating dislocation constructions such as the *sh* marker, the translation toolkits cannot identify the correct dependent (*mashin*) and produce incorrect translations (Google Translate: *Kiana's car hit the door.* Microsoft Bing: *Kiana knocked on the door*).

Mashino Kiana tup-o be dar- esh zad.

Car-râ Kiana ball-OBJ to door-OBJ OBJ-marker hit-3S

our reference Translation: As to the car, Kiana [only] hit its door with the ball. (After(Azizian et al., 2015))

One of the parameters that could be investigated is the distance between the two constituents *mashin* and *esh*, which may play a role in Natural Language Understanding and translations tasks. The frequency of the dislocated constituents can also be another issue that requires investigation. By training our own translation toolkit with calibrated training data enriched with specific examples of dislocations and their relevant translations, we hope to observe frequency thresholds: detect the frequency at which the translation system can "learn" the challenging constituent by fine-tuning.

6 Conclusion

In this paper we have reported a small-scale experiment trying to fine-tune mBART50 for the translations from French into Farsi. We have not tried yet to fine-tune on the Facebook implementation of Cross-lingual Language Model Pretraining (Lample and Conneau, 2019), which has Farsi as one of the 100 languages used for the multilingual training. The baseline results may be more satisfactory for this model than what we observed with mBART50. Our paper is just a small case study that contributes to cross-lingual language understanding (XLU) of these multilingual models. It remains to be seen whether this XLM-100 model developed for Cross-lingual Representation Learning (XLR), which outperforms mBERT (Conneau et al., 2020), would display similar tendencies, since more data was collected for Farsi (13,259 M tokens) than for French (9,870 M tokens) on Common Crawl and Wikipedia. Our main finding is that even a small amount of fine-tuning drastically reduces the number of foreign words in the translations and the number of hallucinations. An important drawback is that our fine-tuned model with French-Farsi parallel data only translates into French, as a direct consequence of the HuggingFace implementation. More research is needed to investigate whether more aligned data in the fine-tuning phase would allow predictions to be semantically more adequate. Taking into account what we have managed to learn with so little data, we would like to be able to evaluate what a system is capable of learning during fine-tuning, and at what cost (at least in terms of the number of examples needed for learning, and – if we have a good idea to avoid that – in terms of "forgetting"). More specifically, we would like to compare the ability of fine-tuning to change :

- the translation of certain tokens (a sort of "lexical" capacity). Here, clearly, the absence of some tokens data accounts for some of the spotted errors, especially for very frequent place names in Farsi.

- the translation of certain grammatical constructions (a sort of "syntactic" capacity)

In both cases, the idea would be to use artificial examples to control exactly what is present in the fine-tuning data and how it impacts the resulting translations. For lexical capacity, we could, for example, create sentences with new words and watch when the system is able to produce them, or "change" the meaning of a word (typically, replace all "green" tokens with "peanuts" in a parallel corpus) and watch when the system's output changes. The assumption is there might be thresholds of frequency in the fine-tuning data to observe this. For syntactic capacity, we could start with the translation of dislocation: we would create an artificial corpus with well-translated dislocations and look at the size of the set that needs to be provided for the system to be able to translate dislocations correctly. To clarify what we mean by "artificial corpus", we have the intuition that we could define a "parallel pattern" like the pattern used to investigate gender bias (the N has finished PRON work) (Wisniewski et al., 2022b) to "model" the translation of a dislocation (in the same way a pattern like DET ADJ NOUN is translated into DET NOUN ADJ) that we would simply instantiate on a lexicon (without taking into account the semantics at the source sentence level, but guaranteeing that the "bilingual links" of the syntactic structure are well preserved). For both experiments, it would be interesting to see what happens on eng-fas, fra-fas, eng-fra pairs to see the impact of the pre-trained model. We have identified the parallel translations of the TED talks which could be used as a starting point for this triangulation.

Author Contributions

Behnoosh Namdarzadeh designed the dislocation test set in Farsi and the reference translations into English and into French and supervised the translation outputs. Sadaf Mohseni provided the aligned data for fine-tuning and contributed to the reference translations and to the analyses of the different translations. Lichao Zhu prepared the OPUS data for ulterior fine-tuning. Guillaume Wisniewski supervised the mBART50 fine-tuning experiments. Nicolas Ballier designed the study, and wrote the first draft of the manuscript. All authors contributed to the analysis of the outputs.

Acknowledgements

We thank the four anonymous reviewers for their input on a preliminary version of this paper. This publication has emanated in part from research supported by a PAUSE research grant to Sadaf Mohseni funded by Collège de France and Université Paris Cité under ANR grant ANR-18-IDEX-0001, Financement IdEx Université de Paris), which is gratefully acknowledged. Nicolas Ballier benefited from a CNRS research leave at LLF (Laboratoire de Linguistique Formelle), for which grateful acknowledgement is made.

References

Aharoni, R., Johnson, M., and Firat, O. (2019). Massively multilingual neural machine translation. *arXiv preprint arXiv:1903.00089.*

Azizian, Y., Golfam, A., and Kambuziya, A. K.-e. Z. (2015). A construction grammar account of left dislocation in Persian. *Mediterranean Journal of Social Sciences*, 6(6 S2):98.

Chronopoulou, A., Stojanovski, D., and Fraser, A. (2022). Language-family adapters for multilingual neural machine translation. *arXiv preprint arXiv:2209.15236.*

Conneau, A., Khandelwal, K., Goyal, N., Chaudhary, V., Wenzek, G., Guzmán, F., Grave, E., Ott, M., Zettlemoyer, L., and Stoyanov, V. (2020). Unsupervised cross-lingual representation learning at scale. In *Proceedings of the 58th Annual Meeting of the Association for Computational Linguistics*, pages 8440–8451, Online. Association for Computational Linguistics.

Dabir-Moghaddam, M. (1992). *On the (In)dependence of syntax and pragmatics: Evidence from the postposition -rá in Persian*, pages 549–574. De Gruyter Mouton, Berlin, New York.

Freihat, A. A. and Abbas, M. (2021). Proceedings of the second international workshop on NLP solutions for under resourced languages (NSURL 2021) co-located with ICNLSP 2021. In *Proceedings of The Second International Workshop on NLP Solutions for Under Resourced Languages (NSURL 2021) co-located with ICNLSP 2021.*

Ghasemi, H. and Hashemian, M. (2016). A comparative study of Google Translate translations: An error analysis of English-to-Persian and Persian-to-English translations. *English Language Teaching*, 9(3):13–17.

Goldberg, A. (1995). *Constructions: A Construction Grammar Approach to Argument Structure*. Cognitive Theory of Language and Culture Series. University of Chicago Press.

Hovy, D. and Prabhumoye, S. (2021). Five sources of bias in natural language processing. *Language and Linguistics Compass*, 15(8):e12432.

Huddleston, R. and Pullum, G. K. (2002). *The Cambridge Grammar of English Language*. Cambridge University Press.

Koehn, P. and Knowles, R. (2017). Six challenges for neural machine translation. In *Proceedings of the First Workshop on Neural Machine Translation*, pages 28–39, Vancouver. Association for Computational Linguistics.

Lample, G. and Conneau, A. (2019). Cross-lingual language model pretraining. *Advances in Neural Information Processing Systems (NeurIPS)*, 33.

Liu, Y., Gu, J., Goyal, N., Li, X., Edunov, S., Ghazvininejad, M., Lewis, M., and Zettlemoyer, L. (2020). Multilingual denoising pre-training for neural machine translation. *Transactions of the Association for Computational Linguistics*, 8:726–742.

Matthews, A., Grasso, I., Mahoney, C., Chen, Y., Wali, E., Middleton, T., Njie, M., and Matthews, J. (2021). Gender bias in natural language processing across human languages. In *Proceedings of the First Workshop on Trustworthy Natural Language Processing*, pages 45–54, Online. Association for Computational Linguistics.

Namdarzadeh, B., Ballier, N., Wisniewski, G., Zhu, L., and Yunès, J.-B. (2022). Toward a test set of dislocations in Persian for neural machine translation. In *The Third International Workshop on NLP Solutions for Under Resourced Languages (NSURL 2022)*, pages 14–21.

Parida, S., Panda, S., Biswal, S. P., Kotwal, K., Sen, A., Dash, S. R., and Motlicek, P. (2021). Multimodal neural machine translation system for English to Bengali. In *Proceedings of the First Workshop on Multimodal Machine Translation for Low Resource Languages (MMTLRL 2021)*, pages 31–39.

Ranathunga, S., Lee, E.-S. A., Prifti Skenduli, M., Shekhar, R., Alam, M., and Kaur, R. (2023). Neural machine translation for low-resource languages: A survey. *ACM Computing Surveys*, 55(11):1–37.

Raunak, V., Menezes, A., and Junczys-Dowmunt, M. (2021). The curious case of hallucinations in neural machine translation. In *Proceedings of the 2021 Conference of the North American Chapter of the Association for Computational Linguistics: Human Language Technologies*, pages 1172–1183, Online. Association for Computational Linguistics.

Schmidt, V., Goyal, K., Joshi, A., Feld, B., Conell, L., Laskaris, N., Blank, D., Wilson, J., Friedler, S., and Luccioni, S. (2021). CodeCarbon: Estimate and Track Carbon Emissions from Machine Learning Computing.

Sennrich, R., Haddow, B., and Birch, A. (2016). Improving neural machine translation models with monolingual data. In *Proceedings of the 54th Annual Meeting of the Association for Computational Linguistics (Volume 1: Long Papers)*, pages 86–96, Berlin, Germany. Association for Computational Linguistics.

Smirnov, A. V., Teslya, N., Shilov, N., Frank, D., Minina, E., and Kovacs, M. (2022). Comparative analysis of neural translation models based on transformers architecture. In *ICEIS (1)*, pages 586–593.

Tang, Y., Tran, C., Li, X., Chen, P.-J., Goyal, N., Chaudhary, V., Gu, J., and Fan, A. (2021). Multilingual translation with extensible multilingual pretraining and finetuning. *Findings of the Association for Computational Linguistics: ACL-IJCNLP 2021*, pages 3450–3466.

Üstün, A., Berard, A., Besacier, L., and Gallé, M. (2021). Multilingual unsupervised neural machine translation with denoising adapters. In *Proceedings of the 2021 Conference on Empirical Methods in Natural Language Processing*, pages 6650–6662, Online and Punta Cana, Dominican Republic. Association for Computational Linguistics.

Wang, M. (2012). An analysis of over-translation and under-translation in perspective of cultural connotation. *Lecture Notes in Information Technology*, 16:129–133.

Wisniewski, G., Zhu, L., Ballier, N., and Yvon, F. (2022a). Analyzing gender translation errors to identify information flows between the encoder and decoder of a NMT system. In *Proceedings of the Fifth BlackboxNLP Workshop on Analyzing and Interpreting Neural Networks for NLP*, pages 153–163, Abu Dhabi, United Arab Emirates (Hybrid). Association for Computational Linguistics.

Wisniewski, G., Zhu, L., Ballier, N., and Yvon, F. (2022b). Analyzing gender translation errors to identify information flows between the encoder and decoder of a nmt system. In *Proceedings of the Fifth BlackboxNLP Workshop on Analyzing and Interpreting Neural Networks for NLP*, pages 153–163.

KG-IQES: An Interpretable Quality Estimation System for Machine Translation Based on Knowledge Graph

Junhao Zhu* zhujunhao@huawei.com
Huawei Translation Center,Dongguan,China
Min Zhang† zhangmin186@huawei.com
Huawei Translation Center,Beijing,China
Hao Yang‡ yanghao30@huawei.com
Huawei Translation Center,Beijing,China
Song Peng Huawei Translation Center,Dongguan,China
Zhanglin Wu Huawei Translation Center,Beijing,China
Yanfei Jiang Huawei Translation Center,Dongguan,China
Xijun Qiu Huawei Translation Center,Dongguan,China
Weiqiang Pan Huawei Translation Center,Dongguan,China
Ming Zhu Huawei Translation Center,Beijing,China
Miaomiao Ma Huawei Translation Center,Beijing,China
Weidong Zhang Huawei Translation Center,Beijing,China

Abstract

The widespread use of machine translation (MT) has driven the need for effective automatic quality estimation (AQE) methods. How to enhance the interpretability of MT output quality estimation is well worth exploring in the industry. From the perspective of the alignment of named entities (NEs) in the source and translated sentences, we construct a multilingual knowledge graph (KG) consisting of domain-specific NEs, and design a KG-based interpretable quality estimation (QE) system for machine translations (KG-IQES). KG-IQES effectively estimates the translation quality without relying on reference translations. Its effectiveness has been verified in our business scenarios.

1 Introduction

QE is an important task in MT research. It directly reflects the quality of MT output in real time during real-world application. Existing popular AQE metrics of MT output include: (1) lexicon-

*Equal contribution, shared first authorship
†Equal contribution, shared first authorship
‡Corresponding Author

Proceedings of Machine Translation Summit XIX, Vol. 2: Users Track, pages 162–170
September 4–8, 2023, Macau SAR, China.

based BLEU (Papineni et al., 2002), which performs n-gram matching between the MT output and reference translations and calculates the matching score; (2) embedding-based BLEURT (Sellam et al., 2020) and BERTScore (Zhang* et al., 2020), which compare the semantic vector distance between the reference translation and MT output. However, both of the metrics need to rely on reference translations, which are scarce in real-world application (Freitag et al., 2022) and require heavy labor costs to construct. In recent years, various metrics have been proposed for reference-free QE. One of the current state-of-the-art metrics is model-based COMET-QE (Rei et al., 2021), which directly calculates the quality score by using the source sentence and the translation through neural network, but leads to poor interpretability. A more interpretable metric is Knowledge-Based Machine Translation Evaluation (KoBE) (Gekhman et al., 2020), a Google-proposed system-level metric based on KG for common domains, which predicts the translation quality by calculating the similarity between bilingual entities in the source and translated sentences and linked entities in the KG. Although this metric has good interpretability and good performance in system-level evaluations of common domains, it is ineffective in specific domains. This is because in specific domains, each paragraph or sentence contains a large number of domain-specific entities, and these entities can only be effectively covered by domain-specific KG, not KG for common domains.

To address these shortcomings, we design a highly interpretable segment-level QE system based on multilingual KG for the Wireless Network[1] domain, that is, an interpretable quality estimation system for machine translation based on knowledge graph (KG-IQES). KG-IQES identifies NEs in the source sentence first, queries the NE translations in the target language from the KG constructed offline, and matches the translated NEs in the KG with NEs in the translated sentence. In this way, the translation quality can be estimated, and the entity alignment details can be displayed (see example in Figure 1).

Overall, our contributions are as follows:

- We design an interpretable QE system for MT output (KG-IQES) and apply it to the Wireless Network domain.
- We propose an effective bilingual entity alignment method for KG-IQES. It achieves much better performance than Fast-Align.
- In the Wireless Network domain, we construct a large-scale multilingual KG, with more than 1.7 million nodes and more than 6 million edges.
- According to experiments in the Wireless Network domain, our system KG-IQES effectively identifies 44.15% of MT bad cases, outperforming KoBE in system-level evaluations.

2 Related Work

Reference-free QE of MT output is a task that predicts quality of the machine translations by scoring the source text and machine-translated text. Many metrics have been proposed in this regard, roughly divided into three categories:

1. Lexicon-based metrics: word-based evaluation metrics that usually use a vocabulary and word statistics. For example, Popović et al. (Popović et al., 2011) designed a bag-of-word translation model, which accumulates the possibility of word pairs aligned with the source text to evaluate the quality of the translation. Specia et al. (Specia et al., 2013) used language-agnostic linguistic features extracted from source texts and translations to

[1]It is the biggest domain of our translation business.

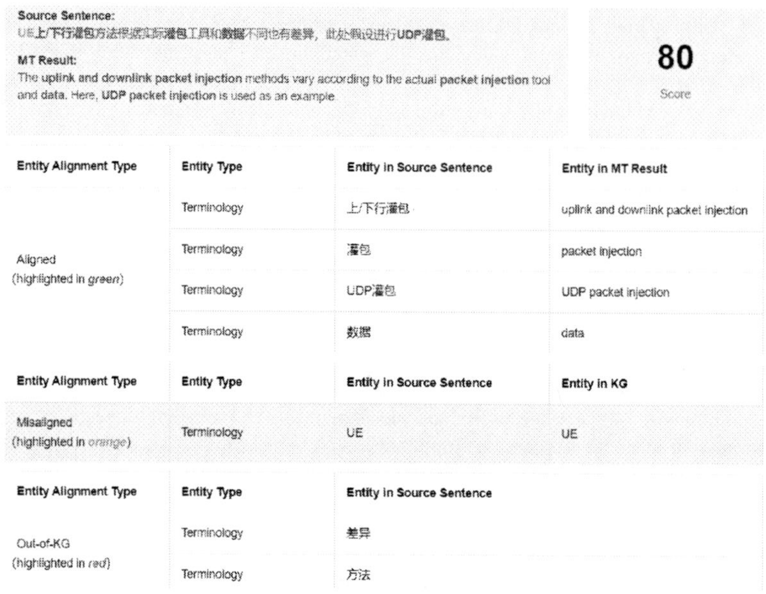

Figure 1: An example of KG-IQES that calculates the score of the MT result. KG-IQES highlights the aligned (green), misaligned (orange), and out-of-KG entities (red) in the source sentence and MT result, and directly shows the details.

estimate quality. KoBE, proposed by Google, calculates the quality score by calculating the recall of entities in the source text and the translation. These metrics are simple and effective, but are restricted by the coverage of aligned words.

2. Embedding-based metrics: word embedding-based evaluation metrics that use a pre-trained word embedding model to evaluate the semantic similarity of MT output. Examples include YiSi-2 (Lo and Larkin, 2020), SentSim proposed by Song et al. (Song et al., 2021), MoverScore metric (Zhao et al., 2019), and XMoverScore (Zhao et al., 2020) proposed by Zhao et al., which perform cross-language alignment directly, but word vectors trained by unsupervised methods during word embedding are usually noisy during their initialization.

3. Model-based metrics: these metrics that use a pre-trained deep neural network to evaluate the syntactic and semantic correctness of MT output. Classic metrics include COMET-QE and UniTE (Wan et al., 2022). The model-based metrics are highly effective when there is a large amount of high-quality manually annotated data. However, in most cases, such data is quite insufficient.

According to current research results, embedding-based and model-based metrics are more effective, but the interpretability is poor. They are not intuitive, and it is difficult to apply them in real world. In this paper, we follow the lexicon-based quality evaluation direction for MT output, and design a highly interpretable QE system KG-IQES. Its effectiveness is verified in the Wireless Network domain.

3 Proposed System

In this section, we provide a description of the KG-IQES system. As shown in Figure 2, the system consists of two subsystems: offline and online subsystems. The offline subsystem mainly constructs a multilingual KG based on the monolingual NER model and NE alignment model from the parallel corpora. The online subsystem provides an interpretable quality score for the MT output.

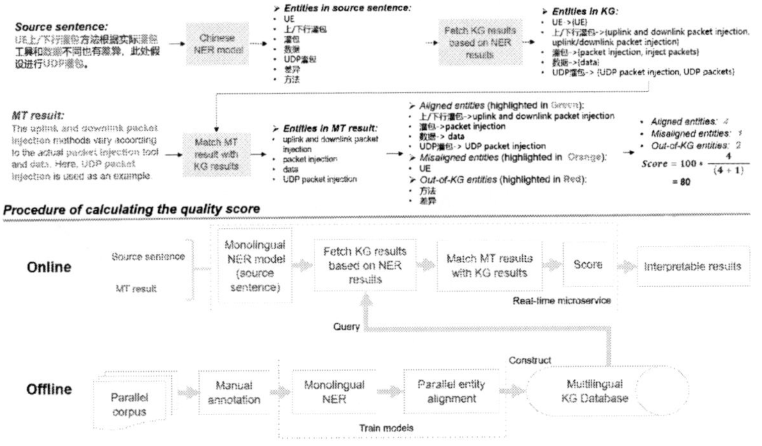

Figure 2: An overview of the KG-IQES system workflow: After offline training of the NER model and entity alignment model, the multilingual KG is constructed. The trained NER model service is deployed online, the KG is queried to obtain the entity translations, and the MT output quality is estimated based on whether the output contains the entity translations.

3.1 Offline Subsystem

The first step of KG-IQES system construction is NE annotation. We preferentially use manual annotation by domain experts who are also professional translators, and then adopt distant supervised annotation as a supplement when a corresponding knowledge base is available. In manual annotation by domain experts, we first obtain domain-specific monolingual corpora of Chinese or English, and then extract some monolingual sentences for manual annotation. Before annotation, we train all domain experts so as to unify the annotation standards. After all the domain experts complete annotating NEs in the monolingual sentences, they conduct cross-checks to reduce incorrect annotations. When a corresponding knowledge base is available, we extract some other monolingual sentences to adopt distant supervised annotation, that is, annotating NEs in these sentences that are matched to NEs in the knowledge base.

3.1.1 NER

To train the NER model, we use the W2NER (Li et al., 2022) model architecture, which consists of three components: encoder layer, convolution layer, and co-predictor layer. In order to improve the training effect of the W2NER model, we use domain-specific data to fine-tune the pre-trained language model in the encoder layer to make it capable of domain-specific encoding. After that, we apply the fast gradient method (FGM) (Miyato et al., 2017) for adversarial training to improve the robustness of the NER model.

3.1.2 Multilingual Domain-specific KG Construction

To construct a multilingual domain-specific KG, we use the cross-lingual NE alignment method to extract bilingual NE pairs from the domain-specific bilingual corpus. We compare the Fast-Align (Dyer et al., 2013) and XLM-RoBERTa (Li et al., 2021) alignment methods. The former needs to use the NER model to identify NEs in bilingual data, and use the Fast-Align tool to extract bilingual NE pairs where NEs in source and translated sentences are aligned. The latter requires a small amount of annotated data to train the alignment model and predicts the bilingual NE pairs in the bilingual data. We choose XLM-RoBERTa, which has a higher alignment accuracy, to build a multilingual domain-specific KG. Also, 30,000 manually annotated bilingual term pairs in the existing knowledge base are used to construct the training dataset of the alignment model, improving performance of the alignment model.

3.2 Online Subsystem

Reference-free QE of MT output refers to scoring the MT output based on the source text. Base on the NER model and the multilingual domain-specific KG, we design an interpretable reference-free QE system for MT output, namely KG-IQES. In the estimation process, we first use the NER model to identify NEs from the source sentence, and then search for bilingual NE pairs from the multilingual domain-specific KG. After that, we classify NEs in the source sentence as aligned NEs (NE count m: $\sum_{i=1}^{m} align_i$), misaligned NEs (NE count n: $\sum_{j=1}^{n} misalign_j$), and out-of-KG NEs (NE count: $count_{out\text{-}of\text{-}kg}$) according to whether the NE translations in the bilingual NE pairs appear in the machine-translated sentence. The translation score $Score$ is the quality score of the machine-translated sentence using KG-IQES. Finally, the score was converted into a 100-point representation.

The formula for calculating the MT output quality score is:

$$Score = 100 \times \max\{\frac{(\sum_{i=1}^{m} \alpha_i \times align_i) - \eta \times count_{out\text{-}of\text{-}kg}}{\sum_{i=1}^{m} \alpha_i \times align_i + \sum_{j=1}^{n} \alpha_j \times misalign_j}, 0\} \quad (1)$$

In the above formula, α indicates the weight of each entity category and η is penalty coefficient for entities that are not in KG. If the weight of each category is the same and the KG can cover most entities, we can set α to 1 and η to a number close to 0 in the above formula.

$$Score = 100 \times \frac{m}{m+n} \quad (2)$$

As shown in Figure 1, m (number of aligned NEs) is 4, n (number of misaligned NEs) is 1, p (number of out-of-KG NEs) is 2, and the $Score$ is $\frac{100\times4}{4+1}$ = 80. It should be pointed out that in our system, p is 0 in most cases because the out-of-KG NEs, if found, will be added to our KG database immediately.

4 Experiments

The following describes the detailed experiment process in the Chinese-English corpus of the Wireless Network domain. First, we carry out NER model training and fine-tuning experiment based on the Chinese corpus of the Wireless Network domain. We then compare two typical cross-lingual NE alignment methods, Fast-Align and XLM-RoBERTa, in the process of building the bilingual KG (Chinese and English) in the Wireless Network domain. Finally, we use our KG-IQES system and Google's KoBE (Gekhman et al., 2020) to estimate the MT output quality of different translation models, and compare the correlation between the two estimation results with direct assessment (DA).

4.1 Data Setup

Before detailed results of each experimental stage are stated, it is necessary to describe the data setup. As shown in Table 1, we collect 6,065,351 Chinese (zh) sentences and 3,523,402 Chinese-English (zh-en) bilingual sentences from the Wireless Network domain.

Corpus Type	Sentences
Wireless zh corpus	6,065,351
Wireless zh-en bilingual corpus	3,523,402

Table 1: Corpus statistics.

4.2 Results

4.2.1 Domain-specific KG

In order to train the Chinese NER and Chinese-English alignment models specific to the Wireless Network domain, we randomly select 1200 Chinese sentences in the Wireless Network domain, and have the contained NEs annotated by domain experts. We use 1000 sentences as the training set and the remaining 200 sentences as the test set. We also use the collected NEs in the Wireless Network domain for distant supervised annotation of 100,000 monolingual sentences in the Wireless Network domain. In the experiments, we compare the results of using only one of these two annotation methods and using them together on NER model training. As shown in Table 2, using them together gets a better training result.

NER Model	Chinese
Manual annotation	70.92
Manual annotation + Distant supervised annotation	73.75
Manual annotation + Distant supervised annotation + In-domain pre-training	80.33
Manual annotation + Distant supervised annotation + In-domain pre-training + FGM adversarial training	**81.80**

Table 2: F1 scores of different NER models on the test set.

To further improve the performance of the NER model on the test set, we not only pre-train the language model used in the W2NER model architecture (we use bert-chinese-base [2] for Chinese NER), but also use FGM for adversarial training in the NER model training phase. As shown in Table 2, in-domain pre-training gets a better result, and the use of FGM adversarial training further improves the NER model training effect.

In the experiment of using the cross-lingual NE alignment method to construct Chinese-English KG for the Wireless Network domain, we compare two alignment methods: Fast-Align and XLM-RoBERTa. When conducting the Fast-Align alignment experiment, we use the Chinese NER model and English NER model to extract NEs from bilingual data, and use the Fast-Align tool to extract bilingual NE pairs where the NEs in Chinese are aligned with their translations in English. When conducting the XLM-RoBERTa alignment experiment, we randomly

[2]https://huggingface.co/bert-base-chinese

select 40,000 bilingual sentences to annotate the bilingual NE pairs, and use 35,000 of them as the training set and the remaining 5,000 as the test set to train the XLM-RoBERTa alignment model. Finally, we use the XLM-RoBERTa alignment model to predict all bilingual sentences and extract bilingual NE pairs. As shown in Table 3, the alignment accuracy of the XLM-RoBERTa method is much higher, so we choose it in our system.

Alignment Method	Accuracy
Fast-Align	75.23
XLM-RoBERTa	**98.09**

Table 3: The accuracy of different cross-lingual NE alignment methods on the test set.

In the end, we construct a Chinese-English KG of the Wireless Network domain with 756,390 Chinese NEs, 958,798 English NEs (English NEs are top 5 translations of the Chinese NEs by occurrence frequency in the bilingual corpus), and 6,738,190 cross-lingual aligned NE pairs as shown in Table 4. In addition, we randomly select 200 Chinese entities, check the corresponding English entities, and find that the accuracy rate of top 1 translations is 96%.

Node	Chinese entities	756,390
	English entities	958,798
Edge	Aligned NE pairs	6,738,190
Top 1 Accuracy		**96%**

Table 4: Multilingual KG statistics.

4.2.2 KG-IQES vs. KoBE

After constructing the KG of the Wireless Network domain in Chinese and English, we also conduct a reference-free QE experiment. In the KoBE and KG-IQES approaches, we use the knowledge base of the Wireless Network domain and the same NER model. We randomly select 1000 bilingual sentences from the corpus as the test set, and use 11 translation systems, including Google, Youdao, Baidu, and our MT systems, for testing. The system-level Pearson correlation coefficients between KoBE and DA and between KG-IQES and DA are calculated. As shown in Table 5, our KG-IQES system has a higher correlation with DA scores.

QE Method	Pearson Correlation Coefficient
KoBE	65.99
KG-IQES	**84.42**

Table 5: System-level Pearson correlation coefficients between the results of different QE methods and DA.

4.2.3 KG-IQES Effectiveness Verification

To further verify the effectiveness of our system in real-world application, we analyze and verify 308 bad cases of the MT system in the Wireless Network domain from the previous 9 months this year. It is found that, except for overtranslation, as shown in Table 6, the KG-IQES system can solve 63.55% of bad cases in two types: undertranslation and mistranslation. The problem of entity overtranslation is not yet solved (see Figure 3). We plan to solve it by extracting NEs from the translation and comparing them with NEs in bilingual NE pairs.

Bad Case Type	Count	Solved	Rate
undertranslation	143	91	**63.64%**
mistranslation	71	45	**63.38%**
overtranslation	94	0	0.00%
Total	308	136	**44.15%**

Table 6: KG-IQES solves 44.15% of MT bad cases in the previous 9 months.

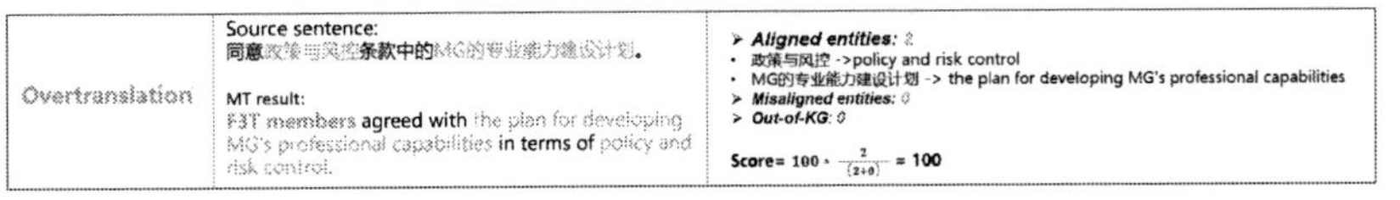

Figure 3: An example of overtranslation case: we do not extract NEs from the translation, so we do not find the entity 'F3T members' in the MT result.

5 Conclusion

We propose the KG-IQES, a simple, efficient, and interpretable system based on KG for estimating the quality of MT output without relying on reference translations. KG-IQES consists of the offline and online subsystems. The offline subsystem mainly constructs a multilingual KG based on the monolingual NER model and NE alignment model from the parallel corpora. The online subsystem provides an interpretable quality score for the MT output. Effectiveness of KG-IQES is verified by experiments in Huawei's Wireless Network domain. In the future, we will mitigate the problem of overtranslation and expand KG-IQES to more languages and more domains.

References

Dyer, C., Chahuneau, V., and Smith, N. A. (2013). A simple, fast, and effective reparameterization of ibm model 2. In *Proceedings of the 2013 Conference of the North American Chapter of the Association for Computational Linguistics: Human Language Technologies*, pages 644–648.

Freitag, M., Rei, R., Mathur, N., Lo, C.-k., Stewart, C., Avramidis, E., Kocmi, T., Foster, G., Lavie, A., and Martins, A. F. (2022). Results of wmt22 metrics shared task: Stop using bleu–neural metrics are better and more robust. In *Proceedings of the Seventh Conference on Machine Translation (WMT)*, pages 46–68.

Gekhman, Z., Aharoni, R., Beryozkin, G., Freitag, M., and Macherey, W. (2020). Kobe: Knowledge-based machine translation evaluation. In *Findings of the Association for Computational Linguistics: EMNLP 2020*, pages 3200–3207.

Li, B., He, Y., and Xu, W. (2021). Cross-lingual named entity recognition using parallel corpus: A new approach using xlm-roberta alignment. *arXiv preprint arXiv:2101.11112*.

Li, J., Fei, H., Liu, J., Wu, S., Zhang, M., Teng, C., Ji, D., and Li, F. (2022). Unified named entity recognition as word-word relation classification. In *Proceedings of the AAAI Conference on Artificial Intelligence*, pages 10965–10973.

Lo, C.-k. and Larkin, S. (2020). Machine translation reference-less evaluation using yisi-2 with bilingual mappings of massive multilingual language model. In *Proceedings of the Fifth Conference on Machine Translation*, pages 903–910.

Miyato, T., Dai, A. M., and Goodfellow, I. (2017). Adversarial training methods for semi-supervised text classification. In *International Conference on Learning Representations*.

Papineni, K., Roukos, S., Ward, T., and Zhu, W.-J. (2002). Bleu: a method for automatic evaluation of machine translation. In *Proceedings of the 40th annual meeting of the Association for Computational Linguistics*, pages 311–318.

Popović, M., Vilar, D., Avramidis, E., and Burchardt, A. (2011). Evaluation without references: Ibm1 scores as evaluation metrics. In *Proceedings of the Sixth Workshop on Statistical Machine Translation*, pages 99–103.

Rei, R., Farinha, A. C., Zerva, C., van Stigt, D., Stewart, C., Ramos, P., Glushkova, T., Martins, A. F., and Lavie, A. (2021). Are references really needed? unbabel-ist 2021 submission for the metrics shared task. In *Proceedings of the Sixth Conference on Machine Translation*, pages 1030–1040.

Sellam, T., Das, D., and Parikh, A. (2020). Bleurt: Learning robust metrics for text generation. In *Proceedings of the 58th Annual Meeting of the Association for Computational Linguistics*, pages 7881–7892.

Song, Y., Zhao, J., and Specia, L. (2021). Sentsim: Crosslingual semantic evaluation of machine translation. In *Proceedings of the 2021 Conference of the North American Chapter of the Association for Computational Linguistics: Human Language Technologies*, pages 3143–3156.

Specia, L., Shah, K., De Souza, J. G., and Cohn, T. (2013). Quest-a translation quality estimation framework. In *Proceedings of the 51st Annual Meeting of the Association for Computational Linguistics: System Demonstrations*, pages 79–84.

Wan, Y., Liu, D., Yang, B., Zhang, H., Chen, B., Wong, D., and Chao, L. (2022). Unite: Unified translation evaluation. In *Proceedings of the 60th Annual Meeting of the Association for Computational Linguistics (Volume 1: Long Papers)*, pages 8117–8127.

Zhang*, T., Kishore*, V., Wu*, F., Weinberger, K. Q., and Artzi, Y. (2020). Bertscore: Evaluating text generation with bert. In *International Conference on Learning Representations*.

Zhao, W., Glavaš, G., Peyrard, M., Gao, Y., West, R., and Eger, S. (2020). On the limitations of cross-lingual encoders as exposed by reference-free machine translation evaluation. In *Proceedings of the 58th Annual Meeting of the Association for Computational Linguistics*, pages 1656–1671.

Zhao, W., Peyrard, M., Liu, F., Gao, Y., Meyer, C. M., and Eger, S. (2019). Moverscore: Text generation evaluating with contextualized embeddings and earth mover distance. In *Proceedings of the 2019 Conference on Empirical Methods in Natural Language Processing (EMNLP)*.

Enhancing Gender Representation in Neural Machine Translation: A Comparative Analysis of Annotating Strategies for English-Spanish and English-Polish Language Pairs

Celia Soler Uguet csuguet@transperfect.com
Fred Bane fbane@transperfect.com
Mahmoud Aymo mahmoud.aymo@transperfect.com
João Pedro Fernandes Torres joao.torres@transperfect.com
Anna Zaretskaya azaretskaya@transperfect.com
Tània Blanch Miró tblanch@transperfect.com
TransPerfect

Machine translation systems have been shown to demonstrate gender bias (Savoldi et al., 2021; Stafanovičs et al., 2020; Stanovsky et al., 2019), and contribute to this bias with systematically unfair translations. In this presentation, we explore a method of enforcing gender in NMT. We generalize the method proposed by Vincent et al. (2022) to create training data not requiring a first-person speaker. Drawing from other works that use special tokens to pass additional information to NMT systems, e.g. by Ailem et al. (2021), we annotate the training data with special tokens to mark the gender of a given noun in the text, which enables the NMT system to produce the correct gender during translation. These tokens are also used to mark the gender in a source sentence at inference time. However, in production scenarios, gender is often unknown at inference time, so we propose two methods of leveraging language models to obtain these labels.

Our experiment is set up in a fine-tuning scenario, adapting an existing translation model with gender-annotated data. We focus on the English to Spanish and Polish language pairs. Without guidance, NMT systems often ignore signals that indicate the correct gender for translation. To this end, we consider two methods of annotating the source English sentence for gender, such as the noun *developer* in the following sentence:
The developer argued with the designer because she did not like the design.

1. We use a coreference resolution model based on SpanBERT (Joshi et al., 2020) to connect any gender-indicating pronouns to their head nouns.

2. We use the GPT-3.5 model prompted to identify the gender of each person in the sentence based on the context within the sentence.

For test data, we use a collection of sentences from Stanovsky et al. (2019) including two professions and one pronoun that can refer only to one of them. We use the above two methods to annotate the source sentence we want to translate, produce the translations with our fine-tuned model and compare the accuracy of the gender translation in both cases. The correctness of the gender was evaluated by professional linguists.

Proceedings of Machine Translation Summit XIX, Vol. 2: Users Track, pages 171–172
September 4–8, 2023, Macau SAR, China.

	Spanish	Polish
Total sentences	577	314
Baseline (no gender annotation in the source)	448	112
'Gold' gender marking	538	175
SpanBERT method	479	168
GPT method	478	158

Table 1: Results of the human evaluation of gender translation.

Overall, we observed a significant improvement in gender translations compared to the baseline (a 7% improvement for Spanish and a 50% improvement for Polish), with SpanBERT outperforming GPT on this task. The Polish MT model still struggles to produce the correct gender (even the translations produced with the 'gold truth' gender markings are only correct in 56% of the cases). We discuss limitations to this method. Our research is intended as a reference for fellow MT practitioners, as it offers a comparative analysis of two practical implementations that show the potential to enhance the accuracy of gender in translation, thereby elevating the overall quality of translation and mitigating gender bias.

References

Ailem, M., Liu, J., and Qader, R. (2021). Encouraging neural machine translation to satisfy terminology constraints. In *Findings of the Association for Computational Linguistics: ACL-IJCNLP 2021*, pages 1450–1455, Online. Association for Computational Linguistics.

Joshi, M., Chen, D., Liu, Y., Weld, D. S., Zettlemoyer, L., and Levy, O. (2020). Spanbert: Improving pre-training by representing and predicting spans.

Savoldi, B., Gaido, M., Bentivogli, L., Negri, M., and Turchi, M. (2021). Gender bias in machine translation.

Stafanovičs, A., Bergmanis, T., and Pinnis, M. (2020). Mitigating gender bias in machine translation with target gender annotations.

Stanovsky, G., Smith, N. A., and Zettlemoyer, L. (2019). Evaluating gender bias in machine translation.

Vincent, S. T., Barrault, L., and Scarton, C. (2022). Controlling extra-textual attributes about dialogue participants: A case study of English-to-Polish neural machine translation. In *Proceedings of the 23rd Annual Conference of the European Association for Machine Translation*, pages 121–130, Ghent, Belgium. European Association for Machine Translation.

Brand Consistency for Multilingual E-commerce Machine Translation

Bryan Zhang bryzhang@amazon.com
Stephan Walter sstwa@amazon.com
Saurabh Chetan Birari sbbirari@amazon.com
Ozlem Eren ozleme@amazon.com
Amazon.com, USA

Abstract

In the realm of e-commerce, it is crucial to ensure consistent localization of brand terms in product information translations. With the ever-evolving e-commerce landscape, new brands and their localized versions are consistently emerging. However, these diverse brand forms and aliases present a significant challenge in machine translation (MT). This study investigates MT brand consistency problem in multilingual e-commerce and proposes practical and sustainable solutions to maintain brand consistency in various scenarios within the e-commerce industry. Through experimentation and analysis of an English-Arabic MT system, we demonstrate the effectiveness of our proposed solutions.

Keywords: multilingual e-commerce, brand consistency, machine translation, data management, Arabic language

1 Introduction

The brand consistency problem in machine translation is often viewed as a terminology enforcement issue. Previous studies (Dinu et al., 2019; Post and Vilar, 2018; Susanto et al., 2020; Wang et al., 2021; Ailem et al., 2021) have proposed terminology constraint mechanisms to tackle this problem. However, these mechanisms assume a static terminology and fail to fully address the challenges encountered in an industry setting. In reality, the localized brand entries in the terminology bank are continuously expanding, being deleted, or undergoing edits, with different aliases taking distinct forms across language pairs.

While brands from larger companies often have well-established localized forms, smaller brands frequently lack such localized versions for specific language pairs. As a result, there is a constant need for fixing or updating brand names in translations. Addressing brand-related issues may require retraining or further fine-tuning of the production machine translation engine (Kanavos and Kartsaklis, 2010; Caskey and Maskey, 2013; Luo et al., 2022), however, the turnaround time to fix these issues can be unacceptable to users and may not align with the business requirements.

To tackle these challenges, we first analyze the brand localization phenomena across various language pairs to simplify the MT brand-handling problem in multilingual e-commerce, then we propose a systematic framework to enforce brand consistency at scale in industrial e-commerce machine translation systems. Furthermore, we provide experimental results showcasing the successful application of our proposed framework in an English-Arabic machine translation setting.

Proceedings of Machine Translation Summit XIX, Vol. 2: Users Track, pages 173–182
September 4–8, 2023, Macau SAR, China.

2 Cross-lingual brand preservation and transformation

To simplify the large-scale MT brand handling problem in E-commerce, we first propose to classify language pairs into two groups based on the major pattern of how brand terms need to be localized for a given language pair. These groups are brand preservation and brand transformation language pairs.

Brand Preservation (BP) language pairs are language pairs where the brand terms from the source language typically remain unchanged in the target language. These language pairs often share similar writing systems, such as English and German. For example, brand term *Adidas* has the same form in English and German. The majority of language pairs belong to this group in the context of E-commerce.

Brand Transformation (BT) language pairs are language pairs where the brand terms in the source language need to be transformed into a different localized form in the target language. This is often the case for language pairs with different writing systems, such as English-Arabic Al'Awadhi (2014), English-Japanese, and German-Greek.

Translation:
Apple - 苹果 [En-Zh]
American Standard - امريكان ستاندرد [En-Ar]
Transliteration:
Adidas - اديداس [En-Ar]
Creation:
G-Star RAW - G-ستار رو [En-Ar]
BMW - 宝马 (precious horse) [En-Zh]

Table 1: Brand Transformations and Examples

We observe brand terms are usually transformed through translation, transliteration and creation as Table 1 illustrates. Same brand terms can be transformed in different ways for different language pairs. For example: *Heineken*-ハイネケン [De-Ja] (Transliteration) and *Heineken*-喜力 [En-Zh] (Creation, meaning Happiness Power).

However, the need for brand transformations can also arise from business requirements or cultural considerations of a given region. For example, customers reading product information in **right-to-left languages** such as Arabic and Hebrew need to alter their reading direction whenever encountering a brand term in Latin-based scripts. In such cases, it is often preferred to have brands transformed in the target language to cater to the reading habits of the customers.

3 Systematic MT brand consistency enforcement for e-commerce translation

An overview of our proposed machine translation (MT) brand consistency enforcement framework is illustrated in Figure 1, the section 3.5 will discuss this framework in detail. The main components of the system are listed as following:

i Brand Mapping (BMCache)

ii Post-editing translation management system (TMS)

iii Heuristics-based approach (HEU)

iv Placeholder approach (PH)

v Data Augmentation approach (DA)

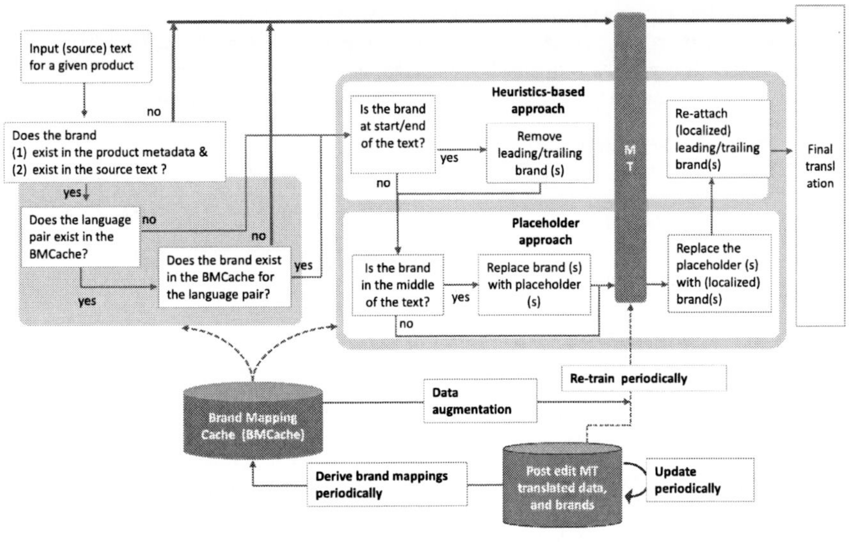

Figure 1: Systematic MT brand consistency enforcement framework for product information texts

3.1 BMCache and Post-editing TMS

The BMCache serves as a comprehensive terminology bank that stores brand terms along with their corresponding localized forms. It is continuously updated with new brand terms, localization forms, and changes derived from a post-editing Translation Management System (TMS). Although detailed discussions about the BMCache and TMS are beyond the scope of this paper, it is worth noting that in the context of e-commerce, brand terms can have multiple valid localized forms in different orthographic variations based on the target language. For instance, English brands can have multiple localized forms in Arabic due to transliteration variations. Similarly, in Japanese, the complexity of the written systems (including Romaji, Kanji, Hiragana, and Katakana)Unger (1996) can lead to multiple localized forms for an English brand, such as *Onitsuka* (Romaji) or オニツカ (Katakana).

To ensure consistency and standardization in brand mappings, a TMS should establish quality assurance guidelines that guide translators to adhere to the localized brand forms available in the BMCache. Once the localized brand forms are validated and accepted as the ground truth, they are stored in the BMCache and can be effectively utilized for communication with various stakeholders.

3.2 Data augmentation (DA) Solution

We first propose the data augmentation (DA) solution which can improve the brand handling capability of MT by incorporating localized brand forms in the target language through regular re-trainings. However, caution must be exercised when augmenting the re-training data with brand mappings from the full BMCache. It is recommended that MT practitioners only utilize brands from the BMCache that do not create ambiguity with generic word translations. For instance, in the Spanish-English language pair, the brand terms "Crema" and "Bebe" should be preserved in the English translation, however, they need to be translated as "cream" and "baby" in English as genetic words. In such cases, MT is expected to learn to disambiguate through parallel training data that contains the brands in the relevant context.

The DA strategy can also be applied periodically to update MT models at a fixed cadence. Alternatively, it can be used in an ad-hoc manner for models that require fixing due to a substantial influx of newer brands that consistently need to be localized in translations.

3.3 Heuristics-based (HEU) solution

Data sample size	Product info type	Brand position in the text		
		Start	*Middle*	*End*
∼half million	Titles	**96%**	3%	1%
∼half million	Desc.	27%	**72%**	1%
∼half million	BP	20%	**75%**	5%

Table 2: Brand term position in the product info texts: Titles, Descriptions (Desc.) and Bulletpointts (BP)

Table 2 provides a breakdown of the positions of brand terms within e-commerce product information. It is worth noting that in 96% of cases, the brand appears at the beginning of the product titles. Exploiting this positional heuristic of brand terms, we propose a straightforward solution based on heuristics. When a brand term is located at the start and/or the end of a title, our approach involves temporarily removing the brand, translating the remaining text using MT, and subsequently reattaching the appropriate localized brand (from the BMCache) to the start or end of the title. This solution eliminates the need for MT re-training or significant engineering modifications while ensuring a quick turnaround time for brand localization fixes.

3.4 Placeholder (PH) Solution

As a robustness feature, we also propose a placeholder solution for other cases where brand terms are located at flexible positions other than the start or the end of product information texts. This is especially useful to product descriptions and bulletpoints where brand terms usually occur in the middle of texts. Based on the previous study Post et al. (2019), we propose to check through the BMCache first, serialize and replace the brand terms with `[PLACEHOLDER]` token(s). The neural machine translation system needs to be placeholder-aware through training for the following steps: (i) read the `[PLACEHOLDER]` token(s) in the source, (ii) predict the position of the `[PLACEHOLDER]` token(s), (iii) place the `[PLACEHOLDER]` token(s) at the predicted position(s) in the target translation. After the machine translation process, the `[PLACEHOLDER]` token(s) is replaced with the proper localized brand form fetched from the BMCache.

This solution adapts to the dynamic nature of the BMCache and localized brand forms across language pairs. It also provides flexibility to fix ad-hoc brand localization issues within short turnover time.

3.5 Overview of the Brand Consistency Enforcement Framework

Given the complexity of the MT brand handling problem in E-commerce and characteristics of the BP and BT language pairs, we propose a systematic MT brand term consistency enforcement framework as shown in Figure 1 to ensure brand localization consistency in translation: This approach consists of all three brand handling solutions described in the previous sections, and a universal **brand handling logic** which enables the three solutions to work independently and in combination to tackle most MT brand handling scenarios in the e-commerce industry setting.

Conditions	BT Lang Pairs					BP Lang Pairs			
(1) Input brand exists (in the product meta data) and (2) Exists in source text	Y	Y	Y	Y	N	Y	Y	Y	N
(3) The language pair exists in BMCache	Y	Y	Y	Y	Y	N	N	N	N
(4) Input brand exists in BMCache	Y	Y	Y	N	-	-	-	-	-
(5) Brand (s) exists at the start or end of source text	Y	N	Y	-	-	Y	N	Y	-
(6) Brand (s) exists in the middle of the text	N	Y	Y	-	-	N	Y	Y	-
Brand Handling Solution (s)									
Heuristics (HEU)-based solution	×		×			×		×	
Placeholder (PH)-based solution		×	×				×	×	
Augmented MT handles directly				×	×				×

Table 3: Systematic MT Brand Handling Logic

Brand handling logic: this logic table contains the conditions and solutions as s Table 3 shown, Figure 1 has more detailed illustrations. This logic table highlights the following scenarios:

Scenario 1: For both BT and BP language pairs, when there is no input brand existing in the product meta data or the input brand does not exist in the source text, augmented MT translates the input text directly and handles the brands. MT can be periodically retrained to improve the capacity to handle brand terms.

Scenario 2: If a language pair does not exist in the BMCache, it will be considered as a BP language pair, both HEU an PH-based solutions can be applied; if it exists in the BMCache, it is considered as a PT language pair. In this case, both HEU and PH-based solutions can be applied only if the input brand exists in the BMCache. Otherwise, augmented MT alone handles brands in the text since there is no established brand localized form for the target language.

Scenario 3: For both BP and PT language pairs, if there is no leading or trailing brand (s), either the augmented MT will handle the brands directly in translation or the PH solution will handle the brands if the PH solution is used for that language pair.

Flexible application solution(s): although PH-based solution can handle brand terms at flexible positions in the texts, including leading and trailing brands that the HEU-based solution focuses on, we propose to keep the two solutions separate for the following reasons: Firstly, the HEU solution can handle most brand handling cases on its own for the texts of certain domain such as product titles. Secondly, the HEU-based solution is simpler and does not require re-training, ensuring that leading and trailing brands have the proper localized form in the translation. Lastly, the two solutions are complementary, and they can be incrementally developed to meet the requirements of various e-commerce scenarios for the MT brand consistency improvement.

Scalability to multilingual MT: Our systematic approach to handling brands in MT can be potentially extended to multilingual models. The BMCache can differentiate between the BP and PT language pairs, and is compatible with both the HEU and PH-based solutions. Therefore, with multilingual MT systems, we can simply provide the input language pair as a signal to the proposed systematic brand consistency enforcement framework, then the multilingual MT can utilize the appropriate localized brand names in the translation for that language pair as an MT system of a single language pair. This approach is easily scalable to any number of languages and provides a straightforward means of maintaining brand consistency across all translated content.

4 Experiment

We experiment with English-Arabic language pair using our proposed framework for brand consistency in machine translation because it has more language-specific complexities and challenges.

4.1 Experiment Setup

We train a transformer-based (Vaswani et al., 2017) MT system that is encoder-heavy (20 encoder and 2 decoder layers) (Domhan et al., 2020) using the Sockeye MT toolkit. We use a vocabulary of 32K BPE (Sennrich et al., 2016) tokens. We optimise using ADAM Kingma and Ba (2015) and perform early-stopping based on perplexity on a held-out dev set. We train a model with in-house generic translation data and e-commerce translation data with the above specifications. The model is fine-tuned with only the in-domain e-commerce translations to create a baseline model, M_0. Below, we describe four more model variants using various components from the Figure 1.

1. M_1: We further obtain millions of the PE product data (in-domain data) and add to the original in-domain data. The newer in-domain data has approximate 13% more brand occurrences than the original, we train an updated model M_1 same way as the baseline model using the newer data. This can show us the effectiveness of simply adding more data with proper brand localized forms without additional brand consistency enforcement.

2. M_2: We further incorporate English-Arabic BMCache data to augment the in-domain data in order to improve the model's ability to learn brand mappings. The English-Arabic mapping data accounts for 5% of the indomain data. This model corresponds to the Data Augmentation approach described in Figure 1.

3. M_3: Building on M_2, we extend the M_2 with the HEU component in our framework.

4. M_4: Building on M_3, we add the PH component in our framework to show the performance of the framework to the full extent.

For each product information type, we obtain approximately half a million test cases together with brands that can match the BMCache. The number of unique brands across three product information types is in the range of 60 K to 120 K.

5 Results

	Titles	Descriptions	Bulletpoints
M_0	-	-	-
M_1	+89.9%	+70.1%	+55.3%
M_2	+96.9%	+72.5%	+57.0%
M_3	+239.4%	+105.3%	+81.8%
M_4	+247.0%	+175.1%	+155.0%

Table 4: Precision of brand terms consistently localized in translation as per entry in BMCache

Table 4 presents the precision scores of the proper localized brand forms in the translations checking against the ground truth in the BMCache. By simply adding more data with brand localized forms without additional brand consistency enforcement, the precision of proper brand localized forms in the translation of M_1 has improved across all titles, descriptions and bullet points compared with the baseline model M_0. Thereafter, we see that M_2 continues to improve when the training data is augmented with the brand data from BMCache.

Finally, after applying the heuristics (HEU) and the placeholder (PH) solutions, the results show that M_3 and M_4 model can achieve close to nearly perfect brand localization consistency in translation for product titles, and precision is also increased by a large margin for product descriptions and bulletpoints. However, we observe cases of missing placeholder tokens in descriptions and bulletpoints, especially when there are three or more placeholder tokens inserted. This issue is also highlighted in the previous study Post et al. (2019) on using placeholder features.

	Titles	Descriptions	Bulletpoints
M_0	-	-	-
M_1	**+90.6%**	+2.6%	+27.8%
M_4	+74.5%	**+6.3%**	**+29.1%**

Table 5: BLEU Scores on Test Sets

	Titles	Descriptions	Bulletpoints
M_0	-	-	-
M_1	**+41.6%**	+0.6%	+41.9%
M_4	+34.3%	**+2.1%**	**+43.0%**

Table 6: ChrF Scores on Test Sets

Table 5 and 6 presents the BLEU and chrF scores of the generic translation quality disregarding the enforcement of consistent brand translations. We see that the M_4 system that makes use of our brand consistency MT framework achieve the best results for product descriptions and bulletpoints but not the titles.

We have further conducted online A/B testing in a store with English-Arabic MT. Customers in this store typically shop in Arabic and use localized versions of brand names while browsing for branded products. Customers are presented with different versions of the product translations from the baseline model (M_0), and the update model (M_4) with three brand handling solutions.

After a 4-week A/B testing experiment, the results have shown that the translations from the MT with brand handling solutions (M_4) had a much larger positive impact on the customers' shopping experiences. This indicates the effectiveness of our approach.

6 Related work

Previous approaches to terminology in machine translation are evaluated on translations in the generic domain (Crego et al., 2016; Dinu et al., 2019; Post and Vilar, 2018; Susanto et al., 2020; Wang et al., 2021; Ailem et al., 2021; Zhang et al., 2022). Other work related to lexical constrained machine translation have focused on general named entities and cross-lingual named entities mapping (Ugawa et al., 2018; Yan et al., 2018; Alankar Jain, 2019).

However, brand handling in the e-commerce machine translation has received little attention in the literature. Previous study Guha and Heger (2014) presents various challenges of "non-standard" source language structure in e-commerce specific texts, they highlight the issue of brand names that are lexically ambiguous, and show that their e-commerce MT systems can manage to preserve brands for 90% of the translations. In the paper, we extend their description of other brand translation issues for e-commerce as presented in Table 3.

Other brand handling studies for e-commerce translations focus on the effects of efficiently standardizing and brand localization Dong et al. (2020); Jeong et al. (2019) on Arabic Benmamoun et al. (2016); Abuljadail and Badghish (2021) and Chinese e-commerce Liu et al. (2016).

7 Conclusions

This study examines brand localization in various language pairs and proposes language groups for brand preservation and transformation to simplify machine translation (MT) brand consistency problem. Then we propose a systematic approach for MT brand consistency enforcement for product info texts translation. This approach consists of a universal brand handling logic as a framework and three MT brand handling solutions which can work independently or in combination to address most MT brand handling cases across language pairs in various e-commerce scenarios. The proposed approach is successfully applied in a case study of MT for English to Arabic, with offline and online experiments showing improved effectiveness and customer experiences.

References

Mohammad Abuljadail and Saeed Badghish. 2021. Exploring type of strategies used by global brands to engage the saudi consumers more in brands' facebook pages in saudi arabia in terms of "like, share and comment". المجلة العربية للإدارة, 41(1):405–416.

Melissa Ailem, Jingshu Liu, and Raheel Qader. 2021. https://doi.org/10.18653/v1/2021.findings-acl.125 Encouraging neural machine translation to satisfy terminology constraints. In *Findings of the Association for Computational Linguistics: ACL-IJCNLP 2021*, pages 1450–1455, Online. Association for Computational Linguistics.

Zachary Chase Lipton Alankar Jain, Bhargavi Paranjape. 2019. Entity projection via machine translation for cross-lingual ner. In *EMNLP/IJCNLP 2019 Computer Science, Mathematics*. EMNLP.

Noura Al'Awadhi. 2014. *Arabic Brand Names: To Translate or Transliterate?* Ph.D. thesis.

Mamoun Benmamoun, Rana Sobh, Nitish Singh, and Francisco Tigre Moura. 2016. Gulf arab e-business environment: Localization strategy insights. *Thunderbird International Business Review*, 58(5):439–452.

Sasha P. Caskey and Sameer Maskey. 2013. https://patents.google.com/patent/US20130007405 Translation cache prediction.

Josep Maria Crego, Jungi Kim, Guillaume Klein, Anabel Rebollo, Kathy Yang, Jean Senellart, Egor Akhanov, Patrice Brunelle, Aurélien Coquard, Yongchao Deng, Satoshi Enoue, Chiyo Geiss, Joshua Johanson, Ardas Khalsa, Raoum Khiari, Byeongil Ko, Catherine Kobus, Jean Lorieux, Leidiana Martins, Dang-Chuan Nguyen, Alexandra Priori, Thomas Riccardi, Natalia Segal, Christophe Servan, Cyril Tiquet, Bo Wang, Jin Yang, Dakun Zhang, Jing Zhou, and Peter Zoldan. 2016. http://arxiv.org/abs/1610.05540 Systran's pure neural machine translation systems. *CoRR*, abs/1610.05540.

Georgiana Dinu, Prashant Mathur, Marcello Federico, and Yaser Al-Onaizan. 2019. https://doi.org/10.18653/v1/P19-1294 Training neural machine translation to apply terminology constraints. In *Proceedings of the 57th Annual Meeting of the Association for Computational Linguistics*, pages 3063–3068, Florence, Italy. Association for Computational Linguistics.

Tobias Domhan, Michael Denkowski, David Vilar, Xing Niu, Felix Hieber, and Kenneth Heafield. 2020. https://www.aclweb.org/anthology/2020.amta-research.10 The sockeye 2 neural machine translation toolkit at AMTA 2020. In *Proceedings of the 14th Conference of the Association for Machine Translation in the Americas (Volume 1: Research Track)*, pages 110–115, Virtual. Association for Machine Translation in the Americas.

Lily C Dong, Chunling Yu, et al. 2020. Globalization or localization: Global brand perception in emerging markets. *International Business Research*, 13(10):53–65.

Jyoti Guha and Carmen Heger. 2014. https://aclanthology.org/2014.amta-users.3 Machine translation for global e-commerce on eBay. In *Proceedings of the 11th Conference of the Association for Machine Translation in the Americas: MT Users Track*, pages 31–37, Vancouver, Canada. Association for Machine Translation in the Americas.

Insik Jeong, Jong-Ho Lee, and Eunmi Kim. 2019. Determinants of brand localization in international markets. *Service Business*, 13:75–100.

Panagiotis Kanavos and Dimitrios Kartsaklis. 2010. https://aclanthology.org/2010.jec-1.3 Integrating machine translation with translation memory: A practical approach. In *Proceedings of the Second Joint EM+/CNGL Workshop: Bringing MT to the User: Research on Integrating MT in the Translation Industry*, pages 11–20, Denver, Colorado, USA. Association for Machine Translation in the Americas.

Diederik P. Kingma and Jimmy Ba. 2015. Adam: A method for stochastic optimization. volume abs/1412.6980.

Sindy Liu, Patsy Perry, Christopher Moore, and Gary Warnaby. 2016. The standardization-localization dilemma of brand communications for luxury fashion retailers' internationalization into china. *Journal of Business Research*, 69(1):357–364.

Chen Luo, Vihan Lakshman, Anshumali Shrivastava, Tianyu Cao, Sreyashi Nag, Rahul Goutam, Hanqing Lu, Yiwei Song, and Bing Yin. 2022. https://www.amazon.science/publications/rose-robust-caches-for-amazon-product-search Rose: Robust caches for amazon product search. In *The Web Conference 2022*.

Matt Post, Shuoyang Ding, Marianna Martindale, and Winston Wu. 2019. https://www.aclweb.org/anthology/W19-6618 An exploration of placeholding in neural machine translation. In *Proceedings of Machine Translation Summit XVII Volume 1: Research Track*, pages 182–192, Dublin, Ireland. European Association for Machine Translation.

Matt Post and David Vilar. 2018. https://doi.org/10.18653/v1/N18-1119 Fast lexically constrained decoding with dynamic beam allocation for neural machine translation. In *Proceedings of the 2018 Conference of the North American Chapter of the Association for Computational Linguistics: Human Language Technologies, Volume 1 (Long Papers)*, pages 1314–1324, New Orleans, Louisiana. Association for Computational Linguistics.

Rico Sennrich, Barry Haddow, and Alexandra Birch. 2016. https://doi.org/10.18653/v1/P16-1162 Neural machine translation of rare words with subword units. In *Proceedings of the 54th Annual Meeting of the Association for Computational Linguistics (Volume 1: Long Papers)*, pages 1715–1725, Berlin, Germany. Association for Computational Linguistics.

Raymond Hendy Susanto, Shamil Chollampatt, and Liling Tan. 2020. https://doi.org/10.18653/v1/2020.acl-main.325 Lexically constrained neural machine translation with Levenshtein transformer. In *Proceedings of the 58th Annual Meeting of the Association for Computational Linguistics*, pages 3536–3543, Online. Association for Computational Linguistics.

Arata Ugawa, Akihiro Tamura, Takashi Ninomiya, Hiroya Takamura, and Manabu Okumura. 2018. Neural machine translation incorporating named entity. In *Proceedings of the 27th International Conference on Computational Linguistics*, pages 3240–3250.

J Marshall Unger. 1996. *Literacy and script reform in occupation Japan: Reading between the lines*. Oxford University Press on Demand.

Ashish Vaswani, Noam Shazeer, Niki Parmar, Jakob Uszkoreit, Llion Jones, Aidan N Gomez, ukasz Kaiser, and Illia Polosukhin. 2017. Attention is all you need. *Advances in neural information processing systems*, 30.

Ke Wang, Shuqin Gu, Boxing Chen, Yu Zhao, Weihua Luo, and Yuqi Zhang. 2021. https://aclanthology.org/2021.wmt-1.85 TermMind: Alibaba's WMT21 machine translation using terminologies task submission. In *Proceedings of the Sixth Conference on Machine Translation*, pages 851–856, Online. Association for Computational Linguistics.

Jinghui Yan, Jiajun Zhang, JinAn Xu, and Chengqing Zong. 2018. The impact of named entity translation for neural machine translation. In *China Workshop on Machine Translation*, pages 63–73. Springer.

Wu Zhang, Tung Yeung Lam, and Mee Yee Chan. 2022. https://doi.org/10.1145/3556677.3556691 Using translation memory to improve neural machine translations. In *Proceedings of the 2022 6th International Conference on Deep Learning Technologies*, ICDLT '22, page 49–54, New York, NY, USA. Association for Computing Machinery.

Developing automatic verbatim transcripts for international multilingual meetings: an end-to-end solution

Akshat Dewan
Michal Ziemski
Henri Meylan
Lorenzo Concina
Bruno Pouliquen {firstname.lastname}@wipo.int
World Intellectual Property Organization, Global Databases Service
34, chemin des Colombettes, CH-1211 Geneva 20, Switzerland

Abstract

This paper presents an end-to-end solution for the creation of fully automated conference meeting transcripts and their machine translations into various languages. This tool has been developed at the World Intellectual Property Organization (WIPO) using in-house developed speech-to-text (S2T) and machine translation (MT) components. Beyond describing data collection and fine-tuning, resulting in a highly customized and robust system, this paper describes the architecture and evolution of the technical components as well as highlights the business impact and benefits from the user side. We also point out particular challenges in the evolution and adoption of the system and how the new approach created a new product and replaced existing established workflows in conference management documentation.

1. Introduction

This paper describes the experience of implementation of a system to automatically create post-factum meeting transcripts and their translations in various languages at WIPO. WIPO is a United Nations (UN) agency in charge of intellectual property and hosts many meetings over the calendar year[1]. These meetings are simultaneously interpreted into the six official UN languages – Arabic, Chinese, English, French, Russian and Spanish (AR, ZH, EN, FR, RU, and ES). Originally, for these meetings, English verbatim reports and their translations were all hand produced, resulting in high cost and delay. Now we deliver automatic transcripts and translations shortly after the end of the meeting.

All automatically produced transcripts and their translations are now published on a newly created public web portal[2], which combines live video, video-on-demand, S2T, MT, and a comprehensive search engine. It is integrated with other WIPO conference room systems, there-

---

[1] WIPO has more than 100 formal meeting days a year

[2] https://webcast.wipo.int/

fore has access to automatic download of media files and meta data which allows for a rich user experience. The solution has also been already adopted by other international organizations.

The backend systems are customized using WIPO data and data gathered from the collaboration of various international organizations. Both neural S2T and neural machine translation (NMT) support all six UN languages and provide transcripts and translations in after-the-fact mode. The MT and S2T components are customized to work well for the language used in the meetings domain of international organizations. Our solution, based on open-source tools, is installed on-premises, allowing us to meet our strong data security and privacy policies, and is even fit for our confidential meetings. We took a conscious decision to cascade S2T with MT instead of end-to-end speech-to-translated-text approach, because it did not meet minimum quality requirements across all language pairs.

Overall, the new solution was well received by the users, creating a new type of product, and replacing existing manual workflows. The users accepted the trade off between potentially lower transcript accuracy for significantly reduced turnaround time. Collected user feedback regarding speed, access and quality shows a positive impact and a transformation of the way transcripts are used. Evaluation included automatic metrics like Word Error Rate (WER) and BLEU (Papineni, 2002) for S2T and MT and other more business-oriented metrics such as fitness for purpose, turnaround time, user experience and cost savings. Further work would be in improving transcript quality, increasing the scope of supported languages, and investigation of open questions such as preference and evaluations of different pathways to arrive at a certain transcript language: e.g., S2T on monolingual interpretation channel vs S2T + MT cascade on multilingual direct floor channel.

2. Background

WIPO, as a specialized UN agency, hosts many international, multilingual meetings each year. Speakers can deliver their interventions in any of the official languages of the UN or in Portuguese. The original speech is then simultaneously interpreted into the remaining official languages.

For all WIPO meetings, originally, verbatim reports were prepared in all UN official languages manually. These were very high quality reports but were costly and time-intensive to produce - anywhere from a month to sometimes 6 months.

With the help of our solution, which is a cascade of an S2T (WIPO S2T[3]), and an MT system (WIPO Translate[4]), we provide machine-generated transcripts and their corresponding machine translations in a couple of hours after the conclusion of a meeting. After running the system in pilot mode for one year for two of its especially important meetings, the WIPO General Assemblies for most of its meetings adopted this system, and it has replaced the manually prepared verbatim reports. This includes the processing of internal confidential WIPO meetings.

Other international organizations are also building speech to text solutions for various use cases, and we are closely collaborating with some. The European Parliament and European Commission are building systems to make their meetings more accessible to a wider audience. The United Nations office of Geneva, International Labour Organization, World

[3]https://www.wipo.int/about-ip/en/artificial_intelligence/speech_to_text.html

[4]https://www.wipo.int/wipo-translate/en/

Trade Organization, and the European Union Court of Justice are also leveraging the WIPO technology to accelerate their work of report writing.

3. Motivation and Design

WIPO's extensive experience in the development of innovative MT models was a major driver behind the efforts to explore S2T for WIPO's needs. When we started our exploration in 2018, we trained an English model from scratch and benchmarked it against other commercial and open-source (Amodei, 2015), (Collobert, 2016) providers on our in-domain test set. We obtained competitive overall accuracy, which along with other business needs for terminology accuracy, turnaround time and strong confidentiality requirements, motivated us to continue developing in-house and guided our design choices.

In 2018, hybrid HMM DNN Kaldi recipes were state-of-the-art (Hadian, 2018), but we chose to use the end-to-end approach using RETURNN (Zeyer, 2018). Our decision relied on the promise (Chan, 2016), (Chiu, 2017), (Doetsch, 2016) of the attention based RNN models and the relative ease of training models in the end-to-end paradigm.

We recognized the fast pace of evolution of the state of the art and kept a modular architecture to easily integrate other providers in our pipeline. Currently, we have RETURNN and ESPnet integrated in our production pipeline. ESPnet[5] Transformer models provide more accurate (lower WER) results compared to RETURNN RNN models. On the other hand, RNN models outperform Transformer models on the metric of adequacy measured in terms of deletion errors.

We can select the model with the highest fitness for purpose. We are also planning to add support for various commercial S2T providers to further increase our options.

4. Training data

A major hurdle for in-house S2T development was obtaining in-domain training data, as the originally collected internal WIPO data was limited in size, especially in languages other than English. To overcome this challenge, we did the following:

1) we collaborated with other international organizations to leverage their historical meetings data,
2) contracted external providers to prepare transcriptions of WIPO in-domain audio,
3) and bought out-of-domain proprietary corpora

Collaboration with International Organizations: As international organizations hold many meetings every year, we targeted meeting audios and their corresponding reports for our needs. Obtaining such data and using it for training poses several hurdles. Using interpretation audio has a potential intellectual property right based legal issue. There are other administrative and technical obstacles before such data becomes available and usable.

Sourcing and filtering: Very often, meeting audio and meeting reports are owned by different business units and thus are stored separately. This can lead to poor mapping between meeting audio and report files. In many cases, the exact type of content varies, and reports can be heavily edited and contain a lot of indirect speech. We filter out such reports to reduce the amount of noise in training data. For text extraction, we have to deal with meeting records that

[5] https://github.com/espnet/espnet

are kept in several different document formats such as Doc, Docx, RTF, and PDF. Extracting text from these documents needs special care or it can lead to noisy data.

Long-term storage and limitations of use: We must also take special care when the partner data is sensitive and not publicly available. E.g., making special arrangements for isolating long-term storage for such data and limiting the use of models trained with such data.

Crowdsourcing transcripts: We also contracted external providers to create some in-domain training data transcripts. Such transcripts were cheaper but suffered from inconsistencies and errors in WIPO terminology. We had to run several iterations of harmonization and cleanup to reach the desired level of accuracy. We also leveraged the Arabic and Chinese speakers at WIPO to collect audio for some of our glossaries and terminology databases.

Commercial corpora: Apart from freely available public corpora – librispeech (Panayato, 2015) (Pratap, 2020), common voice[6], multitedx (Salesky, 2021), m-ailabs[7], open STT[8] etc, we also procured some commercially available corpora for Arabic and Chinese as can be seen in figure 1.

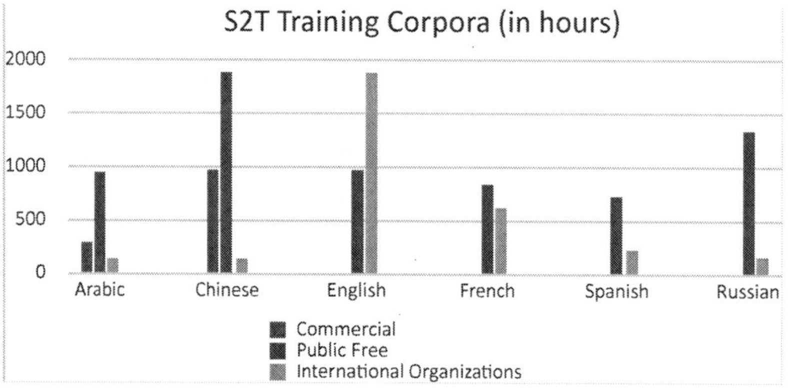

Figure 1: Breakdown of the training corpora for six UN languages in hours of audio.

[6]https://labs.mozilla.org/projects/common-voice

[7]https://www.caito.de/2019/01/03/the-m-ailabs-speech-dataset/

[8]https://github.com/snakers4/open_stt

5. Training S2T

In this section, we describe our pipeline (see Figure 2) to obtain training corpora from the sources data mentioned in section 4.

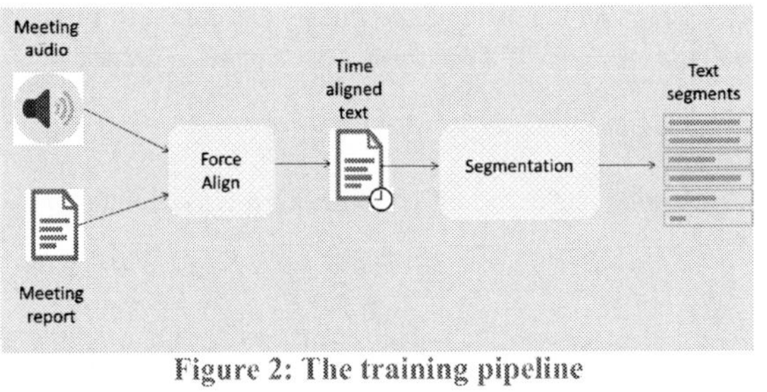

Figure 2: The training pipeline

Audio text alignment /Word level alignment: As each meeting audio file runs for hours and is not compatible with present-day neural architectures, it must be split into segments. To that end, text extracted from meeting reports must be aligned with meeting audio. Gentle[9], with a publicly available Kaldi model is used for English, however, as such models are not readily available for other UN official languages, we trained Kaldi models for ES, FR, ZH, AR and RU. This results in word level alignment of text and audio.

Segmentation / Sentence level alignment: We create training segments using word level timing information obtained from forced alignment. We carry out three distinct kinds of segmentations: 1) linguistic segmentation – based on sentence boundaries; 2) length-based segmentation; and 3) a hybrid of the 1) and 2).

Data augmentation: We use speed perturbation of audio to augment our training data. We also add silence and music examples in the training data with the goal of increasing robustness.

Pre-processing text: We tokenize the text and replace cased text with casing tags to decrease the vocabulary size. In addition, the multilingual nature of our meetings sometimes leads to crosstalk between different channels; therefore, we annotate the foreign language audio with special tags. The training corpora thus prepared are combined, harmonized, and filtered before proceeding for training different RNN, and Transformer models using RETURNN and ESPnet training scripts.

6. Machine translation

We chose to cascade S2T with MT to provide speech to translated text. One reason for this choice was insufficient training data for end-to-end speech translation and another reason was to leverage highly performant MT models for the meetings domain of WIPO. These WIPO Translate MT (Pouliquen, 2017) models are custom-trained using text from WIPO meetings and other documents.

---

[9] https://github.com/lowerquality/gentle

To further customize the MT models for cascading with S2T, we experimented with two methods: 1) denoising models that improve the quality of automatic transcriptions and make them more like the input expected by an NMT system; 2) noising models that replicate errors produced by the S2T system and can be used to introduce errors to the source side of the parallel MT corpora to make the MT systems more robust to automatic transcriptions.

Our initial noising and denoising experiments did not allow us to efficiently model the transcription errors; therefore, we did not further pursue this approach.

7. Decoding pipeline

In this section, we describe our decoding pipeline. Figure 3 illustrates various inputs and outputs of our system.

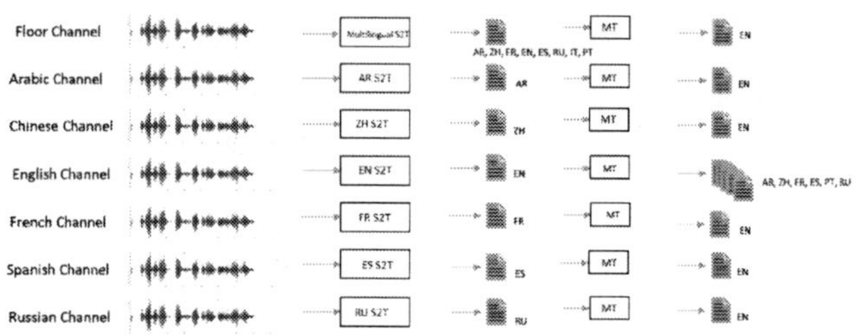

Figure 3: Inputs and outputs

Input videos: As seen in Figure 3, WIPO meetings have 7 audio channels – 6 for the 6 official UN languages plus 1 for the floor. The floor channel is multilingual and has the speaker's original audio while the other 6 channels are monolingual and may contain interpretation. When the language of a monolingual channel matches the language of the multilingual floor channel, the monolingual channel contains the same audio as the multilingual floor channel; otherwise, the monolingual channel has the audio from the interpretation booth.

Meta data: A tight integration with other WIPO systems allows us access to rich meta data to enhance the user experience. The metadata consists of the following items:

- Meeting title and category
- Agenda items and their corresponding timestamps
- Speakers and their corresponding timestamps (this information is more accurate and informative than automatic speaker diarization)
- Speaker information (Flag, Biography etc.)
- List of associated meeting documents

We have a fully automatic pipeline that fetches the meeting video files and metadata from the media server as soon as a meeting concludes.

Output: Outputs constitute S2T transcripts for the 7 audio channels followed by machine translations of the S2T transcripts. Once the media and meta data are available, we run S2T, and MT systems followed by indexing everything in Elasticsearch[10]. Finally, the video, tran-

[10] https://www.elastic.co/

scripts and the translations are published on our public facing webcasting portal. The following bullet points summarize the workflow followed for each of the 7 audio channels:

- Split the several hour-long audio file into 1-20 second segments. We use webRTC[11] or Silero[12] for VAD, and Kaldi[13] for segmentation.
- The segments are then fed to WIPO S2T to generate text, which is then filtered and normalized.
- The English S2T generated text is machine translated into the five remaining UN official language and Portuguese. S2T generated texts in other languages are machine translated back into English (including the multilingual floor channel where each sentence is either copied, if originally in English, or translated into English).
- The audio and the normalized text are force aligned to obtain word level alignment between text and audio.
- Meeting metadata along with the machine transcripts are then indexed in Elasticsearch, which enables a powerful search functionality.
- Some users prefer the rich functionality and familiarity of the Word format to our web interface, so we create exports in a Docx format at the last step.

The output files are uploaded to the webcasting portal[14] as they become available. Typically, this means that the English transcript is online before the other languages.

8. Webcasting Portal

Before 2022, WIPO had two separate websites – one for WIPO S2T and another for meeting live video and VODs. This was not ideal and with the goal of enhancing experience for WIPO stakeholders, we designed and developed a new unified web portal: webcast.wipo.int

The portal offers S2T text that helps in making WIPO meetings content become more available and visible. In addition, it becomes accessible to the hearing impaired. While WIPO meetings are multilingual to start with, the portal further cuts the linguistic barrier by providing machine translation of the S2T generated text. This allows e.g. a non-Chinese user to read the English translation of the original statement made by the Chinese delegation in Chinese. We have also taken particular care to make the portal accessible to the visually impaired by having screen reader friendly web design. The WIPO meetings meta data along with WIPO S2T text allows for smooth navigation and search across the content. The powerful search enables content discovery across the full WIPO meetings library, including records from the past.

Systems Integration: The webcasting portal was envisaged to have a tight integration with other IT systems at WIPO. E.g., the webcasting portal interacts with the videoconferencing

[11] https://github.com/wiseman/py-webrtcvad

[12] https://github.com/snakers4/silero-vad

[13] https://kaldi-asr.org/

[14] https://webcast.wipo.int

software system from Arbor Media called Connectedviews[15] via a web API. Connectedviews itself is integrated with other videoconferencing systems like Televic[16] that provide meta data information like "who spoke when." The WIPO Diplomatic Engagements Team also adds other metadata to the Connectedviews system. This integration reduces the turnaround time of meeting transcripts for our stakeholders. We encountered several hurdles during integration, and some are described here:

Inconsistency in meeting titles: Meeting titles are manually entered in the videoconferencing software, and this can cause some inconsistencies. These inconsistencies could lead to duplicate entries on our public facing portal. To avoid that, we set up a strict naming convention for meeting titles. This, however, does not mitigate all the risks of having duplicates in the web portal, therefore, we need to rely on effective communication between teams to overcome this challenge.

Changes to metadata: Since some meta data is dynamic[17], we have opted for a polling method to update the meta data on our portal continually.

Communication: Continuous communication with the different stakeholders is an important aspect of our work. It is especially important because of the multitude of ways in which the portal can be used. One example is as follows: we decode the 6 monolingual channels using monolingual S2T models while we decode the multilingual floor channel using a multilingual S2T model. Monolingual audio channels contain the same audio as the multilingual floor channel when floor language is the same as the monolingual channel language. This leads to a scenario where one audio has two different transcriptions. This causes confusion for the users, and we solve this by one-on-one user training sessions.

9. Experiments with Whisper

We have also been experimenting with the OpenAI Whisper (Radford, 2022) models. For now, we have focussed on using Whisper only for S2T and we plan to investigate the translation feature in the future. We are investigating customization of pre-trained models for improving performance on in-domain terminology. Customization paths that we currently investigate are:

- Fine-tuning pre-trained models using in-domain data from WIPO and other international organizations.
- Prompting strategies for the pre-trained models to improve performance for WIPO terminology

In our fine-tuning experiments, especially for high-resource languages like English and French, fine-tuning improved the recognition performance on in-domain terminology, but the general accuracy remained unchanged or even slightly worsened. These experiments suggest that it would be difficult to improve performance for high resource languages. However, we plan to run more fine-tuning experiments for languages like Arabic, Chinese and Russian. Whisper models have unpredictable behaviour for multilingual audios, and we are trying to

[15]https://www.arbormedia.nl/products/connected-views

[16]https://www.televic.com/en/conference/markets/institutions

[17] For example, country names can change – e.g., Turkey was recently changed to Türkiye

use speaker diarization to resolve that. We are also investigating prompting strategies (Radford, 2022) to improve in-domain recognition accuracy. Early prompting experiments in English have shown promising but sometimes unpredictable results and we are still working on perfecting our strategies.

10. Evaluation and benchmarking

We evaluate our S2T models on the widely used automatic evaluation metric of WER (and Character Error Rate - CER). Since it penalizes all errors equally, we also evaluate in-domain terminology on a smaller, terminology heavy test set to get a better understanding of perceived WER.

Language	WIPO	GCP	AWS	Whisper Small	Whisper Medium	Whisper Large
EN	0.148	0.123	0.118	0.109	0.102	0.107
FR	0.056	0.171	0.102	0.149	0.094	0.085
ES	0.101	0.126	0.108	0.108	0.079	0.073
ZH	0.071	0.070	0.061	0.193	0.105	0.125
RU	0.145	0.255	0.319	0.278	0.253	0.238
AR	0.191	0.473	0.264	0.487	0.340	0.508

Table 1: WER (CER for ZH) values for various models and services in Dec 2022

We note that our test sets have varied sizes, e.g., EN has 3051 examples while FR has only 252 and this can introduce some bias in our evaluations. We also note that while both AWS and GCP have features to customize the models, we used their off-the-shelf models in our benchmarking.

We also performed human evaluation with the help of linguists to evaluate fitness for purpose where errors were classified as minor or disruptive. Disruptive errors delete or substitute important parts such as nouns, verbs, proper names, time, places, numbers etc. and affect text comprehension. Minor errors do not change the sentence's meaning, for example, errors in function words - pronouns, prepositions, adjectives, and adverbs.

We note that human evaluation for Whisper models and commercial providers has not yet been carried out and is a work in progress.

11. User Feedback

The WIPO General Assemblies (GA) reached a consensus in September 2019 to approve a S2T pilot. It was proposed as a replacement for the verbatim reports for two of nine WIPO bodies. We collected regular feedback during the pilot phase and after its successful completion, WIPO GA in 2021 approved the WIPO S2T for all but two of its meetings. While the users highlight the inaccuracies in certain languages other than English, the overall feedback is extremely positive. The rapid availability and the cost savings are congratulated. It also aligns with the Organization policy for increased digitization. Users also appreciate the user interface, which enables new and improved working methodologies.

12. Conclusions and future work

The deployment of the WIPO S2T and its consolidation into the publicly available WIPO webcast portal created a new type of meeting transcripts, which was well received both internally and externally. Even though the produced texts contain errors, according to user feedback, this was by far outweighed by the speed and convenience of presentation and availability – including various languages and accessibility. This switch also achieved a considerable cost reduction at WIPO.

Automatic workflows and a tight integration with existing systems has proven crucial to the success and adoption of the system. Working closely with the business side in short iterations, and particular focus on communicating the advantages and limitations of the solution have been critical to be able to achieve a positive reception of the final new product, shown by feedback collected.

While most models and components are trained in-house, it remains to be seen which mix of such components will deliver the best possible quality and experience for users in the long term. The modular architecture of the system allows reacting flexibly to user demands and ongoing developments. Especially for high resource languages such as English and French, pre-trained components may be more than competitive to the existing in-house produced. In the short term, we intend to improve in-domain terminology accuracy by using customized Whisper models.

For future work, we would like to make our benchmarking more comprehensive, by including more commercial S2T providers and using the customization features they offer. There are also many open questions: such as the best way to allow for and incorporate the manual edition of pieces of transcripts; and how to best use the multitude of various outputs generated from different audio streams: for example, direct S2T on interpretation channel vs MT cascade.

Acknowledgements

The authors wish to thank Sandrine Ammann, Alessio Corsini, Thomas Gerdes, Roman Grundkiewicz, Sofia Lobanova, Christophe Mazenc, Husaini Mohammad, Andrew Moore, Ha Nguyen, Proyag Pal, Daniel Torregrossa, Tania Romera, Antonella Russo, Jeremy Thille, and Marie-Pierre Vincent for their contributions and invaluable assistance with the project.

References

Amodei Dario, Rishita Anubhai, Eric Battenberg, Carl Case, Jared Casper, Bryan Catanzaro, Jingdong Chen, Mike Chrzanowski, Adam Coates, Greg Diamos, Erich Elsen, Jesse Engel, Linxi Fan, Christopher Fougner, Tony Han, Awni Hannun, Billy Jun, Patrick LeGresley, Libby Lin, Sharan Narang, Andrew Ng, Sherjil Ozair, Ryan Prenger, Jonathan Raiman, Sanjeev Satheesh, David Seetapun, Shubho Sengupta, Yi Wang, Zhiqian Wang, Chong Wang, Bo Xiao, Dani Yogatama, Jun Zhan, Zhenyao Zhu (2015) "Deep Speech 2: End-to-End Speech Recognition in English and Mandarin" Proceedings of The 33rd International Conference on Machine Learning, PMLR 48:173-182, 2016.

Chan William, Navdeep Jaitly, Quoc Le, and Oriol Vinyals, (2016) "Listen, attend and spell: A neural network for large vocabulary conversational speech recognition," in The 41st IEEE International Conference on Acoustics, Speech, and Signal Processing

Chiu Chung-Cheng, Tara N. Sainath, Y. Wu, Rohit Prabhavalkar, P. Nguyen, Z. Chen, A. Kannan, R. J. Weiss, K. Rao, K. Gonina et al., (2017) "State of-the-art speech recognition with sequence-to-sequence models," arXiv preprint arXiv:1712.01769, 2017.

Collobert Ronan, Christian Puhrsch, Gabriel Synnaeve (2016) "Wav2Letter: an End-to-End ConvNet-based Speech Recognition System"

Doetsch Patrick , Albert Zeyer, and Hermann Ney, (2016) "Bidirectional decoder networks for attention-based end-to-end offline handwriting recognition," in International Conference on Frontiers in Handwriting Recognition, Shenzhen, China, Oct. 2016, pp. 361–366.

Galvez Daniel, Greg Diamos, Juan Ciro, Juan Felipe Cerón, Keith Achorn, Anjali Gopi, David Kanter, Maximilian Lam, Mark Mazumder, Vijay Janapa Reddi (2021) "The People's Speech: A Large-Scale Diverse English Speech Recognition Dataset for Commercial Usage" Proceedings of the 34th Neural Information Processing Systems Track on Datasets and Benchmarks

Graves Alex, Santiago Fernandez, Faustino Gomez, Jurgen Schmidhuber (2006) "Connectionist temporal classification: Labelling unsegmented sequence data with recurrent neural networks" Machine Learning, Proceedings of the Twenty-Third International Conference (ICML 2006), Pittsburgh, Pennsylvania, USA, June 25-29, 2006

Hadian Hossein, Sameti, Daniel Povey, Sanjeev Khudanpur (2018) "End-to-end speech recognition using lattice-free MMI." 19th Annual Conference of the International Speech Communication Association

Hannun Awni, Carl Case, Jared Casper, Bryan Catanzaro, Greg Diamos, Erich Elsen, Ryan Prenger, Sanjeev Satheesh, Shubho Sengupta, Adam Coates, Andrew Y. Ng (2014) "Deep Speech: Scaling up end-to-end speech recognition"

Hannun Awni, Carl Case, Jared Casper, Bryan Catanzaro, Greg Diamos, Erich Elsen, Ryan Prenger, Sanjeev Satheesh, Shubho Sengupta, Adam Coates, Andrew Y. Ng (2014) "Deep Speech: Scaling up end-to-end speech recognition" 1412.5567, 2014a. http://arxiv.org/abs/1412.5567

Ko Tom, Vijayaditya Peddinti, Daniel Povey, Sanjeev Khudanpur (2015) "Audio Augmentation for Speech Recognition." 16th Annual Conference of the International Speech Communication Association

Niessen, Sonja, Franz Josef Och, Gregor Leusch, and Hermann Ney (2000) "An evaluation tool for machine translation: Fast evaluation for MT research." Proceedings of the Second International Conference on Language Resources and Evaluation (LREC'00), Athens, Greece: 39-45.

Panayoto V., G. Chen, D. Povey and S. Khudanpur (2015) "Librispeech: An ASR corpus based on public domain audio books" 2015 IEEE International Conference on Acoustics, Speech and Signal Processing.

Papineni, Kishore, Salim Roukos, Todd Ward, and Wei-Jing Zhu (2002) "BLEU: a Method for Automatic Evaluation of Machine Translation." Proceedings of the 40th Annual Meeting on Association for Computational Linguistics, Philadelphia, Pennsylvania, USA: 311-318.

Pouliquen B. 2017 "WIPO Translate: Patent Neural Machine Translation publicly available in 10 languages", invited talk at Patent and Scientific Literature Translation workshop, MT Summit conference, Nagoya, Japan

Pratap Vineel, Qiantong Xu, Anuroop Sriram, Gabriel Synnaeve, Ronan Collobert (2020) "MLS: A Large-Scale Multilingual Dataset for Speech Research". 21st Annual Conference of the International Speech Communication Association

Radford Alec, Jong Wook Kim, Tao Xu, Greg Brockman, Christine McLeavey, Ilya Sutskever (2022) "Robust Speech Recognition via Large-Scale Weak Supervision." Proceedings of the 40th International Conference on Machine Learning, PMLR 202:28492-28518, 2023.

Salesky Elizabeth, Matthew Wiesner, Jacob Bremerman, Roldano Cattoni, Matteo Negri, Marco Turchi, Douglas W. Oard, Matt Post (2021) "The Multilingual TEDx Corpus for Speech Recognition and Translation." 22nd Annual Conference of the International Speech Communication Association

Zeyer Albert, Tamer Alkhouli, Hermann Ney (2018) "RETURNN as a Generic Flexible Neural Toolkit with Application to Translation and Speech Recognition" 56th Annual Meeting of the Association for Computational Linguistics

Optimizing Machine Translation through Prompt Engineering: An Investigation into ChatGPT's Customizability

Masaru Yamada masaru.yamada@rikkyo.ac.jp
College/Graduate School of Intercultural Communication,
Rikkyo University, Tokyo, Japan

Abstract

This paper explores the influence of integrating the purpose of the translation and the target audience into prompts on the quality of translations produced by ChatGPT. Drawing on previous translation studies, industry practices, and ISO standards, the research underscores the significance of the pre-production phase in the translation process. The study reveals that the inclusion of suitable prompts in large-scale language models like ChatGPT can yield flexible translations, a feat yet to be realized by conventional Machine Translation (MT). The research scrutinizes the changes in translation quality when prompts are used to generate translations that meet specific conditions. The evaluation is conducted from a practicing translator's viewpoint, both subjectively and qualitatively, supplemented by the use of OpenAI's word embedding API for cosine similarity calculations. The findings suggest that the integration of the purpose and target audience into prompts can indeed modify the generated translations, generally enhancing the translation quality by industry standards. The study also demonstrates the practical application of the "good translation" concept, particularly in the context of marketing documents and culturally dependent idioms.

1. Introduction

With the advent of ChatGPT, a wider audience, including translation service providers, translators, and non-NLP engineers, can now readily experience the Large Language Model (LLM) capabilities of GPT. Furthermore, GPT-4 has proven to be considerably more powerful than its predecessor, GPT-3.5, overall. This improvement extends to translation tasks using ChatGPT.

In this context, prompt engineering, which is recognized as the key to harnessing the full potential of ChatGPT, also becomes crucial for achieving optimal performance from the LLM. Certainly, proficiency in prompt engineering is required to utilize ChatGPT effectively for translation. Despite it being only a few months since the release of ChatGPT-4 (plus), several papers exploring prompt design to enhance translation efficiency and quality have already been published. However, most of these studies are authored by Natural Language Processing (NLP) researchers, often exploring topics like how ChatGPT prompts might overcome traditional NLP challenges. Consequently, many of these studies aim to improve translation accuracy using ChatGPT prompts, distinguishing our study from theirs.

The primary objective of this research is to investigate the feasibility of generating machine translation outputs suitable for professional translators through the inclusion of suitable prompts in ChatGPT, referencing previous translation studies strategies, translation practices, and ISO documents. Specifically, we aim to examine how the translation output changes when explicitly prompted with translation strategies explored in translation research (e.g., dynamic equivalence vs. formal correspondence). Secondly, we will prompt ChatGPT with a translation specification encompassing parameters such as the purpose of the translation and the target

Proceedings of Machine Translation Summit XIX, Vol. 2: Users Track, pages 195–204
September 4–8, 2023, Macau SAR, China.

audience, to facilitate more flexible integration of generated translations into professional translation workflows. We will examine how these prompts impact the translation process.

Let us illustrate with an example. The Japanese expression, *We are friends who ate out of the same pot*, is currently translated by most MTs verbatim. This literal translation may be suitable if the goal is to help an audience interested in Japanese culture understand unique Japanese expressions. However, adhering to recent translation norms, the phrase might be translated as *We have been through thick and thin together*. In other words, translation isn't a random process; it's determined by the purpose, the target audience, and the established translation strategy. The translation is performed based on this strategy. In this research, we introduce this step-by-step process into ChatGPT via prompts and assess the resulting translation changes.

2. Literature Review

Jiao et al. (2023) analyze ChatGPT's machine translation (MT) competence, revealing it competes with commercial systems in high-resource European languages but struggles with low-resource or distant ones. Notably, pivot prompting enhances translation quality significantly, and ChatGPT fares well in spoken language translation. GPT-4's incorporation further bolsters its capabilities. Gao et al. (2023) develop a new method for translation prompts, involving translation task information, context domain information, and Part-of-Speech tags, improving ChatGPT's performance. Their approach outperforms commercial systems in multiple translation directions using few-shot prompts.

Moslem et al. (2023) underscore the value of consistency and domain-specific terminology adaptation, demonstrating how large-scale language models can improve real-time adaptive MT, particularly for high-resource languages, while aiding less-supported languages via a combination of strong encoder-decoder models and fuzzy matches. Gu (2023) tackles the issue of translating Japanese attributive clauses to Chinese, a consistent problem in current tools. They introduce a pre-edit scheme and a two-step prompt strategy using ChatGPT, achieving significant improvement in average translation accuracy.

Despite these developments, the focus remains primarily on language-specific, low-resource language pairs, and problems conventional MT can't resolve. Industrial translation and pragmatic considerations, such as translation practice and ISO guidelines, aren't well-studied. This highlights a need for future research to address these practical aspects.

3. Translation Pre-Production Process

The purpose of this study, as stated in the introduction, is to enhance the quality of MT through a highly customizable approach using ChatGPT and prompts, which can seamlessly integrate into the Language Service Provider/Translation Service Provider (LSP/TPS) workflow of a practical translation job and also serve as a better computer-assisted translation (CAT) tool for the professional translators. To achieve this, it is crucial to understand the fundamental structure of the translation processes in the industry. Given the limited space, this paper will focus on extracting and elucidating the core concepts.

The translation production process, defined by ISO 17100 (ISO, 2012), is subdivided into three primary stages: pre-production, production, and post-production. The pre-production stage is particularly significant here. It involves defining and determining the requirements of the final translation before the actual translation production process begins. In practical terms, translation does not start immediately after the client provides the source text. Instead, at this stage, the translation project manager, among others, decide on the specifications of the translation, which includes the purpose of the translation, the intended audience, whether there will be a designated glossary, whether the translation will adhere to a style guide and other such aspects. Various documents detail these considerations (ASTM, 2014, ISO 2012, 2017, Onishi and Yamada, 2021). Some of these documents outline the per-word cost and whether a CAT tool should be used. However, these are not items for inclusion in the ChatGPT prompts. Relevant items for the prompts are:

Items related to the target language:

- What is the purpose of the translation?
- Who is the intended audience for the target sentence?
- What is the locale of the target language?
- What is the register?
- Is a style guide available?

The idea that the quality of translation required fluctuates as the translation specifications change is well-established in Multidimensional Quality Metrics (MQM)[1] and Dynamic Quality Framework (DQF)[2]. This notion is widely accepted among TSPs and working translators. However, it has not been a primary concern for the NLP researchers developing MT. Thus far, MTs have not incorporated functions to set or adjust the specifications of the translation as described above, making it challenging for current MT to fit into practical translation workflows.

In response, the Machine Translation Post-Editing (MTPE) method is often adopted in practical translation to modify MT translations. In light of the above discussion, post-editing can be seen as a process to fill in the gaps in translation output due to the MT's failure to set the previously mentioned requirements. In essence, the MT translates the given source text without comprehending the translation specifications, including the purpose of the translation. Consequently, human post-editors are tasked with correcting the MT translation to bridge these gaps.

4. The objective of this paper and method of evaluation

4.1. Objective

The primary objective of this paper is to evaluate the transformation in the translation output when prompts, typically determined during the pre-production phase of translation as per practical translation norms and translation studies outlined in ISO and other standards, are supplied to ChatGPT. The generated translations will be subject to qualitative analysis. Furthermore, the resemblance of the translations to the source text will be examined using the cosine similarity metric applied to the embeddings obtained from OpenAI's embedding API[3]. Note that this validation only deals with a very limited number of samples. The reason for this, however, is that it does not rely on automatic evaluation methods such as the BLEU score.

4.2. Cosine Similarity

Cosine similarity is a method utilized to measure the similarity between two vectors within a high-dimensional space. Essentially, it quantifies how closely two vectors point in the same direction by computing the cosine of the angle between them. For the purposes of this paper, we utilized the *text-embedding-ada-002* provided by OpenAI to calculate the cosine similarity between the source and target texts. This API employs a GPT-3-based model capable of

[1] https://themqm.org/
[2] https://www.taus.net/resources/blog/category/dynamic-quality-framework
[3] https://platform.openai.com/docs/guides/embeddings

understanding text content and generating representative vectors. These vectors are able to encapsulate semantic similarity, indicating whether the texts express comparable content[4].

4.3. Validity and Reliability of Using this Method for Translation Evaluation

Theoretically, it is feasible to gauge the semantic similarity between source and target texts by calculating the cosine similarity of vectors generated using *ada-002*. This technique could be particularly beneficial in determining the accuracy with which a translation preserves the meaning of the source text. However, there are several significant considerations.

First, the quality of a translation should not solely rest on semantic accuracy but should also factor in cultural subtleties and language-specific elements, such as idioms. Moreover, a direct translation is not always the optimal choice. A translation that strictly retains the original meaning may not necessarily constitute a good translation. Different languages have distinct grammatical structures and expressive modes; hence, translations must fully leverage the characteristics of each language. Therefore, this paper also includes a qualitative evaluation performed by a human expert, the author, in conjunction with the aforementioned method.

5. Verification Prompts

Two prompts were utilized for verification purposes. The first prompt is detailed below. All parameters, barring two—Purpose of the translation and Target readers of the translation—were left unset. This was grounded in the author's experience as a professional translator, leading to the conclusion that these two parameters are essential even in everyday translation work. Other items, like a predetermined glossary, are often not provided by the client.

Translate the following Japanese [source text] into English. Please fulfill the following conditions when translating. Purpose of the translation: *You need to fill in.* Target audience: *You need to fill in.* [source text] *You need to fill in.*

Table1: Prompts Specifying the Purpose of Translation and Target Audience

6. Comparative Verification Method

Three reference translations were prepared for comparison: DeepL, Google Translate, and ChatGPT Plus (GPT4) simply using the prompt "Translate to English." The ChatGPT translations, further enhanced by adding the prompts "purpose" and "target reader," were compared to these. We also added the prompt *Please generate three translations* to produce three distinct translations for comparison. For translators in practice, the ability to consider multiple potential translations is crucial.

Pym (1992) posits that the expertise of a skilled translator lies in their capacity to generate as many possible translations of a source text and select the best one— one that adheres to the translation specifications (in this case, the purpose of translation and the target audience). In other words, it is the skill to select the translation that most aptly fulfills the translation specifications. From this perspective, prompting ChatGPT to generate multiple translations aligns well with practical translation methods.

[4] Script to calculate the consine similarity is available at https://github.com/chuckmy/chatGPT_Cosine-Similarity

7. Verification Result 1

The initial step in the verification process involved translating a fictitious marketing statement from Japanese into English. The purpose of the translation and the target audience are outlined below.

Translate the following Japanese [source text] into English. Please fulfill the following conditions when translating. Purpose of the translation: *To market our own brand of cosmetics and to be displayed on our website* Target audience: *Women in their 20s* [source text] *私たちが開発したファンデーションはあなたの自然な美しさを引き立てます。シームレスに肌に溶け込み、まるで素肌そのもののような仕上がりを提供します。*

Table 2: Actual promt specified.

The given statement is part of an advertisement for a women's cosmetic foundation and is typically classified as a "marketing" text type. Translations for marketing differ substantially from those for, say, instruction manuals or contracts. Marketing translations necessitate an understanding of the cultural nuances and conventions of the target market and the crafting of an enticing message. This involves creativity and maintaining brand consistency. Conversely, translations of instruction manuals and contracts must be precise and direct, emphasizing the accurate conveyance of technical details and legal provisions. Therefore, marketing translations demand cultural adaptability, persuasiveness, creativity, and brand consistency, while translations of instruction manuals and contracts prioritize clarity and information accuracy.

Keeping this in mind, it is appropriate to designate the translation purpose as above: *To market our own brand of cosmetics and to be displayed on our website*. Similarly, it is self-evident that the target audience for this translation is *women in their 20s*, which aligns with the product's target demographic. In professional translation practice, the information about the purpose and target audience, as indicated here, will be communicated to the translator. In fact, translating without such contextual information would be deemed unprofessional.

Table 3 presents the three types of translations obtained by employing the above-mentioned prompts. The top three in the table—DeepL (DL), Google Translate (GT), and ChatGPT Plus (GPT) with translation instructions only—are the reference translations for this analysis. The v1, v2, and v3 indicate the three translations generated by the prompt above. 'C.S.' represents 'cosine similarity,' and 'Rank' signifies the similarity order from the most similar to the original source test. The closest to the source is ranked 1 (first).

Given that this translation is for a cosmetic product's marketing, the English translation should also be "stylish". The final portion of DL and GT's translations, *skin itself*, is rather literal. A more unique English translation for this part of the sentence would be preferable. In this aspect, GPT's translation is generally more natural, and its use of the phrase *looks like ... bare skin* at the end outperforms existing MT engines.

Reviewing the types of translations generated by the above prompt, all three translations differ from the baseline translation, an effect attributable to the prompts. However, both v1 and v2 resemble the baseline translation as they employ an expression similar to *enhance ... natural beauty* in the first sentence. In the latter part of the sentence, v1 and v2 also contain *bare skin*, aligning them with the baseline translation. Conversely, the v3 sentence employs a different phrase, *serves to amplify your inherent beauty* instead of *enhance*, and uses *natural skin* in the latter part, distinguishing it from the existing translations. From this standpoint, a professional translator is more likely to select v3 as the fit-for-purpose translation.

Interestingly, the cosine similarity of these sentences revealed that the v3 translation was closest to the source text. The second highest was the ChatGPT baseline translation, while the DL and GT translations exhibited lower values than v1 and v3. This suggests that the appropriate translation choices from a professional translator's standpoint generally align with the cosine similarity ranking. The translation prompted by this marketing translation, considering its purpose and target audience, is likely to be chosen as a more suitable translation than one from an existing translation engine. In other words, this implies that ChatGPT, when combined with suitable prompts, might be able to offer translations that adhere to the specifications outlined in the translation production process.

[source text]
私たちが開発したファンデーションはあなたの自然な美しさを引き立てます。シームレスに肌に溶け込み、まるで素肌そのもののような仕上がりを提供します。

Type	Target sentence	C.S.	Rank
DL	Our foundations enhance your natural beauty. They blend seamlessly into the skin and provide a finish that looks like your skin itself.	0.861	5
GT	Our foundations are designed to enhance your natural beauty. It blends seamlessly into the skin and provides a finish that looks like bare skin itself.	0.868	3
GPT	The foundation we developed enhances your natural beauty. It seamlessly blends into your skin, providing a finish that feels just like your own bare skin.	0.873	2
v1	Our newly developed foundation enhances your natural beauty. It blends seamlessly into your skin, providing a finish that's just like your own bare skin.,	0.870	3
v2	Experience the natural beauty enhancement with our specially designed foundation. Its unique formulation blends effortlessly into your skin, giving the impression of flawless, bare skin.,	0.863	4
v3	The foundation we've created serves to amplify your inherent beauty. Seamlessly melting into your skin, it leaves you with a finish indistinguishable from your natural skin.	0.875	1

Table 3: Results of translations generated with the prompt.

8. Verification 2

Consider another dimension of translation involving culture-dependent idioms and expressions, as initially discussed in this paper. The original source phrase, *we are friends who ate rice from the same pot*, is a Japanese idiom symbolizing a relationship between individuals who have weathered difficult situations together or shared profound experiences. While the literal meaning involves sharing rice cooked in the same pot, the figurative implication refers to enduring hardships together or strengthening bonds through shared experiences.

When translating, such expressions are often embedded in the original text. However, as a direct translation may not be comprehensible, the translation objective is typically set to render these expressions naturally intelligible to English speakers unfamiliar with Japanese culture.

To meet this translation objective, professional translators working in the field would adapt the expression. However, existing MT systems, which do not align with this goal, often produce literal translations that are unfit for use. Therefore, to achieve this objective in a practical working scenario, we set the following prompts:

> Translate the following Japanese [source text] into English. Please fulfill the following conditions when translating.
> Purpose of the translation: *Use natural expressions that can be understood by English speakers who are not very familiar with Japanese culture.*

Target audience: *General English-speaking audience.*
[source text] *私たちは同じ釜の飯を食べた仲です。*

Table 4: Actual prompt specified for cultural-bound expression.

Comparing the three translations acquired with the baseline translations: all translations for DeepL (DL), Google Translate (GT), and ChatGPT Plus (GPT) are essentially literal translations of the source text. In contrast, the translations from v1 through v3, which were generated with prompts, exhibit differences. Nevertheless, the v1 translation still includes *rice* and *the same pot*, differing little from the baseline translation. Consequently, from a professional translator's perspective, v1 does not represent a superior translation in this context. In contrast, v2 and v3 are translations that English speakers could comprehend. Specifically, v2, with *been through thick and thin together*, is deemed appropriate in terms of target acceptability.

Regarding cosine similarity, v2 secures the second position, affirming its semantic proximity. Hence, the result reasserts that including appropriate prompts for purpose and target reader yields a more suitable translation.

[source text] *私たちは同じ釜の飯を食べた仲です。*

Type	Target sentence	C.S.	Rank
DL	We are friends who ate out of the same pot.	0.772	1
GT	We ate rice from the same pot.	0.727	5
GPT	We ate rice from the same pot.	0.727	5
v1	We have shared the same pot of rice.	0.743	4
v2	We have been through thick and thin together.	0.759	2
v3	We've broken bread together.	0.744	3

Table 5: Results of translations of cultural-bound expression

9. Prompt for Dynamic Equivalence

Dynamic equivalence (Nida, 1969/2003) is a translation strategy aiming to balance the reader's response between the source and target texts. Take, for example, the term *Lamb* in the source text, which would be directly translated as *lamb*. However, if the target audience is in Iceland, where sheep are not indigenous, translating the word as *lamb* may not convey the intended nuance. Therefore, to equate the original text reader's reaction with that of the translated text reader, a strategy is employed to transfer the meaning (nuance) of the original text by substituting *lamb* with *seal*. This is somewhat akin to replacing *ate (rice) from the same pot* with *have been through thick and thin together* from the previous example, albeit more extreme.

We aim to examine whether supplying dynamic equivalence prompts to ChatGPT can yield more flexible and creative translations. Presented below are the actual prompts and the source text.

Dynamic equivalence is a strategy for translating from the perspective of equalizing the reader's response to the [source text] and the [target text]. In the example below, the word "Lamb" in the original text would be translated as "lamb" in the literal translation. However, when translating for Iceland, which has no sheep, it is difficult to convey the nuance of the word "lamb". From the standpoint of equalizing the reader's reaction, this is a ruse to translate it as "seal". It is believed that "lamb" in the [source text] and "seal" in the [target text] will evoke the same reaction in the reader.

[source text] Lamb of God
[target text] Seal of God

Following this concept and example, please translate the following [source text] into English using the dynamic equivalent. Please replace the translation with something that would be understood in an English-speaking culture.
[source text] *彼女の歌声は美空ひばりを彷彿とさせる。*

Table6: Actual prompt for dynamic equivalence

The source text translates to *Her singing voice reminds me of Hibari Misora*. The focal point here is the singer H*ibari Misora*. Without understanding who *Hibari Misora* is, the original sentence's meaning becomes unclear. Notably, Hibari Misora (May 29, 1937 - June 24, 1989) was a prominent Japanese singer and actress, revered for her powerful voice and emotional performances. She is widely recognized as a definitive figure in the traditional Japanese "enka" country music style.

After defining the dynamic equivalence, the prompt states, *please replace the translation with something that would be understood in an English-speaking culture*. Who could be a suitable replacement?

[source text] 彼女の歌声は美空ひばりを彷彿とさせる。

Type	Target sentence	C.S.	Rank
DL	Her singing voice is reminiscent of Hibari Misora.	0.876	1
GT	Her singing voice is reminiscent of Hibari Misora.	0.876	1
GPT	Her singing voice reminds me of Misora Hibari.	0.873	2
v1	Her singing voice evokes memories of Judy Garland.	0.830	3
v2	Her singing voice is reminiscent of Billie Holiday.	0.823	5
v3	Listening to her sing, one can't help but think of Ella Fitzgerald.	0.826	4

Table 7: Results of dynamic equivalence prompt

The table reveals that the baseline translations from DeepL (DL) and Google Translate (GT) are identical, and the GPT translations are nearly the same. The part mentioning *Hibari Misora* is directly translated. However, none of the baseline translations meet the dynamic equivalence strategy's objectives. On the other hand, versions v1 through v3 substitute *Hibari Misora* with *Judy Garland*, *Billie Holiday*, and *Ella Fitzgerald*, respectively. These are all interesting choices. In this instance, all translations opted for famed American singers. While the translations succeed in fulfilling the dynamic equivalence goal, the selection of these particular singers, who share a similar era with the original singer, is indeed apt. Yet, from a translator's perspective, it's debatable which—v1 *Judy Garland*, v2 *Billie Holiday*, or v3 *Ella Fitzgerald*—achieves the dynamic equivalence of the original singers most effectively.

Reviewing the cosine similarity rankings, the baseline translations simply transliterate *Hibari Misora* as it is ranked 1st and 2nd. These translations score high on cosine similarity as they semantically align with the source text. However, they do not meet this study's objective. On the other hand, v1, v3, and v2 rank 3rd, 4th, and 5th, respectively. According to this order, v1, which substitutes *Hibari Misora* with *Judy Garland*, achieves the highest score (3rd) among the three alternatives. However, this doesn't necessarily mean that Judy Garland is the singer most similar to *Hibari Misora* based on cosine similarity; this score considers the entire sentence.

Therefore, to determine which of the three English-speaking singers most closely resembles *Hibari Misora* in terms of cosine similarity, we standardized the translation sentence structure to *Her singing voice is reminiscent of*... as generated by DL/GT. We then replaced only the singer's name and analyzed the cosine similarity. The results are outlined in the table below.

Naturally, the baseline translation takes the top spot. However, v3's *Ella Fitzgerald* ranks second, suggesting she is most similar to *Hibari Misora* in terms of cosine similarity. Of course, this doesn't guarantee that the most appropriate dynamic equivalent is *Ella Fitzgerald.* Yet, it does hint at a potential overlap with the rationale employed by professional translators in selecting suitable translations in practical translation. Conversely, these validation results also suggest that it may be advantageous for professional translators to view multiple translation candidates and cosine similarities as part of their Computer-Assisted Translation (CAT) tool.

Type	Target sentence	C.S.	Rank
DL	Her singing voice is reminiscent of Hibari Misora.	0.876	1
v1	Her singing voice is reminiscent of Judy Garland.	0.826	3
v2	Her singing voice is reminiscent of Billie Holiday.	0.823	4
v3	Her singing voice is reminiscent of Ella Fitzgerald.	0.833	2

Table 8: To find out the best 'equivalence' to *Hibari Misora*

10. Conclusion

In this study, we investigated how incorporating the purpose of the translation and the target audience into prompts - key elements of translation specifications defined in the front-end phase of the industrial translation production process - alters the quality of translations generated by ChatGPT. We examined shifts in translation quality when prompts were issued to generate translations meeting these specific conditions. The assessment was conducted from the perspective of a practicing translator, both subjectively and qualitatively. Additionally, we utilized Open AI's word embedding API to calculate cosine similarity, complementing our qualitative evaluation.

Our findings indicated that incorporating the purpose and target readers into prompts indeed altered the generated translations. This transformation, aimed at satisfying the criteria of purpose and target audience, generally improved the translation quality by industry standards. Particularly for marketing documents and culturally dependent idioms, a translation strictly faithful to the source text is not regarded as a "good translation." Thus, by appropriately setting the purpose of the translation, the prompt can be adjusted to produce a translation that is closer to the target culture, favoring intent translation and domestication. This demonstrates the practical application of the "good translation" concept.

Furthermore, we employed strategies like dynamic equivalence, replacing items with high cultural dependency on the target audience. Specifically, we substituted the renowned Japanese singer *Hibari Misora* with *Ella Fitzgerald*, a singer considered her equivalent in English-speaking countries, facilitating a high degree of creative translation. Our results confirmed that prompts can progressively guide creative translations, such as replacing *Hibari Misora* with *Ella Fitzgerald.* These translations may prove more useful than conventional machine-translated ones, even serving professional translators as preliminary translations for post-editing.

Although our study was limited by the development of prompts and a small sample size, further, larger-scale experiments and validations are required to practically apply the results. Nevertheless, our findings confirmed that incorporating appropriate prompts into large language models like ChatGPT can generate flexible translations, an accomplishment yet to be achieved by traditional MT. We anticipate future verifications with great interest.

References

ASTM International. (2014). *ASTM F2575-14. Standard Guide for Quality Assurance in Translation.*www.astm.org DOI: 10.1520/F2575-14

Gao, Y., Wang, R., & Hou, F. (2023). How to Design Translation Prompts for ChatGPT: An Empirical Study. *ArXiv*:2304.02182 [cs.CL].

Gu, W. (2023). Linguistically Informed ChatGPT Prompts to Enhance Japanese-Chinese Machine Translation: A Case Study on Attributive Clauses. *ArXiv*:2303.15587 [cs.CL].

International Standard Organization (ISO) ISO/TS (2012) *ISO 11669:2012 Translation projects–General guidance*.

International Standard Organization (ISO) (2015) ISO 17100. 2015. *Translation services – Requirements for translation services*. First edition.

Jiao, W., Wang, W., Huang, J., Wang, X., & Tu, Z. (2023). Is ChatGPT A Good Translator? Yes With GPT-4 As The Engine. *ArXiv*:2301.08745 [cs.CL].

Moslem, Y., Haque, R., Kelleher, J. D., & Way, A. (2023). Adaptive Machine Translation with Large Language Models. *ArXiv*:2301.13294 [cs.CL].

Nida, Eugene A., and Charles R. Taber. (1969/2003). *The Theory and Practice of Translation*. Brill Academic Pub.

Onishi, N., & Yamada, M. (2021) Metalanguage for Translation Project Management. In R. Miyata, M. Yamada, & K. Kageura (eds.), *Metalanguages for Translation Processes*, (pp. 50 – 62), Routledge.

Pym, A. (1992). Translation error analysis and the interface with language teaching. In C. Dollerup & A. Loddegaard (Eds), *The teaching of translation*, (pp. 279-288). John Benjamins. https://doi.org/10.1075/z.56.42pym

Comparing Chinese-English MT Performance Involving ChatGPT and MT Providers and the Efficacy of AI mediated Post-Editing

Larry P Cady larry.cady@chilin.hk
Chilin (HK), Ltd., Santa Cruz CA, USA
Benjamin K. Tsou btsou99@chilin.hk
Chilin (HK), Ltd. and CityU HK, Hong Kong
John S. Y. Lee jsylee@cityu.edu.hk
City University of Hong Kong, Hong Kong

Abstract

The recent introduction of ChatGPT has caused much stir in the translation industry because of its impressive translation performance against leaders in the industry. We review some major issues based on the BLEU comparisons of Chinese-to-English (C2E) and English-to-Chinese (E2C) machine translation (MT) performance by ChatGPT against a range of leading MT providers in mostly technical domains. Based on sample aligned sentences from a sizable bilingual Chinese-English patent corpus and other sources, we find that while ChatGPT performs better generally, it does not consistently perform better than others in all areas or cases.

We also draw on novice translators as post-editors to explore a major component[1] in MT post-editing: Optimization of terminology. Many new technical words, including MWEs (Multi-Word Expressions), are problematic because they involve terminological developments which must balance between proper encapsulation of technical innovation and conforming to past traditions[2]. Drawing on the above-mentioned reference corpus[3] we have been developing an AI mediated MT post-editing (MTPE) system through the optimization of precedent rendition distribution and semantic association to enhance the work of translators and MTPE practitioners.

1. Introduction

In recent decades we have witnessed spectacular advancements in Machine Translation (MT) technology. More recently, a major turning point has appeared with the introduction of ChatGPT, which is based on a large language model and generative AI.

We pose the following questions: 1. What is the range of variation in the performance of popular MT systems on technical subjects? 2. Are there some clear leaders which perform consistently better than others? 3. What kind of tools can effectively enhance MT results (for

[1] MT post-editing includes several key stages and terminological optimization is the foremost. It entails (1) Identification of canididate constituents for improvement; (2) Appreciation of good available alternatives; and (3) Selection of appropriate alternatives. (See Tsou et al. 2022; Green et al. 2013)
[2] See Tsou et al. 2020.
[3] See also Goto et al. 2013.

Proceedings of Machine Translation Summit XIX, Vol. 2: Users Track, pages 205–216
September 4–8, 2023, Macau SAR, China.

example, post-editing)? 4. How realistic is it for a robotic translator to replace human translator in the foreseeable future?

To answer these questions: 1. We select in this study authoritative and parallel English and Chinese texts with recognized human translations (e.g., parallel bilingual patents) for their technical nature and legal status. 2. We compare translation performance of ChatGPT with the others based on BLEU scores. 3. We focus on terminological deficiency and how to assist human subjects in remedying it. This study draws on novice human translators who would review and select among alternate translations of technical terms with and without reference to their authoritative usage frequencies, and analyze their selections with reference to the gold standards in the filed patents. We conduct C2E and E2C tests with and without access to external resources[4] and analyze the results in the context of questions raised above.

This paper begins with an examination of how ChatGPT 3.5 and 4 compare with some notable MT systems and explores the consequential implications for consumers and providers of MT technology, as well as what might be included in the timely introduction of AI mediated Post-Editing technology. We look at translation between Chinese and English on technical subjects, where there is high demand for quality and where cost is an issue. We first discuss our comparative analysis and some results from a preliminary small-scale study on how lexical improvement in Post-Editing may be achieved.

Our study is based on a set of 3,000 bilingual sentences drawn equally from patent documents involving biotechnology as well as computer science and electronics. We focus on the bidirectional translation between English and Chinese for these sentences among a number of well-known MT systems[5].

2. Comparative Performance of 7 Notable MT Systems

Among the large number of MT systems examined, we report on seven systems: Baidu, ChatGPT3.5, ChatGPT4.0, DeepL, Google, Niutrans and Youdao. Their BLEU scores on the 3,000 sentences in science and technology are taken as the basis for this study. An illustrative sentence and its alternate translations are given in Table 1 based on comparison between their MT ouput and the "Gold standard"[6] of human translation in the filed patents.

Table 1. Alternate Translations of an illustrative sentence[7]

From Chinese Patent	其中 SGLTs 家族中具有葡萄糖转运功能的成员主要分布于肠道和肾脏的近端小管等部位，进而推断其在肠葡萄糖的吸收和肾脏葡萄糖的重摄取等过程中均发挥着关键作用，因而使其成为治疗糖尿病的理想潜在靶点之一。

[4] See Tsou et al. 2022.

[5] The 3,000 test sentences are taken from more than 30 million parallel sentences from the PatentLex corpus developed by Chilin (HK) Ltd in Hong Kong and available from TAUS and LDC (see references). Chilin first cultivated and curated a large corpus of 300,000+ Chinese-English parallel/comparable patents, and from it 30+m bilingually aligned Chinese-English sentences. From that, a large corpus of bilingual multi-word expressions is being cultivated in conjunction within the developments of an AI-mediated Machine Translation post-editing system that makes use of these progressively winnowed databases.

[6] The Gold standard for the 3,000 test sentences is taken to be from the corresponding target language sentences in the filed patents.

[7] From patent WO2004040948A1 (US Priority) "Apparatus and method for controlling registration of print steps in a continuous process for the manufacture of electrochemical sensors"

From English Patent	Members of SGLTs acting as glucose transporters are mainly distributed in the intestine and the proximal tubules of the kidneys, indicating that SGLTs are responsible for the majority of glucose reuptake in the intestine and the kidneys. SGLTs are considered as potential and ideal antidiabetic targets.	
Google	Among them, members of the SGLTs family with glucose transport function are mainly distributed in the proximal tubules of the intestine and kidney, and it is inferred that they play a key role in the process of intestinal glucose absorption and renal glucose reuptake, thus making them It has become one of the ideal potential targets for the treatment of diabetes.	BLEU Score 0.1704
GPT 3.5	Among the SGLT (sodium-glucose co-transporter) family, members with glucose transport function are mainly distributed in the intestine and proximal tubules of the kidneys. It is inferred that they play a crucial role in processes such as intestinal glucose absorption and renal glucose reabsorption, making them one of the ideal potential targets for the treatment of diabetes.	0.2005
GPT 4.0	The members of the SGLTs family with glucose transport functions are mainly distributed in the proximal tubules of the intestine and kidney, thereby hypothesizing that they play a key role in processes such as intestinal glucose absorption and renal glucose reuptake. Therefore, they are considered one of the ideal potential targets for the treatment of diabetes.	0.1876
Niutrans	Among them, the members of SGLTs family with glucose transport function are mainly distributed in the proximal tubules of intestine and kidney, and it is inferred that SGLTs play a key role in the process of intestinal glucose absorption and renal glucose reuptake, which makes them one of the ideal potential targets for the treatment of diabetes.	0.1592
Baidu	Among them, the members of the SGLTs family with glucose transport function are mainly distributed in the intestinal tract and the proximal tubules of the kidney. It is inferred that they play a key role in the absorption of intestinal glucose and the reabsorption of renal glucose, which makes them one of the ideal potential targets for the treatment of diabetes.	0.1718
DeepL	The glucose transporting members of the SGLTs family are mainly located in the proximal tubules of the intestine and the kidney, and are thus hypothesized to play a key role in both intestinal glucose absorption and renal glucose reuptake, thus making them an ideal potential target for the treatment of diabetes.	0.1635
Youdao	Members of the SGLTs family with glucose transport function are mainly distributed in the proximal tubules of the intestine and kidney, and it is inferred that they play a key role in the process of intestinal glucose absorption and renal glucose reuptake, which makes them one of the ideal potential targets for the treatment of diabetes.	0.1911

Even though the range of BLEU scores varies from 0.16 to 0.2 for this example sentence, human evaluation has found these translations to be useful for reference but not as final products.

It will be useful to look at the overall performance of Chinese-English translations of seven among the many MT systems we have evaluated. Figure 1A and 1B show the scores in the bidirectional English-Chinese translations of the seven systems. The error bars are based on one standard deviation.

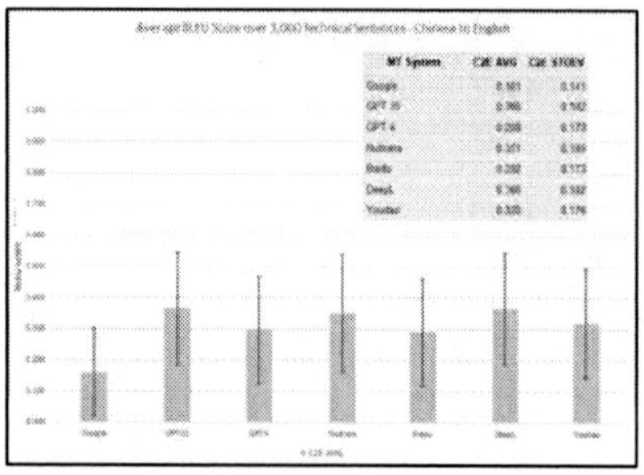

Figure 1A. Average BLEU Scores Chinese to English

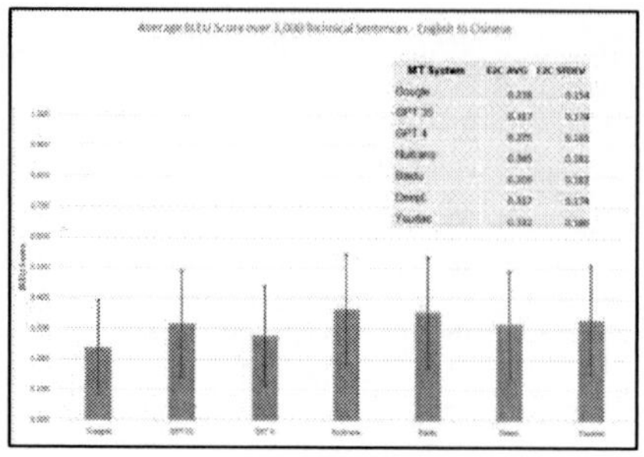

Figure 1B. Average BLEU Scores English to Chinese

We note there is a wide range of overall BLEU scores (0.16 to 0.36) in the translation of this set of 3,000 technical sentences, which are low in general even though the results provide useful references.

3. Pairwise Comparison between common MT Systems and ChatGPT

To make the comparison more meaningful, we did pairwise comparison among the translation systems by plotting the corresponding BLEU scores on a grid. Each axis ranges from 0.0 to 1.0, where 1.0 corresponds to a perfect match versus the reference sentence. Figure 2A shows a comparison between Google and ChatGPT-4 for the Chinese to English direction. Figure 2B shows the English to Chinese direction.

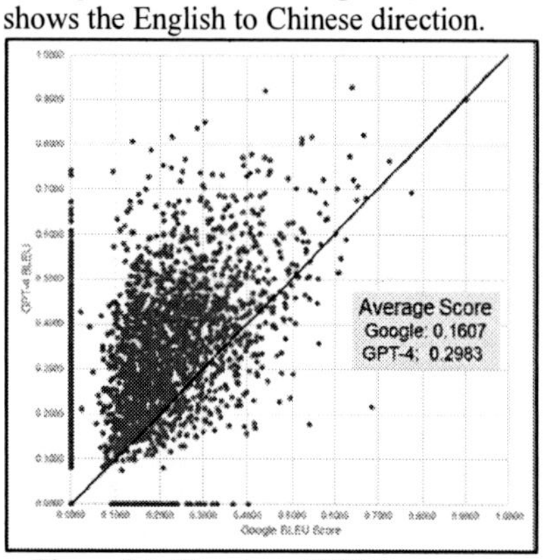

Figure 2A. Google vs GPT-4 : Chinese to English

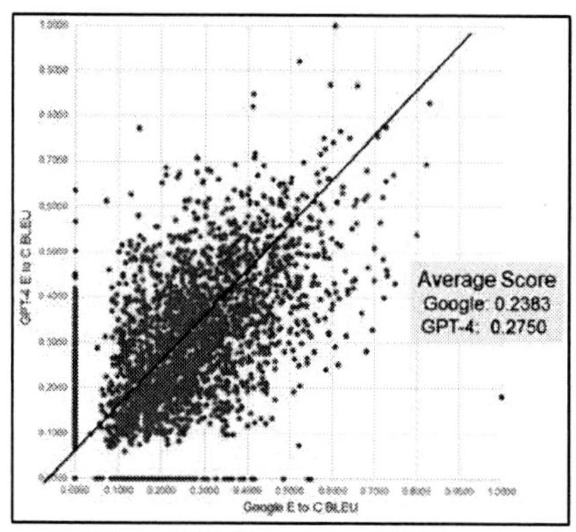

Figure 2B. Google vs GPT-4 : English to Chinese

Note that in the Chinese to English direction, ChatGPT4 outperforms Google. In the English to Chinese direction, they are very close. Note also that the data is widely scattered with many data points on the X and Y axis indicating 0.0 BLEU scores for one of the systems.

Figures 3A and 3B below compare the output of GPT-4 with Baidu.

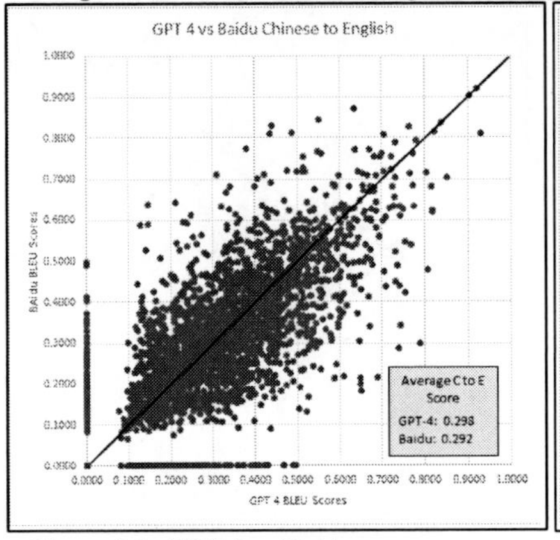

Figure 3A. GPT-4 vs Baidu: Chinese to English

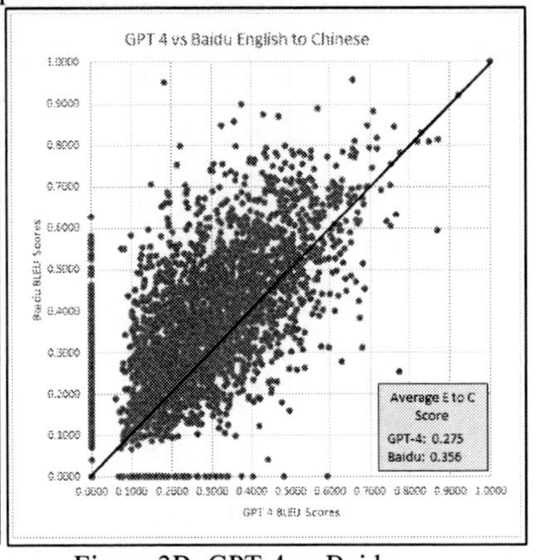

Figure 3B. GPT-4 vs Baidu: English to Chinese

Baidu and GPT-4 are very close for Chinese to English but Baidu outperforms for English to Chinese.

Figures 4A and 4B compare GPT-4 with DeepL.

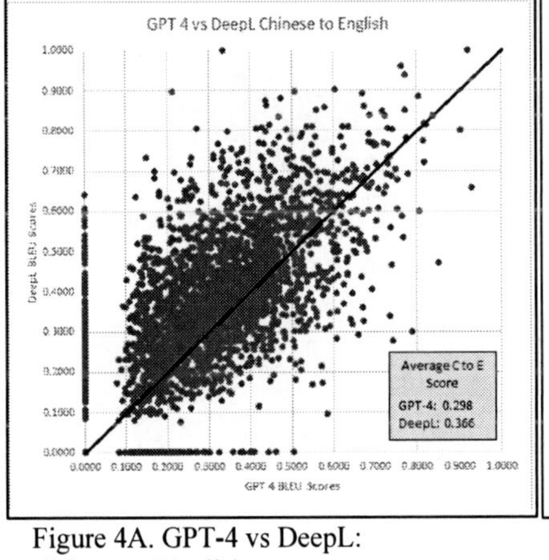

Figure 4A. GPT-4 vs DeepL: Chinese to English

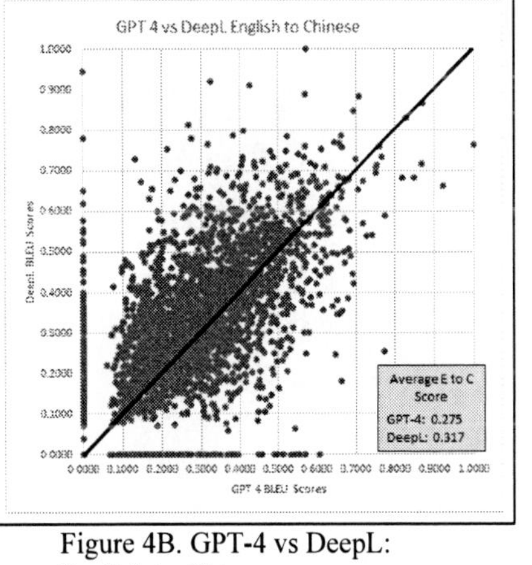

Figure 4B. GPT-4 vs DeepL: English to Chinese

Note that DeepL outperforms GPT-4 in both directions.

Figures 5A and 5B below compare the output of GPT-4 and Niutrans.

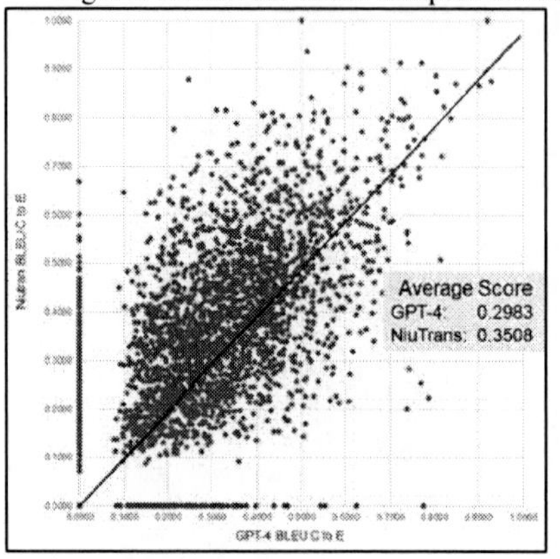

Figure 5A. GPT-4 vs Niutrans:
Chinese to English

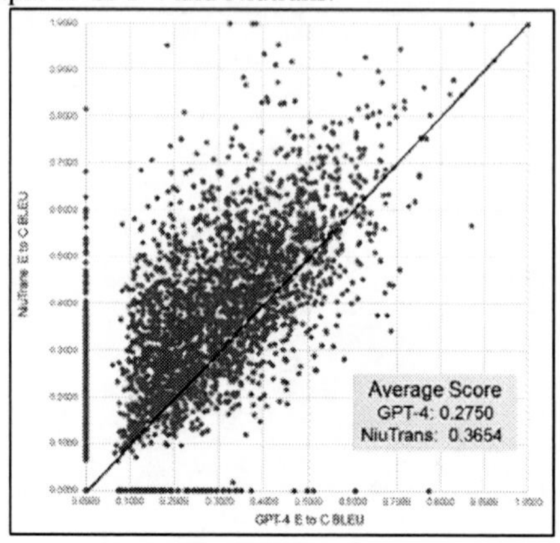

Figure 5B. GPT-4 vs Niutrans:
English to Chinese

Note that Niutrans outperforms GPT-4 in both directions.

Figures 6A and 6B compare GPT-4 with Youdao.

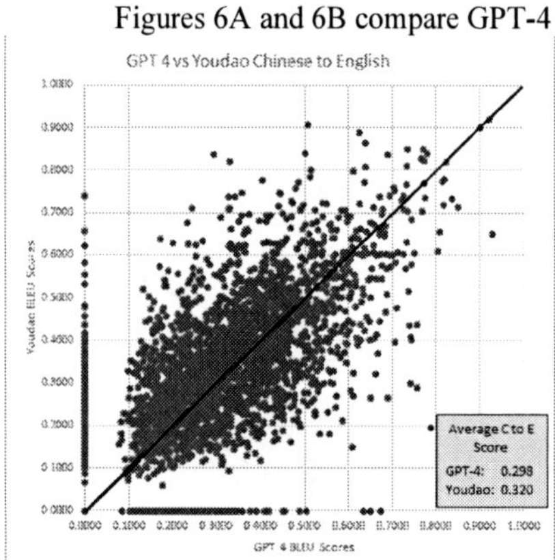

Figure 6A. GPT-4 vs Youdao:
Chinese to English

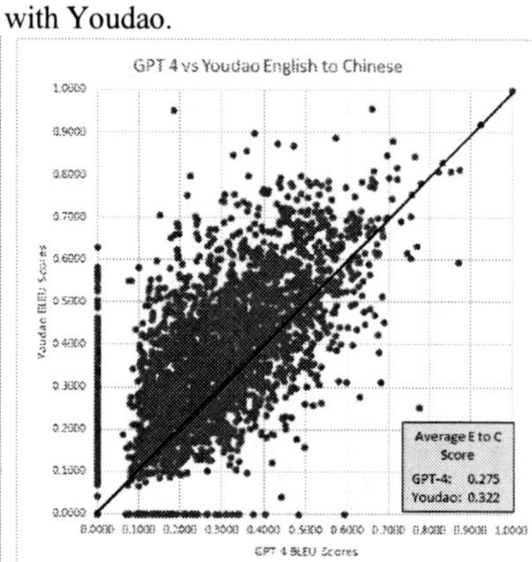

Figure 6B. GPT-4 vs Youdao:
English to Chinese

Youdao performs well in both directions.

Furthermore, the scattered nature of the data points on all the comparison graphs show that there is no single system is consistently above all others.

4. Issues with Automated Scoring

Table 2 shows a second detailed example. Compared with Niutrans, the performances of DeepL and ChatGPT3.5 are at opposite ends of the performance range (0.23 to 0.33). We also note that a recent evaluation by Intento[8] ranked Google highest for Chinese to English and English to Chinese. Intento used a different methodology than we have used. Moreover, ChatGPT-4 performed better than ChatGPT3.5 in this example, as can be seen in the Appendix.

Table 2. Second Example Sentence for MT comparison

From Chinese Patent	合成/对抗疗法药物雷尼替丁的有效率为 82.20%，与制剂 F5 几乎相似，但长期使用会阻止胃液的正常分泌。	
From English Patent	The synthetic/allopathic drug ranitidine showed 82.20% which is almost similar to that of formulation F5 but long use block the normal secretions in the stomach.	
Google	The effective rate of synthetic/confrontation drugs Rennitine is 82.20 %, which is almost similar to the preparation F5, but long -term use will prevent the normal secretion of gastric juice.	BLEU Score 0.2641
GPT 3.5	The efficacy of the combination/antagonist therapy drug Ranitidine is 82.20%, which is almost similar to the formulation F5, but long-term use will prevent the normal secretion of gastric juice.	0.2326
GPT 4.0	The efficacy of the synthetic/antagonistic therapy drug Rennitidine is 82.20%, which is almost similar to Formulation F5, but long-term use may block the normal secretion of gastric acid.	0.2773
Niutrans	The effective rate of synthetic/allopathic drug ranitidine is 82.20%, which is almost similar to preparation F5, but long-term use will prevent the normal secretion of gastric juice.	0.3321
Baidu	The effective rate of the synthetic/antagonistic therapy drug ranitidine is 82.20%, which is almost similar to the formulation F5, but long-term use can prevent the normal secretion of gastric juice.	0.2696
DeepL	The synthetic/allopathic drug ranitidine is 82.20% effective, almost similar to preparation F5, but its long-term use prevents the normal secretion of gastric juice.	0.2326

The major differences involve the appropriate selection of translation for terms such as *synthetic/combination* and *confrontation*/antagonistic/*allopathic*. There are also issues of stylistic variations and anaphora, which affect the BLEU evaluation. However, these features may be important in high-value, high-demand translations in the legal or technical sector. Moreover, it may be noted that the "Gold standard" is not infallible, as it is ultimately human based[9].

[8] See Intento 2023 State of Machine Translation Report. Intento rates Google and DeepL highest for Chinese to English; Google highest for English to Chinese. GPT is rated as competitive.

[9] In the Chilin database, it has sentence ID WO2005063271-100314. The WIPO document is WO2005063271A1 and https://patentscope.wipo.int/search/en/detail.jsf?docId=WO2005063271. The Chinese document is https://patentscope.wipo.int/search/en/detail.jsf?docId=CN83099623. The original application is from India and appears to be in English. In addition to incorrectly using ***USE*** instead of ***USES*** in the English document, the drug name "Ranitidine" is sometimes capitalized and sometimes not capitalized. These are examples of imperfection in the "gold standard" text. This application was filed in several countries (including the US and China) but was only granted in the UK.

The average scores and plots in Figure 1 to Figure 7 are informative, but the widely scattered data and large number of very low scores suggests that MT performance is highly unpredictable.

Given the widely scattered nature of the results, we conclude that the seven systems are all generally competitive with each other, without any system consistently outperforming all others. It should be noted that all MT systems benefit from large data based on past practices and are not sensitive to innovations which are natural in any evolving system as may be found in natural language. In selecting a system for production use, the user should run a suitable test with data that is representative of what he or she will encounter operationally, and examine the results in the light of appropriate criteria and requirements.

Given that MT performance has become very effective, the likelihood of manual preliminary draft translations will diminish quickly. This is especially so for high value documents, such as legal contracts and patent filings, where a careful review and post-editing of the machine translation outputs is inevitable in the foreseeable future. With support from the Hong Kong Innovation and Technology Commission, Chilin (HK) Ltd is developing the PatentLex Translation Assistant (PaTTA) to perform AI-mediated Post-Editing. It utilizes Chilin's large corpus of bilingual technical terms and parallel sentences to help translators review and edit machine translations. Figure 7 shows how PaTTA can identify technical terms and suggest translation options (multiple renditions with frequencies) in post-editing.

5. Towards Terminological Enhancement in Post-Editing

As a consequence of the findings reported above, a new generation of MT post-editors will be needed who would be able to perform the following tasks:

1. Review different MT outputs and identify the most suitable ones for necessary subsequent post-editing before incorporation in the final translation.
2. Improve on the selected output through both light post-editing and heavy post-editing as necessary. A major task or challenge will be to select the best amoung alternate translations of unfamiliar terms to conform to user or client requirements.

In view of these requirements, we have been curating our big database to provide a timely and useful means to improve post-editing results. On this basis, our PatentLex bilingual terminology database provides access to comprehensive alternate renditions of technical terms which should be beyond the usual repertoire of the translator. This is especially true for relatively novice translators who have had insufficient training or exposure relating to technical subjects. It also provides access to additional information such as the authoritative usage frequencies of the alternate renditions in authentic context.

Table 3 summarizes the results of a recent study focused on the post-editing process involving terminological improvement: Translators were asked to look at two sets of uncommon terms and for each given term, two alternate translations taken from the output of two separate MT systems. One of these being the same as that found in the referenced "Gold standard" of the filed patent. Each translator is given two seperate tasks: (1) He/she makes a choice between the two alternative translations in the context of the example sentence given (2 Alt.), and (2) He/she is given additional information on the usage frequency distribution of the two alternate renditions from the massive PatentLex database (2 Alt.+PAT.). The translator's choice is assessed to the "Gold standard". The accumulative results of the two sets are compared to see if the additional PatentLex information provided has helped the translator's final choice in line with the "Gold standard".

The study was conducted among year 3 university students interested in translation from a university among the top 200 out of over 3,000 tertiary institutions of education in Mainland China. They also provided information on their English score and time spent on the exercise.

Table 3. Comparison of Terminological Enhancement in Translation[10]

	2 Alt. (%)	Time (min)	2 Alt. + PAT. (%)	Time (min)	CET4	CET6
C to E	52	17.05	70	17.03	498	430
	65.1	30.17	48.6	26	480	497
	2 Alt. (%)	Time (min)	2 Alt. + PAT. (%)	Time (min)	CET4	CET6
E to C	42.1	18.65	62.9	19.17	496	439
	64.3	17.53	30	18.16	485	497

The student responses show two kinds of opposing tendencies: In C to E tasks, about half of the students, when given the two alternate renditions and additional PatentLex information such as distributional frequencies improve their performance from 52% to 70% with reference to the "Gold standard". For the remaining ones their performance dropped from 65% to 48.6% under similar conditions. Such a contrasting trend is unusual and invites attention and explanation. One could be from the putative observation on the possible correlations between the students' survey performance and their mandatory test score on English: CET4 and CET6. CET (College English Test) is required of university students in China for graduation. It is taken upon entry at university and CET6 is taken subsequently before graduation. CET6 has higher requirements than CET4, and the threshold is usually 425 for most institutions.

Some generizations may be made from Table 3. The set of technical terms used in the exercise contain relatively uncommon words for the students and the results show that those

[10] Alt: alternatives; +: additional usage frequency information among the altenatives in PatentLex; CET: China's College English Test.

students relatively weaker in English readily relied on the additional PatentLex information provided when doing the C to E exercise. Their improvement is from 50% to 70%, and it is northworthy that the time they spent on both tasks is about the same and equal to 17 minutes.

On the other hand, the students relatively stronger in English seemed more engaged with the task and materials given. They spent considerably more time, averaging 26 to 30 minutes (compared to only 17 minutes for the same task by the other group). Despite their strenuous efforts, these year 3 students' limited repertoire in English did not allow them to benefit substantially within the time allotted.

The corresponding exercise on the translation of English terms to Chinese took place after the exercise on Chinese to English term translation. A similar trend may be observed for students relatively weaker in English (as indicated by CET scores) i.e., the extra PatentLex information benefited only one type of students: those relatively weak in English.

In general Students relatively stronger in English seem unable to benefit from the extra information provided. In both cases there could be additional contributing factors which could account for the variations. The CET scores are only for English and not for Chinese, and it shows only one aspect of a student's bilingual ability which is more than simply the combined knowledge of each language. The biggest drop of 34% follows from the introduction of additional PatentLex information in the last part of the exercise. This could be due to the fact that the students whose native language was Chinese were insufficiently stimulated by PatentLex input to help them resolve monolingual lexical issues even in Chinese because they were beyond the students' usual repertoire. This was not dissimilar to the case of Chinese translation to English terms discussed earlier. However, because of the added pressure of time, the stimulation effect of the extra information brought about greater uncertainty and the biggest drop from 64.3% to 30%.

This study has been useful in several ways. It draws attention to the positive impact which the additional PatentLex information could make when directed at appropriately motivated post-editors and that its impact on truly experienced translators as well as the need for the broader process of post-editing to be investigated.

6. Conclusion

Despite the increasingly impressive MT performance of ChatGPT over MT providers, its superior performance is neither exclusive nor consistent. This will likely give rise to the imminent deployment of a new generation of MT post-editors able to make judicious comparisons and revisions, and to replace front-line human translators. The development of AI mediated MTPE systems which provide both important terminological alternatives and the relevant contexts is an crucial direction of development. Our preliminary study shows that well-motivated measures could demonstratably enhance the productivity of suitable MTPE practitioners, and that MTPE can improve speed and quality, as well as versatility (i.e., range of unfamiliar subjects for those already familiar with the grammatical structure of the target language). MTPE will help translators identify sentences that require additional editorial work and will facilitate their subsequent efforts. At the same time, the process of post-editing among different practitioners in terms of experience, linguistic knowledge and attitude deserve further attention just as the capabiities of LLMs and other technologies deserve to be further explored.

We also note the limitations of using BLEU scores to assess translations. BLEU scores are based on matching a translated sentence with reference translations, which are assumed to be the best possible. In reality, there often may be better alternates, especially over time. This means the training databases should be updated regularly and special measures should be made to sensitize the MTPE practioners proactively to the developments, which no robotic system is capable of doing in the foreseeable future.

Acknowledgments

We gratefully acknowledge support from: (1) Hong Kong's Innovation and Technology Commission (ITC) grant to Chilin (HK) Ltd for the PaTTA project (ITC/ESS Project: B/E019/20) and (2) CityU Strategic Research Grant (projects #7005709 and #7005803).

References

Chan, Elsie K. Y., Lee, John S. Y., Cheng, C., and Tsou, Benjamin K. (2023). Post-editing of Technical Terms based on Bilingual Example Sentences. In *Proc. 19th Machine Translation Summit.*

Green, S., Heer, J., and Manning, C.D. (2013). The Efficacy of Human Post-Editing for Language Translation. In *Proc. CHI.*

Goto Isao, Chow, K.P., Lu Bin, Sumita Eiichiro, Tsou Benjamin K. (2013). Overview of the Patent Machine Translation Task at the NRCIR-10 Workshop. *Proceedings of the 10th NTCIR Conference* 18-21 Jun 2013 Tokyo, Japan. pp. 260 -286.

Lee, John S. Y., Tsou, Benjamin K., and Cai, Tianyuan. (2020). Using Bilingual Patents for Translation Training. In *Proc. 28th International Conference on Computational Linguistics* (COLING).

Lu, Bin, Benjamin K. Tsou, Jingbo Zhu, Tao Jiang, and Oi Yee Kwong. (2009). The Construction of an English-Chinese patent parallel corpus. *MT Summit XII: Third Workshop on Patent Translation,* Ottawa (Canada), pp. 17-24.

Tsou Benjamin K., Chow, K.P., Lee, John, Yip, K.F. Ji, Y.X. and Wu, Kevin. (2020). "Bilingual Multiword Expressions, Multiple-correspondence, and their Cultivation from Parallel Patents: The Chinese-English Case". In Minh Le Nguyen, Mai Chi Luong, and Sanghoun Song (Eds.). In *Proceeding of 34th PACLIC Workshop on MWEA*, Hanoi, Vietnam. pp. 589-602.

Tsou, Benjamin. (2022). "Translation 4.5: The Age of Post-Editing Technology" Keynote Speech, 50th Anniversary Translation Lecture Series 2021-22 (5), 9 Apr, HK Translation Society: Hong Kong.

Tsou Benjamin K., Yiu, Elvis, and Mak, Kelly. (2022). "Machine Translation Post-editing and the Role of Big Data in Technical Translation". International Congress on English Language Education and Applied Linguistics (ICELEAL 2022), Dec 6-9, The Education University of Hong Kong.

Chilin PatentLex Bilingual sentence data is available at the University of Pennsylvania Linguistic Data Consortium (LDC) site. https://www.ldc.upenn.edu/language-resources/data, and on the TAUS Data Marketplace https://datamarketplace.taus.net/

"The State of Machine Translation 2023 (inten.to)" https://inten.to/machine-translation-report-2023/ (free with registration) 20 June 2023.

Appendix A. Comparison of the technical translation by GPT-4 and GPT 3.5.

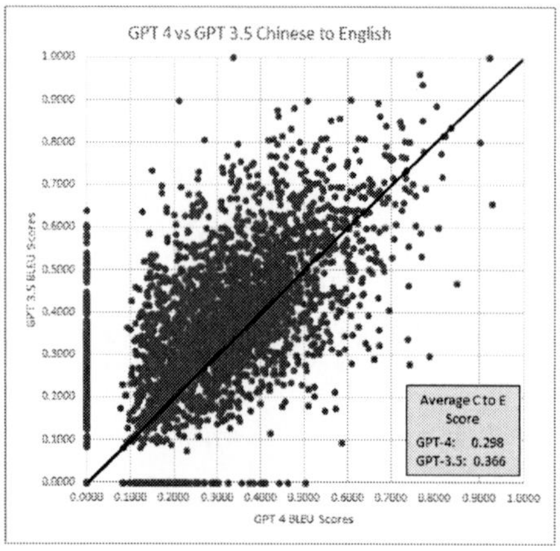

Figure 7A. GPT-4 vs GPT 3.5: Chinese to English

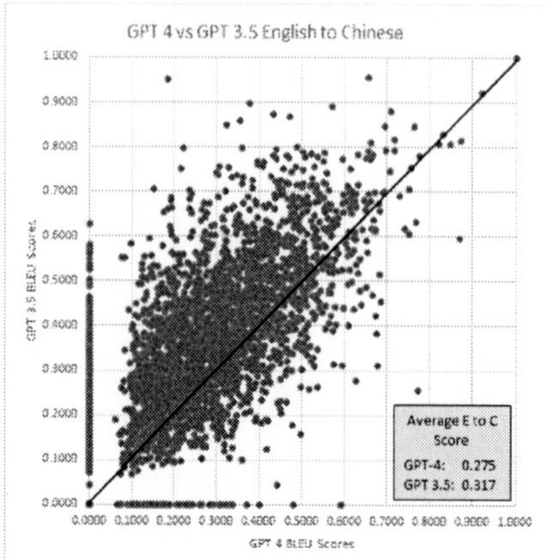

Figure 7B. GPT-4 vs GPT 3.5: English to Chinese

It is notable that GPT-3.5 outperforms GPT-4. On the Chinese to English translation of the source of 3,000 technical sentences between the two are significant. These interesting findings are only tentative but draw attention to the need to better understand the linguistic and related background of those doing translation and post-editing under time constraints. ChatGPT is focused on improvement in the generation of human-like text based on prompts and not strictly on translation. The lower BLEU scores of GPT-4 shows that there is likely a gap between the improved "human-like" output and the practised wisdom embedded in the accumulative database of Patents because of the much larger language models used in the training of the former. This is not surprising because the PatentLex database is retrospective while any successive attempt at human-like output would include innovations and suitable stylistic perferences.

Challenges of Human *vs* Machine Translation of Emotion-Loaded Chinese Microblog Texts

Shenbin Qian s.qian@surrey.ac.uk
Constantin Orăsan c.orasan@surrey.ac.uk
Félix do Carmo f.docarmo@surrey.ac.uk
Centre for Translation Studies, University of Surrey, Guildford, UK

Diptesh Kanojia d.kanojia@surrey.ac.uk
Department of Computer Science, University of Surrey, Guildford, UK

Abstract

This paper attempts to identify challenges professional translators face when translating emotion-loaded texts as well as errors machine translation (MT) makes when translating this content. We invited ten Chinese-English translators to translate thirty posts of a Chinese microblog, and interviewed them about the challenges encountered during translation and the problems they believe MT might have. Further, we analysed more than five-thousand automatic translations of microblog posts to observe problems in MT outputs. We establish that the most challenging problem for human translators is emotion-carrying words, which translators also consider as a problem for MT. Analysis of MT outputs shows that this is also the most common source of MT errors. We also find that what is challenging for MT, such as non-standard writing, is not necessarily an issue for humans. Our work contributes to a better understanding of the challenges for the translation of microblog posts by humans and MT, caused by different forms of expression of emotion.

1 Introduction

User-generated texts (UGT) on social media commonly express sentiments and emotions. The emotion-loaded nature and the non-standard characteristics of UGT make translation difficult. This is true for texts on Sina Weibo[1], the largest Chinese microblog platform, which have their own characteristics due to the unique features of the Chinese language. Since Chinese is a tonal language, there are many characters sharing the same or similar pronunciation, but with quite different meanings. Similar to this feature, homographs that look very similar in writing but with different meanings and pronunciations are also common in Chinese, as there are many logograms and morphograms in Chinese. Netizens use this feature to create emotion-carrying slang by replacing the original character/word with a homophone or homograph character/word to avoid censorship. For example, "草泥马" *caonima*, literally meaning "grass mud

[1]https://weibo.com/

Proceedings of Machine Translation Summit XIX, Vol. 2: Users Track, pages 217–236
September 4–8, 2023, Macau SAR, China.

horse", is coined to refer to a swear word as it shares a similar pronunciation. It is used to show a strong angry emotion, but with some humour (Meng, 2011).

These features of emotion-loaded Chinese microblog texts might pose challenges for human and machine translation (MT), which are different from translating tweets such as hashtags or non-standard orthography in other languages or other types of texts (Saadany et al., 2023). In this paper, we endeavour to investigate the challenges of translating emotion-loaded Chinese microblog texts for humans and MT, with a special focus on answers from professional translators to the question: What are the challenges for humans and MT in the translation of emotion-loaded texts? We also evaluated outputs of an MT engine and compared the problems identified in MT outputs with the challenges mentioned by professional translators.

In the rest of this paper, Section 2 reviews related work in translation studies and MT studies on emotion. Section 3 starts with a description of the dataset used in this paper and explains the methodology for finding out the challenges from both professional translators' perspective and the output of MT. Section 4 shows the results of interviews with translators and the analysis of MT outputs. Section 5 concludes the paper by summarising our findings and indicating future research directions.

2 Related Work

2.1 Translation Studies on Emotion

Early studies related to the translation of emotion focused mainly on the translation of emotional lexical items. For example, Russell and Sato (1995) compared 14 emotional words such as 'happy', 'sad', or 'angry' in English, Chinese and Japanese to study if they were similar or equivalent in these languages. Choi and Han (2008) raised concerns about the equivalence of some emotional concepts, such as *shimcheong* (a combination of empathy, sympathy, and compassion) in Korean. Similarly, Hurtado de Mendoza et al. (2010) questioned the possibility of one-to-one translation of some emotional concepts like 'shame' in English and Spanish. For other language pairs like English and Arabic, Kayyal and Russell (2013) carried out very similar studies, and they found that only one pair (happiness-farah) of emotional words passed their equivalence tests, whereas others somewhat differed in terms of culture and language.

Different from product-oriented translation studies, which focused on the translation of emotional lexica, process-oriented studies paid closer attention to the influence of emotion on translators, which then further affected their translation result. Rojo López and Ramos Caro (2016) carried out an experiment to measure the impact of emotion on translators' performance. They asked students to translate an emotion-loaded text from English to Spanish and gave positive and negative feedback on their translations to different groups. Then, they asked students to translate another text. They found that positive or negative feedback can elicit different processing styles of the text and may affect translation quality, in aspects like accuracy and creativity. Kimovska and Cvetkoski (2021) replicated their experiment in the English-Macedonian pair, and found that positive feedback has a positive impact on creativity and negative feedback has a negative impact on meaning and style. These studies indicate that emotion is an important but difficult phenomenon to deal with during translation.

2.2 MT Studies on Emotion

Most of the research in Natural Language Processing related to emotion focuses on detection and classification of emotions in texts. However, there are some studies investigating the performance of MT systems in preserving sentiment or emotion. Among these studies, Mohammad et al. (2016) examined sentiments in Arabic-English translation of social media texts and evaluated the difference of sentiments before and after translation through human annotation. They found that the change of sentiment was mainly caused by ambiguous words, sarcasm, metaphors, and word-reordering issues. Shalunts et al. (2016) explored the impact of MT on sentiment in German, Russian and Spanish for general news articles. They found that the performance of the sentiment analysis tool on the source and the target was comparable, which means that MT tools do not impact dramatically on the transfer of sentiments. Contrary to their result, Troiano et al. (2020) found that emotions were at least partially lost after back-translation. Similarly, Fukuda and Jin (2022) found that sentiments were distorted by MT tools, with positive sentences tending to stay the same before and after translation, rather than negative and neutral sentences.

Both translation and MT studies on emotion suggest that emotion is difficult to translate and it could be affected by human or machine translation. However, previous studies rarely cover the challenges of emotion translation from the view of professional translators. To the best of our knowledge, no previous study has compared the challenges of emotion translation between human and machine translation in social media texts. This paper intends to contribute to bridging the gap in this area.

3 Data and Methodology

This section introduces the dataset used in the research, and explains the methodology followed to identify challenges when translating emotion-loaded texts.

3.1 Data Description

In order to identify challenges when translating emotion-loaded texts, it is necessary to have access to a dataset that contains numerous emotion expressions. The dataset used in the *Evaluation of Weibo Emotion Classification Technology on the Ninth China National Conference on Social Media Processing* is a good source for our purposes. It was already annotated with six emotion categories, namely, *anger*, *fear*, *joy*, *sadness*, *surprise* and *neutral* (Guo et al., 2021). The dataset had 34,768 Weibo posts, some classified with neutral emotion. We filtered out posts with neutral emotion and randomly sampled 20% of the remaining (about 5500 entries) as the dataset used in this research. Then, we randomly chose 30 entries (each entry is a Weibo post with about 40 Chinese characters), ensuring that in the end we had six entries for each of the five emotion categories, for use in the next stage, which was a translation and interview task.

3.2 Methodology for Studying Challenges for Human Translators

We interviewed professional translators in order to understand the challenges they face when translating emotion-loaded texts. Ten Chinese-English translators with at least one-year professional translation experience[2] were recruited to translate the same 30 selected entries. They were instructed to pay attention to the emotion in the source, and asked to use *PosEdiOn*[3] (Oliver, 2020) to record their actions and translation time during the process. This enabled us to analyse how different their translations were and whether it was difficult for them to translate emotion-loaded texts.

[2]Nine have more than two-year work experience as a translator; one has half-a-year work experience in translating social media texts and half-a-year translation training experience.

[3]An open-sourced software designed for the convenience of translation and post-editing. It is available at https://github.com/aoliverg/PosEdiOn.

These translations were compared by using two types of scores: an n-gram precision score created by BLEU (Papineni et al., 2002); and a cosine similarity score between embeddings obtained from sentence-BERT (Reimers and Gurevych, 2019).

BLEU scores were calculated using the SacreBLEU method (Post, 2018), a variant of BLEU that uses standard tokenisation for the Conference on Machine Translation[4] to improve reproducibility and comparability. To calculate the BLEU scores, one translation from a translator was selected as a reference, and compared with other translations of the same entry from the other translators one by one. This was done iteratively for each translation and each entry, to get 30 matrices of BLEU scores. As BLEU compares the n-grams in the candidate translation with the reference, it focuses more on form and position of words than on meaning. To assess how varied these translations are in terms of meaning, all translations of these 30 entries were embedded into a "semantic" vector space using Sentence-BERT. Cosine similarity was calculated between embeddings of different translations of the same source entry. Then, 30 matrices of similarity scores were obtained using the same process as above. The similarity scores were analysed to see how human translations varied in terms of the "meaning" captured by the embeddings.

After the translation task, one-to-one interviews were conducted online with the translators via Microsoft Teams to ask their opinions about this task. The interviews were semi-structured, and questions used can be found in Appendix B. During the interviews, translators were mainly asked about the challenges of translating emotion-loaded texts and the usefulness of MT for this type of texts. Each interview lasted approximately 30 minutes and was recorded using the Microsoft Teams cloud recording service. The recordings were transcribed by an automatic speech recognition tool, *Whisper* (Radford et al., 2022), and manually checked by the research team. Transcripts of these recordings were imported into an open-sourced software *QualCoder* (Curtain, 2023) for thematic analysis (Braun and Clarke, 2006). All transcripts were first segmented based on interview questions and then coded with different themes[5]. One translator might mention one theme several times for the same question. Similar themes for the same question were merged into broader ones. These themes were extracted and exported for qualitative analyses to identify challenges humans have when translating emotion-loaded texts and problems they think machines might have when translating the same texts. A screenshot of using *QualCoder* can be seen in Figure A.1 in Appendix A.

3.3 Methodology for Studying Problems in MT Outputs

To see the errors present in MT outputs, we used Google Translate[6] to translate the source text of our dataset and recruited two translators to annotate MT errors in terms of emotion preservation, following the framework proposed by Qian et al. (2023). Errors irrelevant to emotions were discarded, as we only focused on translation of emotion. Words or parts of sentences in the source text that relate to the errors were highlighted to analyse the cause for errors in MT.

In order to see how annotators agree with each other or themselves, we randomly sampled 10% (about 550 entries) of the dataset for the inter-annotator agreement check and 100 entries for the intra-annotator agreement check. More details about the framework, error annotation and agreement checks can be found in Qian et al. (2023).

[4]https://www.statmt.org/

[5]We identified some patterned meaning in the transcripts as initial themes or codes, and then refined them during the process.

[6]Results from "https://translate.google.co.uk/" on 30 May 2022.

4 Results and Discussions

This section analyses the data collected in the experiments described in the previous section. Section 4.1 shows results of the analysis of translations and interviews from translators. Section 4.2 summarises results of the analysis of MT outputs and compares similarities and differences of the challenges for translators and MT.

4.1 Analysis of Challenges for Human Translators

4.1.1 Analysis of Translation Data

Before looking into the interview data, we analysed the variations in human translations, by looking at the BLEU and embedding similarity scores.

BLEU Scores Figure A.2 in Appendix A shows 30 heatmaps (one for each entry) of the BLEU score matrix between the 10 translations (excluding comparing with themselves). The numbers on the x and y axes represent different translations (starting from 0). We might expect that, given the same text and enough time to translate, professional translators might produce translations with similar forms. However, most of these matrices are mixed with very light and dark colours, meaning the BLEU scores vary a lot for the different translations of all 30 Weibo posts. Most of these 30 heatmaps are dominated by dark colours—these are associated with low BLEU scores, hence very low similarity between the different translations of each entry.

The most noticeable example is Entry 25, which shows the largest area of black squares. This indicates that the translations of this particular entry are very different among the 10 translators. The source text “淅淅沥沥，沥沥淅淅。也许长大了，胆子就变得小了，想的也愈发多了。内心时常感到惶恐不安，风吹草动，兵荒马乱。心不够沉静，志不够坚强，繁花似锦，稍纵即逝” contains classic Chinese and idiomatic expressions. The first eight characters, bearing the resemblance of rain drops, have been quite often used in literary work to show subtle sad feelings. Many words and phrases such as “风吹草动，兵荒马乱” (showing insecure feelings) should not be interpreted and translated literally. The translators tried to explain them in their own way, and this potentially causes the variation of their translations, as shown in Table A.1 in Appendix A.

Apart from this particular entry, there are other cases in which one version is very different from the other translations of the same entry. Take Translation 7 of Entry 10, for example. BLEU scores between this translation and other translations are very low. This shows that different emotion-loaded texts might influence translators differently, reflected in different levels of variation in the forms chosen by the translators.

Figure A.3 shows the boxplots of these BLEU scores to see the average value (the orange line) and outliers (white circles). Since the matrix of BLEU scores is almost symmetric[7], only the lower half below the diagonal is kept to avoid repetitive plots. Apart from Entries 5, 10, 15 and 29, all entries have outliers. An outlier means that the BLEU score differs significantly and abnormally from others in statistics. Most of the outliers in these entries have abnormally high BLEU scores. This suggests that high agreement among these translations are rare and abnormal. Most of the BLEU scores in each entry have relatively low score values, but a few high-value outliers raise the average level. Entries 5, 10, 15 and 29 are the exceptions, where the emotion-carrying words are straightforward and easy to translate, unlike cultural-loaded words or slang

[7] BLEU score of Translation 1 (T1) as reference and Translation 2 (T2) as candidate can be slightly different (but very similar) from T2 as reference and T1 as candidate, since the distributions of n-grams in T1 and T2 can differ, and their order and frequencies can affect the calculation of precision.

present in the other entries. Take Entry 5 "这个小狗死了没有? 传说疯狗 10 日内必死可怕这个不可大意没事儿少招猫逗狗! 有点恐怖......" for example. The emotion-carrying word "恐怖" literally means "horrible" or "scary", so the translation is less arguable and varied. This can also be seen in Table A.2[8], which shows translations of the source "有点恐怖......". This is also true for the other three entries, where the emotion is strong and clear, and emotion-carrying words are easy to translate.

Embedding Similarity Scores Figure A.4, Appendix A contains 30 heatmaps (one for each entry) of the similarity score matrix between the embeddings of the 10 versions of translations (including comparing with themselves on the diagonal). The colours of these matrices are much lighter than those in the BLEU matrices, which indicates less variation and more consistency in this form of analysis of the different translations of the same entries. As translation is more about rendering the meaning rather than the sentence form or structure, higher similarity scores between embeddings are expected.

Matrices with the lowest similarity scores are Entries 8, 11, and 14. A quick analysis of the source text of these entries reveals that they all contain emotion-carrying slang words, for which it is difficult to find equivalent expressions in English. For example, in Entry 14, there are multiple slang expressions such as "小乃心", "小棉袄", "小傻瓜", and "小宝宝", which all mean "sweetheart" and show similar happy feelings, but in slightly different tones. Some of them are quite unique to the Chinese culture. This might be one of the reasons why similarity scores for the embeddings in this entry are low. Another noticeable point which corresponds to the phenomenon observed in BLEU scores is that similarity scores between Translation 7 and other translations are quite low for Entry 10. This means Translation 7 is dissimilar with others in both word forms or sentence structure and "meaning". This is also the case for Translation 2 and other translations in Entry 10.

Similar to making the boxplots of BLEU scores, the lower half below the diagonal of the similarity matrix is kept for making the boxplots in Figure A.5. Same as the result from the heatmaps, it is easy to see in Figure A.5 that Entries 8 and 14 have low average scores compared to others. Entries with high average scores are also quite noticeable. For example, Entries 20 and 28 have exceptionally high average scores close to 0.9. An investigation of the two entries suggests that both are relatively long compared to others, which means the translators have more context. Another thing they have in common is that most of the text is more informative than emotional. They do contain emotion somewhere in the text, but they mainly describe the event the blogger saw or experienced. This is probably why these translations are more similar in "meaning", as expressed by the embeddings.

From Figure A.5, it can be seen that Entry 15 has more outliers than the others. An analysis of this entry indicates that there are two cultural-specific words "暧昧" and "转正" in the source text. The second word is also a polysemous word, literally meaning "becoming an official member of", which now has been bestowed a new meaning "becoming someone's partner or wife from a mistress" under the modern Chinese culture. Translators may use different translation strategies to translate them in different ways and this may lead to low similarity scores between the embeddings of these translations.

To verify whether emotion-carrying words are the culprit for these variations, Entry 14 was selected since both its average BLEU score and similarity score are low, and it contains many emotion-carrying words. The emotion-carrying words in all translations

[8]Except Translation 7, which is also dissimilar with others in Entry 10.

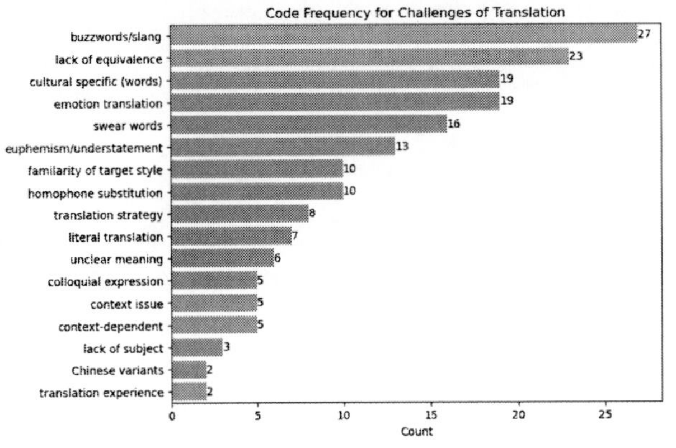

Figure 4.1: Themes Related to What Humans Find Challenging Ordered by Frequency

of Entry 14 were deleted and the BLEU scores[9] between each translation were re-computed to see whether they vary less. Figure A.6 shows the BLEU scores after the deletion of emotion-carrying words in the right boxplot, compared with before deletion in the left. It can be seen that average BLEU scores are improved and there are more high-value outliers, including two extremely high BLEU scores after the deletion of emotion-carrying words. This suggests translators are more likely to agree with each other translating texts without emotion-carrying words.

The analysis above shows that there was ample variation in the translation of Weibo posts by the 10 translators. This suggests that this type of content presents challenges for professional translators, and that emotion-carrying words are one of the sources of such challenges.

4.1.2 Analysis of Interview Data

As described in Section 3.2, interview transcripts were analysed to identify themes mentioned by interviewees in each interview question. The following figures present different themes mentioned in terms of the challenges translators face translating emotion-loaded texts; which aspect in relation to emotion translators find difficult to translate and what problems translators believe MT would have, given emotion-loaded texts.

Figure 4.1 shows the frequency of themes as for the interview question: **Do you think it is difficult to translate emotion-loaded microblog texts? Why?**

The five most frequent themes in the translators' answers are "buzzwords/slang", "lack of equivalence", "cultural specific (words)", "emotion translation" and "swear words". As these Weibo posts are full of buzzwords or slang, and most of them use swear words to show strong emotions, it is clear why these were the top five themes.

"Euphemism/understatement" in the figure is also related to "buzzwords/slang", as Chinese netizens use euphemism or understatement, instead of explicitly using swear words, to make their language more polite and less offensive, but at the same time keeping the same strong emotion. Understatement of emotions on public venues is, as described by interviewees, commonly seen under *"East Asian culture"*, where *"people*

[9]Only BLEU scores were re-computed, not cosine similarity scores, because the deletion of emotion-carrying words made this entry no longer semantically meaningful.

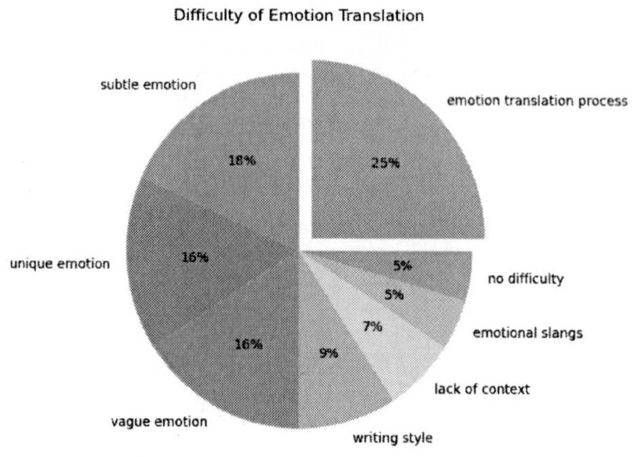

Figure 4.2: Theme Frequency for the Difficulty of Translating Emotions

express feelings in a cute and reserved way". One popular way to create slang expressions or euphemisms in Chinese is "homophone substitution" (King et al., 2013), which is also mentioned as a challenge for translation. Another way to create slang expressions is to use variants of Chinese such as some local dialects to achieve a humorous effect.

However, the use of "buzzwords/slang" may lead to other problems which translators see as challenges as well. "Unclear meaning" and "context issue" are partially caused by the overuse of slang. Some translators indicated that the meaning of some slang expressions are *"context-dependent"*, and that sometimes a blogger uses slang just to show a certain emotion, since he/she *"does not even know what he or she means by saying it"*. This poses some challenges for readers to get the real intention/meaning behind it. Another big challenge for the translation of these texts is "lack of equivalence", because many of these emotion-carrying "buzzwords/slang" are cultural specific. There is no exact equivalent expression in the target context due to cultural differences. Other factors such as "familiarity of the target style", "translation experience" in social media texts, "colloquial expression" and "lack of subject" in the source may also pose challenges for the human translation of emotion-loaded texts.

Two themes worth noticing here are "translation strategy" and "literal translation", which are challenges associated with the choice of the best translation strategy for this type of content. Since cultural specific words are quite common in these texts, translators find it challenging to decide whether to use foreignization, a strategy that is more prone to render the literal meaning, or domestication, which tends to modify the translated text according to the target style and culture. As some of the translators described in the interview, they had to choose *"whether to localise or to keep the features of source"* in the target text.

Figure 4.2 displays the theme frequencies in percentage for the interview question: **Do you think it is difficult to translate the emotion in the source text? Why?**

Excluding the theme related to the impact of emotion in the translation process, the most frequent theme for the difficulty of emotion transferring is "subtle emotion",

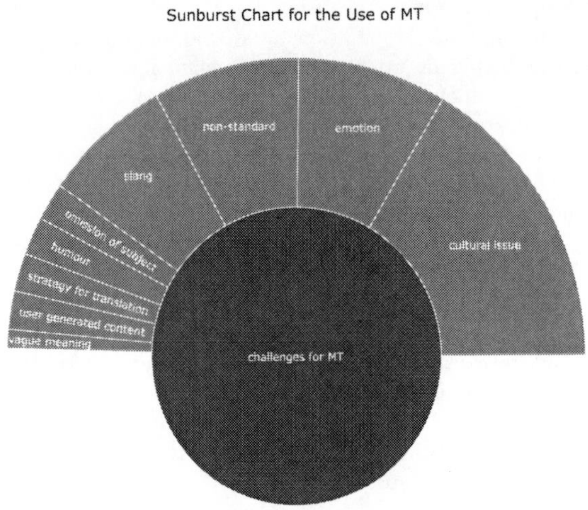

Figure 4.3: Themes Related to Problems for MT in Emotion-Loaded Texts

and then "unique emotion" and "vague emotion". Take Entry 14 for example. The four emotion-carrying words "小乃心", "小棉袄", "小傻瓜" and "小宝宝", meaning "my sweetie", "my warm jacket", "my silly goose" and "my little baby" respectively, are very subtle in expressing emotions. These expressions cause difficulties to translators. Also as discussed in previous literature, some emotions such as "疼", the "heart-aching love" is quite unique to Chinese culture (Sundararajan, 2015). Slang created via homophone substitution is also specific to the Chinese language and culture and very subtle in terms of emotion conveying. These unique and sometimes context dependent emotions raise difficulties for human translation. Likewise, vague or subtle emotions and short context might also pose challenges for understanding and translation, since *"the length of these texts is short"* and some Weibo users accidentally or *"deliberately show their emotion in a vague or subtle way"*. Other frequent themes such as "writing style", "lack of context" and "emotional slang" are also mentioned as difficulties of emotion translation. Only two translators mentioned it is not difficult for them to transfer the emotion as they suggested that they can always find similar expressions of emotion in the target text, without thinking too much about the cultural differences. They mentioned that there are always differences between languages and that translation is a tool for bridging differences, not to eliminate them.

Another frequent theme is "emotion translation process". During the interview, most translators expressed that they were not affected by the strong emotion of the source text, although they felt the same feeling as the source during translation. They remained neutral in the translation process. This does not follow the results of some previous studies, such as Rojo López and Ramos Caro (2016) and Kimovska and Cvetkoski (2021), where emotions affected the translation result.

Figure 4.3 shows themes related to the problems that translators believe MT systems have, when they were asked: **Do you think whether MT tools will be useful for the translation of emotion-loaded social media texts?** The size of segments in the outer layer indicates the frequency of these themes.

The most frequent theme for problems for MT, from the human translators' perspective, are "cultural issue", "emotion" and "non-standard" writing. Translators thought some cultural-specific words are very difficult for MT and end up being translated in a literal way, which severely hinders readers understanding of the emotion of the source. They also stressed that *"machines do not understand human emotions"*, and that unique and subtle emotions in the source are challenging for MT. Different from the challenges for human translators, they think that "non-standard" writing, including the omission of punctuation and subject in some Weibo posts, are difficult for MT, while relatively easier for human translators. Humans can infer the meaning from its context, even if the source does not have punctuation or subject, while machines might not be able to produce good solutions for this. Translators also mentioned that humans might feel relaxed translating the informality as the source is written in a causal way, but machines may have problems in processing this type of content. Another point worth noticing is that one translator mentioned some of the "user generated content" is very *"creative"* in term of the choice of words and writing style. Some of them even use "humour" or other rhetorical devices to convey the meaning or emotion. This also makes the source content challenging for MT.

4.2 Relation between Challenges for Human Translators and Errors in MT Outputs

To study the problems present in MT outputs and test the assumptions of translators regarding the most common sources of MT errors, a task of human evaluation of MT outputs was carried out as described in Section 3.3. This task along with its following results is described in Qian et al. (2023). The results show that besides emotion-carrying words, polysemous words, punctuation, negation, subject/object issues, subjunctive mood and abbreviation are also causes of errors in MT.

In the list of challenges for human translators when translating emotion-loaded texts, and the list of causes of errors in MT outputs of the same type of content, there are two common elements: emotion-carrying words, and subject/object issues.

The differences in these lists of challenges for translators and factors for MT errors can be summarised as follows: 1) MT does not solve correctly issues such as non-standard writing or non-standard use of punctuation; these issues do not pose challenges to human translators, since they can infer meaning from the context; 2) some challenges that humans believe might make themselves and MT struggle, such as the choice of translation strategies, cannot be observed in the MT output; 3) other challenges, such as the translator's familiarity with the target style, are concerns expressed by human translators for themselves, not for the MT. Again, the analysis of MT errors does not give access to such information.

5 Conclusion

Our paper investigates challenges professional translators face when translating emotion-loaded texts, as well as errors MT makes when translating this content. We interviewed 10 professional translators about the challenges they meet when translating this type of texts and the challenges they expect MT to have. We compared results from the interviews with the errors we identified in real MT outputs. We establish that the most challenging problem for both human and MT is emotion-carrying words. We also find that what is more challenging for MT, such as non-standard writing, is not necessarily an issue for human translators. In future work, we plan to explore how these findings can be used to train human translators and improve automatic translation of emotions.

References

Braun, V. and Clarke, V. (2006). Using thematic analysis in psychology. *Qualitative Research in Psychology*, 3:77–101.

Choi, S. and Han, G. (2008). SHIMCHEONG PSYCHOLOGY: A CASE OF AN EMOTIONAL STATE FOR CULTURAL PSYCHOLOGY. *International Journal for Dialogical Science Copyright*, 3:205–224.

Curtain, C. (2023). Qualcoder. `https://github.com/ccbogel/QualCoder/releases/tag/3.2`. Last checked on Jun 22, 2023.

Fukuda, K. and Jin, Q. (2022). Analyzing Change on Emotion Scores of Tweets Before and After Machine Translation. In Meiselwitz, G., editor, *Social Computing and Social Media: Design, User Experience and Impact*, volume 13315, pages 294–308. Springer.

Guo, X., Lai, H., Xiang, Y., Yu, Z., and Huang, Y. (2021). Emotion Classification of COVID-19 Chinese Microblogs based on the Emotion Category Description. In *Proceedings of the 20th China National Conference on Computational Linguistics*, pages 916–927. Chinese Information Processing Society of China.

Hurtado de Mendoza, A., Fernández-Dols, J. M., Parrott, W. G., and Carrera, P. (2010). Emotion terms, category structure, and the problem of translation: The case of shame and vergüenza. *Cognition and Emotion*, 24:661–680.

Kayyal, M. H. and Russell, J. A. (2013). Language and Emotion: Certain English-Arabic Translations Are Not Equivalent. *Journal of Language and Social Psychology*, 32:261–271.

Kimovska, S. K. and Cvetkoski, V. (2021). THE EFFECT OF EMOTIONS ON TRANSLATION PERFORMANCE. *Research in Language*, 19:169–186.

King, G., Pan, J., and Roberts, M. E. (2013). How censorship in China allows government criticism but silences collective expression. *American Political Science Review*, 107:326–343.

Meng, B. (2011). From Steamed Bun to Grass Mud Horse: E Gao as alternative political discourse on the Chinese Internet. *Global Media and Communication*, 7:33–51.

Mohammad, S. M., Salameh, M., and Kiritchenko, S. (2016). How Translation Alters Sentiment. *Journal of Artificial Intelligence Research*, 55:95–130.

Oliver, A. (2020). MTUOC: easy and free integration of NMT systems in professional translation environments. In *Proceedings of the 22nd Annual Conference of the European Association for Machine Translation*, pages 467–468, Lisboa, Portugal. European Association for Machine Translation.

Papineni, K., Roukos, S., Ward, T., and Zhu, W.-J. (2002). BLEU: a Method for Automatic Evaluation of Machine Translation. In *Proceedings of the 40th Annual Meeting on Association for Computational Linguistics*, pages 311–318. Association for Computational Linguistics.

Post, M. (2018). A Call for Clarity in Reporting BLEU Scores. In *Proceedings of the Third Conference on Machine Translation: Research Papers*, pages 186–191, Brussels, Belgium. Association for Computational Linguistics.

Qian, S., Orăsan, C., Do Carmo, F., Li, Q., and Kanojia, D. (2023). Evaluation of Chinese-English Machine Translation of Emotion-Loaded Microblog Texts: A Human Annotated Dataset for the Quality Assessment of Emotion Translation. In *Proceedings of the 24th Annual Conference of the European Association for Machine Translation.* European Association for Machine Translation.

Radford, A., Kim, J. W., Xu, T., Brockman, G., McLeavey, C., and Sutskever, I. (2022). Robust Speech Recognition via Large-Scale Weak Supervision. *arXiv preprint.*

Reimers, N. and Gurevych, I. (2019). Sentence-BERT: Sentence Embeddings using Siamese BERT-Networks. In *Proceedings of the 2019 Conference on Empirical Methods in Natural Language Processing.* Association for Computational Linguistics.

Rojo López, A. and Ramos Caro, M. (2016). Can emotion stir translation skill? Defining the impact of positive and negative emotions on translation performance. pages 107–130. John Benjamins Publishing Company.

Russell, J. A. and Sato, K. (1995). Comparing Emotion Words between Languages. *Journal of Cross-Cultural Psychology*, 26:384–391.

Saadany, H., Orasan, C., Do Carmo, F., Zilio, L., and Quintana, R. C. (2023). Analysing Mistranslation of Emotions in Multilingual Tweets by Online MT Tools. In *Proceedings of the 24th Annual Conference of the European Association for Machine Translation.* European Association for Machine Translation.

Shalunts, G., Backfried, G., and Commeignes, N. (2016). The Impact of Machine Translation on Sentiment Analysis. In *The Fifth International Conference on Data Analytics*, pages 51–56. IARIA.

Sundararajan, L. (2015). *Understanding Emotion in Chinese Culture: Thinking Through Psychology.* Springer.

Troiano, E., Klinger, R., and Padó, S. (2020). Lost in Back-Translation: Emotion Preservation in Neural Machine Translation. In *Proceedings of the 28th International Conference on Computational Linguistics*, pages 4340–4354. International Committee on Computational Linguistics.

Appendices

A Figures and Tables

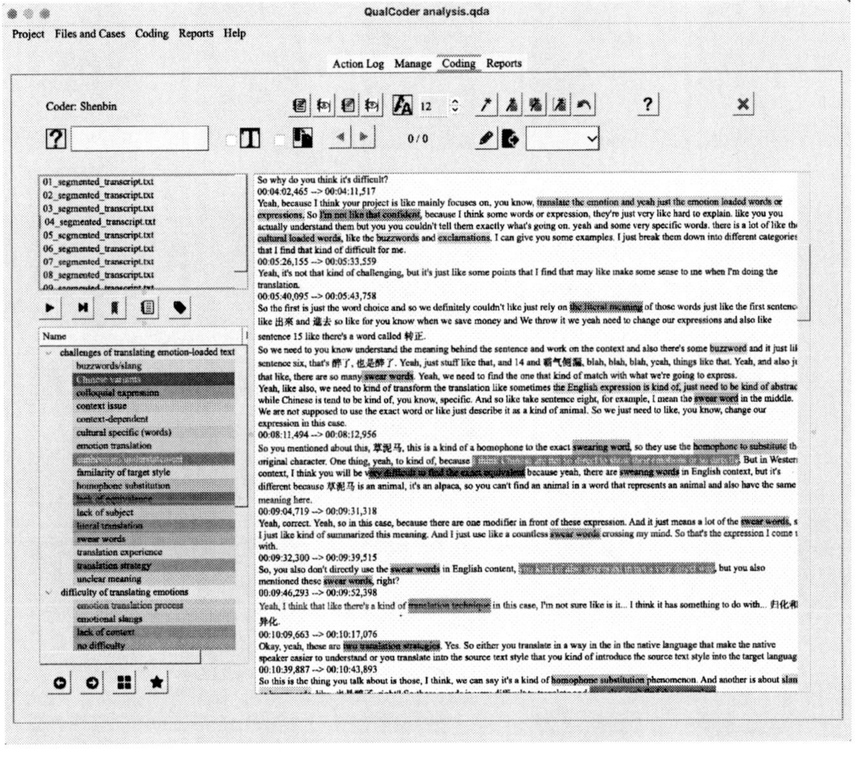

Figure A.1: Screenshot of Using *QualCoder*

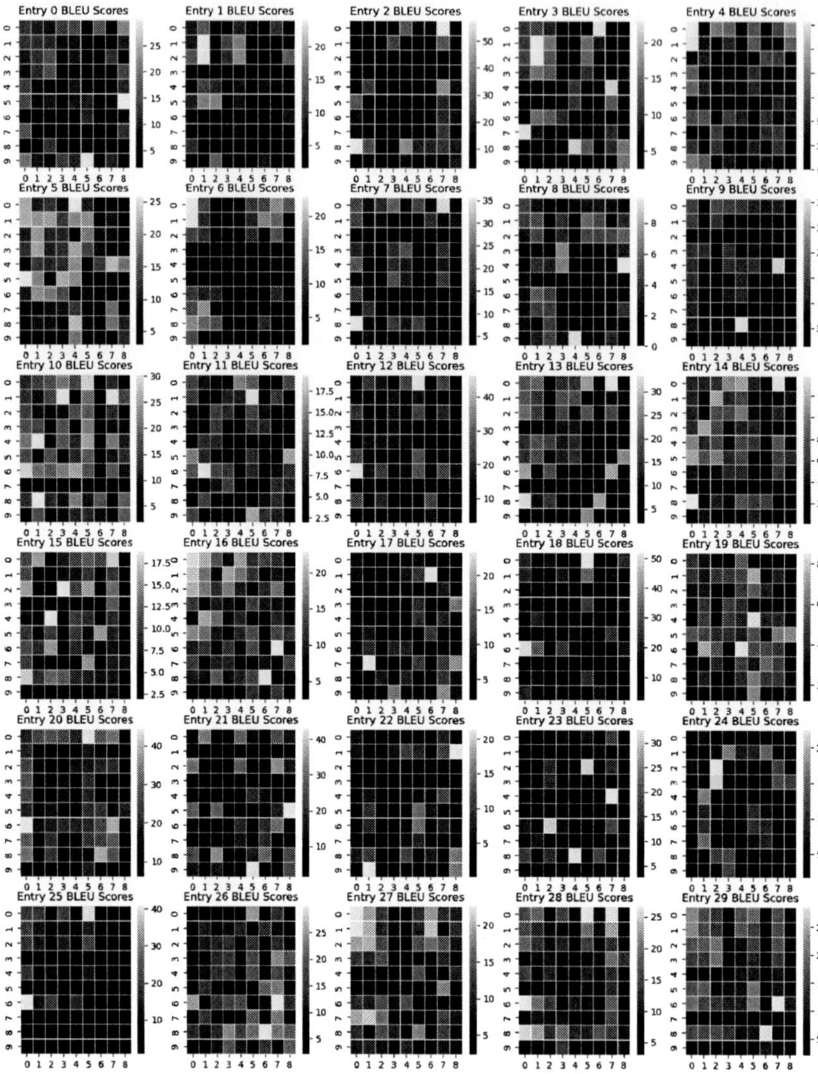

Figure A.2: Heatmaps for BLEU Score Matrices

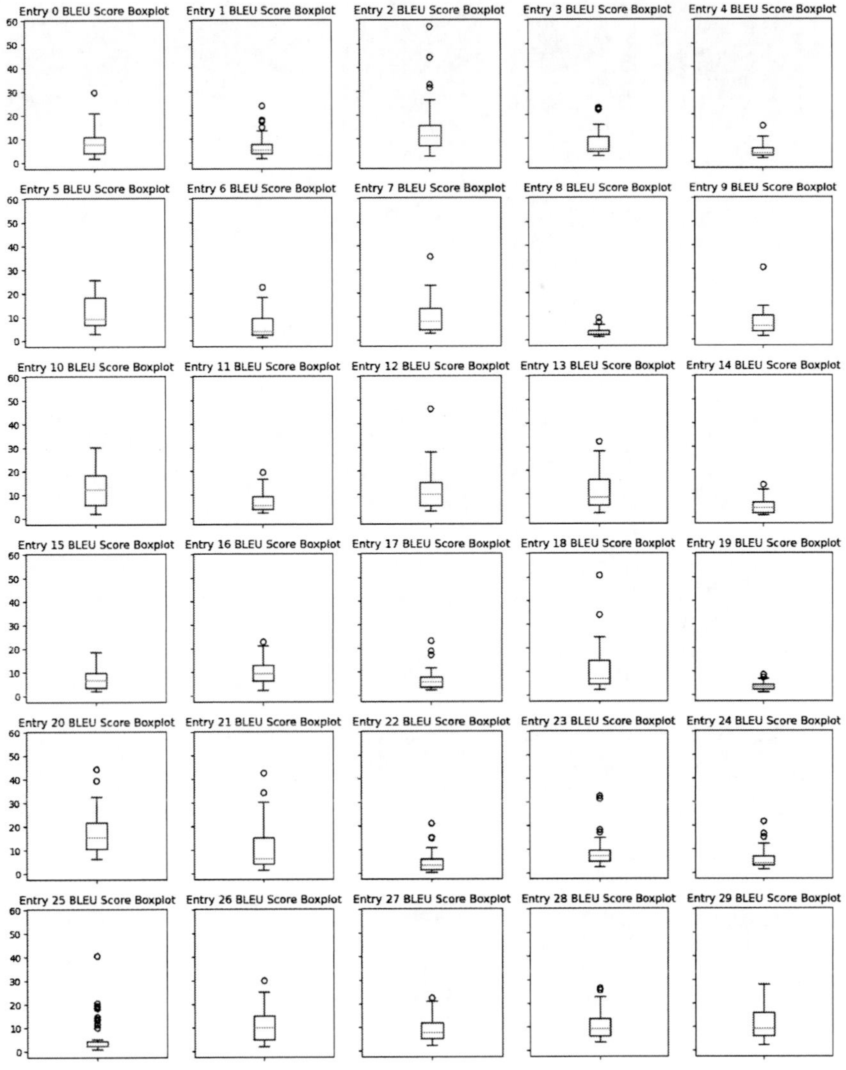

Figure A.3: Boxplots for BLEU Scores

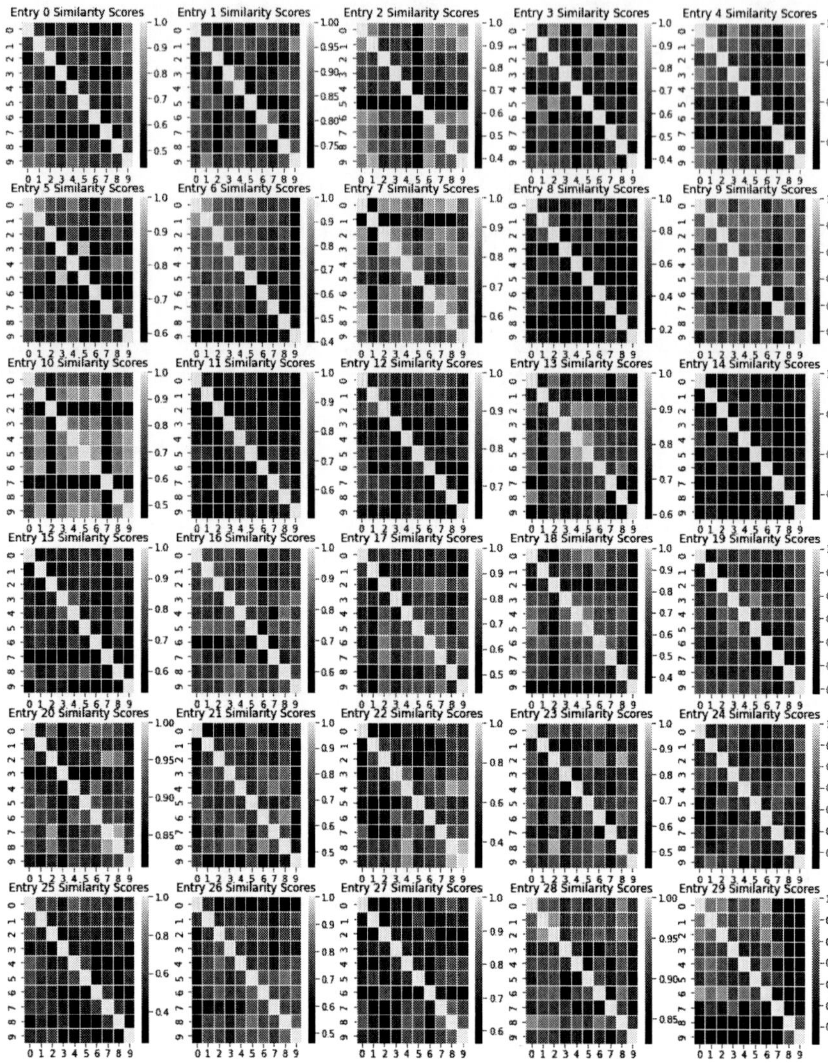

Figure A.4: Heatmaps for Embedding Similarity Score Matrices

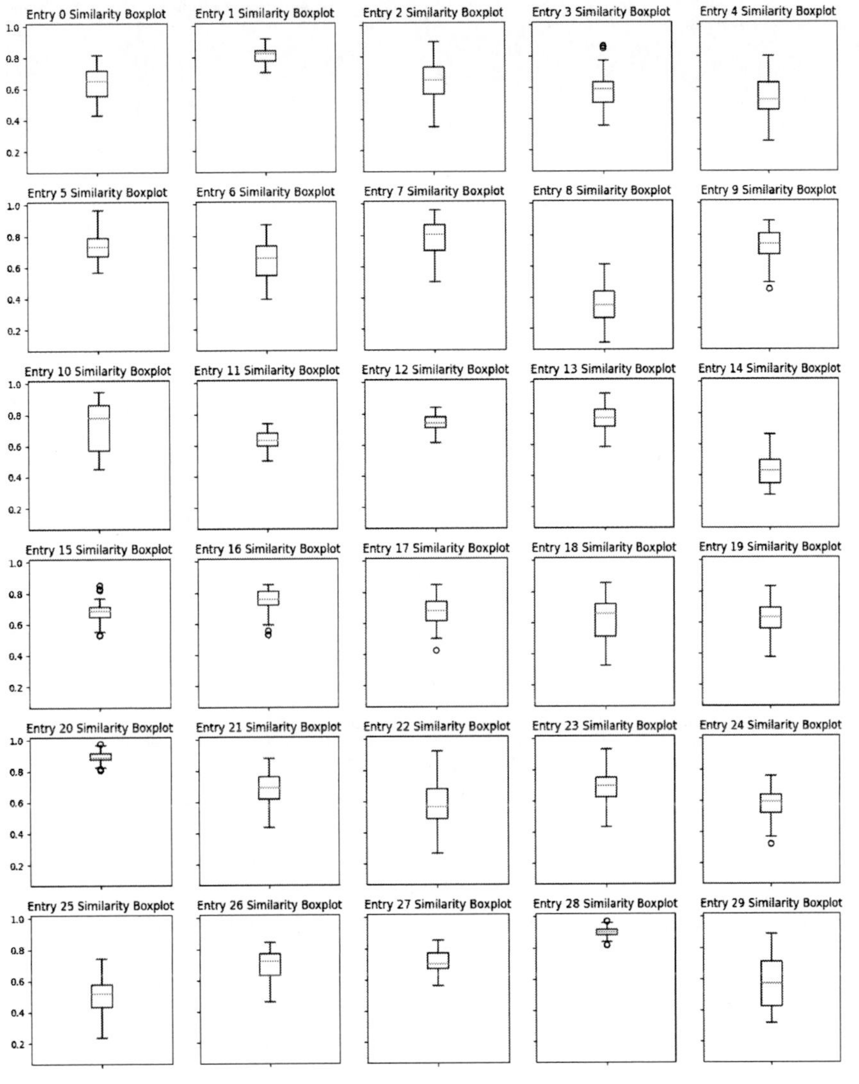

Figure A.5: Boxplots for Embedding Similarity Scores

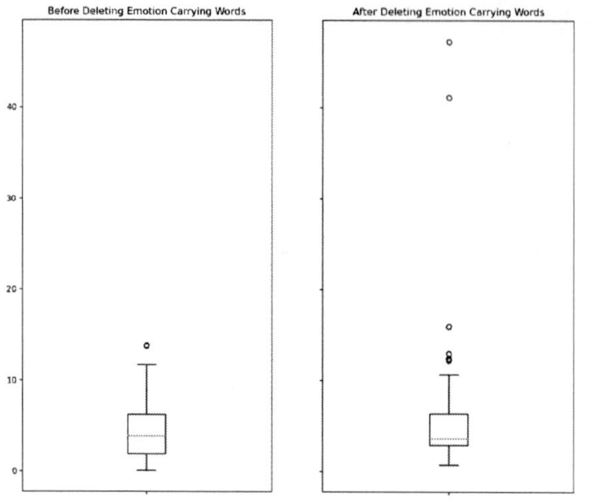

Figure A.6: Entry 14 Boxplots of BLEU Scores **Before (Left)** and **After (Right)** Deletion of Emotion Carrying Words

No.	Translations
0	Drizzling, drizzling, drizzling. Maybe when I grow up, I become less courageous and think more. I often feel panic and uneasiness in my heart, turmoil and chaos. My heart is not calm enough, my ambition is not strong enough. Flowers are in blossom now but will die out every soon.
1	It's drizzling. Maybe people will actually be less brave and have more thoughts when they are getting older. In my mind, I am always worried and being sensitive, just like a nervous wreck. My heart is not calm enough and my spirit is not strong enough. There is no much time.
2	Pattering. Pattering. Maybe I became less bold as I grow older and think more often. I often feel unrest, easy picked and panic. My heart is not calm, my will is not strong. Flourishing flowers dies in a blink of an eye.
3	There is breeze and drizzle, the leaves falling. Maybe when people grow older, they tend to be more intimidated and there is more on their mind. They are easily got fidgety and frightened out of anything unexpected. We may likely to lose those wonderful things we are having in the peaceful state instantly if our mind is in chaos and easily destructive.
4	It's been drizzling for a while. I turn to be more cowardly and think more after I grow up. I often feel panic and anxiety. A little breeze could blow the grass in my heart hard. My heart is in chaos of wars. My heart is not calm enough. My life goal is not clear enough. Though my inside is like a picture of thousands of flowers, it vanishes in a second.
5	It's raining outside. Maybe I lose my guts growing up and I have too many thoughts, and often feel insecure. A small thing in the outside world has an impact in my innner world. I don't have inner peace or strong will. Flowers are blooming, but soon they will be gone.
6	Gradually, time gose by. Maybe when I grow up, I become less daring and think more. I often feel panic and very sensitive. The heart is not calm enough, and the will is not strong enough, such as blooming flowers, transiently.
7	As I get older, I find myself thinking more and accomplishing less. Changes around me frequently astounded me. I wasn't calm or strong enough to deal with these sudden changes.
8	Pitter patter, pitter patter. Maybe being a grown-up makes us more timid. We have loads of ideas, making us afraid and confused. With just a sign of disturbance and trouble, we find it hard to calm down and concentrate. We live like a flash in the pan.
9	Patter, patter. Maybe it's because I grew older, I became not that bold and am always careful with lots of thoughts in my mind. Always feel worried. Any sign could mess my mind. Not calm enough. Neither determined. Shiny as golden hours are, they don't last and very soon pass.

Table A.1: Translations of Entry 25

No.	**Translations**
0	It's a little scary...
1	It's scary......
2	Bit scary......
3	It's a bit intimidating...
4	This is a bit spooky.
5	Horrible...
6	It's scary.....
7	I am not joking.
8	It' s a bit spooky...
9	This is kind of scaring...

Table A.2: Translations of the Emotion-Loaded Part of Entry 5

B Interview Questions[10]

1. Could you tell me about your experience in translation, specifically in translating this type of Weibo posts?
2. Do you think it is difficult to translate this type of emotion-loaded Weibo posts? Why?
3. Are there elements in the Weibo posts that are more difficult to translate? Why?
4. Look at the example in the chat, do you think it is tricky to translate? Why? 管理学真是水的一比，努力的想听，依然坚持不过一分钟...... 考研怎么办呀.
5. How long did it take to translate all the texts?
6. Do you think it is difficult to translate the emotion in the source text? Why?
7. Do you think the strong emotions or those emotional words in the source text makes you concerned more about the overall translation quality? If yes, how might this affect your quality?
8. Do you think whether MT tools will be useful for the translation of emotion-loaded social media texts?
9. Have you tried, as a user, not a translator, the Translate option on social media applications such as Twitter or WeChat?
10. Do you think whether it will be difficult for MT to translate the following sentence in the chat? If yes, which part? 嘤嘤嘤翻牌了开森受宠若惊晚安么么哒.
11. Can you guess the original emotion of the source by looking at the following MT result in the chat? *Tell a woman that she will hurt me for the rest of my life.*

[10] All questions in the interview are listed here, but due to the length of this paper, only questions most relevant to the theme are included in Section 4.1.

Author Index

Association for Computational Linguistics
209 N. Eighth Street
Stroudsburg, Pennsylvania 18360

ISBN 978-1-7138-9037-9

9 781713 890379

CURRAN ASSOCIATES INC.
proceedings.com